Attachment and Loss

VOL. I: ATTACHMENT

Second Edition

ATTACHMENT AND LOSS
VOLUME I

ATTACHMENT

by

JOHN BOWLBY

Second Edition

BasicBooks
A Subsidiary of Perseus Books, L.L.C.

© Tavistock Institute of Human Relations 1969, 1982
Library of Congress Catalog Number: 83-71445
ISBN: 0-465-00543-8 (paper)
Printed in the United States of America

98 99 RRD-H 20 19 18

To
URSULA

Contents

vii

CONTENTS

CONTENTS

Preface

IN 1956 when this work was begun I had no conception of what I was undertaking. At that time my object appeared a limited one, namely, to discuss the theoretical implications of some observations of how young children respond to temporary loss of mother. These observations had been made by my colleague, James Robertson, and together he and I were preparing them for publication. A discussion of their theoretical significance seemed desirable and was destined to form the second part of our book.

Events were to prove otherwise. As my study of theory progressed it was gradually borne in upon me that the field I had set out to plough so lightheartedly was no less than the one that Freud had started tilling sixty years earlier, and that it contained all those same rocky excrescences and thorny entanglements that he had encountered and grappled with—love and hate, anxiety and defence, attachment and loss. What had deceived me was that my furrows had been started from a corner diametrically opposite to the one at which Freud had entered and through which analysts have always followed. From a new viewpoint a familiar landscape can sometimes look very different. Not only had I been deceived in the first place, but subsequently progress has been slow. It has also, I believe, often been difficult for colleagues to understand what I am attempting. It may be of help, therefore, if I put my thinking in a historical perspective.

In 1950 I was asked by the World Health Organisation to advise on the mental health of homeless children. This assignment provided a valuable opportunity to meet with many of the leading workers in the field of child care and child psychiatry and to read the literature. As I wrote in the preface to the resulting report (1951), what struck me amongst those I met was the 'very high degree of agreement existing in regard to both the principles underlying the mental health of children and the practices by which it may be safeguarded'. In the first part of the report I presented evidence and formulated a principle: 'What is believed to be essential for mental health is that the infant and young child should experience a warm, intimate and continuous relationship with his mother (or permanent

xi

mother-substitute) in which both find satisfaction and enjoyment.' In the second part I outlined the measures that, in the light of these principles, are necessary if the mental health of children separated from their families is to be safeguarded.

The report proved timely. It helped to focus attention on the problem, contributed to improved methods of care, and stimulated both controversy and research. Yet, as more than one reviewer pointed out, the report had at least one grave limitation. Whereas it had much to say about the many kinds of ill effect that evidence shows can be attributed to maternal deprivation and also about practical measures that may prevent or mitigate these ill effects, it said very little indeed about the processes whereby these ill effects are brought into being. How does it come about that one or another of the events included under the general heading of maternal deprivation produces this or that form of psychiatric disturbance? What are the processes at work? Why should things happen this way? What are the other variables that affect outcome, and how do they affect it? On all these issues the monograph is silent, or nearly so.

The reason for this silence was ignorance—my own and others'—which could not possibly have been made good in the few months in which the report had to be written. Sooner or later, I hoped, the gap would be filled, though it was unclear when or how.

It was in this frame of mind that I began to give serious attention to observations my colleague James Robertson had been making. With the help of a small grant from the Sir Halley Stewart Trust he had joined me in 1948 to take part in what was intended to be a systematic inquiry into the whole problem of the effects on personality development of separation from mother in early childhood. During an extended reconnaissance of what was at that time largely virgin ground he had observed a number of young children before, during, and after a stay away from home; most of these children were in their second and third years of life and not only were separated from their mothers but for periods of weeks or months were cared for in settings, such as hospital or residential nursery, in which they had no stable mother-substitute. During this work he had been deeply impressed by the intensity of the distress and misery he was witness to whilst the children were away from home and by the extent and duration of the disturbance that was present after they had returned there. No one reading his written reports or viewing the film record he made of one little girl could be left unmoved. Nevertheless, at that time there was no agreement about the significance or relevance of these observations. Some challenged their validity; others recognised that the responses occurred but attributed them to almost anything but loss of mother-figure; yet others conceded that loss was a relevant variable but held that to mitigate its effects was not too difficult and that loss was therefore of less consequence for pathology than we supposed.

My colleagues and I took a different view. We were confident that the observations were valid; all the evidence pointed to loss of mother-figure as a dominant variable, though not the only one; and our experience suggested that, even when other circumstances were favourable, there was more distress and disturbance than was usually recognised. Indeed, we held the view that the responses of protest, despair, and detachment that typically occur when a young child aged over six months is separated from his mother and in the care of strangers are due mainly to 'loss of maternal care at this highly dependent, highly vulnerable stage of development'. From empirical observation we suggested that 'the young child's hunger for his mother's love and presence is as great as his hunger for food', and that in consequence her absence inevitably generates 'a powerful sense of loss and anger'. We were concerned particularly with the great changes in a child's relation to his mother that are often to be seen when he returns home after a period away; on the one hand, 'an intense clinging to the mother which can continue for weeks, months or years'; on the other, 'a rejection of the mother as a love object, which may be temporary or permanent'. The latter state, to which we later came to refer as detachment, we held to be a result of the child's feelings for his mother having undergone repression.

Thus we reached the conclusion that loss of mother-figure, either by itself or in combination with other variables yet to be clearly identified, is capable of generating responses and processes that are of the greatest interest to psychopathology. Not only so, but these responses and processes, we concluded, are the very same as are known to be active in older individuals who are still disturbed by separations that they suffered in early life. Amongst these responses and processes and amongst forms of disturbance are, on the one hand, a tendency to make excessive demands on others and to be anxious and angry when they are not met, such as is present in dependent and hysterical personalities; and, on the other, a blockage in the capacity to make deep relationships, such as is present in affectionless and psychopathic personalities. In other words, it seemed to us that when we observe children during and after periods away from mother and in a strange setting we are witnessing responses, and also effects of defensive processes, that are just those that enable us to bridge the gap between an experience of this sort and one or another of the disturbances in personality functioning that may follow.

These conclusions, which sprang naturally from the empirical data, led to a crucial decision of research strategy. Since our aim was to understand how these pathological processes originate and develop, we decided that henceforward we would take as our principal data detailed records of how young children respond to the experiences of being separated from and later of being reunited with mother. Such data, we had come to believe, are of great intrinsic interest and an essential complement to data of a traditional kind derived from the treatment of older subjects. The thinking underlying this decision and some of the original data are reported in papers published between 1952 and 1954; and a film was published during the same period.[1]

During the years that have elapsed since this decision was taken my colleagues and I have given much time to the scrutiny of data already collected, the collection and analysis of further data, the comparison of these data with data from other sources, and an examination of their theoretical implications. Amongst the fruits of this work already published is a volume, *Brief Separations* (1966), in which Christoph Heinicke and Ilse Westheimer study responses to be seen during and after a brief separation experienced in a defined setting. In that study not only were the responses observed and recorded in a more systematic way than had been possible in earlier studies but the behaviour of the separated children was compared statistically with the behaviour shown by a matched sample of children living in their own homes and not separated. Within its limits the findings of this later study confirm the less systematic but more extensive findings of James Robertson and amplify them at a number of points.

In a series of papers published between 1958 and 1963 I have myself discussed some of the theoretical problems raised by

[1] These papers, from which the passages quoted are taken, are as follows: Robertson and Bowlby (1952); Bowlby, Robertson, and Rosenbluth (1952); Bowlby (1953); Robertson (1953); and Ainsworth and Bowlby (1954). The film is Robertson (1952).

these observations. The present three volumes cover the same ground, but do so in a more rigorous way. There is also much additional material.

Volume I is devoted to problems originally tackled in the first paper of the series, 'The nature of the child's tie to his mother' (1958). In order effectively to present the theory to be advanced, which is attempted in Parts III and IV, it has been necessary to discuss first the whole problem of instinctive behaviour and how best to conceptualise it. The rather long discussion entailed constitutes Part II of the volume. It is preceded by two chapters forming Part I: the first sets out systematically some of the assumptions from which I start and compares them with Freud's; the second reviews the empirical observations on which I am drawing and gives a précis of them. The aim of all the chapters of Parts I and II is to clarify and make more explicit the concepts with which I am working, since these, because they are unfamiliar, have proved puzzling to many clinicians otherwise sympathetic to the work.

Volume II, *Separation*, deals with problems originally tackled in the second and third papers of the series:'Separation anxiety' (1960a) and 'Separation anxiety: a critical review of the literature' (1961a).

The third volume, *Loss*, deals with problems originally tackled in the subsequent papers: 'Grief and mourning in infancy and early childhood' (1960b); 'Processes of mourning' (1961b); and 'Pathological mourning and childhood mourning' (1963).

Throughout this inquiry my frame of reference has been that of psychoanalysis. There are several reasons for this. The first is that my early thinking on the subject was inspired by psychoanalytic work—my own and others'. A second is that, despite limitations, psychoanalysis remains the most serviceable and the most used of any present-day theory of psychopathology. A third and most important is that, whereas all the central concepts of my schema—object relations, separation anxiety, mourning, defence, trauma, sensitive periods in early life—are the stock-in-trade of psychoanalytic thinking, until recently they have been given but scant attention by other behavioural disciplines.

In the course of his explorations Freud followed many different lines of thought and tried many possible theoretical constructions. Since his death the contradictions and ambiguities he left behind have caused unease and there have been attempts to tidy up: certain of his theories have been selected and elaborated, others laid aside and neglected. Because some of my ideas are alien to the theoretical traditions that have become established, and so have met with strong criticism, I have been at some pains to show that most of them are by no means alien to what Freud himself thought and wrote. On the contrary, as I hope to show, a great number of the central concepts of my schema are to be found plainly stated by Freud.

Preface to the Second Edition

The principal reason for preparing a revised edition of this work is that during the past fifteen years there have been major developments in the thinking of biologists studying the social behaviour of species other than man. These developments have necessitated significant changes in a few places in Part II, namely the last two sections of Chapter 3 (especially pp. 53–7), in the sub-section of Chapter 8 on altruistic behaviour (pp. 131–2), and in the opening paragraph of Chapter 9 (p. 141).

Another reason is that, since the publication of the first edition, ideas about attachment have been at the centre of much theoretical discussion and have also provided guidelines for empirical research of the greatest interest. It seemed timely, therefore, to add two new chapters in which certain of the theoretical problems could be clarified and some of the more important research findings described. To provide space, the Appendix reviewing the earlier literature on the nature of the child's tie to his mother has been omitted.

In Part III few changes have been required, though opportunity has been taken to revise the section of Chapter 11 on non-human primates to take account of the most recent findings.

In Part IV a large number of incidental revisions have been called for as a result of the intensive research on the early years of human life undertaken during recent years; and attention is drawn to new findings described in more detail in Chapter 18.

The many new publications referred to in the text are incorporated in the revised References. Indexes also have been revised.

Acknowledgements

IN the preparation of this book I have been helped by many friends and colleagues, and it is a great pleasure to express publicly to all of them my very warmest thanks.

Since the main data on which I have drawn are those of James Robertson, my debt to him is immense. His early observations first impressed me with the great potential of naturalistic studies of how young children behave when temporarily out of mother's care, and his constant concern for accuracy of description and his tireless attention to detail have been of continuous help to me in the presentation and discussion of findings. The systematic observations of Christoph Heinicke and Ilse Westheimer, by making firmer the empirical base from which I am working, have also been of the greatest value.

I am much indebted for help given me also by other colleagues who have worked at the Tavistock Clinic and Tavistock Institute of Human Relations on problems of attachment and loss.

Since she left the Tavistock in 1954, Mary Salter Ainsworth and I have kept in close touch. She has not only been most generous in making available her observations of attachment behaviour, made both in Uganda and in Baltimore, Maryland, but has read most of this book in draft and suggested many improvements, especially to Parts III and IV.

Anthony Ambrose has helped me to clarify points of difficulty and has made many suggestions for improving parts of the text. He also played an invaluable part in helping to organise the four meetings of the Tavistock Seminar on Mother–Infant Interaction, held in London with the generous support of the Ciba Foundation. Anyone familiar with the reports of those meetings will quickly recognise the debt I owe to all those who presented papers and took part in the discussions.

The theoretical schema elaborated stems partly from psychoanalysis and partly from ethology. For my psychoanalytic education I am indebted especially to my own analyst, Joan Riviere, and to Melanie Klein, who was one of my supervisors. Though my position has come to differ much from theirs, I remain deeply grateful to them for grounding me in the object-relations approach to psychoanalysis, with its emphasis on early relationships and the pathogenic potential of loss.

ACKNOWLEDGEMENTS

In 1951, at a sensitive phase in my thinking about problems of separation, Julian Huxley fanned a germinal interest in ethology and introduced me to the just published classics of Konrad Lorenz and Niko Tinbergen. To all three I am grateful for continuing my education and for encouragement.

In seeking to utilise the more recent findings and concepts of ethology I am more indebted than I can say for the time and guidance given me by Robert Hinde. In the course of discussions over many years, and from his comments on drafts, I have received much illumination; and he very kindly loaned me an early version of his *Animal Behaviour*, 1966, which I found invaluable. Whilst he is not to be held responsible for the views I am expressing, without his searching criticism and generous help this book would have been immeasurably the poorer.

Others who have contributed to my thinking and have suggested improvements to parts of the draft are Gordon Bronson, David Hamburg, Dorothy Heard, and Arnold Tustin.

In the preparation of the script my secretary, Dorothy Southern, has been indefatigable. She has typed draft upon draft from abominable manuscript not only with exemplary care but with a devotion and enthusiasm which have never faltered. Library assistance of every kind has been provided with unfailing efficiency by Ann Sutherland. For preparation of the list of references and other editorial help I am indebted to Rosamund Robson, and for the index to Vivien Caplin.

Finally, I express my gratitude to the many bodies that since 1948 have supported the Tavistock Child Development Research Unit and its personnel. Financial help has been received from the National Health Service (Central Middlesex Group and Paddington Group Hospital Management Committees and the North West Metropolitan Regional Hospital Board) and from the Sir Halley Stewart Trust, the International Children's Centre in Paris, the Trustees of Elmgrant, the Regional Office for Europe of the World Health Organisation, the Josiah Macy Jr. Foundation, the Ford Foundation, and the Foundation's Fund for Research in Psychiatry. During 1957–8 I held a fellowship at the Center for Advanced Study in the Behavioral Sciences at Stanford, California, and was thereby enabled to come to grips with some of the fundamental problems presented by the data. Since April 1963, the Medical Research Council has employed me as a part-time member of its External Scientific Staff. Revision of the final chapters was undertaken whilst I was Visiting Professor in Psychiatry at Stanford University.

*　　　*　　　*

ACKNOWLEDGEMENTS

For permission to quote from published works, thanks are due to the publishers, authors, and others listed below. Bibliographical details of all the works cited are given in the list of references at the end of the volume.

Academic Press, Inc., New York, in respect of 'The affectional systems' by H. F. and M. K. Harlow, in *Behavior of Non-human Primates*, edited by A. M. Schrier, H. F. Harlow, and F. Stollnitz; the Clarendon Press, Oxford, in respect of *A Model of the Brain* by J. Z. Young; Gerald Duckworth & Co. Ltd, London, and Alfred A. Knopf, Inc., New York, in respect of the poem 'Jim' from the *Cautionary Tales* of Hilaire Belloc; the Editor of the *British Medical Journal* and Professor R. S. Illingworth in respect of 'Crying in infants and childi en'; the Editor of the *International Journal of Psycho-Analysis* and Professor W. C. Lewis in respect of 'Coital movements in the first year of life'; the Editor of the *Merrill-Palmer Quarterly* and Dr L. J. Yarrow in respect of 'Research in dimensions of early maternal care'; the Editor of *Science*, Dr S. L. Washburn, Dr P. C. Jay, and Mrs J. B. Lancaster in respect of 'Field studies of Old World monkeys and apes' (copyright 1965 by the American Association for the Advancement of Science); Harvard University Press, Cambridge, Mass., in respect of *Children of the Kibbutz* by M. E. Spiro; the Hogarth Press Ltd, London, and the Melanie Klein trustees in respect of *Developments in Psycho-analysis* by Melanie Klein and her colleagues; Holt, Rinehart & Winston, Inc., New York, in respect of 'The social development of monkeys and apes' by W. A. Mason, in *Primate Behavior*, edited by I. DeVore; the International Council of Nurses and Dr Z. Mićić in respect of 'Psychological stress in children in hospital', which appeared in the *International Nursing Review*; International Universities Press, Inc., New York, in respect of 'Psychoanalysis and education' by Anna Freud, and 'The first treasured possession' by O. Stevenson, which appeared in the *Psychoanalytic Study of the Child*; the Johns Hopkins Press, Baltimore, Md, in respect of *Mind: An Essay on Human Feeling* by S. Langer; McIntosh & Otis, Inc., New York, in respect of *The Ape in Our House* by C. Hayes; Methuen & Co. Ltd, London, in respect of 'The development of infant–mother interaction among the Ganda' by M. D. Ainsworth, in *Determinants of Infant Behaviour*, Vol. 2, edited by B. M. Foss; Tavistock Publications Ltd, London, in respect of 'Transitional objects and transitional phenomena' from the *Collected Papers* of D. W. Winnicott; Tavistock Publications Ltd, London, and Liveright Publishing Corporation, New York, in respect of 'Love for the mother and mother love' by Alice Balint, in *Primary Love and Psycho-analytic Technique* by Michael Balint.

ACKNOWLEDGEMENTS

For permission to quote passages from the Standard Edition of *The Complete Psychological Works of Sigmund Freud*, thanks are due to Sigmund Freud Copyrights Ltd, Mrs Alix Strachey, the Institute of Psycho-Analysis, the Hogarth Press Ltd, London, and Basic Books, Inc., New York.

*　　*　　*

In preparing the Second Edition of this work I am once again deeply indebted to Mary Salter Ainsworth for reading through and commenting on new and revised material, to Dorothy Southern for her never-failing secretarial services, and to the constant efficiency of the Librarian and staff of the Tavistock Library.

For extensive help in revising the section of Chapter 11 on the behaviour of non-human primates my especial thanks are due to Barbara Smuts.

For editorial assistance I am indebted to Molly Townsend who has also revised the indexes.

For permission to use three paragraphs from my 1979 Tinbergen Lecture, I am grateful to Baillière Tindall and the Editor of *Animal Behaviour*.

Part I
THE TASK

Chapter 1

Point of View

The extraordinary intricacy of all the factors to be taken into consideration leaves only one way of presenting them open to us. We must select first one and then another point of view, and follow it up through the material as long as the application of it seems to yield results.

SIGMUND FREUD (1915b)[1]

DURING nearly fifty years of psychoanalytic investigation Freud tried first one and then another point of view from which to start his inquiries. Dreams, the symptoms of neurotic patients, the behaviour of primitive peoples were amongst the varied data he studied. But, although in his search for explanation he was in each case led to events of early childhood, he himself only rarely drew for his basic data on direct observation of children. The result is that most of the concepts that psychoanalysts have about early childhood have been arrived at by a process of historical reconstruction based on data derived from older subjects. This remains true even of ideas that stem from child analysis: the events and processes inferred belong to a phase of life that is already passed.

The point of view from which this work starts is different. For reasons that are described in the preface it is believed that observation of how a very young child behaves towards his mother, both in her presence and especially in her absence, can contribute greatly to our understanding of personality development. When removed from mother by strangers young children respond usually with great intensity; and after reunion with her they show commonly either a heightened degree of separation anxiety or else an unusual detachment. Since a change in relations of one or other of these kinds, or even of both compounded, is frequent in subjects suffering from psychoneurosis and other forms of emotional disturbance, it seemed promising to select these observations as a starting-point; and having adopted this point of view to 'follow it up through the material as long as the application of it seems to yield results'.

[1] From the final paragraph of 'Repression'.

3

Because this starting-point differs so much from the one to which psychoanalysts are accustomed, it may be useful to specify it more precisely and to elaborate the reasons for adopting it.

Psychoanalytic theory is an attempt to explain the functioning of personality, in both its healthy and its pathological aspects, in terms of ontogenesis. In creating this body of theory not only Freud but virtually all subsequent analysts have worked from an end-product backwards. Primary data are derived from studying, in the analytic setting, a personality more or less developed and already functioning more or less well; from those data the attempt is made to reconstruct the phases of personality that have preceded what is now seen.

In many respects what is attempted here is the opposite. Using as primary data observations of how very young children behave in defined situations, an attempt is made to describe certain early phases of personality functioning and, from them, to extrapolate forwards. In particular, the aim is to describe certain patterns of response that occur regularly in early childhood and, thence, to trace out how similar patterns of response are to be discerned in the functioning of later personality. The change in perspective is radical. It entails taking as our starting-point, not this or that symptom or syndrome that is giving trouble, but an event or experience deemed to be potentially pathogenic to the developing personality.

Thus, whereas almost all present-day psychoanalytical theory starts with a clinical syndrome or symptom—for example, stealing, or depression, or schizophrenia—and makes hypotheses about events and processes which are thought to have contributed to its development, the perspective adopted here starts with a class of event—loss of mother-figure in infancy or early childhood—and attempts thence to trace the psychological and psychopathological processes that commonly result. It starts in fact with the traumatic experience and works prospectively.

A shift of this kind in research orientation is still unusual in psychiatry. In physiological medicine, on the other hand, it occurred long ago and an illustration drawn from that field may help to illustrate the point. When a study of the pathology of chronic infection of the lungs is undertaken today, an investigator is no longer likely to start with a group of cases all showing chronic infection and attempt to discover the infective agent or agents that are at work. It is more likely that he will start with a specified agent, perhaps tubercle or actinomycosis or some newly identified virus, in order to study the physiological and physiopathological processes to which it gives rise. In so doing he may discover many things which are not immediately relevant to chronic infective pulmonary conditions. Not only may he throw light on certain acute infectious and sub-clinical conditions, but he is almost sure to discover that infections of other organs besides lungs are the work of the pathogenic organism he has selected for study. No longer is his centre of interest a particular clinical syndrome; it has become instead the manifold sequelae of a particular pathogenic agent.

The pathogenic agent the effects of which are to be discussed is loss of mother-figure during the period between about six months and six years of age. Before considering the basic observations that are used, however, it is well to complete the description of the ways in which the approach adopted differs from the traditional one and to discuss a few of the criticisms that it has met with.

Some characteristics of the present approach

One of the differences has already been alluded to. Instead of data obtained in the treatment of patients, the data drawn on are observations of the behaviour of young children in real-life situations. Now such data are sometimes regarded as of only peripheral concern to our science. Occasionally comment implies that, by its very nature, the direct observation of behaviour can provide information of only a superficial kind and that it contrasts sharply with what, it is held, is the almost direct access to psychical functioning that obtains during psychoanalytic treatment. As a result, whenever direct observation of behaviour confirms conclusions reached in the treatment of patients it is regarded as of interest, whereas when it points in some other direction it is apt to be laid aside as of little import.

Now I believe an attitude of this sort to be based on fallacious premises. In the first place we must not overrate the data we obtain in analytic sessions. So far from our having direct access to psychical processes, what confronts us is a complex web of free associations, reports of past events, comments about the current situation, and the patient's behaviour. In trying to understand these diverse manifestations we inevitably select and arrange them according to our preferred schema; and in trying to infer what psychical processes may lie behind them we inevitably leave the world of observation and enter the world of theory. Whilst the manifestations of psychical processes met with in the consulting room are often unusually rich and varied, we are nonetheless still far from having opportunity for direct observation of psychical process.

Indeed, the opposite is probably nearer the truth. Philosophers of mind hold that, in the life of an individual, it is the 'patterns of behaviour' perceptible in infancy that 'must be the original endowment from which the purely mental states develop'; and that what is later regarded as 'inner', be it an emotion, an affect, or a fantasy, is 'a residue' that remains when all forms of associated behaviour are reduced to vanishing point (Hampshire, 1962). Since the capacity to restrict associated behaviour increases with age, it is evident that the younger the subject the more likely are his behaviour and his mental state to be the two sides of a single coin. Provided observations are skilled and detailed, therefore, a record of the behaviour of very young children can be regarded as a useful index of their concurrent mental state.

In the second place, those who are sceptical of the value of direct observation of behaviour habitually underrate the diversity and richness of the data that can be obtained. When young children are observed in situations that lead to anxiety and distress it is possible to obtain data that are plainly relevant to many concepts central to our discipline—love, hate, and ambivalence; security, anxiety, and mourning; displacement, splitting, and repression. It will, indeed, be argued that observation of the onset of detached behaviour in a child who is spending a few weeks in strange surroundings away from his mother is as close as we can get to observing repression actually occurring.

The truth is that neither class of data is intrinsically better than the other. Each is relevant to the problems with which psychoanalysis grapples and the contribution made by each is likely to be enhanced when seen in conjunction with the contribution made by the other. Binocular vision is better than the vision of either eye used separately.

Another way in which the approach adopted differs from the traditional psychoanalytic one is that it draws heavily on observations of how members of other species respond to similar situations of presence or absence of mother; and that it makes use of the wide range of new concepts that ethologists have developed to explain them.

A main reason for valuing ethology is that it provides a wide range of new concepts to try out in our theorising. Many of them are concerned with the formation of intimate social bonds —such as those tying offspring to parents, parents to offspring, and members of the two sexes (and sometimes of the same sex) to each other. Others are concerned with conflict behaviour and 'displacement activity'; others again with the development of pathological fixations, in the form either of maladaptive behaviour patterns or of unsuitable objects to which behaviour is directed. We know now that man has no monopoly either of conflict or of behaviour pathology. A canary that first starts building its nest when insufficient building material is available not only will develop pathological nest-building behaviour but will persist in such behaviour even when, later, suitable material can be had. A goose can court a dog-kennel and mourn when it is overturned. Ethological data and concepts are therefore concerned with phenomena at least comparable to those we as analysts try to understand in man.

Nevertheless, until the concepts of ethology have been tried out in the field of human behaviour we shall be in no position to determine how useful they are. Every ethologist knows that, however valuable a knowledge of related species may be in suggesting what to look for in a new species under investigation, it is never permissible to extrapolate from one species to another. Man is neither a monkey nor a white rat, let alone a canary or a cichlid fish. Man is a species in his own right with certain unusual characteristics. It may be therefore that none of the ideas stemming from studies of lower species is relevant. Yet this seems improbable. In the fields of infant-feeding, of reproduction, and of excretion we share anatomical and physiological features with lower species, and it would be odd were we to share none of the behavioural features that go with them. Furthermore, it is in early childhood, especially the preverbal period, that we might expect to find these features in least-modified form. May it not be that some at least of the neurotic tendencies and personality deviations that stem from the early years are to be understood as due to disturbance in the development of these bio-psychological processes? Whether the answer proves to be 'yes' or 'no' it is only common sense to explore the possibility.

Where Freud Stands

So far four characteristics of the point of view adopted have been described — a prospective approach, a focus on a pathogen and its sequelae, direct observation of young children, and a use of animal data—and reasons have been given for favouring each of them. Because few psychoanalysts adopt this standpoint, however, and because fear is sometimes expressed that to work from it represents a break with tradition that may be dangerous, it is of interest to see where Freud stands. In respect of each of the four characteristics in turn, first Freud's views are described and then the position adopted in this book is elaborated.

In a paper of 1920 Freud discusses the serious limitations of the retrospective method. He notes:

> So long as we trace the development from its final outcome backwards, the chain of events appears continuous, and we feel we have gained an insight which is completely satisfactory or even exhaustive. But if we proceed the reverse way, if we start from the premises inferred from the analysis and try to follow these up to the final result, then we no longer get the impression of an inevitable sequence of events which could not have been otherwise determined. We notice at once that there might have been another result, and that we might have been just as well able to understand and explain the latter. The synthesis is thus not so satisfactory as the analysis; in other words, from a knowledge of the premises we could not have foretold the nature of the result.

A main reason for this limitation, Freud points out, is our ignorance of the relative strengths of different aetiological factors. He cautions:

> Even supposing that we have a complete knowledge of the aetiological factors that decide a given result ... we never know beforehand which of the determining factors will prove the weaker or the stronger. We only say at the end that those which succeeded must have been the stronger. Hence the chain of causation can always be recognized with certainty if we follow the line of analysis, whereas to predict it along the line of synthesis is impossible (Freud, 1920b, *S.E.*, **18**, pp. 167-8).

This passage shows plainly that Freud was in no doubt what the limitations of the traditional method of inquiry are. Though a retrospective method provides much evidence regarding the kinds of factor that are likely to be aetiological, not only may it fail to identify all of them but it is in no position to evaluate the relative strengths of those it does identify. The complementary roles in psychoanalysis of retrospective and prospective studies are indeed only a special instance of the complementary roles in other spheres of knowledge of the historical method and the method of the natural sciences.

Although in every kind of historical study the retrospective method has an established place and many and great contributions to its credit, the method's inability to determine the relative parts that different factors play in causation is an acknowledged weakness. Where the historical method is weak, however, that of the natural sciences is strong. As is well known, scientific method requires that, having examined our problem, we frame one or more hypotheses regarding the causes of the events in which we are interested, and do so in such a way that from them testable predictions can be deduced. On the accuracy of such predictions hypotheses stand or fall.

There can be no doubt that if psychoanalysis is to attain full status as one of the behavioural sciences, it must add to its traditional method the tried methods of the natural sciences. Whilst the historical method will always be a principal method of the consulting room (as it continues to be in all branches of medicine), for research purposes it can and should be augmented by the method of hypothesis, deductive prediction, and test. The material of this book is presented as a preliminary step in the application of this method. Throughout, the aim has been to concentrate on events and their effects on children, and to cast theory in a form which lends itself to predictions that are testable. To frame such predictions in detail and to test even a few of them are tasks for the future.

As both Rickman (1951) and Ezriel (1951) have argued, prediction and test can, if we wish, be employed during the treatment of patients; but such procedures can never test hypotheses about earlier development. For testing the developmental theory of psychoanalysis, therefore, predictions made on the basis of direct observation of infants and young children, and often tested by the same method, are indispensable.

In employing this method it is necessary to begin by selecting a proposed aetiological factor to see whether it indeed has all or any of the effects attributed to it. This brings us to the second feature of the approach—the study of a particular pathogenic agent and its sequelae.

In considering Freud's views on this matter it is necessary to distinguish between his views on aetiological factors in general and his views on the role of the particular factor that has been selected for study here. We start with his general position.

When we examine Freud's views on factors that are causative of neuroses and allied disturbances we find that they centre always on the concept of trauma. This is as much so in his final formulations as in his earliest ones—a fact that has tended to be forgotten. Thus, in each of his very late works, *Moses and Monotheism* (1939) and the *Outline* (1940), he gives a number of pages to a discussion of the nature of trauma, the age-range during which the individual appears to be specially vulnerable, the kinds of event that may be traumatic, and the effects that they seem to have on the developing psyche.

Of these, it is the nature of trauma that is central to Freud's thesis. He concludes, as others have done, that there are two sorts of factor engaged—the event itself and the constitution of the individual experiencing it; in other words, that trauma is a function of interaction. When an experience evokes unusual pathological reaction, Freud argues, the reason is that it makes excessive demands on the personality; it does so, he postulates, by exposing the personality to quantities of excitation greater than it can deal with.

As regards constitutional factors, Freud supposes that individuals must vary in the extent to which they can meet such demands, so that 'something acts as a trauma in the case of one constitution but in the case of another would have no such effect' (*S.E.*, **23**, p. 73). At the same time, he holds, there is a particular phase of life, the first five or six years, during which every human being tends to be vulnerable. The reason for this, he believes, is that at that age 'the ego . . . is feeble, immature and incapable of resistance'. In consequence, the ego 'fails to deal with tasks which it could cope with later on with utmost ease', and instead resorts to repression or splitting. This, Freud believes, is the reason that 'neuroses are acquired only in early childhood' (*S.E.*, **23**, pp. 184–5).

When Freud speaks of 'early childhood', it is important to remember he has in mind a period of several years; in *Moses* he refers to the first five years and in the *Outline* to the first six. Within this span, he thinks, 'the periods between the ages of two and four seem to be the most important' (*S.E.*, **23**, p. 74). The early months are not especially in his mind, and he expresses himself uncertain of their significance: 'How long after birth this period of receptivity begins', he writes, 'cannot be determined with certainty' (*S.E.*, **23**, p. 74).

This, then, is Freud's general theory of aetiology. The particular theory advanced here conforms closely to it. Separation from mother, it is argued, can be traumatic within the definition proposed by Freud, especially when a child is removed to a strange place with strange people; furthermore, the period of life during which evidence shows it to be traumatic coincides closely with the period of childhood that Freud postulates is specially vulnerable. The following brief sketch of how the views advanced about separation from mother fit Freud's concept of trauma affords an opportunity to outline the central thesis of this book.

Freud defines his concept of trauma in terms of causal conditions and of psychological consequences. In both respects separation from mother in the early years fits. As regards the causal conditions, separation in a strange setting is known to induce intense distress over a long period; this is in keeping with Freud's hypothesis that trauma results when the mental apparatus is subjected to excessive quantities of excitation. As regards consequences, it can be demonstrated that the psychological changes that regularly succeed the prolonged distress of separation are none other than repression, splitting, and denial; and these, of course, are precisely the defensive processes that Freud postulates are the result of trauma—are, indeed, the processes to account for which Freud advanced his theory of trauma. Thus, it can be shown that the aetiological agent selected for study is simply a particular example of the kind of event that Freud conceived as traumatic. As a result the theory of neurosis elaborated here is in many respects a variant only of the traumatic theory advanced by Freud.

Nevertheless it must be noted that, although separation from mother fits well with Freud's general theory of neurosis and, moreover, that separation anxiety, loss, and mourning are given an increasingly important place in his theorising, only on rare occasions does he single out an event of separation or loss in the early years as a source of trauma. When he refers to the sorts of event that can be traumatic Freud, in his later writings, is rather guarded; indeed, the terms he uses to describe them are so general and abstract that it is by no means always clear what he has in mind. For example, in *Moses and Monotheism* he states only that 'They relate to impressions of a sexual and aggressive nature, and no doubt also to early injuries to the ego (narcissistic mortifications)' (*S.E.*, **23**, p. 74). Admittedly, a commonly held view is that early separation is to be understood as an early injury to the ego; but, although there is no doubt that early separation can injure the ego, whether this was Freud's view is uncertain. Whilst, therefore, separation from mother in the early years fits perfectly Freud's definition of traumatic event, it cannot be said that he ever gave serious attention to it as a particular class of traumatic event.

The third feature of the approach adopted here is the use made of data derived from direct observation of behaviour; and, as with the first two features, this one also is found to be closely in accord with Freud's views.

First, it should be noted that, although Freud only rarely draws on the data of direct observation, one or two of the occasions when he does so are key ones. Instances are the cotton-reel incident on which he bases much of his argument in *Beyond the Pleasure Principle* (*S.E.*, **18**, pp. 14–16), and the agonising reappraisal of the theory of anxiety that he undertakes in *Inhibitions, Symptoms and Anxiety* (1926). There, when faced with complex and contradictory conclusions about anxiety, Freud seeks and finds *terra firma* in observations of how young children behave when alone, or in the dark, or with strangers (*S.E.*, **20**, p. 136). It is on that foundation that the whole of his new formulation rests.

Secondly, it is interesting to find that twenty years before this, in his *Three Essays on the Theory of Sexuality* (1905), Freud had explicitly commended direct observation of children as complementary to investigation by means of psychoanalysis:

> Psycho-analytic investigation, reaching back into childhood from a later time, and contemporary observation of children combine ... The direct observation of children has the disadvantage of working upon data which are easily misunderstood; psycho-analysis is made difficult by the fact that it can only reach its data, as well as its conclusions, after long détours. But by co-operation the two methods can attain a satisfactory degree of certainty in their findings (*S.E.*, **7**, p. 201).

The fourth feature of the approach adopted here is the use made of animal studies. Whoever may still be sceptical whether knowledge of animal behaviour can help our understanding of man can find no support from Freud. Not only is it known that he made a close study of Romanes's *Mental Evolution in Man* (1888),[1] much of which is devoted to reviewing the significance of animal data, but in his final work, the *Outline*, Freud ex-

---

[1] A copy marked by Freud is in the Freud Library housed at the College of Physicians and Surgeons of Columbia University. In a personal communication Miss Anna Freud has given it as her opinion

presses the opinion that the 'general schematic picture of a psychical apparatus may be supposed to apply as well to the higher animals which resemble man mentally'. And it is possible to detect a note of regret as he concludes, 'Animal psychology has not yet taken in hand the interesting problem which is here presented'(*S.E.*, **23**, p. 147).

Admittedly studies of animal behaviour still have far to go before they can cast light on the kinds of process and structure Freud had in mind. Yet, during the years since Freud wrote the *Outline*, the brilliant studies of animal behaviour that have been made and the new concepts advanced could hardly have failed to attract his attention and arouse his interest.

Theories of motivation

In regard to the four features so far discussed, therefore, the approach adopted in this book, though unfamiliar to many psychoanalysts and as yet unexploited, is one with which Freud plainly would have found no difficulty. Nevertheless, there are certain other features of the approach that do differ from Freud's. Of these by far the main one concerns the theory of motivation. Since the theories that Freud advanced regarding drive and instinct are at the heart of psychoanalytic metapsychology, whenever an analyst departs from them it is apt to cause bewilderment or even consternation. Before going further, therefore, let me orient the reader as to the position taken. The work of Rapaport and Gill (1959) provides a useful point of reference.

In their 'attempt to state explicitly and systematically that body of assumptions which constitutes psychoanalytic metapsychology', Rapaport and Gill classify assumptions according to certain points of view. They identify five such viewpoints, each of which requires that whatever psychoanalytic explanation of a psychological phenomenon is offered must include propositions of a certain sort. The five viewpoints and the sort of proposition each demands are held to be the following:

The Dynamic: This point of view demands propositions concerning the psychological forces involved in a phenomenon.

The Economic: This demands propositions concerning the psychological energy involved in a phenomenon.

The Structural: This demands propositions concerning the

---

that her father's marginal markings were probably made during 1895 when he wrote his *Project for a Scientific Psychology* (*S.E.*, **1**).

abiding psychological configurations (structures) involved in a phenomenon.

The Genetic: This demands propositions concerning the psychological origin and development of a phenomenon.

The Adaptive: This demands propositions concerning the relationship of a phenomenon to the environment.

Now there is no difficulty with the structural, the genetic, and the adaptive. Propositions of a genetic and adaptive sort are found throughout this book; and, in any theory of defence, there must be many of a structural kind. The points of view not adopted are the dynamic and the economic. There are therefore no propositions concerning psychological energy or psychological forces; concepts such as conservation of energy, entropy, direction and magnitude of force are all missing. In later chapters an attempt is made to fill the resulting gap. Meanwhile let us consider briefly the origins and status of the points of view abandoned.

A model of the psychical apparatus that pictures behaviour as a resultant of a hypothetical psychical energy that is seeking discharge was adopted by Freud almost at the beginning of his psychoanalytical work. 'We assume,' he wrote many years later in the *Outline*, 'as other natural sciences have led us to expect, that in mental life some kind of energy is at work...' But the energy conceived is of a sort different from the energy of physics and consequently is termed by Freud 'nervous or psychical energy' (*S.E.*, **23**, pp. 163–4). Because it is necessary clearly to distinguish this kind of model from those models that, whilst presupposing physical energy, exclude any other sort of energy, the model conceived by Freud is referred to henceforward as a 'psychical energy model'.

Although from time to time details of the psychical energy model underwent change, Freud never considered abandoning it for any other kind of model. Nor have more than a handful of other analysts. What, then, are the reasons that have led me to do so?

First, it is important to remember that the origin of Freud's model lay, not in his clinical work with patients, but in ideas he had learned previously from his teachers—the physiologist Brücke, the psychiatrist Meynert, and the physician Breuer. These ideas stemmed from Fechner (1801–1887) and Helmholtz (1821–1894), and before them from Herbart (1776–1841); and, as Jones remarks, by the time Freud became interested in them, they were already 'both familiar and widely accepted throughout the educated, and particularly the scientific world' (Jones, 1953, p. 414). The psychical energy model is, therefore, a theoretical model brought by Freud to psychoanalysis: it is in no way a model derived by him from the practice of psychoanalysis.[1]

Secondly, the model represents an attempt to conceptualise the data of psychology in terms analogous to those of the physics and chemistry current in the second half of the nineteenth century. Impressed especially by the use physicists were making of the concept of energy, and by the principle of its conservation, Helmholtz held that, throughout science, real causes must be thought of as being some kind of 'force'; and he was busy applying such ideas to his work in physiology. Accordingly Freud, eager to frame his concepts in terms of a proper science, borrowed and elaborated a model that had been built with these concepts by Fechner. The principal features of Freud's model are: (a) that 'in mental functions something is to be distinguished—a quota of affect or sum of excitation—which possesses all the characteristics of a quantity . . . . which is capable of increase, diminution, displacement and discharge' and which is pictured as analogous to an electric charge (Freud, 1894, *S.E.*, **3**, p. 60); and (b) that the mental apparatus is governed by two closely related principles, the principle of inertia and the principle of constancy, the former stating that the mental apparatus endeavours to keep the quantity of excitation present in it as low as possible, and the latter that it tends to keep it constant.[2]

[1] Apart from Freud's own writings, the best guides to the origins of Freud's model are Bernfeld's papers (1944, 1949); the first volume of Jones's biography (1953), especially Chapter 17; the Introduction, by Kris, to the volume of Freud's letters to Fliess (Kris, 1954); and a commentary by Strachey (1962), 'The emergence of Freud's fundamental hypotheses' (*S.E.*, **3**, pp. 62–8). A longer historical perspective is given by Whyte (1960) who, amongst other things, emphasises the high prestige enjoyed by the quantitative form in which Herbart expressed his ideas.

[2] In those early days the principle of inertia was held by Freud to be primary and to govern the system when stimulation of external origin is received: 'This process of discharge represents the primary function of the nervous system.' The principle of constancy was regarded as secondary and as an elaboration required to enable the system to deal with stimulation of internal (somatic) origin (Freud, *Project for a Scientific Psychology*, *S.E.*, **1**, p. 297).

Subsequently, Freud's thinking about these two principles underwent

Thirdly and most important, the psychical energy model is logically unrelated to the concepts that Freud, and everyone since, regards as truly central to psychoanalysis—the role of unconscious mental processes, repression as a process actively keeping them unconscious, transference as a main determinant of behaviour, the origin of neurosis in childhood trauma. Not one of these concepts bears any intrinsic relation to a psychical energy model; and when this model is discarded all four remain intact and unchanged. The psychical energy model is a possible model for explaining the data to which Freud drew attention: it is certainly not a necessary one.

The points to be emphasised are, first, that Freud's psychical energy model originated outside psychoanalysis, and, secondly, that a main motive for his introducing it was in order to ensure that his psychology conformed to what he believed to be the best scientific ideas of the day. Nothing in his clinical observations required or even suggested such a model—as a reading of his early case studies shows. No doubt partly because Freud adhered to the model throughout his lifetime and partly because nothing compellingly better has been available most analysts have continued to employ it.

Now there is nothing unscientific in utilising, for the interpretation of data, any model that seems promising; and there is therefore nothing unscientific either in Freud's introduction of his model or in his own or others' employment of it. Nevertheless, the question arises whether there may by now be an alternative better suited for the purpose in hand.

Within the psychoanalytic movement itself there have, of course, been several attempts either to augment or to replace Freud's model. Amongst these attempts are a number that concentrate on the individual's strong tendency to seek relationships with other persons, or parts of other persons, and that regard this tendency as representing a primary principle and therefore either of equal importance in psychical life to the discharge (Nirvana) principle and the pleasure principle, or as an alternative to them. Unlike the psychical energy model,

revision though no essential change. In his final formulation the principle of inertia remains primary; it is attributed to the death instinct and renamed the Nirvana principle. The principle of constancy is to some extent replaced by the pleasure principle which, like its forerunner, is regarded as secondary; the pleasure principle is held to represent a modification of the Nirvana principle by action of the life instinct (see editor's footnote, *S.E.*, **14**, p. 121).

it should be noted, object-relational models are derived from clinical experience and from the data obtained during analysis of patients. Once the importance of transference material is recognised, indeed, some model of this kind is forced upon us; and from Freud onwards some such model is present in the thinking of all practising analysts. The issue, therefore, is not whether this type of model is useful but whether it is used as a supplement to a psychical energy model or as a replacement of it.

Of the many analysts since Freud who have contributed to object-relations theory probably the four most influential have been Melanie Klein, Balint, Winnicott, and Fairbairn. Though the versions of theory each advances have much in common, they also differ in a number of ways. For present purposes the most important difference between them is the extent to which a theory is a pure object-relational theory or a composite theory in which object-relational concepts are combined with concepts of psychical energy. Of the four theories, Melanie Klein's is the most complex because of the emphasis she places on the role of a death instinct; and Fairbairn's is the most pure because of his explicit rejection of all non-object-relational concepts.[1]

Because the theory advanced here derives from object-relations theory, it owes much to the work of these four British analysts. Nevertheless, it adopts the position of none of them closely and at some points differs greatly from each. It differs from all four, moreover, in one principal way: it draws on a new type of instinct theory.[2] An absence of any alternative theory of instinct to Freud's constitutes, I believe, the biggest single shortcoming of each of the current object-relations theories.

The model of instinctive behaviour employed is, like Freud's, imported from neighbouring disciplines and, also like his, is

---

[1] A second way in which the theories differ is in regard to the period of life during which a child is held to be at his most vulnerable. In this respect there is a gradation from Melanie Klein's view to Balint's. In Melanie Klein's theory almost all the crucial steps in development are assigned to the first six months of life; in Fairbairn's theory they are assigned to the first twelve months, and in Winnicott's to the first eighteen months; in Balint's theory all of the first few years of life are considered to be of about equal importance.

[2] The term 'instinct theory' is used here in preference to such terms as 'drive theory' or 'motivation theory'. Reasons are to be found in Chapter 3 and following chapters.

a reflection of the scientific climate of the times. It derives partly from ethology and partly from such models as those suggested by Miller, Galanter, and Pribram in *Plans and the Structure of Behavior* (1960) and by Young in *A Model of the Brain* (1964). In the place of psychical energy and its discharge, the central concepts are those of behavioural systems and their control, of information, negative feedback, and a behavioural form of homeostasis. The more complex forms of instinctive behaviour are regarded as resulting from the execution of plans that, depending on the species, are more or less flexible. Execution of a plan, it is supposed, is initiated on the receipt of certain information (derived by the sense organs either from external sources or from internal sources, or from a combination of the two) and guided, and ultimately terminated, by the continuous reception of further sets of information that have their origin in the *results of the action taken* (and are derived, in the same way, by the sense organs from external, internal, or combined sources). In the determination of the plans themselves and of the signals that control their execution, both learned and unlearned components are assumed to enter. As regards the energy necessary to make the whole work, none is postulated, except, of course, the energy of physics: that is what differentiates the model from the traditional theory.[1]

These, in short, are a few of the essential features of the model employed. In Part II of this volume (after some empirical data have been considered in the next chapter) the model is amplified. Meanwhile, a brief indication is given of three shortcomings that are present, it is thought, in a psychical energy model and are avoided, or at least reduced, in the new model. They concern the way in which the theory deals with termination of action, the theory's testability, and the relation of the concepts used to those of current biological science.

Comparison of Old and New Models

Action not only starts but stops. In a model that employs psychical energy the start is thought of as resulting from an accumulation of psychical energy and its ending is thought of as due to an exhaustion of that energy. Before a performance can be repeated, therefore, a fresh supply of psychical energy

[1] Mr James Strachey has called my attention to the possibility that the theory advanced in this book is not quite as different from Freud's as I, and others, might suppose (see the final section of this chapter, p. 22).

must be accumulated. A great deal of behaviour, however, is not easily explained in this way. For example, a baby may cease to cry when he sees his mother and resume soon afterwards when she disappears from sight; and the process may be repeated several times. In such a case, it is difficult to suppose that cessation of crying and its resumption are caused by first a drop and then a rise in the amount of psychical energy available. There is a similar problem about the nest-building of birds. When the nest is complete the bird stops building; but if the nest is then removed it soon repeats its performance. Again, it is not easy to suppose that the repetition is due to a sudden access of a special energy—and one that would not have occurred had the nest been left *in situ*. In each case, on the other hand, the change of behaviour is readily understood as due to signals arising from a change in the environment. The matter is discussed further in Chapter 6.

The second shortcoming of the psychical energy model of psychoanalysis, as of other similar models, lies in its limited degree of testability. As Popper (1934) has argued, what distinguishes a scientific theory from other sorts of theory is not how it originates but the fact that it can be and is tested, not only once but over and over again. The more frequently and rigorously a theory has been tested and has stood up, the higher its scientific status; from which it follows that, other things being equal, the better testable a theory the better is it for purposes of science. In physics, energy is defined in terms of an ability to do work, and work can be measured in foot-pounds or their equivalents. The theory of physical energy, therefore, can be, and frequently has been, subjected to test by determining whether predictions about work deduced from it prove valid or false. So far, of course, the many predictions tested have proved valid. For Freud's theory of psychical energy, on the other hand, as for all similar theories, no tests of an analogous kind have yet been proposed. Thus the theory of psychical energy remains untested; and until it is defined in terms of something that can be observed, and preferably measured, it must be regarded as still untestable. For a scientific theory this is a serious shortcoming.

The third shortcoming of the model stems, ironically, from what must have seemed to Freud its main strength. For Freud the psychical energy model was an attempt to conceptualise the data of psychology in terms analogous to those of the physics and chemistry current at the time he began his work, and thus was thought to have the great virtue of linking psychology to science proper. Nowadays it has precisely the opposite effect. Models of motivation that assume the existence of a special form of energy distinct from physical energy do not commend themselves to biologists (Hinde, 1966); nor is it supposed that the principle of entropy applies to living as it does to non-living systems. Instead, in biological theory today, the operation of physical energy is taken for granted, and the main emphases are on concepts of organisation and information, which are concepts independent of matter and energy, and on the living organism as an open not a closed system. As a result the psychical energy model, so far from integrating psychoanalysis with present-day science, has the opposite effect: it is a barrier.

The model employed in this book does not, it is claimed, suffer from these shortcomings. By utilising the concept of feedback, it gives as much attention to the conditions that terminate an act as to those that initiate one. Through being closely related to observable data it is testable. By being cast in terms of control theory and evolution theory, the model links psychoanalysis to the main corpus of present-day biology. Finally, it is claimed, it can give a simpler and more consistent explanation of the data with which psychoanalysis is concerned than does the psychical energy model.

These, it is realised, are large claims and may not be readily acceptable. The purpose in stating them is to explain why this new model is employed and why, therefore, certain of the main metapsychological concepts of psychoanalysis are not utilised. Thus Freud's instinct theory, the pleasure principle, and the traditional theory of defence are three examples out of many that could be cited of formulations which, because they are cast in terms of a psychical energy model, are regarded as unsatisfactory as they stand. At the same time, it is clear, no analyst will discard such theories unless at least two conditions are fulfilled: first, that the data the theories are intended to explain are respected, and, secondly, that new theories at least as good as the old ones are available as alternatives. These are stringent conditions.

It is evident that the difficulties confronting anyone who attempts a reformulation of this kind are numerous and big. One difficulty especially should be called to the reader's attention. During the seventy years since psychoanalysis was born the traditional model has come to be applied to almost all aspects of mental life; and as a result it now provides an explanation, more or less satisfactory, for most of the problems met with. In this regard, obviously, no new theory can compete. To start with, inevitably, each new theory can show its paces only in selected areas—much as a new political party can compete in only a few constituencies. Not until it has proved itself in a limited area can a theory's application be extended and its more general usefulness be tested. How widely applicable and useful the theory advanced here will prove to be is therefore a matter for investigation. Meanwhile, the reader is asked to judge the theory, not on what it has yet to tackle, but on the measure of success it achieves within the limited field to which it is so far applied. 'The extraordinary intricacy of all the factors to be taken into consideration leaves only one way of presenting them open to us. . . .'

To conclude this orienting chapter it may be of interest to consider how Freud might have been expected to greet these innovations. Would he have found them alien to his conception of psychoanalysis or would he, perhaps, have found them strange but legitimate as alternative ways of ordering the data? A reading of his work leaves little doubt what the answer would be. Time and again he emphasises the very tentative status of his theories and recognises that scientific theories, like other living things, are born, live, and die. He writes:

> a science erected on empirical interpretation . . . will gladly content itself with nebulous, scarcely imaginable basic concepts which it hopes [either] to apprehend more clearly in the course of its development or . . . to replace by others. For these ideas are not the foundation of science, [which] is observation alone . . ., but the top of the whole structure and they can be replaced and discarded without damaging it (*S.E.*, **14**, p. 77).

In his *Autobiographical Study* (1925) he speaks in the same vein, referring blithely to the 'speculative superstructure of psycho-analysis, any portion of which can be abandoned or changed without loss or regret the moment its inadequacy has been proved' (*S.E.*, **20**, p. 32).

The two questions to which we must constantly address ourselves are, therefore, how adequate to the data is this or that theory and how can we submit it most effectively to test? It is hoped that the theories advanced here will be scrutinised and criticised with these questions in mind.

Note on the concept of feedback in Freud's theorising

As remarked in the footnote to page 18 it is possible that in some respects the theory of motivation advanced in this book is not quite as different from some of Freud's ideas as I, and others, might suppose.

In recent years there has been renewed interest in the neurological model presented by Freud in his *Project for a Scientific Psychology*, written in 1895 but unpublished in his lifetime. A neurophysiologist, Pribram (1962), calls attention to many features of the model, including negative feedback, that, even by today's standards, are sophisticated. Strachey (1966), in his Introduction to the new translation, also draws attention to resemblances between Freud's early ideas and modern concepts: for example, 'there is, in Freud's account of the mechanism of perception, the introduction of the fundamental notion of feedback as a means of correcting errors in the machine's own dealings with the environment' (*S.E.*, 1, pp. 292–3).

The presence of these ideas in the *Project* leads Strachey to believe that the model of instinctive behaviour advanced here, especially the concept of action being terminated by the perception of environmental change, is less different from Freud's than I had supposed:

> In the *Project* at all events Freud would say that the 'action' was started as a result of a perception from outside and was stopped because of a fresh perception from outside and was started again because of yet another perception from outside (Strachey, personal communication).

The idea of feedback may also be discerned in Freud's concepts of the aim and the object of an instinct. In his paper on 'Instincts and their vicissitudes' (1915a), he describes these concepts as follows:

> The aim of an instinct is in every instance satisfaction, which can only be obtained by removing the state of stimulation at the source of the instinct . . . The object of an instinct is the thing in regard to which or through which the instinct is able to achieve its aim (*S.E.*, 14, p. 122).

The removal of a state of stimulation at source by means of a relationship with an object is readily understood in terms of feedback; to the concept of discharge it is alien.

It is of much interest to find the concept of feedback at these points in Freud's theorising, yet the concept is always shadowed and often excluded by concepts of a quite different kind. As a result the concept of feedback has never been exploited in psychoanalytic theorising; usually indeed, for example in the account of metapsychology presented by Rapaport and Gill (1959), it is conspicuous by its absence.

In searching for current ideas in the thinking of a previous generation there is always a danger of reading in more than is there. For example, it is doubtful whether it is legitimate to regard Freud's principle of inertia as a special case of the principle of homeostasis, as Pribram suggests: 'Inertia is homeostasis in its baldest form.' There appears to be a vital difference between the two principles. Whereas Freud's principle of inertia is conceived as a tendency for the level of excitation to be reduced to zero, the principle of homeostasis is conceived not only as a tendency for levels to be maintained between certain positive limits but as working to limits set mainly by genetic factors and at points that maximise the likelihood of survival. The one is conceived in terms of physics and entropy, the other in terms of biology and survival. As a concept resembling homeostasis the principle of constancy seems more promising than the principle of inertia.

Chapter 2

Observations to be Explained

A child forsaken, waking suddenly,
Whose gaze afeard on all things round doth rove,
And seeth only that it cannot see
The meeting eyes of love.
                                        GEORGE ELIOT

FROM time immemorial mothers and poets have been alive to the distress caused to a child by loss of his mother; but it is only in the last fifty years that, by fits and starts, science has awoken to it.

Apart from a few early references, some of them by Freud, no series of observations of how infants and young children behave when separated from mother was on record until the early 1940s. Then the first observations, made in the Hampstead Nurseries during the Second World War, were reported by Dorothy Burlingham and Anna Freud (1942, 1944). They cover children in the age-range from birth to about four years who were healthy and who, after separation, were cared for in conditions as good as could be created in a wartime nursery. Because these were pioneer studies, reporting is not systematic and the exact conditions of care, which changed considerably during the years, are not always described. Nevertheless, much that is recorded is now known to be typical and the vivid accounts presented have become famous.

The second series of observations are those made by René Spitz and Katherine Wolf on about one hundred infants of unmarried mothers who were cared for in a penal institution (Spitz and Wolf, 1946). Except for a few infants observed up to the age of eighteen months, observations in this series are limited to behaviour occurring during the first twelve months of life. Until they were between six and eight months old all the babies studied were cared for by their own mothers. Then, 'for unavoidable external reasons', a separation occurred which lasted 'for a practically unbroken period of three months, during which the child either did not see its mother at all, or at best once a week'. During this period the child was cared for either

24

by the mother of another child or by a girl in the later stages of pregnancy. Unlike most other studies of the sort, in this one, except for the changes of mother-figure, the child's environment remained much the same during separation as it had been before.

Since these two early studies there have been a number of others. In the years 1948–52 my colleague, James Robertson, who had himself been on the staff of the Hampstead Nurseries, observed a number of children, mostly between the ages of eighteen months and four years, who had gone either to a residential nursery or to a hospital, some of them for a week or two only and some for much longer periods. As many as possible he observed not only during their stay away but also at home before and afterwards. Some of his observations are recorded in papers and a film published between 1952 and 1954.[1] Robertson (1962) has also published a number of descriptions by parents of how their young children have reacted during and after a period in hospital: most of these children were in hospital without mother, but in a few instances mother was there too.

Since Robertson's observations two other studies have been conducted by my colleagues in the Tavistock Child Development Research Unit, the first by Christoph Heinicke (1956) and the second by Christoph Heinicke and Ilse Westheimer (1966). In both studies the children were aged between thirteen months and three years, and the separation occurred when they were placed in a residential nursery; most of the children returned home after about a fortnight but a few stayed away longer. Although in each of these investigations only a handful of children were observed (six in the first and ten in the second), the studies are unique for the care of their design and the amount of systematic observation. Moreover, for each sample of separated children a contrast group was selected and observed: in the first it was a fairly well-matched group of children observed during their first weeks of attendance at a day nursery; in the second it was a similarly matched group of children observed whilst living in their own homes. Heinicke and Westheimer treat their data statistically and also describe in some detail the behaviour of individual children.

During the past decades a number of other studies have been

[1] Robertson and Bowlby (1952); Bowlby, Robertson, and Rosenbluth (1952); Bowlby (1953); and Robertson (1953). The film is Robertson (1952).

reported. For example, in Paris Jenny Aubry (formerly Roudinesco) and her associates observed a number of young children, in their second year of life, soon after they had been received into the care of a residential nursery (Appell and Roudinesco, 1951; David, Nicolas, and Roudinesco, 1952; Aubry, 1955; Appell and David, 1961). Later, members of this group studied children aged from four to seven years during a stay of one month in a holiday camp (David, Ancellin, and Appell, 1957).

The findings of all these studies of well children in a nursery setting, including their own, have been systematically considered by Heinicke and Westheimer in later chapters of their book *Brief Separations* (1966). A very substantial degree of agreement between findings is apparent.

A number of studies of the behaviour of young children during and after a stay in hospital are also on record. Some have been by paediatricians: for example, in the United States by Prugh *et al.* (1953); in England by Illingworth and Holt (1955); in Jugoslavia by Mićić (1962); and in Poland by Bielicka and Olechnowicz (1963). Others have been carried out by psychologists, and include a study in Scotland by Schaffer of the responses of children under a year old both on admission to hospital and on return home (Schaffer, 1958; Schaffer and Callender, 1959), and a comprehensive investigation in Czechoslovakia by Langmeier and Matejcek (1963). A comprehensive review of the hospital literature has been published by Vernon *et al.* (1965).

The subjects of the various studies differ in many respects. For example, they differ in age, in the type of home from which they come, in the type of institution to which they go and the care they receive there, and in the length of time they are away. They differ, too, in whether they are healthy or sick.[1] Despite all these variations, however, and despite the different backgrounds and expectations of the observers, there is a remarkable uniformity in the findings. Once a child is over the age of six months he tends to respond to the event of separation from mother in certain typical ways. Since the observations on which the theoretical work presented here is based are mainly those

[1] It should be noted that in two principal studies of children in hospital, those by Robertson and Schaffer, a child more than transiently affected by fever, pain, or other feature of the illness was excluded. Most of the children were admitted either for investigation or for a minor operation.

of James Robertson, the account given derives largely from his work.

His basic data are observations of the behaviour of children in their second and third years of life whilst staying for a limited period in residential nurseries or hospital wards and there cared for in traditional ways. This means that the child is removed from the care of his mother-figure and all subordinate figures and also from his familiar environment and is cared for instead in a strange place by a succession of unfamiliar people. Further data are derived from observations of his behaviour in his home during the months after his return and from reports from his parents.

In the setting described a child of fifteen to thirty months who has had a reasonably secure relationship with his mother and has not previously been parted from her will commonly show a predictable sequence of behaviour. This can be broken into three phases according to what attitude to his mother is dominant. We describe these phases as those of Protest, Despair, and Detachment. Though in presenting them it is convenient to differentiate them sharply, it is to be understood that in reality each merges into the next, so that a child may be for days or weeks in a state of transition from one phase to another, or of alternation between two phases.

The initial phase, that of protest, may begin immediately or may be delayed; it lasts from a few hours to a week or more. During it the young child appears acutely distressed at having lost his mother and seeks to recapture her by the full exercise of his limited resources. He will often cry loudly, shake his cot, throw himself about, and look eagerly towards any sight or sound which might prove to be his missing mother. All his behaviour suggests strong expectation that she will return. Meantime he is apt to reject all alternative figures who offer to do things for him, though some children will cling desperately to a nurse.

During the phase of despair, which succeeds protest, the child's preoccupation with his missing mother is still evident, though his behaviour suggests increasing hopelessness. The active physical movements diminish or come to an end, and he may cry monotonously or intermittently. He is withdrawn and inactive, makes no demands on people in the environment, and appears to be in a state of deep mourning. This is a quiet stage, and sometimes, clearly erroneously, is presumed to indicate a diminution of distress.

Because the child shows more interest in his surroundings, the phase of detachment which sooner or later succeeds protest and despair is often welcomed as a sign of recovery. The child no longer rejects the nurses; he accepts their care and the food and toys they bring, and may even smile and be sociable. To some this change seems satisfactory. When his mother visits, however, it can be seen that all is not well, for there is a striking absence of the behaviour characteristic of the strong attachment normal at this age. So far from greeting his mother he may seem hardly to know her; so far from clinging to her he may remain remote and apathetic; instead of tears there is a listless turning away. He seems to have lost all interest in her.

Should his stay in hospital or residential nursery be prolonged and should he, as is usual, have the experience of becoming transiently attached to a series of nurses each of whom leaves and so repeats for him the experience of the original loss of his mother, he will in time act as if neither mothering nor contact with humans has much significance for him. After a series of upsets at losing several mother-figures to whom in turn he has given some trust and affection, he will gradually commit himself less and less to succeeding figures and in time will stop altogether attaching himself to anyone. He will become increasingly self-centred and, instead of directing his desires and feelings towards people, will become preoccupied with material things such as sweets, toys, and food. A child living in an institution or hospital who has reached this state will no longer be upset when nurses change or leave. He will cease to show feelings when his parents come and go on visiting day; and it may cause them pain when they realise that, although he has an avid interest in the presents they bring, he has little interest in them as special people. He will appear cheerful and adapted to his unusual situation and apparently easy and unafraid of anyone. But this sociability is superficial: he appears no longer to care for anyone.

We had some difficulty in finding the best term to denote this phase. In early papers the term 'denial' was used. This gave rise to difficulties, however, and was abandoned in favour of the more purely descriptive term 'detachment'. An alternative is 'withdrawal'; but this has two disadvantages for the purpose. In the first place there is a danger that withdrawal might convey the picture of an inactive child withdrawn from the world, a picture the opposite of what often obtains. In the second, in psychoanalytic writing withdrawal is commonly associated with libido theory and the idea of instinct as a quantity of energy that can be withdrawn, a model that is not being used. Not only does the term 'detachment' have neither of these disadvantages, but it is a natural counterpart of 'attachment'.

It is plain that both the intensity of the reactions to be seen and the particular forms they take are influenced by the many variables already referred to. Thus the more isolated a child and the more he is confined in a cot, the more vigorous the protest; whereas the less strange the environment and the more he is in the care of a single mother-substitute the less intense the distress. Features that seem regularly and effectively to reduce the intensity of reaction are either the presence of a sibling, even a very young one (Heinicke and Westheimer, 1966) or care by a single mother-substitute, especially when the child has met her beforehand in the presence of his mother (Robertson and Robertson, 1967).

A variable that is found regularly to be associated with increased disturbance, both during separation and after return home, is the length of a child's separation. Such association stood out in the study by Heinicke and Westheimer (1966) and, as they show, is reported regularly by almost all other workers (*ibid.*, pp. 318–22).

Though there is good evidence that by far the most important variable in determining the behaviour described is absence of familiar mother-figure,[1] this view is not always accepted. Instead, other variables are held responsible. Amongst those that have been suggested are: a strange environment, the condition of the mother, and the kind of relationship a child has had with his mother previously. Thus, it is pointed out that in many of the studies reported the child is not only in the care of strange people but also in a strange place; that when a healthy child is sent to a residential nursery it is often because his mother is going into hospital to have a new baby; and that many other children go to a nursery because relations at home are unsatisfactory. May not the behaviour be due, therefore, not to loss of mother but to the strange environment, or to the expectation of a rival, or to a previously unsatisfactory relation with mother?

Were these objections to carry weight, the case for regarding

[1] Although throughout this book the text refers usually to 'mother' and not to 'mother-figure', it is to be understood that in every case reference is to the person who mothers a child and to whom he becomes attached. For most children, of course, that person is also his natural mother.

separation *per se* as of importance would crumble. There is, however, good evidence regarding the influence of each class of variable and in no case does it support the sceptics. Let us consider it.

Although in many studies, including those of Robertson, the children are confronted not only with strange people but with a strange place also, there are some studies in which this does not occur. One is the study by Spitz and Wolf already referred to. The infants whose behaviour led Spitz to delineate the syndrome 'anaclitic depression' remained in the same institution during the absence of mother. Not only so, but, provided it occurred within three months, only one change was necessary to restore them to something like their previous condition—the return of mother.

Two other reports confirm that, whatever effects change of environment may have, a main variable is always absence of mother-figure. One is a report by Helene Deutsch (1919) of a little boy who was brought up by nannies because his mother was working. When he was just two years old his first nurse left and was replaced by a second. Despite the fact that he remained at home and that his mother was there every evening, the behaviour he showed after his familiar nurse's departure conforms to pattern. On the night of her going he cried a great deal, was sleepless, and insisted on his mother remaining with him. Next day he refused to let the new nurse feed him, and he reverted to being wet and dirty. During each of the subsequent four nights his mother had to stay with him and assure him of her love, and his daytime behaviour continued disturbed. Not until the sixth day did much of his behaviour return to normal and not until the ninth did he appear to be himself again. Although there was clear evidence that he was missing his familiar nurse, he never once mentioned her by name and seemed reluctant in any way to refer to her absence.

A similar case is reported by Spiro (1958). This describes the behaviour of another little boy of about the same age who was brought up in an Israeli kibbutz and was left there for several weeks whilst his parents were away. In this case the child was left in his familiar environment with his familiar nurse and playmates. Nevertheless, as the following extract from his mother's account shows, he was much upset by his parents' absence.

> We have just returned to the kibbutz. Our absence was very painful for Yaakov. The nurse tells me that many evenings he

did not sleep. One night the watchman found him standing in front of our door, with his thumb in his mouth. When his father, who returned a week before me, came home, Yaakov would not let him leave the house in the evening, and cried when he did leave. When I returned, Yaakov did not recognise me, and he ran to his father. Now when I leave him in the evening, he always asks me: 'You'll never leave me again, never?' He has deep fears about being left alone again. He has begun to suck his thumb . . . I have to stay with him at night until he falls asleep.

Spiro reports further that the same boy reacted with anger when his father went on a trip at a later date. Yaakov, now a few months older, says to his mother: 'Father went to Tel Aviv. All the children will be very angry with my father.' His mother asks if *he* is angry with his father, and he replies: 'All the children will be angry with Father.'[1]

This evidence is sufficient to show that the sequence of behaviour with which we are concerned cannot be attributed simply to a change of environment. Undoubtedly a strange environment is of consequence, but what matters much more to a child is whether his mother is present or absent. That conclusion is strongly supported by observations of how a young child behaves when he is in a strange environment but is with his mother.

Family holidays provide a vast array of anecdotal evidence of how young children behave in strange surroundings when they are accompanied by mother. It is true that a few children, especially those in their second year, are disturbed by such conditions; nevertheless, as long as the familiar mother-figure is present, it is rare for the disturbance to be serious or to persist.[2] On the contrary, most young children enjoy a family holiday because of the changed surroundings it offers, not in spite of them.

Another class of evidence that also supports the position that, so long as mother is present, strange surroundings are either not disturbing or only slightly so derives from observation of how young children behave in hospital.

There are now a number of studies which leave no doubt that,

---

[1] In the quoting of this report a few minor changes have been made, to avoid the use of proper names.

[2] A report by Ucko (1965) suggests that young children who are upset during family holidays are frequently children who at birth had been found to be suffering from asphyxia.

when a child is accompanied into hospital by his mother, he shows little or none of the disturbed behaviour so typical of a child who is there alone. One such case, that of a little girl of two, has been recorded on film by Robertson (1958). Several other reports come from paediatricians, for example MacCarthy, Lindsay, and Morris (1962) and Mićić (1962). The latter records the dramatic change in behaviour that occurs when a child who has been in hospital for a few days without his mother is joined there by her. Mićić gives the following account of a little girl aged thirteen months who was in hospital for broncho-pneumonia:

> Dzanlic was well developed and well nourished. She was admitted without her mother and was alone for a couple of days. She lay listlessly all the time and did not want to eat, but she only cried in her sleep. During examinations she did not resist. I raised her into a sitting position but she at once turned away and lay down again.
>
> On the third day her mother came. The moment she saw her mother the child got up and started to cry. Then she calmed down and became ravenously hungry. After being fed she started to smile and play. When I went into the ward the next day I did not recognise the child, the change was so complete. She was smiling in her mother's arms whereas I had expected to see a sleeping child lying there. It was inconceivable that a child who had been psychologically depressed and had slept continuously could turn overnight into so happy a little girl. Everything pleased her and she smiled at all.

That this remarkable change is no chance effect is attested by many other similar accounts, including those written by parents and collected by Robertson (1962).

A systematic study by Fagin (1966) of thirty children who had been accompanied in hospital by mother and of a matched sample of children who had been in hospital alone (though visited daily) points firmly to the same conclusion. On return home after a few days in hospital all the unaccompanied children showed responses typical of young children who have undergone a short separation in a strange environment: increased clinging, increased upset during any further brief separation, relapse in sphincter control. The accompanied children, by contrast, showed none of these disturbances.

A strange environment, therefore, is certainly not the principal cause of a separated child's distress. That in the absence of mother it exacerbates distress is, however, certain. These issues are discussed further in the second volume.

Mother's pregnancy and the expectation of a new baby can also be ruled out as anything but minor factors. In the first place, as is clear from the cases reported, children whose mothers are not pregnant habitually show typical responses when they are separated. In the second, in the study reported by Heinicke and Westheimer (1966) it was possible to make a direct comparison of the behaviour of thirteen children whose mothers were about to have a new baby with that of five children whose mothers were not pregnant. When a detailed comparison was made of the ways in which children in these two groups behaved during the first fortnight of their separation no significant differences were found between them.

Finally, there is no evidence that it is only those children whose relationship with mother previous to the separation was unfavourable who are distressed by the event. In each of the studies referred to some of the children who were acutely distressed had come from homes in which family relationships, including that between child and mother, were almost certainly excellent. Some of the best-documented evidence on this matter comes from the study by Heinicke and Westheimer (1966). In this study, Ilse Westheimer, an experienced psychiatric social worker, paid numerous visits to the homes of the separated children immediately before the separation (whenever possible), during it, and after the child had returned home. In this way she came to know the families well and to have a fairly clear picture of the relationship between child and mother. Relationships varied from reasonably good to indifferent. Although the researchers had expected to find corresponding differences in the ways in which the children responded during and after their separation, findings were otherwise. Such connection as they did find supports the view, expressed earlier by Robertson and Bowlby (1952), that an absence of fretting during separation is seen mainly in children who have had previously a very unsatisfactory relationship with mother; or, in other words, the more affectionate the relationship has been the greater a child's manifest upset during separation.

In view of this substantial body of evidence we believe it safe to conclude that, whatever part is played by other variables in determining the distress described, by far the most weighty is the loss by a child of his mother. This being so, a number of problems are posed. Why should a young child be so distressed simply by the loss of his mother? Why after return home does he become so apprehensive lest he lose her again? What psychological processes account for his distress and for the phenomenon of detachment? Before all, how do we understand the nature of the bond that ties a child to his mother? These are the problems to which these volumes are addressed. But before broaching them it is necessary to give space to an account of the model of instinctive behaviour that is employed in place of the energy model proposed and used by Freud.

Part II

INSTINCTIVE BEHAVIOUR

Chapter 3

Instinctive Behaviour: An Alternative Model

> I am altogether doubtful whether any decisive pointers for the differentiation and classification of the instincts can be arrived at on the basis of working over the psychological material. This working over seems rather itself to call for the application to the material of definite assumptions concerning instinctual life, and it would be a desirable thing if these assumptions could be taken from some other branch of knowledge and carried over to psychology.
>
> SIGMUND FREUD (1915a)

> There is no more urgent need in psychology than for a securely founded theory of the instincts on which it might then be possible to build further. Nothing of the sort exists, however. . . .
>
> SIGMUND FREUD (1925)

Introduction

During the half-century since Freud sought a well-based theory of instinct and lamented his inability to find one, striking progress has been made. To this progress many disciplines have contributed. A long-awaited theoretical breakthrough has been achieved by analytical biology and control theory, which together have elucidated the basic principles that underlie adaptive, goal-directed behaviour. Exploiting the breakthrough have been three empirically based sciences: ethology (the study of animal behaviour by zoologists), experimental psychology, and neurophysiology—Freud's own first love. Each of these three disciplines has its own distinctive origins and also its own distinctive fields of interest, methods, and concepts; and it is, therefore, no wonder that for some years there was little exchange between them and some misunderstanding. In recent times, however, a greater familiarity with the control systems approach and with each other's work has shown how each has its own unique contribution to make and how effectively the three complement one another. What was formerly a source of weakness has become a source of strength—and at last the principles of a unified behavioural science are beginning to emerge.

Behaviour of even the simplest animals is enormously complex. It varies in systematic ways from members of one species to those of another, and in less systematic ways from individual to individual within a species. Moreover, the behaviour of a single individual when adult is different from its behaviour when young, and it differs too from season to season, from day to day, and from minute to minute. Yet there are many regularities of behaviour and certain of these regularities are so striking and play so important a part in the survival of individual and species that they have earned the name 'instinctive'. Provided we do not imply by it any particular theory of causation and use it as an adjective purely descriptively, the term instinctive continues to be of value. Its limitations, and also the difficulties to which the noun 'instinct' gives rise, are discussed in Chapter 8.

Behaviour that traditionally has been termed instinctive has four main characteristics:

a. it follows a recognisably similar and predictable pattern in almost all members of a species (or all members of one sex);

b. it is not a simple response to a single stimulus but a sequence of behaviour that usually runs a predictable course;

c. certain of its usual consequences are of obvious value in contributing to the preservation of an individual or the continuity of a species;

d. many examples of it develop even when all the ordinary opportunities for learning it are exiguous or absent.

In the past a discussion of this class of behaviour has often been bedevilled by fruitless argument as to whether one or another example of it is innate or acquired (by learning or by other means). Now, it is realised, the antithesis 'innate versus acquired' is unreal. Just as area is a product of length multiplied by width so every biological character, whether it be morphological, physiological, or behavioural, is a product of the interaction of genetic endowment with environment. Terms like innate and acquired must therefore be cast into limbo and a new terminology employed.

The terminology used here is one introduced by Hinde (1959). Any biological character that in its development is little influenced by variations of environment is termed 'environmentally stable'; any that in its development is much influenced by such variations is termed 'environmentally labile'. Examples of environmentally stable characters include most of the common morphological characters, such as colour of eyes and shape of limbs, physiological characters such as blood pressure and body temperature, and behavioural characters such as the nest-building of birds. Examples of environmentally labile characters are body weight and the colour of a salamander's skin, physiological characters such as immunity reactions, and behavioural characters such as show-jumping and playing the piano. Between the examples given, which are deliberately extreme cases, there lies, of course, a multitude of biological characters of intervening degrees of stability and lability. From the environmentally stable to the environmentally labile is, in fact, a continuum: characters commonly termed innate belong to the stable end, and those commonly termed acquired belong to the labile end or to the middle ranges.

Behaviour traditionally described as instinctive is environmentally stable, or at least is stable so long as the environment remains within the range of that in which the species usually lives. In such an environment, therefore, it appears in a predictable form in all members of the species, and so is often termed 'species characteristic'.

Whether in man there is any behaviour that can reasonably be described as instinctive is sometimes disputed. Man's behaviour, it is claimed, is infinitely variable; it differs from culture to culture; nothing resembling the stable and predictable patterns of lower species is to be found. I do not believe this view can be sustained. Man's behaviour is very variable, it is true, but not infinitely so; and, though cultural differences are great, certain commonalities can be discerned. For example, despite obvious variability, the patterns of human behaviour, often very intensely motivated, that result in mating, in the care of babies and young children, and in the attachment of young to parents are found in almost all members of the human race and seem best considered as expressions of some common plan and, since they are of obvious survival value, as instances of instinctive behaviour. For it must be emphasised that in all higher species, and not in man alone, instinctive behaviour is not stereotyped movement but an idiosyncratic performance by a particular individual in a particular environment—yet a performance that nonetheless follows some recognisable pattern and that in a majority of cases leads to some predictable result of benefit to individual or species. It is not only for man but for all higher species, including birds, that a theory of instinctive behaviour based on the concept of stereotyped movement is wholly inadequate.

Those who dispute the view that there is in man behaviour homologous with what in other species is traditionally called instinctive have a heavy onus of proof on their hands. In respect of man's anatomical and physiological equipment a continuity in structure with that of other species is unquestionable. In respect of his behavioural equipment continuity of structure may be less evident, but were continuity to be totally absent all we know of man's evolution would be contradicted. What is far more probable than absence of continuity is, therefore, that the basic structure of man's behavioural equipment resembles that of infra-human species but has in the course of evolution undergone special modifications that permit the same ends to be reached by a much greater diversity of means. The Romans could reach York by few routes; today we can select from hundreds. The ancient Sanskrit language provided only limited means of expression; its modern successors provide astonishing, seemingly infinite, variety. Yet in each case the structure of the modern equipment, whether roads or language, is founded on and derived from the ancient structure. The early form is not superseded: it is modified, elaborated, and augmented but it still determines the overall pattern. This is the view of instinctive behaviour in humans that is advanced. Its basic structure is assumed to derive from some prototype or prototypes that are common to other animal species; that they have been augmented and greatly elaborated in certain directions is taken for granted.

What, then, can these prototypic structures be like? What sorts of system can we imagine that, in less elaborated forms, can account for instinctive behaviour, say, in fish, that in some more elaborated forms can account for such behaviour in birds and mammals, and that, in forms still more greatly elaborated, can account for instinctive behaviour in man? The search for prototypes is comparable to the search for a prototypic pelvic girdle by a comparative anatomist whose problem starts with the specialised pelvic girdle of a horse.

Models that promise to make great contributions to our understanding of the prototypic structures of instinctive behaviour are models developed by control theory. This is a body of knowledge that has grown fast in the past twenty-five years and, apart from its innumerable applications in engineering, has already proved of great value when applied to problems of physiology (Grodins, 1963). Although it would be naïve to assume that such theory can already solve behavioural problems of the degree of complexity that confront the clinician, or even that it will do so soon, its usefulness in the analysis of simple movements is already demonstrated and it holds high promise of casting light on more elaborated sequences.

In presenting ideas derived from control systems theory we shall work from the simplest systems to the more complex. This has the advantage of introducing, first, features that are basic to this class of system and of showing, thence, how a design that starts by being simple and easily understood can be increasingly elaborated so that the resulting system can achieve effects that are more and more complex and increasingly well adapted to requirements. But this mode of presentation has also a disadvantage. It means that the systems first described are so elementary and so restricted in their performance that a sceptical reader may be tempted to dismiss any suggestion that their study can help him to understand human behaviour. Other readers, it is hoped, will be more patient.

Some principles of control systems

Let us first, then, consider certain basic features of those special systems known as control systems. The two features we shall start with concern the age-old problem of purposiveness and the modern concept of feedback.

At one time to attribute purposiveness to animals or to build a psychology of human behaviour on the concept of purposefulness was to declare oneself a vitalist and to be banned from the company of respectable scientists. The development of control systems of increasing sophistication, such as those that control a homing missile, has changed that. Today it is recognised that a machine incorporating feedback can be truly goal-directed. Thus it comes about that nowadays to attribute purposiveness to behaviour and to think, if not teleologically, at least teleonomically (Pittendrigh, 1958)[1] is not only common sense, as it always was, but also good science.

The special feature that enables a machine to behave in a purposive way, in the sense of achieving a predetermined goal by versatile means, is feedback. This is simply a process whereby the actual effects of performance are continuously reported

[1] At the end of Chapter 8, in the section 'Problems of Terminology', the terms 'purposive' and 'teleonomic' are discussed further.

back to a central regulating apparatus where they are compared with whatever initial instruction the machine was given; the machine's further action is then determined by the results of this comparison and the effects of its performance are thus brought ever closer to the initial instruction. Like an athlete intent on running a four-minute mile who trains with stopwatch in hand to check his time round each lap, the machine is constantly checking the effects of its own performance and basing its further action on the extent to which these effects conform with instruction.

The simplest form of control system is a regulator, the purpose of which is to maintain some condition constant. A well-known example is a room thermostat, the purpose of which is to maintain the room at a set temperature. To achieve this the system is so designed that its behaviour is dictated by the results of comparing the actual temperature with what is set. To make this comparison the system requires, first, an initial setting and, secondly, continuous information about what the room temperature actually is. This information is derived from a thermometer, readings of which are relayed back (fed back) in an appropriate form to be compared with the initial setting.

A regulator may be an extremely simple device like an ordinary room thermostat that does no more than switch on heat when temperature falls below the set level and switch it off when temperature rises above that level. But a simple device of this sort has great limitations. If there is a sudden fall of outside temperature, room temperature may fall sharply too and the system will take time to adjust, and if the room temperature rises above set temperature the system has no means of reducing it. To overcome these limitations and to provide a system that maintains temperature much closer to the one set a number of elaborations can be introduced. For example, when temperature rises the thermostat could not only switch off heat but switch on refrigeration. When temperature drops it could be designed to take account not merely of the fact that actual temperature is below that set but also of the magnitude of the discrepancy, and act so that the bigger the discrepancy the more heat is switched on, and vice versa. In addition, it could be constructed to take account not only of absolute magnitude of temperature difference but also of the rate at which a difference is increasing or decreasing. And to make additionally sure that temperature is kept at an exact level, all the machinery could be duplicated or triplicated, using perhaps analogous but not identical processes; for example, heating arrangements could include an oil-fired as well as an electric installation.

This description of an elaborated room thermostat may seem a far cry from a description of human instinctive behaviour. It is given at this stage of the exposition for two reasons: first, to introduce the concepts of setting (or instruction), set-goal, and feedback as they are used in control systems,[1] and, secondly, because it is now known that systems designed along these very lines underlie much physiological functioning. To keep blood sugar at a constant level, for example, a control system using all the sorts of component so far described is at work (Goldman, 1960). This shows not only that living organisms incorporate control systems in their design but that they are utterly dependent upon them for a number of vital functions.

Nevertheless, a regulator of the type so far described is a relatively static type of system and hardly begins to provide a model for even the simplest form of instinctive behaviour. It is a system operating at but one setting that remains constant; all it has to do is to keep actual performance as close as possible to the one it is set for. A type of control system more promising for our purpose is the servo-mechanism. In this case the setting is repeatedly or even continuously changed and the task of the system is to bring performance into line with the setting every time the setting changes. A well-known example of this is power-steering on a car. By turning his steering wheel the driver sets the position in which he wishes his front wheels to be and the servo-unit has the task of ensuring that the wheels are brought into line with that setting. The unit does so by first comparing actual position of front wheels with that now set, and then acting so that the discrepancy is reduced and actual position becomes the same as the set position. When the driver again turns his steering wheel he changes the previous setting to a new one and the servo-unit again has the task of first comparing actual position with that required and then acting in such a way that actual becomes the same as required.

[1] Although the *concepts* of setting, or instruction, and set-goal are both integral parts of control theory, the *terms* 'setting' and 'set-goal' are not. For what is here termed 'setting' or 'instruction' control systems engineers commonly use the term 'command signal', and for what is here termed 'goal' or 'set-goal' they commonly use 'equilibrium level'. Some reasons for preferring the terms to be used will be found in sections of later chapters, namely 'Types of Behavioural System' (Chapter 5) and 'Problems of Terminology' (Chapter 8).

It will be noticed that in the control systems discussed thus far the setting is done by a human agent. The thermostat is not set at any particular temperature until a man sets it; likewise the front wheels of a car. But it is possible so to design a control system that the settings are themselves derived from another system. For example, the settings to which the servo-units of an anti-aircraft gun are working can be derived from a radar instrument which is so designed that it tracks the aircraft, and not only tracks it but extrapolates from present knowledge of how the aircraft is moving to predict the aircraft's future position. In this way the gun is kept pointing constantly in such a way that a shot fired is likely to hit the aircraft. This type of system also is replicated in living organisms. There is reason to think that our possession of systems of this kind, appropriately linked and integrated, enables us to hit a moving tennis ball, and that similarly linked systems enable a falcon to seize a flying bird. Henceforward the objective of hitting the ball (or the aircraft) or seizing the bird is termed the set-goal of the system.

Control systems and instinctive behaviour

At this point in elaboration of the design the concept of control system is perhaps just beginning to do justice to one of the simpler forms of instinctive behaviour. The seizure by a falcon of a bird in flight conforms in fact to the usual criteria of instinctive behaviour: in every individual falcon the stoop conforms to a recognisable pattern; it appears without opportunity for learning; and it is of obvious survival value. Though we may be a very long way from understanding how integrated control systems of this kind come to develop within a growing bird, there is nothing intrinsically inexplicable about it—or at least little more inexplicable than there is about how a physiological system of comparable complexity comes to develop. Just as within the ordinary expectable environment of a species genic action ensures that a cardiovascular system comes to develop, with its amazingly sensitive and versatile components for controlling blood supply to the tissues in constantly changing conditions of organism and environment, so can we suppose that genic action ensures that a behavioural system develops, with components of equal or greater sensitivity and versatility for controlling a particular sort of behaviour in conditions that also constantly change. If instinctive behaviour is regarded as the result of integrated control systems operating within a certain kind of environment, therefore, the means whereby they

44

come into being present no special problems—that is, problems no greater than those in respect of physiological systems.

It is well known, however, that although the instinctive behaviour of all members of a species (with only very few exceptions) conforms to a common overall plan, the particular form it takes in any one individual is often distinctive, and may in fact be quite unusual. For example, a bird of a species that habitually nests in trees may nest on cliffs when no trees offer: buzzards in Norway are an example. A mammal of a species that habitually congregates in flocks may be ungregarious if brought up away from its kind: the sheep brought up by the farmer's daughter is a case in point. These illustrations show how the development of a behavioural system that appears to be environmentally very stable (as nesting in trees and gregariousness unquestionably are) may nonetheless be open in some degree to influence by the environment in which development occurs. The same could well be true of physiological systems. For example, an embryonic cardiovascular system could have the property that the form into which it develops in the adult is determined in some measure by the barometric pressure to which the individual is subjected when young. The fact that a system is in general environmentally stable is in no way inconsistent with its being influenced in some degree also by variations in the environment.

Indeed, environmentally stable though the form taken by any system responsible for instinctive behaviour commonly is, there is hardly a species studied in which the form taken in the adult is not significantly influenced in one way or another when the environment, especially the juvenile environment, deviates greatly from what is found in nature. Even ants, which put other ants into two categories, friend and foe, and treat them very differently, have to learn which is friend and which foe. If by experiment they are brought up in a colony of another species, they treat these others as friends and members of their own species as foes. Instinctive behaviour is not inherited: what is inherited is a potential to develop certain sorts of system, termed here behavioural systems, both the nature and the forms of which differ in some measure according to the particular environment in which development takes place.

In practice it is found that there are great differences between species in the degree to which behavioural systems are environmentally stable or labile. In carnivores and higher primates many of them are notably labile; but even within a single species there are likely to be differences in this respect between one behavioural system and another. To ensure maximum chances of survival a nice balance between stability and lability must be struck. A design for behavioural equipment that determines adult form without allowing for any modifications dependent on environment has the advantage that the equipment can be complete and ready at the moment in the life-cycle at which it is required; whereas a design that provides for modification dependent on environment may result in the equipment's taking longer to develop and not being ready so promptly. On the other hand, a design that permits of modification according to environment is likely to result in equipment that is better adapted and more efficient in its working than equipment based on a general purpose and fixed design can ever be;[1] although with modifiability goes also a risk of curious twists of development that can lead to an outcome as bizarre as that of a goose courting a dog-kennel. In any case, whether the design does or does not permit of modifiability by environment, it is important to remember that no system whatever can be so flexible that it suits all and every environment.

The recognition that behavioural equipment, like anatomical and physiological equipment, can contribute to survival and propagation only when it develops and operates within an environment that falls within prescribed limits is crucial to an understanding of both instinctive behaviour and psychopathology. The anatomical equipment of the whale is admirable for life in the great oceans but a terrible handicap elsewhere; the digestive equipment of the cow is excellent when abundant herbage is available but of no use when the cow is fed with meat; in the same way the behavioural equipment of a species may be beautifully suited to life within one environment and lead only to sterility or death within another. In an environment that provides no nesting-holes tits cannot breed; in an environment in which a source of light is a naked flame moths fly to their death. In all such cases the reason that the equip-

[1] Held (1965) points in addition to the fact that bodily growth entails that during an animal's development there has to be modification of sensory organisation to take account of increasing distance between eyes and between ears, and also modification of motor organisation to take account of longer bones. Held's experiments suggest that such modifications occur as a result of the sensory feedback that accompanies an animal's active movements. Were it not to occur by these means, he points out, a great increase in genetically coded information would be required.

ment proves so unsuccessful is that it is being required to operate within an environment to which it is not adapted.

In the case of man-made control systems, structure is designed in the light of explicit assumptions about the kind of environment in which it is to operate. In the case of biological systems, structure takes a form that is determined by the kind of environment in which the system has in fact been operating during its evolution, an environment that is of course usually, though not necessarily, much the same as that in which it may be expected to operate in future. In each case, therefore, there is a particular sort of environment to which the system, whether man-made or biological, is adapted. This environment I propose to term the system's 'environment of adaptedness'. Only within its environment of adaptedness can it be expected that a system will work efficiently. In any other environment it cannot be expected to do so. In some such cases a system may in fact work reasonably well; in others it does not work at all; and in others again it gives rise to behaviour that is at best unusual and at worst positively unfavourable to survival.

It is important to recognise that an environment of adaptedness exists not only for each species but for each single system of each species; and that any one environment of adaptedness can be more or less narrowly defined in terms of a number of variables. The cardiovascular system of a cat will work efficiently within a certain range of oxygen and carbon dioxide tensions and within a certain range of pressures and temperatures; the cardiovascular systems of a monkey or a man will work efficiently within ranges of these variables similar to but perhaps not identical with those that are relevant for the cat. In the same way, behavioural systems responsible for maternal behaviour in a species will work within certain ranges of social and physical environment and not outside them, and these ranges too will differ from species to species.

For a number of reasons the concept of adaptation in biology is a difficult one. When the issue concerns an animal's behavioural equipment it is especially difficult, and when it concerns the behavioural equipment of man such difficulties are doubled. Because of this and because the concept 'environment of adaptedness' is central to the argument of this book, the final section of this chapter (p. 50) and the whole of the next are given to discussion of these terms.

Whilst all the instinctive systems of a species are so structured that as a rule they promote the survival of members of that species within its own environment of adaptedness, each system differs in regard to the particular part of that environment with which it is concerned. Some behavioural systems are so structured that they bring an organism into a certain kind of habitat and retain it there; others are so structured that they lead the organism to eat particular foodstuffs; and others again that they bring the organism into special relations with other members of its own species. On some occasions the relevant part of the environment is recognised by perception of some relatively simple character, such as a moving flash of light; far more often, however, recognition entails the perception of pattern. In all such cases, we must suppose, the individual organism has a copy of that pattern in its CNS and is structured to react in special kinds of way when it perceives a matching pattern in the environment and in other kinds of way when it perceives no such pattern.

In some cases evidence suggests that the way the pattern comes to exist in the CNS is very little influenced by variations of environment, as for instance when a mallard duck recognises and responds in a characteristic way to the green head of a mallard drake, though she has never seen a mallard drake before; whereas in other cases the pattern that is responded to in special ways is environmentally much more labile, the form it takes being sometimes especially sensitive to the environment met with at a particular period of life. One of the best-known examples of the latter is the pattern that a young goose acquires when it becomes imprinted to a moving object. Once it has learned the pattern of that object during the process of imprinting, its behaviour when alarmed (and in certain other conditions) changes in a dramatic way; then, whenever the gosling perceives the pattern in the environment it follows it, and whenever it cannot perceive the pattern it searches until it does so. Though to design systems with these characteristics would still tax the ingenuity of engineers, the advance of control theory and techniques brings their design within the bounds of reasonable possibility.

As well as having equipment that enables them to recognise certain special parts of their environment, members of all but the most primitive phyla are possessed of equipment that enables them to organise such information as they have about their world into schemata or maps.[1] Even laboratory rats will not apply

[1] Though neither protozoa nor coelenterates appear to have this capacity, insects show it unmistakably (Pantin, 1965).

themselves to maze-running until they have had time enough to acquire a more generalised knowledge of their environment, a knowledge of which they make good use when given opportunity. Higher mammals, for example dogs and primates, can acquire such knowledge of the terrain in which they live that they are able to take the quickest way to a given spot within it—a house or a group of trees—on starting from any point in the surrounding area. Man's capacity to build up a detailed representation of the world in which he lives, a topic to which Piaget has devoted a lifetime's work, is obviously far greater than that of other species—and its accuracy for prediction has been vastly increased of recent times by the discovery and application of scientific method.

The achievement of any set-goal, then, requires that an animal is equipped so that it is able to perceive certain special parts of the environment and to use that knowledge to build up a map of the environment that, whether it be primitive or sophisticated, can predict events relevant to any of its set-goals with a reasonable degree of reliability. It requires, in addition, that the animal is possessed of much effector equipment.

Effector equipment comprises not only anatomical and physiological structures but also, and just as important, control systems that organise and direct their activities within the environment of adaptedness. Only by the action of such equipment does an animal maintain towards particular parts of that environment, for either long or short stretches of time, those special sorts of relationship that lead to survival and reproduction.

Both to enter into some form of temporary relationship, as in caring for young, and to maintain a relationship over a long period, as in possession of territory, obviously imply that the animal has at its disposal one or more techniques of locomotion—walking, running, swimming, flying. They imply also that, in addition to these general purpose techniques, it possesses a repertoire of behavioural techniques of more specialised kinds, for example, singing, threatening a rival, attacking a predator. Finally, they imply that it is equipped with means by which behavioural systems and the order in which they are activated are so organised that within the environment of adaptedness the whole performance as a rule has effects that promote the survival of individual and/or its kin.

The types and sequences of behaviour that lead a pair of birds to reproduce their kind illustrate the sort of problem that any theories of instinctive behaviour must solve. All the following behaviour, and more, is required if outcome is to be successful: male identifies territory and nest-site; male ejects intruding males; male attracts female and courts her; male and/or female build(s) nest; pair copulate; female lays; male and/or female brood(s); pair feed young; pair ward off predators. Each of these activities entails a number of movements and behavioural sequences for each bird, each movement and each sequence of which is complex in itself, like singing or building, yet so executed as to be adapted to the special circumstances of the locality and to the other inhabitants thereof; and each of these activities must be performed at such times and in such sequences that the whole performance leads to a successful outcome more often than not. In what way do we imagine all this to be organised? What principles of organisation are necessary if behaviour is to attain these ends?

Answers to these questions entail consideration of the various ways in which behavioural systems themselves are structured and also of the various ways in which the activities of one behavioural system can be dovetailed to those of another. Before either of these problems can be discussed, however, it is necessary to clarify the concepts 'adaptation', 'adapted', and 'environment of adaptedness', especially as they apply to man.

Adaptation: system and environment

The Concepts of Adaptation and Adaptedness

In the previous section it was emphasised that no system whatever can be so flexible that it suits all and every environment. This means that, when the structure of a system is considered, the environment within which it is to operate must be considered simultaneously. This environment is termed the system's environment of adaptedness. In the case of a man-made control system the environment of adaptedness is the environment within which the system is explicitly designed to operate. In the case of a biological system it is the environment within which the system gradually became evolved. Because of this distinction, it is sometimes useful to refer to the environment of adaptedness of a man-made system as its environment of *designed* adaptedness and to that of a living organism as its environment of *evolutionary* adaptedness.

Let us consider further the nature of biological adaptation and adaptedness.

There are many reasons why the concepts of adaptation and adaptedness give rise to difficulty. One is that the words themselves—adapt, adapted, adaptation—carry more than one meaning. A second is that in biological systems the condition of being adapted is achieved by unusual means, an understanding of which is constantly hindered by the ghost of teleology. A third reason, which obtains when man's biological equipment is under discussion, is that modern man has an extraordinary ability to change his environment to suit himself. Because of these difficulties it is necessary to start with first principles.

Let us consider first the condition of being adapted, and, secondly, the process of becoming adapted.

To define a *state of adaptedness* three terms are required: (i) an organised structure; (ii) a specified outcome to be attained; (iii) an environment within which the structure is to attain that outcome. Whenever the organised structure is able to attain the specified outcome when acting within a particular environment the structure is said to be adapted to that environment. Thus the property of being adapted belongs to the structure; its definition entails reference both to a specified outcome and to a specified environment.

The *process of becoming adapted* refers to a change of structure. Such change can be one of two distinct kinds. First, a structure can be changed so that it continues to attain the same outcome but in a different environment. Secondly, a structure can be changed so that it attains a different outcome in the same or a similar environment.

It should be noted that the term 'adaptation' is used to denote not only the process of change that leads a structure to become adapted (either to a new environment or to a new outcome) but sometimes also the condition of being adapted. To avoid confusion, however, the latter is better termed 'adaptedness' (Weiss, 1949); hence 'environment of evolutionary adaptedness'. These points can be made clearer by illustration.

A first example is taken from the world of man-made objects. A certain small car, it might be said, is well adapted to London streets. This means, of course, that as a mechanical structure the car attains a specified outcome, namely convenient transport, in a certain sort of urban environment. It is able to do so because it has a number of properties connected with size, speed, acceleration, braking, turning circle, and so on, properties each of which not only is within certain ranges but bears a certain relation to the others. The car, in fact, has been specially designed to suit London streets.

Whether or not it will also suit other environments, however, is unknown. Each motoring environment that differs appreciably from the London streets poses a new and different question. Is the car well adapted to motorway conditions? to Alpine roads? for use within the Arctic Circle? for the Sahara? Plainly, to provide convenient transport in all these other environments the car needs many properties not relevant in London, and perhaps even at variance with what is required in London. It would hardly be surprising, therefore, if a model well adapted to London streets failed in one or more of the other environments. Until it is shown to be more extended, it is wise to assume that the car's environment of adaptedness is limited to London streets.

Nevertheless, the structure of the car might readily be changed to enable it to provide convenient transport in one or other of these different environments. In that case the structure would undergo a process of adaptation so that it became suited to the new environment, which would then become its new environment of adaptedness. Many different changes (adaptations) to suit many different new environments are obviously possible.

Adaptations considered thus far are all of one kind, namely a change of structure that enables the system to attain one and the same outcome, transportation, but in a series of different environments. Because, however, adaptedness is relative not only to environment but also to outcome, it is possible to change the car's adaptedness in a quite different series of ways. For example, the car's structure could be changed so that, instead of providing transport, it provided power for an electric generating set. In that case the structure would have been adapted to attain a different outcome, though perhaps still in the original environment.

Although change to suit a new environment and change to suit a new outcome are quite distinct kinds of change, each is habitually described as an adaptation. This can easily lead to confusion.

A further difficulty, and an even greater one, arises from the fact that a structure can sometimes be enabled to attain its specified outcome more effectively if a change is made in the environment in which it is to operate. Since to use the terms 'adapt' and 'adaptation' to denote such environmental changes would lead to even greater confusion, other terms are required. I shall, therefore, use 'modify' and 'modification' to refer to any change of environment that is made so that a system can operate more effectively. This leaves the terms 'adapt', 'adapted', and 'adaptation' to refer only to changes occurring in the system itself.[1]

The distinction between adapting a system and modifying an environment can be illustrated by further reference to the small car. Let us assume that in certain conditions of the London streets the car has a tendency to skid. This failing could be dealt with in one of two ways: either a change could be made in the car, e.g. in its tyres, or a change could be made in the environment, e.g. in the road surface. The first is described as adapting the car, the second as modifying its environment.

Let us now consider biological structures and their environments of adaptedness.

Biological Adaptation

It has long been evident not only that animals and plants are very complex structures but that with an astonishing precision members of each species are suited for life in a particular environment—often called the ecological niche. Furthermore, the more carefully an individual is studied the clearer it becomes that almost every detail of its structure, whether morphological, physiological, or, in the case of animals, behavioural, is adapted so that survival of that individual and its kin is secured in that environment. Famous examples of such studies are those of Darwin, who showed that the detailed flower structure of each species of orchid is such that one particular species of insect is attracted to it and, following visits by the same insect to different flowers, during which it comes into contact with special parts of each flower, fertilisation of the orchid seed is achieved. These studies showed clearly, first, that biological structure is unintelligible unless it is considered in terms of survival within a very particular environment; and, second, that, once it is recognised that survival is the outcome that all biological structures are adapted to attain, biological features that hitherto have appeared only as beautiful or curious or bizarre come to have a new meaning: each feature is found to contribute, or to

[1] In selecting these terms 'adapt' and 'modify' and using them in distinct ways, I am aware that I am not following common usage, which is to apply both words without discrimination to both kinds of change.

have contributed, to survival in the environment inhabited by the species.

Darwin was explicit that what was true of the parts of a flower was true also of the behaviour of animals. In a chapter of *The Origin* (1859) entitled 'Instinct' he notes that each species is endowed with its own peculiar repertoire of behaviour in the same way that it is endowed with its own peculiarities of anatomy, and emphasises that 'Instincts are as important as corporeal structure for the welfare of each species'. Translated into the terminology used in this chapter this would be rendered as 'environmentally stable behavioural systems are as necessary as morphological structures for the survival of each species'.

Thus Darwin and his successors came to the epoch-making realisation that the ultimate outcome for which all structures of a living organism are adapted is neither more nor less than survival. Whereas in the case of man-made structures the outcome to be attained can be one of an almost limitless array—transport, power, amusement, shelter, and so on—in the case of biological structures the outcome to be attained is, in the long run, always the same—namely, survival. Thus, when the adaptedness of a species of plant or animal to a particular environment is under consideration, the issue in question is whether or not its structure is such that, in that environment, survival can be attained. When it can be, members of the species are said to be adapted to that environment; when it cannot be, they are unadapted.

Until Darwin's day, and even later, it proved impossible to understand how the structure of an animal or a plant can become so effectively adapted that it attains the outcome that it so patently does attain. For long, theories of supernatural intervention or of teleological causation held the stage. Now, a century after Darwin proposed the solution, the problem is regarded as solved. The adaptedness of any biological structure, be it morphological, physiological, or behavioural, is seen as the resultant of natural selection's having, in a particular environment, led to the successful reproduction, and therefore preservation, of the more-adapted variants, and simultaneously to the less successful reproduction, and therefore dropping out, of the less-adapted variants.

Though a theoretical viewpoint of this kind has long been applied to the morphological and physiological equipment of animals, it is only in comparatively recent times that it has been applied also in a systematic way to their behavioural equipment. For this development we are indebted to the ethologists. Recognising, as Darwin the founding father of ethology himself did, that the behavioural repertoire of each species is as unique as are its morphological and physiological characteristics, ethologists have sought to understand behavioural equipment by reference to the contribution it makes to the survival of members of the species and their kin in the natural habitat of that species. To their following of this principle so consistently are largely due the distinctive and distinguished contributions that they have made to an understanding of behaviour. A main thesis of this book is that the same principle must be followed equally consistently if we are to understand the instinctive behaviour of man.

The Biological Unit that is Adapted

During the 1960s a revolution took place in the biological study of social behaviour. Until then there had been much confusion about the identity of the biological unit that is adapted. Darwin's phrase 'the welfare of each species' suggests that it is the whole species that is adapted. Others, recognising that most species exist as a number of distinct breeding populations, have suggested that the unit of adaptation is the interbreeding population (as indeed was proposed in the first edition of this book). Another closely related line of thinking, very prevalent until quite recently, pointed to the existence of social groups the organisation of which appears to bring benefit to the group as a whole though not necessarily to individuals in it. The most notable examples are colonies of certain species of termites, ants and bees, but schools of fish and herds of mammals have often been thought to have similar properties. As a result the belief has arisen that the unit of adaptation is the social group itself.

All these ideas are now discredited, however. That is the consequence of a more rigorous examination of the data and of the application to them of the genetical theory of natural selection, known as the Neo-Darwinian theory, that was developed by Ronald Fisher, Jack Haldane and Sewall Wright during the 1930s.

The basic concept of the genetical theory of natural selection is that the unit central to the whole process is the individual gene and that all evolutionary change is due to the fact that certain genes increase in number over time whereas alternative genes decrease or die out. What this means in practice is that, through the process of differential breeding success, individuals that are carrying certain genes increase in numbers whilst individuals that are carrying others diminish. A corollary is that the adaptedness of any particular organism comes to be defined in terms of its ability to contribute more than the average number of genes to future generations. Not only, therefore, does it have to be designed so that it is capable of individual survival but so that it is capable also of promoting the survival of the genes it is carrying. This is commonly done through reproducing and promoting the survival of offspring. An additional, or alternative, method is through promoting the survival of any other kin likely to be carrying the same genes.

Although the survival of the genes an individual is carrying must always be the ultimate criterion when biological adaptedness is being evaluated, it is often convenient to consider the adaptedness of any part of an organism's equipment in terms of some proximate outcome. Thus the adaptedness of a cardiovascular system within a given environment is commonly considered in terms of the efficiency with which the system maintains an individual's blood supply in those conditions; and the adaptedness of an immunological system in terms of its efficiency in maintaining an individual's freedom from infection. In the same way with behavioural systems, the adaptedness of systems responsible for feeding behaviour, for example, can be considered in terms of the adequacy with which the feeding behaviour maintains an individual's nutrition in a particular environment. (Thus the feeding behaviour of swallows is well adapted to an English summer, when there are plenty of airborne insects, but ill adapted to an English winter.) Nevertheless the outcome of blood supply, freedom from infection, or nutrition is in each case no more than a proximate outcome; and the same is true of each instinctive behavioural system. Whether outcome for the individual is food-intake, selfprotection, sexual union or defence of territory, the ultimate outcome to be attained is always the survival of the genes an individual is carrying.

Note on Literature

Few references are given in the body of this chapter or in the remaining chapters in Part II. Those wishing to read further are advised to consult the following sources from which most of the ideas and the illustrative examples are culled.

AN ALTERNATIVE MODEL

The concept of biological adaptation is examined by Sommerhoff in his *Analytical Biology* (1950). He shows how the phenomena that have given rise to teleological thinking can be understood in terms of control theory.

For the application of control theory in biology generally, see *Living Control Systems* (1966) by Bayliss, *Control Theory and Biological Systems* (1963) by Grodins, and the symposium on *Self-organising Systems* (1960) edited by Yovits and Cameron, especially the articles by Goldman and Bishop.

For the application of a control systems approach in behavioural science, see Young's *A Model of the Brain* (1964) in which he sets out to describe the nervous system as an engineer would describe the control system of a homeostat, and also McFarland's *Feedback Mechanisms in Animal Behaviour* (1971).

For a sketch of how ideas derived from control theory, especially the concept of 'plan', can be applied to human behaviour, see the very stimulating *Plans and the Structure of Behaviour* (1960) by Miller, Galanter and Pribram.

The genetical theory of natural selection is clearly described by Williams in his *Adaptation and Natural Selection* (1966). In it he demonstrates how the many forms of social behaviour observed in animals can be understood in terms of gene selection, making it unnecessary to invoke a theory of group selection to account for them. A recent more popular account is given by Dawkins in his *Selfish Gene* (1976). Wilson's *Sociobiology: The New Synthesis* (1975) is comprehensive and of great interest, though some of his few comments on human social behaviour have proved injudicious.

Many of the ideas developed in this and subsequent chapters derive from Hinde's *Animal Behaviour* (1970), in which an integration of the work and ideas of ethology and comparative psychology is presented. Illustrative examples from the field of animal behaviour are drawn principally from Hinde's book. Other sources are Tinbergen's *Study of Instinct* (1951), Thorpe's *Learning and Instinct in Animals* (1956, 2nd edition 1963), and Hediger's *Studies of the Psychology and Behaviour of Captive Animals in Zoos and Circuses* (1955).

Chapter 4

Man's Environment of
Evolutionary Adaptedness

IN the previous chapter it is emphasised that no system can be expected to operate effectively except in its environment of adaptedness. Because of this, when we come to consider with what instinctive behaviour—or, more properly, with what behavioural systems mediating instinctive behaviour—humans may be endowed, a first task is to consider the nature of the environment within which they are adapted to operate. This poses unusual problems.

Two main characteristics of man are his versatility and his capacity for innovation. Exercising these gifts he has in recent millennia extended the environments in which he is capable of living and breeding to include extremes of natural conditions. Not only this, but he has also, more or less deliberately, changed these conditions so as to create a series of entirely new man-made environments. These modifications to the environment have, of course, led to a spectacular increase in the world population of the species; and they have simultaneously made the biologist's task of defining man's environment of evolutionary adaptedness far more difficult.

At this point, it should be recalled that our problem is to understand man's instinctive behaviour. Thus, whilst full recognition must be given to man's remarkable versatility, his capacity for innovation, and his achievements in modifying his environment, none of these attributes is our immediate concern. Instead, we are concerned with the environmentally stable components of man's behavioural repertoire, and the relatively stable environment of adaptedness in which they were in all likelihood evolved. What, then, is the nature of that environment likely to be, or to have been?

For most species of animal the natural habitat not only is of limited variation but also changes only slowly. As a result each species is living today in an environment little different from the one in which its behavioural equipment was evolved and within which the equipment is adapted to operate. In consequence it is usually fairly safe to assume that the habitat occupied by a species today is either the same as or close to its environment of evolutionary adaptedness. For man this is not so. First, the range of habitats in which man lives and breeds at present is enormous. Secondly, and more important, the speed at which man's environment has been diversified, especially the speed in recent centuries of man-made change, has far outstripped the pace at which natural selection is able to work. We can therefore be fairly sure that none of the environments in which civilised, or even half-civilised, man lives today conforms to the environment in which man's environmentally stable behavioural systems were evolved and to which they are intrinsically adapted.

This leads to the conclusion that the environment in terms of which the adaptedness of man's instinctive equipment must be considered is the one that man inhabited for two million years until changes of the past few thousand years led to the extraordinary variety of habitats he occupies today.[1] Identification of that environment as man's environment of evolutionary adaptedness carries no suggestion that such primeval environment is in some way better than present-day ones or that ancient man was happier than present-day man. The reason for it is simply that the primeval natural environment of man, which can probably be defined within reasonable limits, is almost certainly the environment that presented the difficulties and hazards that acted as selective agents during the evolution of the behavioural equipment that still is man's today. This means that man's primeval environment is, almost certainly, also his environment of evolutionary adaptedness. If this conclusion is correct, *the only relevant criterion by which to consider the natural adaptedness of any particular part of present-day man's behavioural equipment is the degree to which and the way in which it might contribute to population survival in man's primeval environment.*

What, then, of the adaptedness, or lack of it, of man's

[1] Tobias (1965) dates the emergence of an early species of man, *Homo habilis*, to the very beginning of the Pleistocene, about two million years ago. Since the introduction of agriculture occurred a mere ten thousand years ago, the period during which any men have lived in modified environments is no more than 0·5 per cent of the time man has been in existence. Though these changes have led to some easing of selective pressures, there can be little doubt that the genotypes of present-day human strains are in most respects the same as they were in pre-agricultural times.

behavioural equipment to the innumerable other environments occupied by man today? To raise this question, as one must, is in fact to raise a series of new and distinct questions— just as the question whether a small car adapted for transport in urban streets is adapted also for transport in other motoring environments poses a series of new and distinct questions. It may, in fact, be that all parts of man's behavioural equipment are well adapted not only to man's primeval environment but to all his present-day environments also. But it may not be so, and certainly cannot be assumed to be so. Only research can give the answers.

At this point it might be urged that animals of species other than man also change the environment to suit themselves and that man is not so unusual after all. Insects and birds build nests, rabbits make burrows, and beavers dam streams. These environmental modifications, however, being themselves the products of instinctive behaviour, are of limited degree and relatively stereotyped in form. As a result an equilibrium has come to obtain between each of these species and its modified environment. The modifications that man makes to his environment are of a different character. None is a product of instinctive behaviour; instead, each is the product of some cultural tradition, learned afresh and sometimes laboriously by members of each new generation. A difference that is vastly more important, however, is that in recent centuries, thanks to technological innovation, most cultural traditions have become subject to rapidly accelerating changes. As a result the relation between man and his environment has become increasingly unstable.[1]

The upshot of the argument is, therefore, that, enormously important though they are, all questions as to whether man's present behavioural equipment is adapted to his many present-day environments, especially urban environments, are not strictly relevant to this book, which is concerned only with elemental responses originating in bygone times. What matters here is that, if man's behavioural equipment is indeed adapted to the primeval environment in which man once lived, it is

[1] This is a theme to which Vickers (1965) gives attention. He points out that modification of environment by technological means leads to a population explosion, and that a population explosion demands further and more far-reaching technological change. So far from feedback being negative and leading to stability in the system, feedback is positive and is leading to increasing instability.

only by reference to that environment that its structure can be understood. Just as Darwin found it impossible to understand the structure of an orchid flower until he knew what insects flourished and visited it in its environment of adaptedness, so, it is held, it is impossible to understand man's instinctive behaviour until we know something of the environment in which it evolved. For a picture of this we need to turn to anthropological studies of human communities living in the least modified of human environments, to archaeological studies of early man, and to field studies of the higher primates.

Few peoples on earth today still obtain their food solely by hunting and gathering, and even fewer good accounts of their social life exist.[1] The evidence available shows, nevertheless, that without exception all live in small social groups comprising individuals of both sexes and all ages. Whereas some social groups are reasonably stable, others change in size and composition. But whether the larger group is stable or not, the tie between a mother and her children is always present and virtually unchanging.

Many anthropologists have argued that the basic and elementary social unit of mankind is the nuclear family. Fox (1967) points out, however, that, though in every human society females and young are constantly accompanied by mature males, the accompanying males are not always the fathers of the young or even the mates of the females; they may be father, uncle, or brother. This, and other considerations, led Fox to the view that the basic social unit of man is a mother, her children, and perhaps her daughter's children, and that the way societies differ is in whether, and in the extent to which, fathers become attached to this unit: in some societies they are fairly permanently attached to one such unit, in others—polygamous societies—to several such units, and in other societies again they are hardly attached at all, e.g. the freed-slave societies of the West Indies. If Fox is right, the elements of human social life are remarkably similar to those of man's nearest sub-human relatives.

In any case it seems clear that man's primeval way of living can fruitfully be compared with the ways of living of the other large ground-living species of higher primate. Differences between man and sub-human species there certainly are; but for

[1] An exception is the pygmy people of the African rain forests, whose way of life is admirably portrayed by Turnbull (1965).

purposes of this book, it is argued, their similarities are equally important, and perhaps more so than their differences.

It is characteristic of all large ground-living species of higher primate, including man, that they live in social groups made up of members of both sexes and all ages. Groups vary in size from one or two families to some two hundred members. Females and immatures are never found without adult males (except amongst chimpanzees) and adult males are rarely found on their own. The social group usually remains stable throughout the year, though it may divide and re-form from time to time; only occasionally do individuals change from one group to another. With few exceptions, individuals spend their whole life in close proximity to other familiar individuals.

The social group inhabits a range varying from a few square miles to a hundred or more, and, though there may be some overlap of ranges, each group tends to remain strictly within its own range. For sub-human primates diet is mostly vegetarian but meat is eaten when occasionally it is available. Man is unusual because meat constitutes a larger proportion of his diet. Nevertheless there are few societies in which meat forms more than 25 per cent of the diet, and in many it constitutes a much lower proportion. The advantage of an omnivorous diet, including meat, is that it enables a species to survive in conditions of temporary drought and so to extend the variety of habitat in which it can live.

Virtually every species of animal shares its habitat with a number of potentially very dangerous predators and, to survive, needs to be equipped with behavioural systems resulting in protection. In the case of the ground-living primates, predators are the great cats (especially leopards),[1] wolves and jackals, and birds of prey. In achieving protection from these predators the organised social group characteristic of the terrestrial primate plays an essential part. When members of the group are threatened, the mature males, whether monkeys or men, combine to drive off the predator whilst the females and immatures retire. Thus only individuals found alone are likely to fall victim. By having evolved this co-operative technique of protecting themselves, ground-living primates are capable of prospering in many different habitats instead of being confined to areas containing the trees and cliffs that are necessary for the protection of other primate species.

[1]For evidence that early man was preyed on by leopards see C. K. Brain (1970) in *Nature*, **225**, 1112–19.

Sexual relations vary greatly in the ground-living primates. In many species there is a good deal of sexual promiscuity within a group, though even in baboons there are periods during which a consort pair is formed. Man is unusual in that the female is continuously receptive and there is commonly, though not always, a family life based on prolonged male–female relations and an incest taboo. Exogamy between neighbouring social groups making up a tribe occurs in man. In sub-human species something similar occurs as a result of an occasional male or female changing from one band to another.

Of the many behavioural features that we think of as especially characteristic of man, some are common also in other ground-living species and others are found in embryonic form amongst them. Amongst those found commonly in sub-human species as well as in man are: a large repertoire of calls, postures, and gestures that act as means of communication between members of a group; tool use; and a long period of immaturity during which customs typical of the social group are learned. Those found only very rarely in sub-human species include: adult males combining to hunt food animals, and tool-making. The most notable feature specific to man is speech. Others are a protected home base, temporary or permanent, in which sick members can remain throughout the twenty-four hours, and the related practice of sharing food. In man, differentiation of role between the sexes and between mature and immature members, already well developed in other primate species, is carried much further.

This thumb-nail sketch, based largely on the work and publications of Washburn and DeVore,[1] is believed to give a tolerably accurate picture of the social life of pre-agricultural humans and of ground-living species related to man. In all of them the organised social group serves at least one important function, that of protection from predators: in no situation are the organisation of the group and role differentiation within it more apparent than when a predator threatens. As a result, immatures are enabled to live a protected existence whilst they learn skills necessary for adult life. A second function of the social group, but one almost certainly developed much later, is that of facilitating food-getting by co-operative hunting.

It is against this picture of man's environment of evolutionary

[1] Washburn (ed.), *The Social Life of Early Man* (1961); DeVore (ed.), *Primate Behavior: Field Studies of Monkeys and Apes* (1965); see also Southwick (ed.), *Primate Social Behavior* (1963).

adaptedness that the environmentally stable behavioural equipment of man is considered. Much of this equipment, it is held, is so structured that it enables individuals of each sex and each age-group to take their places in the organised social group characteristic of the species.

The concept of 'man's environment of evolutionary adaptedness' outlined here is, of course, a version of Hartmann's concept of 'man's ordinary expectable environment' (Hartmann, 1939), but one that is defined more rigorously in terms of evolution theory. Not only does the new term make even more explicit that organisms are adapted to particular environments but it draws attention to the fact that not a single feature of a species' morphology, physiology, or behaviour can be understood or even discussed intelligently except in relation to that species' environment of evolutionary adaptedness. Given constant reference to man's environment of evolutionary adaptedness, the vagaries to which human behaviour is liable become, it is held, much less incomprehensible than they are when the nature of that environment is ignored. In later chapters, in which the behavioural systems that tie child to mother are considered, further attention is given to the environment in which early man is believed to have lived and in which our present behavioural equipment is likely to have been evolved. Responses to loss are considered in the same light.

Note: Those not concerned with the details of the model of instinctive behaviour can turn forward to Part III, 'Attachment Behaviour'.

Chapter 5

Behavioural Systems Mediating
Instinctive Behaviour

In the 'thirties it did not seem to us that there *was* any
way of studying behaviour 'scientifically' except through
some kind of experimental intervention . . . Even poking
an animal would surely be better than just looking at it:
that would lead to anecdotalism: that was what bird-
watchers did.

Yet it was also what the pioneers of ethology did.
They studied natural behaviour instead of contrived
behaviour, and were thus able for the first time to discern
natural behaviour structures or episodes . . .

P. B. MEDAWAR (1967)

Types of behavioural system

So far in this exposition pride of place is given to behavioural
systems that, in controlling behaviour, are structured to take
account of discrepancies between initial instruction and the
effects of current performance, a comparison made possible by
means of feedback: to such systems only is the term goal-
directed, or better, goal-corrected, applied. The reason for this
pride of place is twofold. First, it is evident that a great deal
of behaviour, especially in man, is governed by systems having
these properties, and secondly, it is the elucidation of the
principles underlying these systems that has led to a revolution
in the biological sciences. It would, however, be a mistake to
suppose that all behavioural systems are of this degree of
sophistication. Some are very much simpler; and there are
advantages in giving these others attention before considering
further the mode of action of the goal-corrected ones.

Fixed Action Patterns

One of the simpler types of system and one to which much
attention has been paid by ethologists is the type that governs
a Fixed Action Pattern. This is a structured pattern of movement which, though different examples differ in their degree
of complexity, is not unlike a reflex. In one respect, however,

65

a fixed action pattern differs radically from a reflex: whereas the threshold of activation of a reflex is constant, the threshold of a fixed action pattern varies according to the state of the organism. Examples are some of the weaving movements used by canaries in building a nest, and many of the social displays of birds and fish that occur during social interaction and that often are responded to in predictable ways by other members of the species. As their name implies, fixed action patterns are highly stereotyped and, once initiated, follow their typical course to its completion almost irrespective of what is happening in the environment. From this it can be inferred with confidence that the type of system responsible for a fixed action pattern operates without the aid of feedback from the environment via exteroceptors (eyes, ears, nose, and touch receptors).

The system responsible for a fixed action pattern could be structured in accordance with one of two principles. One is for the system to be dependent entirely on a pre-set programme within the CNS; the other is for it to be in part dependent on a pre-set programme, but dependent in some part also on aid from proprioceptive feedback derived from sense organs in the musculature, feedback that serves to signal the progress of the behavioural sequence and to ensure that it runs true to type. Without further research, however, it is not possible to know which of these arrangements is the commoner.

Fixed action patterns can vary in complexity from those which, like yawning and sneezing, appear little more than glorified reflexes to those which, like certain social displays in birds, give the impression of an elaborate ritual. In comparison with birds, the higher primates, including man, are poorly equipped with them. To the student of human behaviour fixed action patterns are of interest because of the important roles they play throughout life in controlling facial expression (Tomkins, 1962), and especially during infancy before any systems responsible for more sophisticated types of behaviour become available. Rooting, grasping, crying, and smiling when they first appear are probably all examples of fixed action patterns and all play an important part in the earliest phases of social interaction. The existence of fixed action patterns not only is a reminder of the relative complexity of movement which can be controlled by a system dependent on a programme existing centrally (with or without proprioceptive feedback), but also provides a baseline from which to consider systems of greater degrees of flexibility and adaptedness.

Behaviour that is one degree more flexible than the fixed action pattern occurs when a fixed action pattern is combined with a simple sequence of movements that is dependent on feedback from the environment. A well-known example is the behaviour shown by a goose whose egg has rolled outside the nest. The behaviour with which the goose responds to the situation can be divided into two components. One component, that of placing the bill over the egg and drawing it slowly towards the breast, continues once it has started, even though the egg is removed. The other component, that of moving the bill from side to side in a way that takes account of the irregular movements of the egg, occurs only in response to tactile stimuli from the egg and ceases when the egg is removed. The actual behaviour, a combination of both components, though clumsy, usually results, if repeated often enough, in the egg's being returned to the nest.

This illustration serves to introduce two large and interrelated issues: one is the directedness of behaviour and the ways by which it is achieved, the other is the problem of goals. Apart from intrinsic difficulties, each raises a number of terminological problems.

Two Sorts of Predictable Outcome

A first question to settle is whether or not to use the term 'goal' to denote the reasonably predictable outcome of the egg-rolling behaviour of the goose, namely a return of egg to nest. There are in fact good reasons for not doing so. This is readily explained by comparing the means by which this outcome is achieved with the means by which interception of prey is achieved by a peregrine.

When a peregrine stoops on its prey its movements are constantly influenced by its sight of the prey. By use of vision the peregrine is provided with a continuous stream of information that enables it to make an almost continuous comparison between its own position, speed, and direction and those of the prey, and to modify its flight accordingly. The behavioural system controlling the stoop is thus structured in such a way that it takes continuous account of discrepancies between instruction (intercept prey) and performance. The more or less predictable outcome of interception is a natural result of reducing this discrepancy to zero.[1]

[1] Although the account given is probably correct, the peregrine's performance has not in fact been subjected to critical analysis.

The pair of behavioural systems responsible for egg-rolling by the goose, on the other hand, are structured quite differently. The movements are in no way influenced by sight of nest and there are no calculations of discrepancy between position of egg and position of nest. In this task the more or less predictable outcome is a result of nothing more elaborate than a fixed action pattern operating in combination with an alternating movement governed by immediate tactile feedback from the egg, both being in action whilst the goose itself remains sitting on the nest. Were the goose to be sitting elsewhere than on the nest the egg would, of course, arrive not at the nest but elsewhere.

Thus in each of the two examples a more or less predictable outcome follows the behaviour; but the reasons for its doing so differ radically. In the case of the peregrine the behaviour can legitimately be termed goal-directed, for the same principles govern the way it stoops at prey and the way a footballer shoots at goal. The behaviour of the goose, on the other hand, is better not termed goal-directed. It is, in fact, no more goal-directed than is the behaviour of a child at a fairground who pays sixpence to be allowed to walk blindfold down some mysterious passage. Whilst walking, and keeping on course by means of tactile feedback from the walls, the child has no idea where he is going and so has no goal. Even so an onlooker might with confidence predict the outcome—perhaps arrival in the presence of a beautiful fairy (or something less agreeable). This, and the egg-rolling example, show that outcome may be highly predictable even though behaviour is not goal-directed.

Since it is imperative we keep precise the distinction between behaviour that is goal-directed and other behaviour, an exact usage of terms is important. A first question to settle is the term to be used to denote the outcomes of goal-directed behavioural systems. At first sight it might appear that the word 'goal' could itself be used in this sense were it to be carefully defined. There appear, however, to be two weighty reasons for not using it. One is that the word 'goal' may suggest a temporally finite end towards which action is directed, and is commonly used by psychologists in that sense. Although the term sought must be applicable to such temporally finite ends, it must be applicable also to conditions that extend over time, and for this broader purpose the word 'goal' is not very suitable. A second reason for not selecting 'goal' is that in common parlance it is often used to refer to an object in an environment, and the references with which we are concerned are never that. What is required is a term that can be used to refer generically both to a temporally finite event that is to be brought about through the interaction of an animal with some parts of its environment, for example seizure of prey, and to some condition that continues through time, for example a specified relationship of distance between an animal and some part of its environment.

For these reasons, which are amplified in Chapter 8, I propose the term 'set-goal'. Set-goal denotes either a time-limited event or an ongoing condition either of which is brought about by the action of behavioural systems that are structured to take account of discrepancies between instruction and performance. In this definition, it should be noted, a set-goal is *not* an object in the environment but is either a specified motor performance, e.g. singing a song, or the achievement of a specified relation, of short or long duration, between the animal and some object in or component of the environment. Thus the set-goal of the peregrine's stoop is not the prey stooped at but interception of that prey. In the same way, the set-goal of some other behavioural system might be the continuous maintenance by an animal of a certain distance between itself and an alarming object in the environment.

To describe behavioural systems structured in terms of set-goals, the adjective 'goal-directed' remains useful. A better term, however, is 'goal-corrected'. First, it emphasizes the fact that the behaviour controlled by such systems is constantly corrected by reference to whatever discrepancy exists between current performance and set-goal. Secondly, it may help the reader to remember that some such systems may be concerned with set-goals that extend over long periods of time. Thirdly, it helps to keep behaviour that is organised to achieve a set-goal distinct from behaviour that is precisely oriented in space and is therefore truly directed, though it may or may not be goal-corrected (see later in this chapter).

To refer to an object that is a constituent part of a set-goal the term 'goal-object' is sometimes useful.

From the discussion it will be seen that the more or less predictable and beneficial[1] outcomes to which differently structured behavioural systems can lead are of at least two sorts: set-goals and those that are not set-goals. For the latter there

[1] Most forms of behaviour have several fairly regular consequences, not all of which are beneficial. This fact and the related problem of function are discussed in Chapter 8.

appears to be no agreed term. Both sorts of outcome can, however, be referred to generically as 'predictable outcomes', provided it is realized that the prediction is contingent on a number of conditions and that, if these change, the prediction is falsified. The term 'predictable outcome' must therefore always be read as short for 'conditionally predictable outcome'. Set-goals are one class of predictable outcome.

Goal-corrected Behaviour

It is easy to suppose that the behaviour of a simple organism is goal-corrected when it is seen to use many different responses before it finally attains some particular outcome. To reach a predictable outcome, however, is no criterion of goal-correctedness; as has been seen, such outcome can be attained in many other ways. What characterises a goal-corrected system is not that it reaches a predictable outcome but that it does so by a special process: from a large repertoire of stereotyped or variable movements, the system selects movements in a non-random manner and in such a way that they bring the animal progressively nearer the set-goal. The more sophisticated the process the more economical the behaviour. Efficient goal-corrected behaviour is variable, not necessarily in the sorts of behaviour used, but in the large number of starting-points from which the set-goal can be reached (Hinde, 1966).

Not unexpectedly, a behavioural system responsible for goal-corrected behaviour is much more complex than is one responsible for other behaviour. Two vital components of a goal-corrected system are: (a) a means of receiving and storing instructions regarding the set-goal, and (b) a means of comparing the effects of performance with instruction and changing performance to fit.

Before the days of computers a major difficulty was to imagine by what possible means the kinds of detailed instruction required for the execution of instinctive behaviour could be drawn up and stored, and then made available for use at the required time and place. Now the means whereby they come to be stored and made available are no longer wholly beyond the powers of imagination, even though the processes used appear to be far more intricate and ingenious than any that man has yet learned to employ.

The way the instructions 'reach' the organism, however, still remains difficult to imagine. In the case of the computer the instructions are fed to it. In the case of the organism, one must suppose, the instructions come to exist within it as a result of its development within a particular environment, development which is a product of the interaction of the animal's genetic endowment with that environment, and a resultant of epigenetic processes in general and of all the processes termed learning as well.

Instructions regarding a set-goal may contain only one type of constituent specification. For example, the system that enables a human singer to maintain a particular note is structured to utilise auditory feedback: the results of the singer's performance are listened to by the singer himself and his performance is continuously modified slightly so as to correct any deviation between performance and instruction. Here the system governing vocal performance would appear to require an instruction comprising but a single type of specification, in terms of pitch, volume, etc.

More frequently, instructions regarding a set-goal include more than one type of specification. For example, in the case of the peregrine's stoop they comprise two types: (i) a specification of potential prey in terms, presumably, of size, shape, movement, etc., and (ii) a specification of the relationship required to the prey in terms such as proximity, interception, etc. Each type of specification can vary in its degree of precision from rather general to very exact.

In addition to the specific instructions that are required for an animal to achieve any set-goal, there is often another and more general requirement. This is that the animal should have at its disposal some schematic representation of the topography of the environment in which it is living. Only by reference to such a cognitive map is an animal able to find its way quickly from any one part of its familiar environment to another. Rapid retreat to a place of safety by a troop of baboons is an example.

Though reference to a reasonably accurate cognitive map is essential if certain goal-corrected systems are to operate successfully, there is no one-to-one relationship between reference to map and goal-corrected system. On the contrary, whereas goal-corrected systems that do not entail locomotion operate successfully without reference to a map, there are behavioural systems built on simpler lines that nonetheless require such reference.

Maintenance of Spatial Relations over Time

Past discussions of instinctive behaviour have tended to concentrate on sequences that have a dramatic and time-limited outcome, such as orgasm, and to neglect behaviour the outcome of which is an ongoing relationship, such as maintenance of a specified distance over a comparatively long period. There can be no doubt, however, that the latter sort of behaviour is of great frequency and vital importance in the life of most animals. Examples are brooding behaviour, in which proximity to eggs and nest is maintained over weeks, territorial behaviour, in which location within a certain bit of the environment is maintained over months and sometimes over years, and alarm behaviour, in which a certain distance between an animal and a predator threatening it is maintained over minutes or hours.[1]

A main reason for past neglect of this sort of behaviour is that it cannot readily be understood in terms of such concepts as 'drive' or 'energy discharge'. When the present set of concepts is applied, on the other hand, possible solutions are not too difficult to see.

Behavioural systems resulting in the maintenance of specified distance over time could be organised on less or on more sophisticated lines. An example of a simple version would be a system that leads to movement towards a specified goal-object, that comes into play whenever distance between animal and object increases, and that ceases when distance is zero. Such a system would of course lead to permanent contiguity unless it were balanced by one or more other systems that from time to time led to movement away from the goal-object. The result might then be some sort of oscillation, as one or other system gained ascendancy.

Another kind of system and one that would lead to less oscillation would be a system organised to maintain a set-goal specified in terms not only of a goal-object but of an exact (though not necessarily constant) distance from the object. In that case the set-goal would be an equilibrium point.

In Chapter 13 a system of the simpler sort is postulated to account for a young child's maintenance of proximity to mother.

Orientation of Behaviour

The discussion of set-goals has already touched on the second main issue referred to earlier, that of the directedness of behaviour. Any behaviour entailing locomotion controlled by

---

[1] Hediger (1955) gives many examples of the great part played in the lives of animals by behaviour that maintains them at more or less constant distances either from members of their own species or from potential predators.

systems that are goal-corrected is, of course, inherently directed, both in the sense of being oriented in space and in the sense of having an objective, namely a set-goal. Since behaviour that has no set-goal, and is therefore not directed in that sense, can also be oriented in space, there is need to discuss the problem of orientation independently of set-goal. The term 'orientation' refers simply to the spatial axes on which the behaviour is organised, the reference points of which are commonly objects in or components of the environment.

Since behaviour takes place in space all behaviour has some orientation. Some behaviour appears to be oriented purely at random, but more often it is oriented in a non-random way. There are a number of means whereby this is achieved, some of which will already be evident.

In the case of the peregrine's stoop and all other goal-corrected behaviour in which the set-goal includes a specified part of the environment to or away from which the animal moves, orientation results from a continuous comparison of performance with set-goal. In those cases the system responsible is working on a 'homing' principle, as in the case of a homing missile.

In other closely related cases the animal itself does not move, but either its whole body or some part of it, for example eyes, is turned towards an object in the environment. In those cases the system responsible may be working on a 'tracking' principle, as in the case of a radar receiver set to lock on to and track an aircraft. An example of tracking followed by an aimed movement is the way in which a toad catches a fly by shooting out its tongue towards the fly. Here orientation is achieved by the toad's turning its head towards the fly in a tracking movement. The tongue itself, on the other hand, does no more than extrude straight from the toad's mouth and is oriented in no other way. Systems responsible for this form of orientation are working on the same principle as a man-aimed gun. In each case the aim is a result of movement controlled by a goal-corrected tracking system, and the subsequent movements of tongue and of bullet result from the action of a simple fixed-action type of system.

In other cases of non-random orientation, for example many instances of bird migration, orientation is determined not by direct reference to a set-goal but by reference to other items in the environment, such as landmarks, sun and stars. Systems responsible for this form of orientation are working on a 'navigatory' principle, as in the case of ship navigation, and depend on the presence in the organism of a cognitive map.

Behaviour oriented on this principle leads to its predictable outcome only when the items used for navigation bear a fixed relationship to some spatial component of that predictable outcome, for example a nest-site. This is illustrated by the case of the digger wasp which finds its inconspicuous nesting-hole by means of navigation. Provided a pattern of landmarks in the nest's vicinity remains unchanged, the wasp flies direct to its hole, which is thus a major component of predictable outcome; the wasp's ability to find its hole, experiment shows, is due to its having first learned the spatial relationship between nesting-hole and landmarks. If the position of the landmarks is changed, therefore, inevitably the wasp flies to a point removed from its nesting-hole. An outcome of a similar kind may occur to a man-navigated ship should buoys get out of position.[1]

No doubt there is also oriented behaviour controlled by systems working on principles yet other than those described. Enough has been said, however, to indicate the many different means whereby behaviour can be oriented in space and organised so that predictable outcomes are reached. It is a virtue of modern instinct theory that, whilst remaining a strictly scientific discipline, it is able to give full weight to such crucial features of behaviour as orientation, predictable outcome, and set-goal.

In concluding this section it is important to note that nothing has yet been said about what causes a movement of any kind to start or to stop. Instead, we have been concerned solely with patterns of movement and with the means whereby patterned movements are oriented in space and structured so that predictable outcomes are reached. In the next section this discussion continues, with special reference to the principles by which a number of behavioural systems come to be organised and co-ordinated over a span of time. Only after that (in Chapter 6) are the activation and termination of behavioural systems given attention. It will be seen then that to understand them raises new issues, of a different kind from those so far discussed.

Co-ordination of behavioural systems

Just as there are many different types of behavioural system so there are a number of different ways in which their activities can be co-ordinated.

[1] The various methods by which birds do, or may, orient their flight either when homing or during migration are classified by Schmidt-Koenig (1965).

Perhaps the simplest method of organising behaviour that has to change in a specified way over time is by means of a chain, each link of which is a behavioural system. When this is done behaviour proceeds in the correct sequence because the effects produced by the action of one behavioural system, when fed back centrally, not only terminate that system but also activate the system next in the chain. As a result one activity stops and another starts.

The effects produced by the first activity may be registered by proprioceptive sense organs or by exteroceptive ones, or by both together. An example of a behavioural sequence that is dependent on proprioceptive feedback is walking. Here the end of the first phase of the alternating action is registered proprioceptively and, when fed back to the controlling system, simultaneously inhibits the first phase of movement and initiates the second. Most of the more complex and interesting instinctive sequences, however, are dependent on feedback from exteroceptors, notably eyes, ears, and nose. Many examples are given in the ethological literature. The re-actions of a foraging honey bee provide a good illustration: links in the chain of responses have been identified by experimental work using models.

The collection of honey by a honey bee starts with a visually controlled behavioural system; on perceiving, often at a considerable distance, a flower-shape of colour yellow or blue the bee flies towards it until it reaches within 1 cm. The next link in the chain is controlled by olfactory stimuli: on perceiving an odour that lies within a certain range the bee settles on the flower and explores its shape. The third link is controlled by tactile stimuli: on perceiving structures of a certain shape the bee inserts its mouth parts and begins to suck. In the ordinary course of events the collection of nectar results. Thus the behavioural equipment of the bee is so organised that within the environment of evolutionary adaptedness behaviour resulting from the action of one behavioural system leads to a situation which simultaneously terminates that system and activates the next in a series of steps such that the final result is a gathering of nectar.

Many intricate and beautifully adapted sequences of behaviour are now known to be due to systems organised in simple chains of this kind. Yet, remarkable though the achievement of systems so organised may be, such an organisation is subject to grave limitations. For example, the whole organisation fails in its purpose if the action of one link in the chain miscarries. If, because of a chemical spray, the flower's odour cannot be detected, the second behavioural system in the chain is not activated and the bee moves elsewhere without finding the honey to which it came so near. Thus, only when the environment conforms exactly to the environment of evolutionary adaptedness does each of the behavioural systems in the chain produce its effect and the whole organisation lead to behaviour of survival value. As in other chains, the strength of the organisation is no greater than that of its weakest link.

There are, however, ways by which a chain-linked organisation of behavioural systems can be made more flexible. For example, at any point in it a chain can have one or more alternative links so that, whenever activation of the first of a set of alternative behavioural systems fails to achieve results that activate the succeeding system in the chain, one of the other systems of the set becomes active. In this way it may happen that the same outcome is attained by any of a number of alternative behaviours.

A further point to remember regarding the potentialities of chains is that any particular link in a chain can be a behavioural system of any degree of complexity. Thus, whilst the chain itself is always strung together without goal-correction, any or even all of the individual links in it can be a goal-corrected system. For instance, it is not unlikely that, in many species of bird, nest-building behaviour is organised in this way: whereas each of the distinct phases of behaviour required to make a nest is goal-corrected, transition from one phase of behaviour to the next is by chain. Thus, parts of a behavioural sequence may be goal-corrected even when the whole is not. By these means sequences of behaviour with predictable outcomes that are remarkably adapted can be organised on the chain principle.

Nevertheless organisation of systems on a chain-linked principle is by no means the only principle of organisation used by living creatures. Another principle is for a number of behavioural systems all to share a common causal factor. Such causal factor might be the level in the body of a particular hormone or the sight in the environment of a particular object. Tinbergen (1951) has referred to this mode of organisation as hierarchical. Since its understanding entails consideration of factors that activate and terminate behavioural systems, its discussion is postponed to the next chapter (p. 88).

Yet another mode of organisation and one that, when developed, is capable of giving a much greater degree of flexibility than either of those so far mentioned is also hierarchical in form, though it is organised on a hierarchical principle entirely different from Tinbergen's causal hierarchy. Following Miller, Galanter, and Pribram (1960) it is conveniently termed a plan hierarchy.

In considering the ways in which the behaviour of humans may be organised, Miller and his associates advance the concept of 'plan', an overall goal-corrected behavioural structure made up of a hierarchy of subordinate structures (termed by them 'totes'). Although in the model they propose each of the sub-structures is conceived as goal-corrected, this is neither essential to their concept nor likely to be found empirically. Indeed, sub-structures of any of the types described in the previous section would be consistent with their main proposal. The distinctive feature of a plan hierarchy is that the overall structure, within which sub-structures of any number and kind are integrated, is goal-corrected.

The great merit of the contribution of Miller, Galanter, and Pribram is that they have shown how some of the most complex and flexible sequences of behaviour could in principle be organised by means of a hierarchy of systems, the highest of which, the plan, is always goal-corrected and many of the subordinates of which are likely to be so as well. Moreover, their concept of plan is such that it can be applied as readily to behaviour that is environmentally labile as to behaviour that is environmentally stable, and that it can be applied to behaviour organised in terms of a very simple map of the environment as well as to behaviour organised in terms of a highly sophisticated map.

To illustrate what is meant by organisation of behaviour in terms of a plan hierarchy it is convenient to use first a sequence of learned human behaviour. A second illustration of this mode of organisation is drawn from the literature of sub-human behaviour.

The illustration drawn from learned human behaviour is the kind of routine each of us follows on rising of a morning. Between leaving bed and arriving at work each of us is likely to behave in a certain fairly predictable way. At one level of description it can be described as 'getting to work'; and at a level rather less general as a sequence of leaving bed, washing, dressing, breakfasting, and travelling. Each of these activities, however, can be even further specified. In the ultimate analysis activities would be specified to the finest movement of the smallest muscle.

Now in real life we are usually concerned only with the overall operation of getting up and going to work, or at most with the main activities and sub-activities entailed; and each day we may follow a more or less regular routine. But to suppose the operation is organised as a chain of responses would certainly be wrong. For one thing the activities can follow each other in changed order—breakfasting before dressing, for example; for another, the components of any one activity can be greatly changed without the overall plan being changed—a breakfast, for example, can be either big or small, or skipped altogether. The essential difference from organisation by chain is, however, that, whereas in the case of a chain the whole sequence is not goal-corrected, in the case of a plan the whole sequence is goal-corrected. In the example given the set-goal of the plan is 'arrival at work'. The whole sequence is then conceived as governed by a master plan structured to achieve a long-range set-goal, the master plan itself being made up of a number of sub-plans each with its more limited set-goal, and each of the sub-plans in turn being made up of sub-sub-plans, and so on right down to miniscule plans (or, more probably, systems of simpler type) that control the most elementary units of behaviour. In order to get to work the complete master plan must be executed, but the sub-plans and other subordinate systems that go to make it up can, within limits, be varied.

In a hierarchical system of this sort, each plan and sub-plan is to be regarded as a set of instructions for action. As in the case of a military operation, the master plan gives only main objective and general strategy; each commander down the hierarchy is then expected to make more detailed plans and to issue more detailed instructions for the execution of his part in the master plan. By leaving detail to subordinates not only does the master plan remain simple and intelligible but the more detailed plans can be developed and executed by those with knowledge of current local conditions. With plan hierarchy there can more easily be flexibility.

The overwhelming advantage of an organisation of this sort is, of course, that the same set-goal can be achieved even though circumstances vary over a wide range. To return to our original illustration, on any one morning we may be confronted with over-sleeping, a dirty shirt, no coffee, or a bus-strike; but by drawing on one of many alternative sub-plans we can deal with each hazard and execute the overall plan. Yet even when behaviour is organised as a plan hierarchy there is a limit to the extent to which deviations of environment can be coped with. When the environment deviates too greatly from that presupposed by the master plan—no clothes or no transport—the plan cannot be executed and the set-goal cannot be achieved.

The first example of behaviour organised on the principle of a plan hierarchy has been drawn from the learned behaviour of a relatively sophisticated adult human, and represents a very advanced form of hierarchically planned organisation of behaviour. In animals below the level of man no sequences of anything like this degree of elaboration are likely to exist (except possibly in the great apes). Nevertheless, there is evidence that some behaviour in many species is organised on this principle.

An elementary example is the running of a maze by a rat. When rats are subjected to spinal or cerebellar operations in such a way as to interfere with their locomotor co-ordination they may nevertheless make error-less runs employing quite novel locomotory movements. In such a case it is evident that their master plan for running the maze is unimpaired and that, when the usual locomotory systems are not in working order, locomotory systems of a novel kind can be invented and executed.

Evidence available at present suggests strongly that, whilst certain behavioural sequences in some species are organised in fixed chains and other behavioural sequences in other species are organised by means of causal hierarchies or plan hierarchies, a great deal of behaviour is organised using a mixture of methods. So far from the methods being mutually incompatible, they are plainly complementary to one another. There is no reason, moreover, why similar behaviour, for example nest-building, should not be organised as a chain in one species, as a causal hierarchy in another, and as a plan hierarchy in a third; or why the same behaviour should not be organised as a chain or a causal hierarchy in immature members of a species and reorganised in terms of a plan hierarchy in the adult members.

A progression from organisation by chain to organisation by hierarchy is, indeed, a striking feature of the development, both phylogenetic and ontogenetic, of behavioural equipment. The biological success of insects has been founded on behavioural systems that are environmentally stable, responsive to simple cues, and organised in chains. In the higher vertebrates behavioural systems are more often environmentally labile, responsive to more complex cues, and in their means of integration more likely to include causal or plan hierarchies. In man these trends have been carried a very long way further.

Higher processes of integration and control

Working Models

Earlier in this chapter reference is made to the cognitive map that an animal must have of its environment if it is to achieve a set-goal that requires it to move from one place to another. Clearly such maps can be of all degrees of sophistication from the elementary maps that we infer hunting wasps construct to the immensely complex world-picture of an educated Westerner. In addition, however, to a knowledge of the world, an individual requires, if he is to frame effective plans, a knowledge of his own capabilities.

Let us consider first his knowledge of the environment.

A map is a coded representation of selected aspects of whatever is mapped. Selection is unavoidable, partly because the environment is so enormously complex, partly because our sense organs provide us with information about only a limited aspect of it, and partly because, to be usable, a map needs to concentrate on those aspects of the environment that are most relevant to the achievement of set-goals.

To call our knowledge of the environment a map is, however, inadequate, because the word conjures up merely a static representation of topography. What an animal requires is something more like a working model of its environment. The notion that brains provide such models has been explored by, amongst others, Young (1964), who writes:

> An engineer makes a model of the structure he proposes to build, so that he may test it, on a small scale. Similarly the idea of a model in the brain is that it constitutes a toy that is yet a tool, an imitation world, which we can manipulate in the way that will suit us best, and so find out how to manipulate the real world, which it is supposed to represent.

The use to which a model in the brain is put is to transmit, store, and manipulate information that helps in making predictions as to how what are here termed set-goals can be achieved. The notion that brains do in fact provide more or less elaborate models that 'can be made to conduct, as it were, small-scale experiments within the head' is one that appeals to anyone concerned to understand the complexities of behaviour and especially of human behaviour. Though to some steeped in extreme behaviourism the idea may seem fanciful, it is far from being so. For example, to electrical engineers familiar with analogue computers the notion is an obvious possibility. And the same is true in the case of researchers like Young, himself a biologist engaged in studies of brain and behaviour. In considering the idea, Young emphasises that models 'are often constructed out of unit parts, components that are individually unlike those of the structure represented but can be assembled to make the finished, working model'. With this in mind he advances the hypothesis that

> the varied cells of the brain provide sets of such components, and that these are assembled during learning to make the model. The characteristics of each component are specified in the main by the forms of their dendritic branches.
>
> The evidence for this hypothesis, slender as it is, comes from study of the brains and behaviour of octopuses and cats.

Those who wish to examine the evidence should read Young (1964). The position taken here is not only that it is reasonable to postulate that the brain builds up working models of its environment but that in order to understand human behaviour it is difficult to do without such a hypothesis—which squares, of course, with such introspective knowledge of our own mental processes as we have. In later chapters, and especially in Volumes II and III the hypothesis is frequently called upon.

A number of measures are required if an organism is to exploit usefully a working model. First, the model must be built in accordance with such data as are or can be made available. Secondly, if the model is to be of use in novel situations, it must be extended imaginatively to cover potential realities as well as experienced ones. Thirdly, any model, whether applicable to an experienced world or to a potential one, must be tested for internal consistency (or, in technical language, for compliance with the axioms of the theory of sets).[1] The more adequate the model the more accurate its predictions; and the more comprehensive the model the greater the number of situations in which its predictions apply.

[1] Here and elsewhere in Part II I am indebted to help from Professor Arnold Tustin.

If an individual is to draw up a plan to achieve a set-goal not only must he have some sort of working model of his environment, but he must have also some working knowledge of his own behavioural skills and potentialities. Someone crippled or blind must make plans different from those made by the fit and sighted. Someone who drives a car or rides a bicycle has an array of potential plans larger than the array available to someone who can do neither.

Henceforward the two working models each individual must have are referred to respectively as his environmental model and his organismic model.

To be useful both working models must be kept up-to-date. As a rule this requires only a continuous feeding in of small modifications, usually a process so gradual that it is hardly noticeable. Occasionally, however, some major change in environment or in organism occurs: we get married, have a baby, or receive promotion at work; or, less happily, someone close to us departs or dies, a limb is lost, or sight fails. At those times radical changes of model are called for. Clinical evidence suggests that the necessary revisions of model are not always easy to achieve. Usually they are completed but only slowly, often they are done imperfectly, and sometimes done not at all.

The environmental and organismic models described here as necessary parts of a sophisticated biological control system are, of course, none other than the 'internal worlds' of traditional psychoanalytic theory seen in a new perspective. As in the traditional theory so in the theory advanced, much psychopathology is regarded as being due to models that are in greater or less degree inadequate or inaccurate. Such inadequacy can be of many kinds: a model may be unserviceable, for example, because it is totally out-of-date, or because it is only half revised and therefore remains half out-of-date, or else because it is full of inconsistencies and confusions. Some of the pathological sequelae of separation and bereavement can be understood in these terms (see Volumes II and III).

There is one further property of environmental and organismic models that is of great importance in psychopathology. Reflection suggests that many of the mental processes of which we are most keenly conscious are processes concerned with the building of models, with revising or extending them, checking them for internal consistency, or drawing on them for making a novel plan to reach a set-goal. Although it is certainly not necessary for all such processes always to be conscious, it is probably necessary that some should be so sometimes. In particular it seems likely that revising, extending, and checking of models are ill done or done not at all unless a model is subjected from time to time to whatever special benefits accrue from becoming conscious.[1] These matters are discussed further in Chapter 7.

Language

A special and unique feature of man's behavioural equipment is language. An obvious benefit it confers is that, instead of each one of us having to build his environmental and organismic models entirely for himself, he can draw on models built by others. Another benefit, though less obvious because independent of communication, is the use each individual makes of language for organising his own behaviour by means of plans, sub-plans, and sub-sub-plans in the way already illustrated by the routine of getting up and going to work. A new plan of action, if it is of any complexity, is first thought out in words and may later be written down in words. Furthermore, verbal instructions are also the means whereby individuals are able to combine together to construct and execute a joint plan that draws upon a shared environmental model and shared models of the skills of each participant. Thus the possession of language enables the organisation of behavioural systems in plan hierarchies to be carried to astonishing lengths.

Once behavioural systems are organised hierarchically by means of language and can draw on sophisticated models of organism and environment, results are protean in their variability. In consequence a very great deal of man's behaviour cannot, by any stretch of the term, be called instinctive. Yet, because much behaviour of adult men and women is organised in complex learned hierarchical integrates, it does not follow that there are present within it no simpler, more environmentally stable or chain-linked systems. The contrary is, of course, far more probable. Since the time when Freud himself was a neurophysiologist, neurophysiologists have been emphasising on what conservative lines the central nervous systems of higher species are built. So far from the neural equipment of early

[1] MacKay (1966) has discussed the idea that 'conscious experience is the correlate of what might be called metaorganizing activity—the organization of internal action upon the behavioural organizing system itself ... The unity of consciousness would on this basis reflect the integration of the metaorganizing system ...'

design being scrapped, the neural equipment of higher species incorporates within itself all the earlier design features and then adds to it new systems that modify, and sometimes override, the activities of the old; in that way more complex and elaborate behaviour becomes possible. If the early and simpler versions of neural equipment are an integral part of neural equipment of advanced design, it is more than likely that the same applies to behavioural equipment. It would indeed be very strange if, even in the most advanced behavioural equipment of which we know, early design features did not play a significant part.

There is in fact good reason to think that in the early infancy of man most of the behavioural systems in working order are simple ones and integrated as chains. As development goes forward, goal-corrected systems become more evident, environmental and organismic models are elaborated, and integrates become organised as plan hierarchies. Linguistic skill soon enables models to become more adequate and hierarchical organisation to be extended, yet young children (and also older ones) are still quick to resort to behaviour organised in relatively simple ways. Because there is evidence that much psychopathology originates in early life, the ontogenesis of man's behavioural equipment is of special interest to psychoanalysis. In later chapters discussion of this theme is resumed.

So far the discussion has been confined, first, to a description of the kinds of control system that may account for units of instinctive behaviour and, secondly, to the principles on which such control systems may be organised so as to produce the kinds of complex and purposive behavioural sequences that are to be observed in real life. It is time now to consider more systematically a little of what is known of the conditions that lead an animal at any one moment to behave in one way rather than another; or, in other words, what is known of the causal conditions that underlie some particular behaviour. This discussion, it will be found, takes us back repeatedly to the organisation of behaviour. The way in which instinctive behaviour is initiated and the way in which it is organised are in fact closely interconnected.

Chapter 6

Causation of Instinctive Behaviour

Activation and termination of behavioural systems

Starting and Stopping: Classes of Causal Factor

At the present stage of exposition an adult animal is pictured as possessing an elaborate behavioural equipment that comprises a very large but finite number of behavioural systems that are organised in chains or hierarchies, or a mixture of the two, and that, when activated, lead to behavioural sequences of greater or less complexity each of which commonly promotes survival of individual and/or species. The precise forms the systems take in a particular individual are, as always, a product of gene action and environment; and, dependent on species and system, the forms they take are more or less stable environmentally. In addition to the more stable behavioural systems responsible for instinctive behaviour, animals are equipped with many others that are environmentally labile and in the development of which learning plays a very large part (though they are not our concern here). Given this varied equipment, then, the question that confronts us is why one part of it is in action at one time and another part at another.

The first thing to recognise is that, so long as an animal is alive, one or another part of its behavioural equipment is bound to be in action. Animal life is behaviour, even if it is only the behaviour of sleep. Since our task as psychologists is not that of solving the riddle of life, we are not called upon to explain why an animal behaves but only why at any one time it behaves in this way rather than that, and why, when it is behaving in any particular way, it does so more intensely at some times than at others.

One approach to the problem is to consider the activity of physiological systems. Most physiological systems are in constant simultaneous activity. The cardiovascular system, the respiratory, the excretory, are permanently at work; and, whilst the digestive and the reproductive are more episodic in their operation, their activities are not usually incompatible with those of other physiological systems and so can be in operation simultaneously with them. In other words, physiological systems can all be in action together: there is no problem of stopping one in order to start another.

Nevertheless, when we come to consider activities comprised within any one physiological system, issues of starting and stopping do arise: this is because one activity is often incompatible with another. For example, ever since Sherrington formulated the principle of reciprocal inhibition it has been recognised that, if a limb is to be extended, not only must the extensor muscles be contracted but simultaneous contraction of the flexors must be avoided. The mechanism controlling extension therefore sends out two signals, one that activates extensors and another that inactivates flexors. When flexion is required an opposite pair of signals is sent out. Reciprocal activity of an analogous kind occurs in the cardiovascular system. During muscular exertion blood supply to the muscles is increased by dilation of blood vessels and, because blood volume is limited, blood supply to the viscera is decreased by contraction of visceral blood vessels. After a heavy meal the position is reversed. Any one pattern of physiological activity, therefore, occurs only episodically, the reason being that the activity of one pattern is commonly incompatible with activity of others.

The activity of behavioural systems is similarly episodic and for the same reason. Though it is often possible to do two things at once, more than a limited number are not possible simultaneously, and not infrequently to behave in one way is incompatible with behaving in another. Sometimes two sorts of behaviour compete for the same effectors: a bird cannot simultaneously build a nest and search for food. Sometimes two sorts of behaviour require different sorts of environment: a rabbit cannot simultaneously graze grass and hide in a burrow. Sometimes two sorts of behaviour lead to contrary consequences: to attack another creature is not compatible with protecting it. Again and again, therefore, to behave in one way entails not behaving in very many others. This means that in order to understand the working of behavioural systems it is necessary to explain why one system starts up and another stops. It is also necessary to know how it comes about that one system is selected for action in preference to another and what happens when two or more systems are in action at once.

In the determination of why one behavioural system is activated rather than another at least five classes of causal factor are at work. Some are relatively specific to particular behavioural systems, others are more general. The most specific are the way in which the behavioural systems are organised within the cns and the presence or absence of special objects in the environment. Hormones, also, are fairly specific in their influence on behaviour. The least specific factors are the current state of activity of the cns and the total stimulation impinging at the time. As a rule all five classes of factor are acting together. Since, moreover, each class of factor interacts with all the others, the texture of causal conditions is as intricate as a Persian carpet.

Some schools of behaviour theory favour the concept of a limited number of rather general drives; Hinde (1966), on the other hand, argues strongly against it. His is the position adopted here; reasons are set out in the latter half of Chapter 8.

Roles of Specific Causal Factors

In considering the parts played by causal factors having fairly specific effects let us start with the role of hormones. In birds and mammals the presence in the blood stream of high levels of one or another sex hormone is apt to be accompanied by certain typical sorts of sexual behaviour, whilst at the same time behaviour of other sorts is conspicuous by its absence.

In members of both sexes of the three-spined stickleback, for example, the presence of high levels of male sex hormones makes all the following activities more probable:

Fighting:	biting
	threatening
	fleeing
Nest-building:	collecting
	glueing
	boring
Courting:	zig-zag dance
	leading, etc.

Simultaneously, a number of other activities are made less probable, either by the direct action of the hormone itself on the cns or because the stickleback is too busy fighting, nest-building, or courting to engage in them. Included in the less probable are schooling with other sticklebacks and migrating to fresh territories.

Research shows that in this species members of both sexes are equipped with behavioural systems that can give rise to masculine behaviour (and also to feminine) and that the particular set of systems that becomes active is in large part determined by hormone level. Yet at any one time, with a given level of male hormone, only one or two of the many possible masculine activities that are potentiated are in fact executed; which shows that causal factors other than hormone level are at work also. In this and similar examples some of the other causal factors that are of particular importance are environmental ones. Thus the presence of another male is likely to lead to fighting behaviour, whereas the presence of a ripe female is likely to lead to courting. This shows how the exhibition of each particular bit of behaviour is determined neither by hormone level alone nor by environmental stimulus[1] alone but by both acting in co-operation (and in co-operation not only with each other but with other factors as well).

In this example, it is to be noted, the role of hormone and the role of environmental stimulus are different: whereas hormone level potentiates a large number of behavioural systems (and 'depotentiates' others), environmental stimuli tend to activate particular systems. Thus there is a hierarchical organisation of causes and the hormone is acting at a higher point in it. In other cases, as we shall see, the roles of hormone and environment may be reversed: for example, stimuli from the environment may in large part determine hormone level.

Before we examine further the role of environmental factors, it may be useful to consider briefly the organisation of behaviour by means of causal hierarchy, a principle to which Tinbergen (1951) first drew attention.

In the example of stickleback behaviour just given it was seen that the causal factor acting at a high point in the causal hierarchy is hormone level. In the next example the 'senior' causal factor is of a different sort: it is excitation at a particular part of the CNS.

By means of experiments using electrical stimulation of the brain-stem of an intact animal (chicken), von Holst and von St Paul (1963) have analysed the ways in which the behavioural repertoire itself comprises a very large but finite number of behavioural units, such as clucking, crowing, pecking, fleeing, sitting, feeding, standing still. Not only can each of these units be made to occur in isolation but most of them can be made to occur as parts of a number of different and more complex sequences. Sitting, for example, can be a part of sleeping or of

[1] The term 'environmental stimulus' begs a number of questions: see discussion at the end of this chapter (p. 102).

brooding, and it may also occur as pure sitting; cackling can succeed fleeing as well as egg-laying; looking around, standing up, or running can occur as parts of numerous different behavioural sequences. These findings, with other ones, lead the authors to conclude that in the chicken there are at least three levels at which behaviour is integrated, ranging from the simple unit to the level of a complex sequence of units. Some features of this integration could be organised by means of chains, but it is evident that any chain-organised sequences must be subordinate, in a hierarchical sense, to some other organisation which determines which of several possible chain-linked sequences are to be performed. Were there not this superordinate control system, behavioural unit Q would always have to be preceded by P and followed by R, whereas observation shows that unit Q can in fact appear in many other contexts.

Another feature in the causal organisation of behaviour which this series of experiments illustrates is the critical part played by environmental stimuli of special sorts. Thus it is possible to stimulate a chicken's brain in such a way that simple sequences of behaviour are exhibited, but certain of the more complex sequences cannot (at least at present) be made to occur by electrical stimulation alone. For example, if attack by a cock on a rival or on an enemy is to be exhibited, the presence of at least a suitable dummy is required. This shows again how behavioural systems are designed to fit particular environments and, in this case, how the behaviour to which a system gives rise may be unable to occur unless the environment provides the 'right' stimulation.

In other cases, on the other hand, hormone level and/or the state of the CNS may be such that an activity may occur even in the absence of the 'right' stimulation from the environment. This leads to the so-called vacuum activities. An example, described by Lorenz, is of a starling that obtained all its food from a dish but nonetheless from time to time went through all the aerial motions of chasing, catching, and swallowing a fly, even though there was no fly there.

The part played by the way in which behavioural systems are organised within the CNS was touched on in the preceding chapter. When systems are organised as chains with proprioceptive or exteroceptive feedback, the signals that terminate one sort of behaviour are often the same as those that activate the system next in the chain. The way in which the CNS is organised can also influence the priorities of different systems by other means. Thus, whenever behaviour of one sort occurs the probability of its occurring again is likely to be either increased or decreased; and the change may even be in one direction in the short run and in the opposite direction over a longer period. For example, after a male has copulated with ejaculation the likelihood of his copulating again soon is usually much reduced, though over a longer period it may be raised. As a rule, too, the performance of one sort of behaviour influences in one direction or another the likelihood of other sorts of behaviour being exhibited. After becoming adult an aphid flies for a while and then settles to lay eggs. Research shows that initially the aphid is not disposed to settle, even when a suitable leaf is provided, but only to fly. Once it has flown for a time, however, it becomes less prone to fly and more prone to settle; indeed, the longer it flies the more prone does it become to settle and the longer will it remain settled. Thus the activity of flying lowers the threshold for settling.

It has already been said that not only do the different classes of factor, hormones, characteristics of CNS, and environmental stimuli, contribute jointly towards disposing an animal to behave in one way rather than another, but that the classes of factor interact constantly with each other. Hormone output is influenced by environmental stimuli and by autonomous processes in the CNS; environmental stimuli are encountered because behaviour initiated by hormones or by other changes in the CNS brings the animal into new environmental situations; how behavioural systems in the CNS come to be organised is determined in part by the particular environmental stimuli met with and in part also by hormone levels occurring during development.

Hormones influence behaviour by acting in one or both of two different ways: sometimes a hormone acts directly on a particular part or parts of the CNS, making some behavioural systems more responsive and others perhaps less so; sometimes it acts on certain peripheral organs, for example on one sort of sensory nerve-ending in a particular skin area, thereby making that area, and so the animal, more sensitive to particular stimuli coming from the environment. To illustrate a few of these complex interconnections, two examples are given. The first concerns nest-building and egg-laying by canaries; the second, maternal behaviour of the rat.

The causal factors leading to nest-building and laying by a female canary have been the subject of systematic research by

Hinde (1965b). In the female canary, as in many other bird species, changes in the environment (increased light and/or raised temperature) cause changes in the female's endocrine state as a result of which she associates with a male. Next, stimuli from the male accelerate oestrogen production in the female and this causes her to build a nest. Thenceforward the presence of the male continues to be of great importance, whilst the existence of a partly built nest, within which the female is prone to sit, plays a prominent and additional causal role in her behaviour. Because of the endocrine changes that have already taken place, the female's breast has become defeathered and vascular and is more sensitive to the tactile stimulation that reaches her when she sits in the nest. This tactile stimulation from the nest-cup then has at least three different effects on her behaviour. Immediately, such stimulation influences certain of her nest-building movements. Over a period of minutes, it influences the frequency of her visits to the nest and the nature of the nest material that she selects. Over a longer period, it causes further endocrine changes that result in her laying her eggs earlier than she would otherwise do. At the next stage of the reproductive process stimulation reaching the female from the nest and eggs plays a part by affecting her incubating behaviour.

In this sequence of behaviour, executed over a period of many weeks, successive behavioural systems become first active and later inactive. The activation of some systems is caused largely by endocrine levels and that of others largely by environmental stimulation, but, in addition to this, endocrine level is itself largely a result of environmental stimulation, and the particular stimulation received from the environment is itself a result of actions, or of an increased sensitivity, the cause of which was a previous endocrine level. Complex though the series of interactions depicted is, this description is in fact an oversimplified version of the real thing.

Complex series of interactions of a comparable kind between hormone level, environmental stimulation, and organisation within the CNS are now known to play causal roles also in the behaviour of lower mammals. Amongst a number of investigators who have studied the reproductive behaviour of the laboratory rat, Beach (e.g. 1965) has been a pioneer and has contributed much to an understanding of sexual behaviour. More recently Rosenblatt (1965) has analysed further some of the causal factors that elicit maternal behaviour. In particular, he has been interested to discover how the behaviour of a mother rat is changed so that at each phase of the offspring's development her behaviour is appropriate to them.

Maternal behaviour in the rat has three main components: nest-building, nursing, and retrieving. Over a period of about four weeks one or more of these components are to be seen; after that they are seen no more. The whole cycle of maternal behaviour can be divided into some four phases during each of which details of behaviour differ. These four phases are:

i. the final days of pregnancy during which a very little nest-building may occur;

ii. the three or four days starting at parturition during which all components of maternal behaviour are shown, and the mother initiates almost all interaction with the pups;

iii. the remaining days of the first fortnight, a maintenance period, during which the whole repertoire of maternal behaviour continues to be exhibited at full strength, still mostly on the initiative of the mother;

iv. the third and fourth weeks after parturition during which the mother increasingly leaves the initiative for interaction to the young, and during which the amount of nest-building, retrieving, and nursing she does is steadily reduced until finally it disappears altogether.

In the ordinary course of events these phases of maternal behaviour are nicely synchronised to suit the condition of the pups. Until the end of the second week the pups are without sight and hearing, and rely mainly on contact stimulation. Though they are able to crawl rather earlier, not until the end of the second week are they able to walk. Once they are two weeks old, however, the pups become much more independent. They start leaving the nest, they initiate suckling and also social interaction with litter-mates. After four weeks they can fend for themselves.

Now in analysing the maternal behaviour cycle it is useful to distinguish between maternal state and maternal behaviour. Any particular bit of maternal behaviour is very sensitive to stimuli from the environment: for example, when the nest is disarrayed nest-building starts at once; when a pup has strayed, it is retrieved. Even so, such behaviour occurs only when the mother is in a certain condition, termed here 'maternal state'.[1]

---

[1] Rosenblatt uses the term 'maternal mood', but as a rule the term 'mood' is used to refer to a condition that lasts for a shorter period than the days or weeks of 'maternal state'.

What this means is that certain causal factors are operating at a higher point in a hierarchical organisation and are thus determining maternal state, whilst another set of causal conditions is operating at a lower level and is thus determining the particular behaviour that is shown.

The questions the researchers set out to answer were: What causal factors account for a mother rat's developing a maternal state? What causal factors account for the subsequent changes in and ultimate disappearance of maternal state? And to what extent are these changes due to hormonal changes occurring in the mother irrespective of environmental stimuli and to what extent to stimulation coming from the pups, stimulation which, of course, changes as the pups get older and more active? To answer these questions a series of experiments was conducted in which test pups of various ages were placed with mothers at different phases of the maternal cycle, whilst the mother's own pups either remained with her or were removed from her for periods of days at different phases of the cycle.

The main conclusions to be drawn are as follows:

(a) Even when given newborn test pups, females still pregnant do not nurse or retrieve and do hardly any nest-building, whereas they do all these things immediately after parturition. This shows that stimulation from pups cannot be the main cause of the onset of maternal state. The causal factor may be some proprioceptive feedback from the pelvic tissues occurring during the process of parturition itself or, and probably more likely, it may be a shift in hormonal balance that occurs abruptly after parturition, when placental hormones are cut out; but both factors could well play a part.

(b) Since maternal state wanes rapidly if pups are removed from mother for a few days immediately after parturition, stimulation from pups evidently plays an important part in maintaining the maternal state during those days—probably by ensuring that hormonal levels are maintained.

(c) Since removal of pups for a similar length of time at later phases of the cycle has much less effect on maternal state, it seems that after a few days hormonal levels are much less dependent on stimulation from pups. Even so, it is found that, should pups be removed from the mother nine or more days after parturition, maternal state wanes more readily than it does when pups remain with her; this shows that maintenance of the maternal cycle continues to be dependent in some measure on stimulation received from pups.

(d) In the final phase of the cycle, maternal state wanes inexorably and this occurs even when the mother's own 'elderly' and active pups are replaced by young ones for test purposes. This shows that initiation of this phase of the cycle is influenced only slightly by the changing stimulation coming from the increasingly active pups and is due presumably to autonomous internal changes in the mother.

Thus once again it is found that a change occurring within an animal, in all likelihood a change in hormonal level, leads to changes in her behaviour, e.g. care of young, that result in her receiving stimulation from the environment, which itself has an effect on her hormonal level, and that that again influences her behaviour, and perhaps her sensitivity, and so the kind of stimulation that she receives. The more adequately any sequence of instinctive behaviour is analysed the more certain are interactive cycles of this kind to be found. Since they occur in lower mammals, it must be expected that in due course they will be identified in higher mammals, in primates, and in man himself.

Throughout these chapters the fact that behaviour is not only initiated but also terminated has been emphasised; no action persists for ever. The factors that cause behaviour to cease are clearly just as complex as those that cause it to start. All potential for maternal behaviour in the rat is absent when hormonal level has fallen below a certain level, or at least when hormonal balance has changed. Nest-building by a canary ceases when stimulation is received from the nest just completed—for it is resumed immediately should that nest be removed. Feeding behaviour of a dog ceases when there is nutrient food in the stomach and long before there has been any absorption of it into the blood stream. Thus different sorts of behaviour in different species are terminated by one or another different class of factor—in these examples by hormonal level, by exteroceptive stimulation, and by interoceptive stimulation, respectively. Termination is due not to a running down of some clockwork mechanism or to the running out of some psychical energy but to a specific signal. A game of football ends because a whistle blows, not because the players' energy is exhausted. A stream of cars stops because they meet a red light, not because they have run out of petrol. So with behavioural systems.

The signals responsible for the termination of a sequence of behaviour are usually termed by ethologists 'consummatory stimuli', though as the opposite of eliciting or initiating stimuli they are better called 'terminating stimuli'. As the examples already given show, terminating stimuli are of as many different kinds as those that initiate behaviour and those that orient it. In each case, signals are received by the behavioural systems concerned by way of any of the three classes of sense organ —exteroceptive, proprioceptive, and interoceptive—and sometimes by more than one class of sense organ at once.

Sometimes the stimuli that terminate a sequence of behaviour are received by an animal when and because it performs a particular act. This act, known as a consummatory act, is readily identifiable for systems in which the predictable outcome is a time-limited event. Orgasm is a well-known example. For systems in which the predictable outcome is a condition that extends indefinitely over time—location in a particular territory, for example—it is not possible to identify any consummatory act and the concept does not apply.

In the case of goal-corrected behavioural systems it is necessary to distinguish carefully between stimuli that guide behaviour towards a set-goal, i.e. orienting stimuli, and stimuli that bring a sequence of behaviour to an end, i.e. terminating stimuli. Because both classes of stimuli are likely to originate in the same source, namely the goal-object, they are easily confused. An example will help to make clear the distinction. In following a moving object, a young gosling is oriented by reception of visual and/or auditory stimuli from the object, on which it is homing. The stimuli that terminate the behaviour may, however, be of another kind, namely tactile; if the gosling is alarmed it is only when it receives tactile stimuli of a certain sort that following behaviour ceases. In this case visual and auditory stimuli from the goal-object orient behaviour, whereas tactile stimuli from the same goal-object terminate it.

Terminating stimuli must also be distinguished from inhibitory stimuli. Sometimes all the causal factors necessary for a behavioural system to be active are present but it is in fact inactive because of the simultaneous presence of inhibiting stimuli. Whereas terminating stimuli bring a sequence of behaviour to an end, inhibitory stimuli prevent its being started.

Thus a behavioural system may be inactive for two quite different reasons:

i. the causal factors necessary for its activation are not all present; or, which is the same thing, the causal factors leading to its termination are present;

ii. the necessary activating factors are present and the terminating factors absent, but there are present also inhibitory stimuli that prevent the activating factors having an effect.

Such inhibitory stimuli usually originate in some other behavioural system that is also on the brink of activity. This leads to a consideration of what happens when incompatible behavioural systems are activated simultaneously—the topic of a later section of the chapter.

Roles of Non-specific Causal Factors

Thus far little has been said about causal factors that have a general effect on behaviour rather than a specific one. The factors concerned are the arousal state of the CNS and the total level and/or patterning of stimulation that the animal is receiving. As usual the two are closely interrelated.

The effects that these general factors have on behaviour are chiefly to determine: (a) whether a stimulus is responded to at all, (b) the degree of sensory discrimination shown, (c) the speed of response, and (d) whether the response is organised or disorganised. There is no evidence that these factors have much influence on which behavioural system is activated and which not.

Evidence shows that, if a specific stimulus is to be responded to by behaviour, the mammalian cortex must be in a state of arousal (as measured by EEG), and shows also that the condition of the cortex is in great measure determined by the condition of the brain-stem reticular formation, which, in turn, is much influenced by the total stimulation received by the animal, irrespective of sensory mode. Up to a certain threshold, the more stimulation, through any of its sense organs, that an animal is receiving the greater its arousal and the more efficient its behaviour: sensory discrimination improves and reaction time is shortened. Above a certain level, however, efficiency may be diminished; and, when in an experimental situation total stimulation is very greatly increased, behaviour becomes completely disorganised. The same occurs when stimulation is much diminished, as in sensory deprivation experiments. These findings strongly suggest that there is an optimum level of sensory input at which responsiveness and efficiency are at their best. This optimum level may well be different for different sorts of behavioural system.

Some workers have interpreted these findings to indicate that the most significant variable is the total quantity of stimulation an animal receives, and have postulated 'general level of activation' and 'general drive' as useful concepts. As we have seen, Hinde (1966) calls these conclusions in question. He emphasises that in sensory deprivation experiments not only is the quantity of stimulation reduced but patterning is greatly diminished also. The same is probably true in experiments on the effect of sensory overload: bombarded by excessive stimulation an animal's pattern-recognition may fail. Hinde tends to the view that integrated behaviour is probably dependent more on regular relationships between patterned sensory inputs than on quantitative factors alone—a view supported by the results of neurophysiological experiment (Pribram, 1967).

Incompatible behavioural systems : results of simultaneous activation

In the previous section it was tacitly assumed that behavioural systems tend to be active only one at a time. It is, however, by no means uncommon for more than one system to be active at once. Here we consider some of the behaviour that results when two or more systems are active simultaneously.

The behaviour to which the activation of one behavioural system leads may be highly compatible with the behaviour to which activation of another system leads; or it may be highly incompatible with it; or some parts of one may be compatible with some parts of the other, whilst other parts of each are incompatible with each other. It is not surprising, therefore, that the kind of behaviour that results when two systems are active at once varies very greatly. Sometimes elements of both behavioural patterns are exhibited, sometimes elements of only one, and sometimes elements of neither. In some cases the resulting behaviour is excellently suited to the situation, in others it is the reverse. In some cases, indeed, the behaviour that results when two incompatible behavioural systems are active simultaneously is of a kind that suggests pathology.

To simplify presentation in this section a new terminology is used. Whenever there are grounds for believing that a certain behavioural system is active though the behaviour to which it gives rise is hardly apparent, it will be said that the animal has a 'tendency' of a certain sort, for example a tendency to flee.

Now to postulate a tendency to a certain sort of behaviour when such behaviour is hardly apparent raises methodological problems to which attention must be given. How do we know, it will be said, that any such tendency is present? What kind of evidence makes it legitimate to infer that a behavioural system is active even when the behaviour for which it is ordinarily responsible is absent? The methodological problem is, of course, familiar to psychoanalysts who often maintain that, even though a person's overt behaviour is of one sort, motivation of quite another sort is present as well.

It is not without interest that the two disciplines, ethology and psychoanalysis, when confronted with the same methodological challenge, give the same answer. Whether the behaviour occurs in animal or man, the main reason for inferring the presence of a hidden tendency is that that tendency reveals itself in occasional and incomplete sequences of behaviour. Sometimes such behaviour, or a fragment of such behaviour, occurs simultaneously with the dominant behaviour and results in slight oscillation. At other times the hidden tendency can be inferred because, after the dominant behaviour is completed, a short sequence of the other sort is seen; in other cases behaviour expressing a hidden tendency may appear briefly before the dominant behaviour takes command. For both the ethologist and the psychoanalyst it has been attention to such details of behaviour that has given insight and led to scientific advance.

Psychoanalysts, it is true, use an additional class of data in making inferences regarding hidden tendencies, a class of data not available to ethologists. This comprises reports made by a patient regarding his thoughts and feelings. Since the place that thoughts and feelings are assigned in the present theoretical schema is described in the next chapter, further discussion of them is postponed.

To return now to the behavioural data that psychoanalysts share with ethologists: a few of the many types of behaviour that can result when two tendencies are present simultaneously but are in some degree incompatible with one another are described below.

Behavioural Sequences deriving from Both Tendencies are Exhibited

Alternating behaviour. In some cases behaviour deriving from both tendencies is exhibited in such a way that behaviour of one sort alternates with that of the other sort. Although it sounds as though the result would be unfavourable, it is by no means necessarily so. There are, for example, many instances of this type in the courtship behaviour of fish and birds, since in very many species courtship is found to be a complex alternation of aggressive, sexual, and escape behaviour. A male chaffinch, for example, starts his courtship by being aggressive, then gradually becomes subordinate to the female and behaves as though afraid of her. Henceforward there is conflict between his tendency to flee from her and his tendency to make sexual advances, and his behaviour alternates between expressions of the one and of the other. Copulation, nonetheless, is commonly achieved.

Intention movements, combined behaviour, and compromise behaviour. Not infrequently when in a conflict situation an animal, unable to express fully one of its tendencies, nevertheless shows an incomplete movement belonging to that tendency; for example, when in a conflict between staying and flying, a bird may repeatedly exhibit most of the behaviour of take-off without actually doing so. This is termed an 'intention movement'.

Intention movements are common in mammals, including man. They afford important clues whereby we judge the motives and likely behaviour of other people.

On occasion, intention movements derived from two conflicting behavioural tendencies may be present together and result in behaviour that is a patchwork of both. On other occasions an intention movement or other behavioural element that is common to both tendencies is exhibited on its own.

Behavioural Sequences deriving from only One Tendency are Exhibited

Perhaps the commonest outcome of conflict is that the behaviour shown derives entirely from one tendency and not at all from the other; in other words, the expression of the second tendency is completely inhibited. A small bird quietly feeding may, for example, dash for cover when a hawk appears. Since we can presume that factors causing feeding are still present and that the small bird would have continued feeding had the hawk not appeared, it seems safe to conclude that, though feeding behaviour is inhibited, the tendency to feed persists. An outcome of this kind is in fact so frequent as to be commonplace; and there are probably a multitude of different ways by which inhibition of one of two such conflicting tendencies is effected—from automatic processes of which we are unaware to conscious deliberation and decision. Since very many behavioural systems are incompatible with each other, it seems probable that for most animals a state in which one or more systems are being inhibited is the usual one.

Although in such cases the behavioural outcome is commonly unequivocal and of obvious survival value, there are other cases where it is not. For example, inhibition of a competing tendency may be unstable or inefficient and the result be alternating behaviour of a non-functional kind. Another outcome may be the sort of behaviour that is known to psychoanalysts as 'displacement' and to ethologists as 'redirection'. Here the individual, seized by conflicting tendencies, exhibits a behavioural sequence that is a true expression of one of the two tendencies but directs it towards an object other than that which elicited it. A familiar example is when a dominant animal threatens a subordinate and so elicits in the latter both attack and escape behaviour; the subordinate animal may then express attack but do so not towards the dominant animal but towards an animal still more subordinate. Such redirection of aggression towards a subordinate animal has been observed frequently in primate groups in the wild and is, of course, extremely common in human groups.

A special sort of redirected behaviour to which humans are prone but which is not met with in lower animals occurs when the object towards which behaviour is redirected is a symbolic one. Examples are aggression directed towards an effigy of the original object and attachment behaviour directed towards a national symbol, e.g. flag or anthem.

The Behavioural Sequences Exhibited derive not from the Conflicting Tendencies but from Others

Sometimes when two tendencies are present, e.g. to turn to the left and also to the right, they cancel each other out and no behaviour of any sort results.

Not infrequently, however, although behaviour deriving from neither tendency is exhibited, the animal does something quite different. For example, during a battle between two gulls, each of which has tendencies both to attack the other and to fly away, one bird may suddenly start preening or nest-building. Such behaviour appears entirely irrelevant to the situation and is termed by ethologists a 'displacement activity'.

How this apparently irrelevant behaviour is caused has been and still is the subject of much debate. One idea was that a displacement activity is caused by factors different from those producing the same behaviour in a normal context; and the notion of a 'spark-over' of energy from one (or both) of the conflicting tendencies not expressed became current. Now that this type of explanation has been abandoned, together with the energy model from which it sprang, a number of alternatives are under consideration.

One explanation derives from the fact that most displacement activities are activities, such as grazing or preening, that the animal performs frequently and that are easily elicited. One of them occurs as a displacement activity, it is suggested, because causal factors which normally activate its behavioural system are present most of the time but, during quite long periods, the behaviour itself is inhibited because other activities are taking priority. Once two such priority activities cancel each other out, however, through being in conflict with each other, the previously inhibited behaviour has its chance: it becomes disinhibited.

Much experimental evidence supports the disinhibition hypothesis. A common displacement activity in birds is preening their feathers, and one of the conflict situations in which it occurs is when a gull has tendencies both to incubate eggs and to flee from something alarming. Experiments aimed to determine in exactly what conditions such displacement preening occurs suggest that it does so when the two tendencies are in balance, for example when both incubation and escape tendencies are strong or when both are weak, so that they exactly cancel each other out. Furthermore, the fact that displacement preening, like ordinary preening, occurs more frequently during and after rain shows that it is influenced by the same external factors as ordinary preening is.

Whilst many displacement activities seem to be due to disinhibition, others seem to be a by-product of autonomic activity that has been aroused in the conflict situation. For example, during a territorial tussle, in which a bird is torn between tendencies to attack and to flee, it may suddenly start drinking. This, it is suggested, may be a result of dryness of the throat, which is itself a consequence of the autonomic activity associated with fear responses.

Yet other explanations have been advanced to account for the occurrence of displacement activities. It may well be that different types of displacement activity are caused in different ways.

Activities which appear completely out of context and are therefore similar to the displacement activities of ethology are, of course, common in human neurosis. Recognition of their existence was, indeed, one of the principal reasons that led

Freud to advance a theory of instinct that pictured psychical energy as being conducted down pipes and as apt to be diverted from one pipe to another—on the analogy of water. The changing views of ethologists about displacement activities are of much interest as showing not only that in their theorising ethologists are struggling with problems very similar to those that confront psychoanalysts, but also that theories other than those based on psychical energy have been elaborated and are ready for consideration by clinicians.

The same may be said of regression, namely, the return to juvenile behaviour by an adult when adult behaviour is thwarted, either by conflict or in some other way. It is now well known that such behaviour occurs as readily in animals as it does in man. To explain it, ethologists have considered two sorts of theory. The first is that the animal, when faced with a problem, is returning to a way of solving it that had proved successful during its immaturity. The second is that regression is a special form of displacement activity: when adult patterns of behaviour cancel one another out a juvenile pattern, always latently active, gets an innings. It is not improbable that both these explanations, and perhaps others also, are required to account for all cases of regressive behaviour.

Sensory input and its transformation

Throughout the chapter so far the term 'environmental stimulus' has been employed to refer to environmental events that play a role in activating or terminating instinctive behaviour. The concept of stimulus, however, is not a simple one. Events that act as stimuli to behaviour in one animal are perhaps not noticed by another. Events that are seen as alarming by one individual are treated as of no account by another. What then is a stimulus and how is it related to happenings in the environment?

Research by neurophysiologists during the past two decades has drawn attention to the way in which sensory input is regulated and transformed by the activity of the CNS. When first received sensory input, derived from an environmental event, is assessed. If judged of no importance, it is blanked off. If judged otherwise, it is amplified and, if then judged relevant (and not too overwhelming in its implications), its import for action is determined; appropriate messages are then forwarded to motor areas.

Such assessing and regulating of sensory input are major and skilled activities of the sensory areas of the brain. Once decided upon, a reduction or an amplification of sensory input is effected by means of efferent messages, carried by special efferent nerves that travel from the sensory areas of the brain either to the sense organs themselves or to ganglia situated on the efferent tracts; the moment-to-moment responsiveness of sense organ or ganglion is thereby controlled (Livingston, 1959).[1]

Experimental evidence suggests that the regulation of receptor events can be carried out at one or at several of many levels in the nervous system. For example, a blinding flash leads to constriction of pupil and closing of lids. It may lead also to averting of face and flight. Conversely, sight of an attractive girl may lead to an opposite series of responses. In each case, some responses are organised as reflexes, others as fixed actions, and others again perhaps as plans, and control of the response is exercised either peripherally or more centrally.

Assessing of input, whether it be initial unregulated input or subsequent regulated input, is a skilled task. It necessitates interpreting the input in terms either of standards established by previous experience or of such other previously stored information that appears relevant, itself a skilled job of information retrieval, and then judging the resulting interpretation in terms of action to be taken. Such assessing and judging, it seems likely, are also carried on at many levels of the cns, in some instances at one level only, in others at several successively. The higher the level at which processes are dealt with the more discriminated the behaviour that can be selected, including behaviour organised as plans with set-goals. To make such plans requires, of course, reference to models of environment and organism (see Chapter 5).

Not infrequently in man the processes of assessing and judging are conscious and the interpreted input is experienced in terms of value, such as 'interesting' or 'uninteresting', 'pleasant' or 'disagreeable', 'satisfying' or 'frustrating'. This leads to a consideration of feeling and emotion.

[1] The significance for the theory of defence of central control of sensory input and processing is discussed in Volume III.

Chapter 7

Appraising and Selecting:
Feeling and Emotion

The movements of expression in the face and body, whatever their origin may have been, are in themselves of much importance for our welfare. They serve as the first means of communication between the mother and her infant; she smiles approval, and this encourages her child on the right path, or frowns disapproval. The movements of expression give vividness and energy to our spoken words. They reveal the thoughts and intentions of others more truly than do words, which may be falsified. . . . These results follow partly from the intimate relation which exists between almost all the emotions and their outward manifestation. . . .

CHARLES DARWIN (1872)

Introduction

In clinical circles it is usual for affects, feelings, and emotions to be referred to as though they were causative of behaviour. That is one reason for discussing them at this point. Another is that every good clinician uses the language of feeling and emotion to communicate with his patients—as everyone does in his communication with others in everyday life. Both the clinician and other readers may therefore already be impatient to know the place that feeling and emotion are assigned in the theory of instinctive behaviour advanced.

Briefly, the view taken is that all, or at least most, of what are termed (rather indiscriminately) affects, feelings, and emotions are phases of an individual's intuitive appraisals either of his own organismic states and urges to act or of the succession of environmental situations in which he finds himself. These appraising processes have often, but not always, the very special property of being experienced as feelings, or, to use better terminology, as felt. Because an individual is often aware of these processes, they commonly provide him with a monitoring service regarding his own states, urges, and situations. At the same time, because they are usually ac-companied by distinctive facial expressions, bodily postures, and incipient movements, they usually provide valuable information to his companions.

A central part of this thesis is that, since these appraising processes may or may not be felt, it is the appraising pro-cesses rather than the feeling and emotion that require first attention. The fact that appraising processes are not always felt provides a clue to understanding the ambiguous but clinically useful concept of 'unconscious feeling'.

Appraising processes, then, are conceived as having three roles. The first is that of appraising changing environments and organismic states, including tendencies to act; as such, whether felt or unfelt (conscious or unconscious), the processes are play-ing a vital role in the control of behaviour. The second is that of providing a monitoring service to the individual as a sentient being. The third is that of providing a communicative service to others.

The first and third roles do not require the processes to be conscious. The second, of course, does.

Amongst features of the view advocated is that, although affects, feelings, and emotions are commonly treated as though they were discrete entities, it is quite inappropriate so to treat them. To speak of 'an affect', 'a feeling', or 'an emotion', as though it were an atom or an orange, is as inadmissible as it would be to speak of 'a redness' or 'a squareness'. Instead, feeling is regarded as a property that certain processes con-nected with behaviour from time to time come to possess. Any phrase that reifies feelings or emotions is, therefore, held inadmissible.

Before our thesis is developed further, it is well to clarify terminology. Traditionally, 'affect' has been used to denote a wide range of feeling experience—feelings pleasurable, dis-tressed, and sad as well as loving, fearful, and angry. In addition, the word 'feeling' itself is often used in this broad way. 'Emotion', on the other hand, is always used more restrict-ively: as a rule it is confined to feelings or affects such as loving, hating, being frightened or hungry, that are inherently connected with one or another form of action.

In what follows the word 'feeling' is used always as a general purpose term. It is preferred to both 'affect' and 'emotion' because it is the only one of the three words to derive from a verb (to feel) having exactly the same meaning as itself. The word 'affect' is used only in the discussion of traditional theories; the word 'emotion' is used in the restricted sense referred to above.

Let us start by considering briefly some of the philosophical problems that beset us when we move from the purely behavioural account of instinctive behaviour so far adopted to an account that attempts to include also awareness of feeling.

Philosophical problems

Langer (1967) writes:

> The vexing question in the philosophy of the biological sciences is how something called 'feelings' enters into the physical (essentially electro-chemical) events that compose an animal organism. . . . The fact that we feel the effects of changes in the world about us, and apparently in ourselves, too, and that all such changes are physically describable, but our feeling them is not, presents a genuine philosophical challenge.

To this challenge there have been many answers. Most can be classified as variants of two main schools of thought: the mentalist and the epiphenomenalist.

The mentalist school, stemming from Descartes and appealing not only to humanists but also to neurophysiologists, including both Hughlings Jackson and Freud (Jones, 1955), postulates two distinct entities, a body and a mind, each of equivalent status, which are harnessed together in ways still unfathomable. By contrast, the epiphenomenalist, appealing to scientists and acclaimed as hard-headed, treats only the physical world as real. To an epiphenomenalist thoughts and feelings are no more than shadows playing no real part in life's drama; of aesthetic interest perhaps, of scientific relevance none.

Few today are satisfied with either of these answers. Lampooning the mentalist philosophy as 'the dogma of the Ghost in the Machine', Ryle (1949) argues that it derives from a category mistake based on the assumption that human body and human mind belong to the same logical category: both are things though each a different sort of thing. 'The logical mould into which Descartes pressed his theory of the mind . . . was the self-same mould into which he and Galileo set their mechanics.' As a result Descartes tended to describe minds in terms and idioms that are the counterpart of those used in mechanics but that are usually their mere negatives. Thus minds 'are not in space, they are not motions, they are not modifications of matter, they are not accessible to public observation. Minds are not bits of clockwork, they are just bits of non-clockwork' (Ryle, *ibid.*).

Based on a logical fallacy, the mentalist outlook, when applied to empirical problems by, amongst others, Freud, has led to checkered results: thus justice has been done to the place of feeling and emotion in human life, but the methodological problem of formulating hypotheses in a testable form has not been solved. Consequently no science of the mind comparable to physical science has been built. Equally checkered, though in a different way, have been the results of epiphenomenalists, who usually sail under the flag of extreme behaviourism. Testable hypotheses have been framed, it is true, yet the price paid has been high. All the more exciting reaches of human experience are ruled out of bounds; moreover, the theoretical schema presented is found to be of little use to those, clinicians and others, who deal with ordinary people living everyday lives.

It must of course be recognised that by no means all those who in their research adopt a behaviourist strategy are epiphenomenalists. On the contrary, many take a position similar to that taken many years ago by J. S. Haldane (1936). For the present, they would explain, we do not deal with feelings, meaning, conscious control, and suchlike, important though they plainly are, for the very good reason that so far we do not see how the facts relating to them can be combined with the other material of biological and behavioural study to make a coherent system of scientific thought. One of these days, they would continue, the time to tackle these problems will be ripe; meanwhile the field appears to lie beyond the reaches of the 'art of the soluble'.

Prudent though that position undoubtedly is, clinicians, whether psychiatrists or neurologists, find it impractical. Day in day out a clinician must deal with what each patient tells of his private experience—whether he has a pain in his stomach, whether a limb feels numb, what thoughts and feelings he has about his parents, his employer, his girl-friend. Such accounts from the private eye of personal experience are part and parcel of the practice of medicine.

Since, then, a clinician must perforce adopt some viewpoint, what is it to be? How is he to picture the relation of private to public, of subjective to objective, of feeling to physics, of body to mind?

The viewpoint adopted here, with the diffidence necessary in a field so strewn with boulders, is well expressed in Langer's recent book on the subject (1967). Langer takes her cue from some reflections of a neurologist concerned to understand voluntary control of muscle. 'It will be with feeling that we shall be largely concerned,' writes Gooddy (1949), 'for sensory symptoms so commonly are a complaint of patients with dysfunction of voluntary movement. "My hand feels funny when I try and move it."' Pondering on this, Gooddy notes that 'the natural use of the words "feel", "seems", "numb", "clumsy", "heavy", "helpless", "stiff", [is] to describe what turns out to be motor dysfunction'. Gooddy then asks the troublesome question of how it is that events neurophysiological can 'break through to feeling'.

At this point Langer notes that 'feel' is a verb, and to say that what is felt is 'a feeling' may well be deceptive: 'the phenomenon usually described as "a feeling" is really that an organism feels something, i.e. something is felt. What is felt is a process . . . within the organism.' This leads on to Langer's main proposition: '*Being felt*', she concludes, '*is a phase of the process itself*' (my italics).

By 'phase' Langer means one of the many modes in which something may appear without anything having meanwhile been added to or substracted from it. As an illustration she considers the heating and cooling of iron:

> When iron is heated to a critical degree it becomes red; yet its redness is not a new entity which must have gone somewhere else when it is no longer in the iron. It was a phase of the iron itself, at high temperature.
>
> As soon as feeling is regarded as a phase of a physiological process instead of a product of it—namely a new entity metaphysically different from it—the paradox of the physical and the psychical disappears.

Thus, continues Langer, the question is no longer one of 'how a physical process can be transformed into something nonphysical in a physical system, but how the phase of being felt is attained, and how the process may pass into unfelt phases again'.

If Langer's seems a good viewpoint from which to approach the problem, it leaves us still far from being able to answer the question posed. How, indeed, does the phase of being felt occur? Yet, unanswerable though that question remains,[1] there is another question related to it that is both more answerable and of more immediate relevance to our thesis. Of what sort are the processes that commonly attain the phase of being felt?

Processes that are felt

At the end of the previous chapter it was pointed out that sensory data regarding environmental events reaching an organism via its sense organs are immediately assessed, regulated, and interpreted. Only after that can their relevance for action be determined. The same is true of sensory data derived from the internal state of the organism. Once their general relevance for action is determined, moreover, much else may be subjected to appraisal before co-ordinated action occurs; that includes, especially, the probable effects on environmental situation and on organism of actions of different kinds. Furthermore, even after co-ordinated action is begun, the processes of appraisal do not cease. First, the progress of action is itself monitored and, finally, the consequences of action are judged and noted for further reference.

[1] Though insoluble at present, the problem may one day yield to study. Tustin, an electrical engineer, points to a historical parallel:

> Not many decades ago a man put together for the first time that particular pattern of pieces of iron, copper and cotton-rag that constituted a dynamo, and when this special mechanical object was rotated a new field of phenomena became apparent. The dynamo became, as we say, electrically alive. It revealed electrical phenomena, rarely exhibited, and never previously recognised anywhere else. We now know that a variety of inter-relations exist between particular structures of 'mechnical' parts and the field of electrical phenomena, and these mechanical parts themselves must now be understood as in some sense more primarily electrical than mechanical, so that ultimately the two fields are one.
>
> Is it conceivable that just as electrical phenomena were unrecognised until a particular structure of mechanical parts showed interaction with them as something that could no longer be neglected in our account of reality, so evolution, in the elaboration of the kind of brain that corresponds with the mechanist conception, chanced upon a rare linkage with phenomena of a different kind, and turned this to biological account? If this speculation should happen to have resemblance to the truth it would give grounds to hope that patient investigation may ultimately give us some understanding of these phenomena, although such an account would not be wholly in terms of the concepts of present-day physics (Tustin, 1953).

Each of these processes of appraisal, it seems, may reach a phase of being felt; and we shall consider them one by one. At the same time it must be emphasised that not all appraisal processes are, in fact, felt. In all that follows, therefore, it is necessary to keep constantly in mind that, whilst appraisal is an integral part of the operation of any control system, and the more sophisticated the system the more appraisal enters in, whether or not any particular appraisal process is felt is a distinct question. Like a school of dolphins that is at one moment visible and at another not, some appraisal processes may change phase, being active at times above our threshold of awareness and at times below. Others, like cod, may remain permanently below until unusual conditions draw attention to them.

One difficulty of exposition is that each sort of appraisal process can be conducted at any one of several levels. Thus, sensory input may be only crudely discriminated and interpreted, and what is felt only crudely differentiated; by contrast, input may be finely discriminated and interpreted and what is felt differentiated in high degree. Furthermore, some sequences of behaviour, especially those organised as reflexes or fixed action patterns, may proceed, once begun, without much further appraisal. In what follows attention is given principally to behaviour organised in a more discriminating and differentiated way.

A great deal of evidence relevant to these problems has been collected during the last two decades by neurophysiologists, using techniques of ablation and of recording from microelectrodes placed with exactitude in particular loci of the brain, and also techniques of direct stimulation of parts of the brain, including parts of the human brain during the course of surgical operations. In these and other ways a much more adequate picture of cerebral organisation and activity has been obtained; and in particular the role in the organisation of behaviour and in the appraisal of organismic states and situations of the midbrain nuclei and limbic system has been clarified (MacLean, 1960). The significance of this work for a theory of feeling and emotion has been reviewed in much detail by Arnold (1960). Her two volumes, *Emotion and Personality*, contain also a comprehensive review of the psychological literature. Throughout this chapter I am much indebted to Arnold's work and to her introduction of the term 'appraisal'.[1]

[1] Although Arnold does not present her ideas in terms of control theory, most of them can be translated fairly readily into those terms. A

Interpretation and Appraisal of Sensory Input

Sensory input is of two main classes: that which relates to the state of the organism and that which relates to the state of the environment. Input of both classes, to be useful, must be interpreted and appraised. We start with input deriving from change in the environment.

As soon as sensory messages begin to be received they are assessed and regulated (see previous chapter). Assuming they are not blanked off they are next interpreted. Taken alone sensory input is inadequate: on the one hand, it is over-abundant and must be scanned for parts that are relevant; on the other, it is insufficient and must be supplemented with matching information from the organism's memory store. Only by these means is raw sensory input deriving from the environment transformed into perception of objects interacting with each other in a space-time continuum. Because of his large store of relevant information about the appearance and habitats of birds and plants, the experienced naturalist sees far more than does a tyro. In perception as elsewhere 'To him that hath shall be given'.

Sensory input deriving from the organism itself goes through comparable processes of selection and supplementation. Feeling hot, feeling cold, feeling hungry are not raw sensations but phases of certain sensory inputs in the course of being appraised. Occasionally such appraisals are mistaken: what is first appraised as very hot may later and rightly be appraised as very cold.

Arnold points out that very frequently the interpreted and appraised input, whether from environment or from organism, is experienced inherently in terms of value, as pleasant or unpleasant, nice or nasty, likeable or unlikeable. Interpreted input of organismic origin when very unpleasant is experienced

---

serious shortcoming of her position is a failure to distinguish between function and set-goal (see next chapter). As a result some of her formulations are flawed by teleology. In addition, I do not find useful the distinction she draws between 'instincts', e.g. feeding and mating, which 'are aroused even without a suitable object', and 'emotions', e.g. anger and flight, which are aroused only 'after an object has been appraised'. Activation of all these behaviours, it is held, is produced by varying combinations of all five causative factors discussed in the previous chapter, and the classification proposed by Arnold seems rather arbitrary.

as pain; and the same is sometimes true of input of exteroceptive origin, e.g. a painfully loud noise.

Not infrequently a felt appraisal attributes some quality to person or object in the environment—'a nice man', 'a nasty smell'. At other times no external attribution is made, but reference is to a state of the organism itself—'it makes me feel funny all over'.

The rough and ready sorting of input into pleasurable and painful, nice and nasty, is a result of comparing input with internal set-points or standards. Some of these standards may remain unchanged through life; more often they vary in a regular way to reflect the current state of the organism. Thus olfactory input sorted as nice when we are hungry may be sorted as unpleasant when we are replete. Similar shifts of standard occur in the judging of input that relates to temperature, according to whether we are at the time warm or cold.

When these temporary and regular shifts are taken into account, many of the set-points applied to sensory inputs are probably environmentally stable during development and reasonably similar from one individual to another. Others are clearly environmentally labile, the setting being determined in part by experience. They are then termed acquired tastes.

Once interpreted input has been appraised as nice or nasty, certain sorts of behaviour usually follow. Whatever is appraised as nice is likely to be maintained or sought after; whatever is appraised as nasty is likely to be reduced or avoided.

Thus, appraisal is a complex process in which two main steps can be distinguished: (a) *comparing* input with standards that have developed within the organism during its lifetime; (b) *selecting* certain general forms of behaviour in preference to other forms in accordance with the results of comparisons previously made.

Since many of the basic standards used for comparisons and many of the simpler behaviours of approach and withdrawal that follow comparison are environmentally stable, much of this behaviour can be classified as instinctive. A very great deal of it, of course, is of a kind likely to promote species survival because what is classified as 'nice' tends to correspond with what is advantageous to an animal and vice versa. Nevertheless these are only statistical probabilities, and the question of the survival value of any particular sort of behaviour is a distinct and important issue of its own, to a discussion of which the next chapter is given.

Sensory input of organismic origin is of many kinds. Some, when interpreted and appraised, arouse desire—for example desire for warm clothes, desire for fresh air, desire for food, desire for a member of the opposite sex. How this is best conceptualised is discussed below.

More Refined Appraisals of Persons and Objects: Emotion

Not only is interpreted sensory input of environmental origin sorted into the crude categories of pleasant–unpleasant, nice–nasty, but parts of it are sorted also in much more refined ways. Of special relevance to our discussion is the sorting of interpreted input into categories that potentially signal activation of one or another of the behavioural systems that mediate instinctive behaviour. (Whether a system is in fact activated turns, of course, on other factors, e.g. hormone levels and signals of organismic origin.) When such categorisation occurs the subject is likely to experience emotion—alarm, anxiety, anger, hunger, lust, distress, guilt, or some other comparable feeling depending on which behavioural system is being activated.

It is not very easy to be sure at what exact point in the sequence of processes of input appraisal and behaviour activation, emotional feeling begins to be experienced. That, indeed, has been a major source of controversy since James and Lange advanced the view that emotion is experienced only *after* behaviour has begun and that it is simply a result of feedback from voluntary muscles and viscera.

There can, of course, be no doubt that once behaviour has begun emotion is very often experienced: when running away we may feel very frightened; when turning on an adversary we may feel very angry; whilst preparing an overdue meal we may feel very hungry. Nor can there be much doubt that feedback from voluntary muscles (though probably not from viscera) augments whatever emotion is felt: an aggressive stance seems to increase courage. Yet such evidence is hardly relevant to the issue. For it may still be that emotional feeling is experienced also at the very start of behavioural activation, or, indeed, as an alternative to behavioural activation (Pribram, 1967).[1] It is likely, for example, that the very process of categorising a person or object or situation as one fit to elicit one or another class of behaviour is itself experienced emotionally; in which case, perhaps, the processes of centrally regulating sensory input

[1] Pribram points out that the word emotion comes from the Latin *emovere*, which means to be 'out of' or 'away from' motion.

according to the results of initial appraisal would be so experienced.

This view is in keeping with an impression that, even before action is elicited, we tend to categorise our environment in terms of our potential behaviour, e.g. into 'that attractive woman', 'that frightening dog', 'that appetising meal', 'that hateful man', 'that cuddly baby'. Furthermore, the class of behaviour selected is usually specified initially only in broad terms. Thus it may well be that after someone has made us angry we deliberate for long on what actually to do about it. Not infrequently, many alternative plans are concocted, their potential consequences imagined (on the basis of models of environment and organism) and the consequences of each plan appraised. Only after that is any particular plan put into operation. Nevertheless, angry feelings are experienced from the very start.

The hypothesis that the process of categorising parts of the environment in terms of fitness to elicit a particular class of behaviour is itself experienced as coloured by the appropriate emotion finds support also from dreams. Emotionally coloured dreams are always concerned with action, but the dreamer is usually in fact inactive. Only when emotional feeling becomes very strong is the dreamer liable to shout out or start whatever action would be appropriate were the dream to represent reality.

The fact that emotional feeling can be experienced during sleep is a reminder that not all processes having an emotional feeling phase originate in the environment. As remarked above, sensory input of organismic origin may, when interpreted, give rise to desire. Put another way this means that sensory input of organismic origin may be categorised as fit to activate a behavioural system mediating instinctive behaviour in much the same way as sensory input of environmental origin may be so categorised. And, also in the same way, such processes of categorisation and activation are commonly experienced in terms of one or another emotion, depending on the category into which interpreted input has been sorted.

Appraisal of Progress of Current Behaviour

Once a behavioural system is activated the progress of the behavioural sequence elicited is usually monitored and this is always so when the behaviour is organised as a plan. Feeling varies according to whether progress is appraised as smooth, halting, or stopped. Qualities of feeling vary over a range from pleasurable exhilaration when things are going well, through displeasure when they are going badly, to utter frustration when they are brought to a standstill.

Not only is progress of the overall activity monitored but progress of each bit of it is monitored as well. This is illustrated by Gooddy's findings already referred to. The sensory symptoms of which his patients complained—feeling 'numb', 'clumsy', 'stiff', etc.—are reports that sensory feedback from voluntary muscles in action is abnormal in one or more of various ways. By contrast, when our voluntary musculature is performing well we usually have a sense of physical wellbeing.

Appraisal of Consequences of Behaviour

Finally, certain of the consequences of behaviour are monitored and appraised.

The consequences of any one bit of behaviour are of many kinds (see the next chapter), and not all are likely to be monitored. In particular, long-term effects may go unnoticed. Of those that are monitored, it is possible to discern at least two kinds, both short-term, each of which often has a feeling phase.

One kind refers to some of the immediate changes in the environment and/or in the organism's own state that the behaviour has brought about. Such changes are determined by sensory input that, as usual, must undergo interpretation before it can be appraised. When applied to consequences, appraisal processes are often experienced in terms of pleasurable–painful, liked–disliked, good–bad.

A second kind of short-term consequence refers to whether or not a set-goal has been achieved. Appraisal of those consequences is often experienced in terms of satisfying–frustrating.

The distinction between these two kinds of short-term consequence is illustrated by someone saying 'I'm glad I got to the top, but the view was disappointing'.

Regular monitoring both of behavioural progress and of consequences is of course necessary if the organism is to learn. That is a large and controversial field and one not for discussion here. It may, however, be noted that the more strongly an appraised process is felt, and the more keenly, therefore, the consequences of some behaviour are experienced as pleasurable or painful, the quicker and more persistent is the ensuing learning likely to be. Since the formation of affectional bonds is commonly experienced as intensely pleasurable, it comes as no surprise that bonds often develop rapidly and, once made, are apt to be long-lasting. As Hamburg (1963) puts it, 'they are easy to learn and hard to forget'.

Is feeling or emotion causative of behaviour?

The notion that affect, feeling, emotion is in some way causative of behaviour, namely, causes us to act, is widespread. It is enshrined in many colloquial phrases—'patriotism led him to do so and so', 'she did that out of jealousy'—and is deep in much psychoanalytic thinking (despite Freud's having abandoned the idea in his later work).[1] Is it a valid notion? And, if so, in what sense?

If the view taken here is on the right lines, feeling is a phase of an appraisal process, in a way analogous to that in which redness is a phase of iron when heated. In considering our problem, therefore, we must first distinguish between feeling and the processes of which it is a phase. It is easier to start with processes.

Plainly, in the causation of any particular class of behaviour, the processes of appraising sensory input (whether of environmental or organismic origin or, and most frequently, of both combined), and of selecting a class of behaviour appropriate to it, are vital links. Thus, in the causation of a behavioural sequence such as comforting a crying baby, appraising the baby as something to be comforted is a necessary step. For there are various alternatives to that appraisal: for example, the crying

[1] In a valuable review Rapaport (1953) describes three phases in the development of Freud's theory of affects. During a first phase, when the concept of catharsis was central, affect is equated with a quantity of psychical energy (later conceptualized as 'drive-cathexis'): here affect is plainly given a causal role in promoting behaviour. During a second phase, affects are conceived as alternatives to behaviour through serving 'a safety-valve function when discharge of drive-cathexes by drive-action meets opposition' (Rapaport). During a third phase, developed in *Inhibitions, Symptoms and Anxiety* (1926), affects are conceived 'as ego-functions, and as such are no longer safety-valves but are used as signals by the ego' (Rapaport). The conception is akin to the one developed in this chapter.

Psychoanalytic theory has, of course, continued to be formulated in terms of drives and energy levels; and, notwithstanding Freud's changed views on affects, theory still sometimes treats affect as something that can be dammed up, drained away, or discharged. As a result it is perhaps small wonder that in clinical circles affect continues sometimes to be regarded as constituting in some way a driving force.

baby might be appraised as something to be ignored or even as something to be shouted at. Appraising sensory input plays a similar role in the causation, for example, of so simple a response as sharp withdrawal of hand from a hot surface.

We must conclude therefore that the processes of interpreting and appraising sensory input must unquestionably be assigned a causal role in producing whatever behaviour emerges. Like the other causal factors already discussed they are necessary but not often sufficient.[1]

Whether the feelings experienced as a phase of such appraising should also be assigned a causal role is a much more difficult question. In the example given, sympathy for the baby may well be experienced (in contrast, say, to irritation or anger) at the moment the baby is appraised as 'fit to be comforted'. Yet it is not clear that sympathy is necessary for the behaviour to be elicited. With some mothers, for example, comforting a crying baby might be so much a matter of course that the behaviour is engaged in without any particular feeling. If the matter were left there, feeling and emotion, as such, would be assigned little or no causal role.

Yet on other occasions a mother might feel keen sympathy for her crying baby and, to an outside observer, the way she comforted him might seem to reflect it. For example, the mother might seem to go to special trouble on the baby's behalf. If that is a true estimate, how should that effect be assessed?

Feeling, attention, and consciousness go together. The question that confronts us therefore is an aspect of a much larger one: namely, whether a person being feelingly aware of what he is doing adds anything to the process itself, and, if so, what. To discuss that would take us beyond the bounds of this volume. It seems fairly certain, however, that, provided feeling is not too intense, keen feeling goes with alert attention, with refined perceptual discrimination, with considered (though not necessarily well-judged) planning of behaviour, and with the well-registered learning of results. Thus, whether or not appraisal processes are felt is probably of considerable consequence for the behaviour that emerges. In particular, that they be felt seems to be of special importance if there is to be any reassessment and

[1] The causal role of appraisal processes has led Tomkins in his two-volume work on *Affect, Imagery, Consciousness* (1962–63) to postulate that 'affects constitute the primary motivational system', defining a motive as 'the feedback report of a response'.

modification of standards of appraisal and of models of environment and organism, and if there are to be changes in future behaviour; for it is a clinical commonplace that only after a patient has become emotionally aware of how and what he is feeling can therapeutic change be expected.

That, however, would still not be to say that feeling itself plays a causal role in *present* behaviour. For, if the view adopted is correct, the conclusion to be drawn might be that all the more discriminating appraisal and reappraisal processes can occur only in conditions that give rise to conscious feeling, a conclusion that might be analogous to the fact that certain manipulations of iron are possible only in conditions that give rise to redness. If that were so, feeling would play no more of a causal role than does the redness.

There the matter must be left. The appraising processes of which feeling may be a phase undoubtedly play a causal role. To what extent and in what way feeling itself plays such a role remains undemonstrated.

Nevertheless we are still left with such statements as 'patriotism led him to do so and so' and 'she did that out of jealousy'. How then are they to be understood?

That question is examined by Ryle (1949). His conclusion is that a statement such as 'jealousy led Tom to do so and so' describes not the cause of Tom's having done so and so but only what in common parlance might be called a 'reason' for his having done it.

In drawing the distinction between a cause and a reason Ryle uses as an illustration a stone breaking a sheet of glass. 'There are at best two quite different senses in which [such] an occurrence is said to be "explained",' notes Ryle. In answer to the question, 'Why did the glass break?', one can reply either 'because the stone hit it' or 'because the glass was brittle.' Only the first of these answers refers to a cause, however: in that case the explanation given is in terms of an event, namely stone hitting glass, which stands to fracture of glass as cause to effect. In the case of the second answer, by contrast, no event is referred to and no cause, therefore, is given. Instead, the second answer asserts only 'a general hypothetical proposition about the glass', namely that *if* sharply struck the glass *would* fly into fragments and *would not* do such things as stretch or evaporate or remain intact. As a conditional statement it tells us, of course, nothing whatever about why the glass happens to have flown into fragments at one particular moment; instead it tells us that in certain specified conditions it would be likely to do so. Thus it gives no cause, though it does give some sort of reason.

The statement 'Tom bit his little sister because he was jealous' is logically equivalent to the statement 'the glass broke because it was brittle'; and, as such, it also gives no cause. 'Jealous', Ryle points out, is a dispositional adjective: it carries the meaning that if certain circumstances obtain, for example if mother attends to little sister and not to Tom, Tom *would* be likely to attack his little sister in some way or other and *would* probably *not* play contentedly or caress her. The statement tells us, in fact, nothing whatever about the particular events that led up to this particular bite: what it says is that in certain conditions such an action is likely.

Since misunderstanding of this sort is of importance for clinical theory it may be useful to put the statement about Tom and his little sister into the structure of theory advocated in this book. In Tom, it can be said, there is a tendency to appraise certain situations in such a way that a behavioural system is activated that results in his attacking his little sister and biting her. Further, the conditions that lead to this appraisal and so activate the system are specifiable, at least roughly. They comprise, perhaps, a combination on the one hand of a situation of mother attending to little sister and not to Tom and, on the other, of certain organismic states of Tom, themselves brought about by specifiable conditions, such, for example, as a rebuff from father, or fatigue, or hunger. Whenever certain combinations of these conditions obtain, it is predicted, a certain appraisal will be made, a certain behavioural system will be activated, and Tom will bite.

To what then, within this framework of theory, does the word 'jealous' in the original statement refer? As a dispositional adjective, 'jealous' in the context refers, not to Tom's behaviour, but to the postulated presence in Tom of structures that lead Tom to appraise situations in certain ways and thence to act in roughly the way described. To say that 'Tom bit his little sister because he was jealous', is simply, therefore, an inexact conversational shorthand.

But, inexact though it is, it is very convenient; since it enables a witness of the scene to communicate a good deal about Tom and his behaviour without having to spell out laboriously the technical rigmarole of the preceding paragraph. We shall return at the end of the chapter to the tremendous convenience of the vernacular language of feeling. Before doing so, let us consider the expressive role of feeling—that is a role of the greatest importance and one that, in comparison with the issues considered in this section, is less difficult and less controversial.

The communicative role of feeling and emotion

In everyday living we take for granted that to some extent we can tell how our friends are feeling, and also, though with decreasing confidence, how acquaintances and strangers are feeling. In doing so we note facial expression, posture, tone of voice, physiological changes, tempo of movement, and incipient action, all with reference to the situations in which they occur. The stronger the feeling being experienced by our companion and the clearer the situation, the more confident are we that we can identify what is going on.

No doubt some observers are much more accurate than others, and some subjects much easier to judge than others. No doubt also every observer is often mistaken, either because expression is ambiguous or the situation is misunderstood, or because of deliberate deception. Yet for most observers most of the time the mistakes are probably few compared with the successes.[1]

What, then, is our criterion of success? There is a difficulty here because, in attributing feeling to someone, we are making one or both of two distinct statements. On the one hand, we may be making a prediction about his behaviour; on the other, we may be describing how and what we suppose him to be aware of feeling. For some purposes the prediction of behaviour is all that matters; for others, the question of whether a person is aware of how he is feeling and of how he is likely to behave is also of importance.

[1] The patent shortcomings of experiments that purport to show that observers of emotional expression fail to agree and are hopelessly inaccurate have been discussed by Hebb (1946a) and Arnold (1960). Shortcomings include restricting observers to still photographs or to short movies of unfamiliar subjects seen without social context. Hebb points out that, because emotional expression reflects changes in responsiveness, diagnosis requires opportunity to observe how someone's behaviour changes over time. Taking these considerations into account, Hamburg and his colleagues (1958) have demonstrated that, when independent observers are asked to rate the affect shown by patients during sessions each lasting three hours held on four successive days, a high level of agreement is attained. Trained observers agree on which affect is predominant at any occasion and on level of affect. Their agreement is especially high on change in direction of affect.

Let us start with feeling as a prediction of behaviour, partly because it is squarely within the realm of the testable and partly because it has tended to be neglected (except by ethologists).

To ascribe feeling is usually to make a prediction about subsequent behaviour. Thus to describe a person (or an animal) as amorous, angry, or afraid is to predict that during the coming minutes certain behaviour is much more likely than any other sort—provided always the situation does not change.

Words descriptive of feeling are readily grouped according to the types of prediction that they imply. 'Amorous', 'angry', and 'afraid' belong together because in each case the prediction is short-term, is fairly precise, and is limited to the situation obtaining. Such words are usually classed as denoting emotions. In contrast are words classed as denoting moods—for example, 'elated', 'depressed' or 'hopeless', 'cheerful', 'confident' or 'calm'. When a mood is attributed to a person (or an animal) the prediction is more general than in the case of an emotion: it refers to the types of response likely to be shown in any of a variety of situations that may be met with over a longer period of time—perhaps only a day, but possibly a week or longer. In some cases mood words are used to refer to the style of behaviour predicted of a person over even longer periods of time; they are then regarded as referring to his temperament.

The fact that words denoting feeling are predictive of behaviour means that they can be used in a rigorously scientific way not only of humans but also of animals. They provide in fact an indispensable shorthand for what would otherwise be long-winded, clumsy, and inadequate descriptions. Hebb (1946a) was amongst the first to make this point explicit. In studies of chimpanzees in which different ways of describing an animal's state were compared, it was found that good predictions of behaviour were obtained when an observer used 'frankly anthropomorphic concepts of emotion'; whereas attempts at more detailed 'objective' description yielded only a series of specific acts that were useless for prediction.

The clues used in judging emotion and making predictions arise from several classes of behaviour. Some are specific social signals such as a smile or a cry. Others are intention movements or physiological changes of an analogous sort. Others again are displacement activities (see Chapter 6). Hebb argues convincingly that our knowledge of how one emotion differs from another is derived, not from any intuitive awareness of our own feelings, but from observations of other people behaving emotionally; only later do we come to apply the learned categories to ourselves.

That the feeling states an individual perceives in his companions are predictive of their behaviour is, of course, made use of when he decides how to behave towards them. The same is true for members of other species, especially primates. Only if an animal, human or sub-human, is reasonably accurate at assessing the mood of another is he able to participate in social life: otherwise he might treat a friendly animal as likely to attack or an angry animal as unlikely to. The fact is that most individuals grow up to be reasonably competent in making the right predictions, partly probably because of innate bias to develop so and partly because mistakes are soon revealed and there is plenty of opportunity to learn from them. In clinical work the predictive value of overtly expressed feeling and emotion is obvious. So, too, is the value of a patient's reports of how he feels, especially when they are in terms of how he appraises situations and what he then feels like doing.

To the individual who feels, what is felt is a reflection of how he is appraising the world and himself, how he is appraising particular situations, and what kinds of behaviour are from time to time being activated within him. Thus, to the subject, feeling provides a monitoring service of his behavioural state (as it does also of his physiological state). All this he may be able to note and report; and in so far as he can he will naturally adopt the language of feeling. This gives a clue to why the language of feeling is so valuable in clinical work.

When a patient is with us he is unlikely to be actually doing the things that he is motivated to do. He may be angry with his wife but we are unlikely to see him attack her. He may be reliving a time when he yearned for his mother, but we do not see him seeking her. He may be jealous of another patient but we do not witness him trying to eject the other patient from our room. In other words the behavioural systems mediating such sequences of behaviour are not being given their head. Nevertheless they are in a state of activation and, because of that, can be monitored. A patient who has insight into his feelings can therefore report that he feels angry with his wife, is still grieving for his mother, or is jealous of the other patient. And if he has no insight we may be able, by taking note of how he behaves and of what he says, to infer what behavioural systems are currently activated within him and to communicate to him our inferences—in terms again of how we suspect he may be feeling, or of how we suspect he would feel were he to be aware either of how he is appraising a situation or of what behavioural systems within him are being activated.

Thus the language of feeling is an indispensable vehicle for talking about ways in which a situation is appraised and about behavioural systems in a state of activation, whether activation is leading to overt behaviour or whether, because of inhibition, the behaviour activated remains incipient.

The language of feeling has certain dangers, however. A principal one is that, instead of being regarded as indices of how situations are being appraised and what behaviours are being activated, feelings are reified. Then there is a danger of therapist and patient alike supposing that recognition that the patient is angry, or sad, or jealous is enough, and omitting to determine exactly what situation the patient is appraising or what the patient is now disposed to *do*—for example, to hurt his wife in certain ways, or to seek his mother in certain places and at certain times, or to oust another patient from the room. When the language of feeling becomes an obstacle to recognising that feeling entails action of particular sorts, it is best abandoned and replaced temporarily by a language of behaviour.

The issues touched on in this chapter are obviously fundamental for an understanding of human nature, especially of all the more complex and sophisticated parts of it. Though the account given is no more than a sketch, it is hoped it will be enough to show that the model of instinctive behaviour adopted, which by itself may appear remote from issues of real life, is capable of being used as a foundation on which theory of more immediate day-to-day relevance can be erected.

Chapter 8

Function of Instinctive Behaviour

The mechanists were undoubtedly right in rejecting the teleology of the vitalists as scientifically sterile and as making nonsense of physical science. Yet they undid all they had gained by failing to realise that the unique manner in which vital phenomena appear to be tailored to the application of teleological concepts, and positively invite their use, points to very real differences between animate and inanimate matter. . . .

G. SOMMERHOFF (1950)

Functions of behavioural systems and other consequences of their activity

Function Distinguished from Causation

Throughout these chapters it has been emphasised that in a species' environment of evolutionary adaptedness instinctive behaviour commonly has effects that contribute in an obvious way to the survival of the individual or of the species. Nutrition, safety, reproduction, each is a vital requirement and each is served by its own special and efficient behavioural systems. Instinctive behaviour is organised to achieve a predictable outcome and any attempt to reduce it to something simpler evades the issue. Yet, if we are not to be trapped in theories of a teleological kind, it is necessary to walk warily. The task of theory, in fact, is to 'discover how to express the concerns of the vitalists in the exact scientific language of the mechanists' (Sommerhoff, 1950).

A teleological theory is one that not only recognises that an active biological system, whether physiological or behavioural, tends in a species' environment of adaptedness to result in a predictable outcome that is usually of value to the species, but accounts for its reaching that outcome by supposing that in some way the outcome is itself an immediate cause of the physiological reaction, or of the behaviour, that leads to it. 'The bird builds a nest to have somewhere to rear young' is a teleological statement when it carries the meaning that the bird needs to have somewhere to rear young and that such need causes it to build its nest. And, because such a theory entails supposing that the future determines the present through some form of 'finalistic causation', it lies outside the realm of science. Yet to say that a bird builds a nest to have somewhere to rear young is not necessarily unscientific—in fact no more unscientific than to say that a predictor-controlled gun aims and fires in order to destroy enemy aircraft. The puzzle has always been to understand how an action which has such predictable and useful results can be the effect of causes conceived in terms that are compatible with hard-headed science.

The secret lies not in the immediate causes of the action but in the mode of construction of the agent—the animal or the predictor. Provided the agent is constructed in a very special way and provided it is operating within its environment of adaptedness, a certain particular and predictable consequence is likely to follow when it is set in action. In the case of a man-made system this particular consequence is what the system is designed to do. Any other consequence, of which there may be many, is more or less accidental.

In biology that consequence which a system appears as though designed to achieve is usually termed the system's 'function'. Thus to maintain blood supply to the tissues is the function of the cardiovascular system. To provide a convenient place to brood eggs and rear young is the function of behavioural systems responsible for nest-building. In the same way, to destroy aircraft is the function of a predictor-controlled anti-aircraft gun. The function of a system determines the way it is constructed.

Once the system is in existence it can be either active or inactive. Some of the sorts of factor that activate behavioural systems were considered in Chapter 6—hormone levels, organisation and autonomous action of the CNS, and environmental stimuli of special sorts. None of them, it is to be noted, include the system's function (though it is not by accident that they are related in special ways to the system's function). The kinds of factor that activate a predictor-controlled gun are environmental stimuli, such as the presence within range of an aircraft, and the pressing of various switches. Again the causal factors do not include the system's function, though once again they are in special ways related to it.

Thus the immediate causes of a system's activation are one thing; the function of that system is quite another. Functions are the special consequences that arise from the way a system is constructed; causes are the factors that lead the system to become active or inactive on any one occasion.

When this distinction is applied to the problem of instinctive behaviour, it is seen that the causes of any behaviour are those factors that activate that particular behavioural system; whereas the function of that behaviour derives from the structure of the system, which is such that, when it is in action in its environment of evolutionary adaptedness, a consequence that promotes survival commonly follows.

If psychopathological theory is to fulfil its own function of doing full justice to its empirical data and at the same time to formulate theory in a form that is truly scientific, nothing is more important than that it draws, and rigorously maintains, the distinction between the causes of behaviour and its function. All too often they are still inextricably confused.

Whilst it is a great advance to recognise that function stems from a system's structure and has nothing to do with the immediate causes of activity, it still leaves the problem of understanding how in living organisms such ingenious structure comes into existence.

In the case of man-made systems this is no real problem. The way in which a predictor-controlled gun comes to be structured so that a common consequence of its action is the destruction of enemy aircraft is intelligible in terms of skilled engineers building the system in conformity with certain recently understood principles. The way in which an animal, say a bird, comes to be structured so that a predictable consequence of its actions is a completed nest is perhaps less readily intelligible. Yet, as already remarked, the existence in an animal of behavioural systems that when activated result in nest-building poses problems no greater than does the existence in the same animal of physiological systems that result in a well-regulated blood supply. The existence of each, it is confidently believed, can be understood in terms of evolution. Those organisms that develop physiological and behavioural systems that fulfil their functions more efficiently in the environment occupied by the species survive better and have more offspring than do organisms whose systems are less efficient. Thus current structure of behavioural systems is conceived as a product of natural selection's having, during evolution, incorporated into the gene pool of a species genes that, in the environment of adaptedness of that species, determine the more efficient variants of those systems; whereas genes responsible for variants that are less efficient in that environment have been lost.

In the case of a biological system, therefore, the function of a system is that consequence of the system's activity which led to its having been evolved, and which leads to its continuing to remain in the equipment of the species.

When it is active, of course, any system is likely to have many consequences in addition to its functional consequences. By no means all consequences, therefore, are to be regarded as functional. The predictor-controlled gun is likely to make a loud noise, but no one supposes it to be designed so as to achieve that result. In the same way, a behavioural system is bound to have many consequences besides that for which we believe it to have been evolved, namely the particular consequence that during evolution conferred on animals equipped with it a selective advantage. Thus, when a bird broods its eggs, one consequence is that it may go without food for long periods; when it migrates one consequence is that it may arrive exhausted. Plainly the behavioural systems leading to brooding and migration did not undergo positive selection during evolution because of those consequences. Quite the contrary. We suppose that in each case some other consequence confers such advantage that the behavioural system in question is selected for positively in spite of its having adverse consequences, such as food deprivation or exhaustion.

Function Distinguished from Predictable Outcome

The fact that quite often some of the consequences of the activity of a behavioural system are adverse is of much importance for an understanding of pathology. What is of far greater importance, however, is that, for a number of reasons to be discussed, the activity of any one behavioural system in some given individual may sometimes not, or even *never*, be followed by its functional consequence. Examples are not far to seek. When a baby sucks a dummy no food-intake results; when a male courts another male no conception results. In each case, though the behavioural system is active and both the resulting behaviour and the predictable outcome conform fairly closely to type, the usual functional consequence is missing. In the case of the baby's sucking the functional consequence is likely to be absent on some occasions only: on other occasions he sucks a nipple and food-intake results. In the case of a confirmed homosexual the functional consequence is absent on all occasions. (Contraception practised during heterosexual relations is, of course, a deliberate though reversible plan to avoid functional consequences.)

The point to note is that *in the individual* a behavioural system becomes active, reaches a more or less typical predictable outcome, and then becomes inactive, all without reference to the system's function. Thus, *in the individual performer, instinctive behaviour is absolutely independent of function*; this is a point constantly emphasised by Freud. *In a population of individuals*, on the other hand, the position is different. Although in many individuals for a part, or even much, of the time behavioural systems may be active without their functions being fulfilled, so long as the population survives it must happen that in some individuals for at least some of the time the functions are being fulfilled. Though some individuals starve and others fail to reproduce for other reasons, enough remain nourished and have offspring for the population to persist. Thus, as with adaptation, *an understanding of function requires a study of the behaviour of a population of individuals and is impossible if the unit of study is the individual alone.*

A sharp distinction can, then, be drawn between the predictable outcome of a behavioural system's activity and the function that it may or may not fulfil. Predictable outcome is a property of a particular system in a particular individual. Function is a property of that system in a population of individuals. Whereas if a population is to survive it is essential that the predictable outcome of a system should in a sufficient number of individuals be consonant with function being fulfilled, if an individual is to survive this may be of no matter.

There are two main reasons why the activity of a behavioural system can achieve a predictable outcome yet fail to be followed by its functional consequence:

(a) Whilst the system itself is in functionally effective order, namely capable of achieving functional consequences, the current environment deviates in greater or less degree from the environment of evolutionary adaptedness and so does not conform to that required for function to be fulfilled.

An example is when a hungry baby is given a dummy to suck. The reason that food-intake does not follow has nothing to do with the system responsible for sucking but is because the particular object sucked contains no food. Another example is when two tom-cats meet each other unexpectedly; for instance, when each simultaneously rounds the same corner from a different direction. The usual territorial fights, which occur when the animals have warning of each other's presence, consist mainly of threats and feints and no damage results. In the statistically rare event of sudden confrontation fights may be savage and damaging.

(b) The second reason is much more serious than the first because relatively permanent: it arises when the behavioural system itself is not in functionally effective order so that, even in the environment of evolutionary adaptedness, the functional consequence is never (or only rarely) achieved. This needs further discussion.

There are many reasons why, in the course of development, one or another feature of an animal's diverse biological equipment may fail to develop satisfactorily. Anatomical structures may be deformed or missing, physiological systems may be in poor working order or, in the case for example of vision or hearing, not working at all. Though occasionally one or more genes are responsible for the failure, more often some anomaly of the embryo's environment is the cause—a virus, a chemical, a mechanical trauma, and so on. It is probably the same with failures in development of behavioural systems. Whilst genes may well account for some forms and cases of failure, anomalies of a juvenile's environment beyond those to which behavioural equipment is adapted are likely to be the cause of most of them.

In Chapter 3 it was emphasised that in the higher vertebrates most behavioural systems are to some extent environmentally labile, namely, the form they take in an adult turns in some degree on the kind of environment in which that adult is reared. The advantage of this is that the form ultimately to be taken by the system is in some degree left open so that it can, during development, become adapted to the particular environment in which the individual finds himself. Such flexibility, however, is not without its price. Provided the environment met with during development lies within certain limits, the ultimate form of a behavioural system may be well adapted, namely be such that, when activated, it commonly achieves a functional consequence. But when the environment in which development takes place falls outside those limits the form taken by the system may be ill adapted, namely be such that, when activated, it fails often or always to achieve a functional consequence. There are now countless examples of this in the literature of animal behaviour—motor patterns that take a functionally ineffective form, behaviour that follows a functionally ineffective sequence, objects towards which behaviour is directed that are ineffective for function to be fulfilled, and so on. In each such case the behavioural system has, during development, become organised so that a particular predictable outcome is reached, but that outcome happens to be of such a kind that the function of the system is never fulfilled.

In vertebrates there is probably hardly any behavioural system that could not, by suitable manipulation of environment, be diverted in its development to become functionally ineffective in form. Systems responsible for locomotion, for nest-building, for courtship, for parental behaviour, all are on record as having developed in such a way that functional consequences rarely or never follow their activation. Whereas some behavioural systems, e.g. those responsible for food-intake, must be in reasonably effective functional order if the individual is to survive, others, notably those responsible for sexual and parental behaviour, need not be. This is perhaps one reason why so much of psychopathology is concerned with behavioural systems responsible for sexual and parental behaviour: whenever it is concerned with a more immediately vital function the individual dies before a psychiatrist sees him. Another and no less important reason is that sexual and parental behaviour of a functionally effective kind are in each case a product of a very large number of behavioural systems organised in very special ways. And, since much of the development and organisation of these behavioural systems takes place whilst the individual is immature, there are plenty of occasions when an atypical environment can divert them from developing on an adaptive course. The result is that the adult is equipped with a system that, although in working order and capable of reaching a quite specific predictable outcome, is not capable of fulfilling the system's function.

An example of a system or rather integrate of systems that is in working order but not in functionally effective working order is the integrate responsible for sexual behaviour in an adult who is a confirmed homosexual. In such a case all components of behaviour may be performed efficiently but, because the object towards which they are directed is inappropriate, the functional consequence of reproduction cannot follow. The integrate not only has a predictable outcome, namely sexual orgasm with a partner of the same sex, but is so organised that the outcome is achieved. What makes it functionally ineffective is that for some reason the system has developed in such a way that its predictable outcome is unrelated to function. Were a similar error to have crept into the design of a radar and predictor-controlled anti-aircraft gun, it might lead to the gun's firing efficiently but aiming so that it always destroyed a friendly plane and never an enemy one. These examples show clearly that the distinction between predictable outcome and function is a crucial one. Usually structure is such that when the predictable outcome is reached function is at least sometimes fulfilled, but mistakes can occur—especially when structure is environmentally labile. Some of the developmental processes at work and the ways in which they can go wrong are discussed in Chapter 10.

The upshot of all this is that, in a particular individual, the activity of any one behavioural system may have consequences that fail to promote the survival of the species, or even of the individual, and may even be inimical to the interests of one or both. Either because the present environment deviates significantly from the species' environment of evolutionary adaptedness or because during development the system has itself taken an unadapted form, the usual function of the system remains unfulfilled. Nevertheless, because the individual is part of a population, the species is likely to survive. Provided that the environment of some individuals of the population, both during development and currently, conforms to that to which the species is adapted, the activity of behavioural systems will, in a sufficient number of individuals, have appropriate functional consequences. As a result the species persists, and potential to develop the behavioural systems is preserved in its genic equipment.

Altruistic Behaviour

In the history of psychology the existence of altruistic behaviour has sometimes been regarded as a problem; and many psychoanalytic formulations suggest that by nature individuals seek only selfish ends and that they are altruistic only when constrained to be so by social pressures and sanctions. A biological approach to instinctive behaviour shows this view to be false. Once the criterion in terms of which a system's function is to be considered is recognised to be the survival of the genes carried by the individual concerned, the fact that much behaviour has an altruistic function is no surprise. On the contrary, from a biological point of view, behaviour that has an altruistic function is perhaps understood a little *more* readily than is behaviour the function of which appears more egotistic.

Let us consider two apparently contrasting patterns of instinctive behaviour. Some instinctive behaviour is so structured that it commonly achieves food-intake and good nutrition, and as such may appear to fulfil a function of value only to an individual. This is unlikely to be so, however, since behaviour that achieves the good nutrition of an individual is likely also to enable that individual sooner or later to contribute to the survival of the genes he is carrying. Although at first sight the behaviour might appear intelligible only in terms of individual survival, reflection shows that it is no less intelligible in terms of gene survival.

By contrast there is other instinctive behaviour that is so structured that it commonly fulfils a function of obvious benefit to some other individual though of no benefit to the performer. An example is the caregiving behaviour of parents towards their young. Other examples include the helpful behaviour of individuals towards kin other than offspring, notably siblings, nephews and nieces, and sometimes cousins. In every case the behaviour is readily intelligible in terms of gene survival. Offspring carry half the genes of each parent; and, on average, siblings have half their genes in common. For first cousins the proportion of genes in common averages one quarter. In each case the helper is either older and therefore stronger than the individual helped or else is in a temporarily more favourable situation, so that the sacrifice entailed is proportionately less than the benefit conferred. The extreme case of the lifelong behaviour of worker bees, which are sterile and spend their lives caring for the queen and her progeny, is to be explained in the same way. Worker bees are females that, having been produced by parthenogenesis, are identical genetically with the queen whose offspring they tend. This means that their caregiving behaviour is equivalent biologically to that of a parent.*

* There are also occasions when an individual animal is helpful to some other animal even though it is not kin. In species other than man such helpfulness takes two forms. One occurs when an animal directs parental caregiving to some individual other than its offspring. This can be understood as the result of the behaviour being misdirected, as it were by mistake. The other form occurs only between individuals that have a long-term friendly relationship; and it can be explained in terms of the genetical theory of natural selection on the principle of reciprocal altruism. Provided that help given to a friend is occasionally reciprocated, a tendency to behave altruistically will be favoured by natural selection. Conscious calculation is not required, though in man, of course, it may occur.

Thus, once gene survival is recognised as the true criterion in terms of which the function of instinctive behaviour is measured, some old-standing problems evaporate. That some instinctive behaviour has a function of direct and immediate benefit to kin is only to be expected; that other forms of instinctive behaviour have a function of immediate benefit to individual survival and of only indirect benefit to gene survival is no less intelligible. Whether classified as 'egotistic' or as 'altruistic' the ultimate function is the same.

This means that altruistic behaviour springs from roots just as deep as does egotistic, and that the distinction between the two, though real, is far from fundamental.

How the Function of a System is Determined

So far we have spoken as though the function of every behavioural system is so obvious that it can be taken for granted. No one bothers to ask what the function of eating is—or that of brooding or migration. Nevertheless, there are a number of long-recognised behavioural systems the functions of which remain obscure. A notable one is the territorial behaviour of many species of bird and mammal. No one doubts that such behaviour falls into the general class we are calling instinctive, yet the exact advantage (or advantages) that it confers on a species often remains unclear. Nevertheless it is characteristic of contemporary biological thought that any instinctive behaviour is confidently presumed to have some particular function (or functions) that aids survival, even though the nature of that function is not yet agreed by students of the subject.

The task of determining precisely what the function of a certain piece of instinctive behaviour is may be considerable. First, it has to be established that in a species' environment of evolutionary adaptedness individuals so equipped have more progeny than do those not so equipped, and, secondly, the reason for their doing so has to be discovered. Ideally the necessary research is carried out in the wild. Procedure is to intervene experimentally so that certain individuals of a species are unable to behave in the usual way and then to compare their survival rate and breeding success with those of individuals not interfered with. In recent years Tinbergen (e.g. 1963) has been carrying out experiments of this sort on certain details of the breeding behaviour of gulls. Without such experiments, either in the species with which we are concerned or at least in closely related species, any discussion about which of the many common consequences of a piece of instinctive behaviour is its functional consequence is apt to become unfruitfully speculative.

In Chapter 12 it is argued, first, that the behaviour of the young human child that leads him to maintain proximity to his mother-figure (and that is termed attachment behaviour) is an example of instinctive behaviour, and, secondly, that its function has been little discussed and is still a matter on which agreement has to be reached. A hypothesis that hitherto has been little considered in clinical circles is advanced.

Problems of terminology

Now that an alternative theory of instinctive behaviour has been outlined it is time to discuss briefly the usefulness, or otherwise, of some traditional terms.

In the introduction to Chapter 3 it was remarked that so long as the word 'instinctive' is used descriptively as an adjective it is useful, but that difficulties are encountered when the noun 'instinct' is employed. Let us consider why this should be so.

The theory of instinctive behaviour advanced conceives such behaviour to be a result of the activation within a particular environment of behavioural systems that are integrated, either in chains or in hierarchies or in a mixture of the two; and each behavioural system and each integrate of behavioural systems is conceived as being so constructed that, as a rule, when activated it achieves a consequence that has survival value. Now to what entity is the substantive noun 'instinct' to be applied? Is it to be to the behaviour itself? Or to the behavioural system? Or to the causal conditions that activate a behavioural system? Or to its predictable outcome? Or, perhaps, to the function that it fulfils?

The fact is that workers of repute have applied the term instinct to all these different things. At one extreme it has been used to refer narrowly to relatively fixed action patterns, such as 'turning head', and to movements, such as seizing prey, that occur at the end of a longer sequence of instinctive behaviour. At another extreme the term has been used to refer very broadly to forces, regarded as causal factors, that lead to states as general as life or death. Sometimes it refers to the predictable outcome of a sequence of instinctive behaviour, as in 'nest-building instinct' and 'sexual instinct', or to its biological function, as in 'reproductive instinct'. Occasionally the term is used to refer to an emotion that commonly accompanies behaviour, as in 'instinct of fearing'.

It will be at once plain that this varied and mixed usage leads only to confusion. Yet it may still be asked whether perhaps some standard usage could not be agreed. There are, in fact, two good reasons why this cannot be. First, a term that has been employed in so many different ways is not easily redefined and used anew in an exact sense. Secondly, the existence of integrates of behavioural systems of every level of complexity makes it extremely difficult to draw a line and to decide that all integrates below that line in complexity are to be termed instincts and all integrates above that line are not to be so termed. Such an exercise would resemble the task of dividing industrial concerns into two groups in terms of their level of organisational complexity and giving those of less complexity a special name. The difficulty of the task needs no emphasis; but the real question is of what use would the result be were it to be done.

To select by whatever criteria certain integrates of behavioural systems and to term them instincts would serve no useful purpose. Not only that, but it would perpetuate the widespread error of supposing that the systems that come within any one integrate of systems have all their causal conditions in common and that these conditions are usefully conceived as 'drive'.

In Chapter 6 an account was given of some of the various interacting factors that activate the behavioural systems leading to nest-building in canaries, and this research provides an apt illustration also for the point now to be made. The nest-building of canaries can be analysed into gathering material, carrying it to the nest, and building while sitting in the nest. Since these activities fluctuate more or less together, it could be argued that all are governed by a 'nest-building drive'. Analysis of the factors causing them shows that all three components do in fact share certain causal factors: all are influenced by oestrogen level and all are inhibited by stimuli from the nest. Yet correlation between the three activities is not absolute: each has causal factors specific to it, and the sequence in which the activities appear is probably due to the self-suppressing effect that accompanies the performance of each activity. The concept of a single nest-building drive is plainly inadequate. The same would be true were we to postulate a separate drive for each component activity of nest-building, since each of these activities can be analysed into a number of constituent movements each of which varies in some degree independently of the others.

The truth is that the better we come to understand the causal factors influencing instinctive behaviour the less useful the concept of drive becomes. So long as the springs of action are unknown it is easy and perhaps inevitable to suppose that some special force drives the behaviour forward, perhaps not only initiating it but also directing it in a mysterious yet beneficent way. But, if we are right in believing that behaviour is a result of the activation of behavioural systems and that the activation is caused in the ways described, the mystery evaporates and the need to postulate drives disappears. Engineers have no need to postulate a special 'aircraft-shooting drive' to account for the behaviour of a predictor-controlled gun, nor physiologists a 'blood-supply drive' to account for the action of the cardiovascular system.

In what follows, therefore, neither the concept of instinct as an entity nor that of drive is employed.

The descriptive term 'instinctive behaviour' remains useful, however, to refer in a rough and ready way to behaviour that in the environment of evolutionary adaptedness has consequences that are vital to the survival of the species and that is controlled by systems which in that environment are usually fairly stable. At the same time it must be recognised that even when 'instinctive' is used purely descriptively it is apt to bring with it two related dangers. The first is a risk that it may be supposed that every kind of instinctive behaviour is controlled by behavioural systems of but a single type; the second is a risk of creating a false dichotomy between instinctive behaviour and all other kinds of behaviour. The truth is that behaviour that is traditionally described as instinctive is controlled by systems of many different types and that these systems lie on a number of continua ranging from the most stable systems to the most labile and from those that are most necessary for species survival to those that make only a marginal contribution to it. There can, therefore, be no cut-off point between what is called instinctive behaviour and what is not.

In certain psychoanalytic theorising (e.g. Schur, 1960a and b) the adjectives 'instinctive' and 'instinctual' have been used in special ways: the term 'instinctive' is reserved for behaviour of the kind also termed here instinctive, and the term 'instinctual' is applied to a postulated 'psychical drive energy' that is held to be discharged by means of such instinctive behaviour.

FUNCTION

Since in the theory advanced in the present work no psychical drive energy is postulated, the adjective 'instinctual' is not used at all;[1] the adjective 'instinctive' is used to refer both to behaviours of a certain kind and to the behavioural systems responsible for them.

A number of other terms used in discussions of instinctive behaviour and of psychopathology require consideration. They include such terms as 'need', 'wish', 'aim', 'purpose', and many others. How, it may be asked, does each fit into the present schema and how do they relate to concepts such as predictable outcome, set-goal, and functional consequence?

To avoid commitment to any particular theory of instinctive behaviour and to indicate the apparently purposive character of behavioural systems, the term 'need', or 'need system', is sometimes used. It is not a satisfactory term, however, because it is readily taken to mean something required for survival—a vital need; and a further complication is that this, in turn, may lead to teleological thinking. Let us look at these difficulties more carefully.

It has been emphasised in this chapter that the existence in an animal of a particular species of any one environmentally stable behavioural system comes about because the activity of that system commonly has a consequence that is of survival value to the species. Systems responsible for eating behaviour commonly have food-intake as a consequence. Systems responsible for mating behaviour commonly have reproduction as a consequence. Since the activities of these systems so commonly and so plainly fulfil a biological need, why then not term them 'need systems'?

There are at least three good reasons for not doing so. First, in each instance the activity of the behavioural system in question may have consequences of quite other kinds. In a particular individual a system that is obviously connected with food-intake may have as its main consequence the sucking of a thumb or a pipe.[2] In another individual a system obviously connected with mating may have as its main consequence sexual

[1] In earlier published work on anxiety and grief, the term 'instinctual response systems' was in fact used to refer to behavioural systems that are responsible for instinctive behaviour. For the reasons given above, terminology is changed in the revised versions of this material that appear in Volumes II and III.

[2] Some sucking, however, is essentially non-nutritive; see Chapters 13 and 14.

activities directed towards a fetish or an individual of the same sex. In such instances the activity of the system has no survival value whatsoever. To call the system a need system is therefore confusing; and the confusion is only made worse if, to meet the difficulty, new needs, e.g. to suck, are postulated. Secondly, as already remarked, there are a number of species-characteristic behavioural systems the biological functions of which are still unclear. This fact is obscured when every behavioural system is termed a need system, because the term 'need' tends to imply that the usefulness of the system is self-evident. Finally, the term 'need system' can readily lead to an assumption that the need plays some sort of causal role in activating the system, the fallacy of teleology.

A legitimate usage of the term 'need' is to restrict it to refer to the requirements of species survival. If the species is to survive, an animal can be said to need food, warmth, a nesting-site, a mate, and so on. Obviously none of these needs is a behavioural system, nor does any of them cause the activation of a behavioural system. On the other hand, many behavioural systems have the function of meeting one or other of these needs; and it is because, if that species is to survive, those functions have to be fulfilled that those particular behavioural systems have been evolved. Needs, therefore, are not the causes of instinctive behaviour. What they do is to determine the functions that behavioural systems have to serve. Thus they constitute the selection pressures under which behavioural systems evolve.

Just as needs are not causes of instinctive behaviour so wishes and desires are not causes either. The terms 'wish' and 'desire' refer to a human subject's awareness of the set-goal of some behavioural system or integrate of systems that is *already* in action, or at least alerted for action. The statements 'I wish for food' or 'I desire food' indicate that an integrate of behavioural systems that has food-intake as its set-goal has been activated, perhaps only incipiently, and that I am aware that this is so. Such reports are usually trustworthy, but psycho-analysts know well that that is not always so. A subject may in fact mis-identify the set-goal of a behavioural system currently active—and such mis-identification may itself be the result of interference by an active system that has a set-goal which is incompatible with the first. This leads to the concept of unconscious wish.

To say that a wish is unconscious indicates that, in the person of whom it is said, a behavioural system or integrate of systems having such and such a set-goal is active but that the person is not aware of the fact.

Whilst the term 'wish' refers to the set-goal of a behavioural system, the term 'intent' refers usually to some stage on the way to the set-goal. When I say I *intend* to do such and such it commonly indicates that such and such is part of the plan that guides my present behaviour (this point is elaborated by Miller, Galanter, and Pribram, 1960).

There are a number of different terms in use to refer to what in this chapter is termed 'predictable outcome', with its sub-category of 'set-goal'. They include 'purpose', 'aim', and simply 'goal'. The defects of 'goal' have already been dealt with (see Chapter 5).

A difficulty about both 'purpose' and 'aim' is that each tends to carry overtones of teleological causation. A more serious difficulty about them, moreover, is that each is habitually used in ways that fail to distinguish between a system's predictable outcome and its function—a fatal confusion. For this reason neither is used in the present work. Although the English word 'aim' is commonly employed in both these senses, it is of interest that when Freud defined the aim of an instinct he was alive to some of the problems. For example, in 'Instincts and their vicissitudes' (1915a) he recognised the basic distinction between terminating stimuli, on the one hand, and function, on the other, and confined his usage of the term 'aim' to what in the terminology used here is 'reaching the terminating conditions of the behavioural system in question'.

Other technical terms have been introduced to refer to what is here termed predictable outcome or set-goal. Sommerhoff's 'focal condition' is very nearly co-terminous with my 'predictable outcome', though it may exclude the predictable outcome of very simple types of behaviour, for example egg-rolling. A German term, introduced by Mittelstaedt and used by Hinde, that refers to certain types of set-goal is *sollwert*, namely the 'should be' state, or the state that a system is set to reach and/or maintain. A disadvantage of the term may be that it was introduced to refer to set-goals the instructions for reaching which require only one type of constituent specification, e.g. the position of a limb or the singing of a note, and may not be so easily applied to more complex set-goals, instructions to reach which require two or more constituent specifications. Another possible disadvantage of *sollwert* is that a 'should be' state might, perhaps, be misinterpreted to imply that that state is a norm that contributes to survival. In fact, as has been repeatedly emphasised, the set-goal or *sollwert* of a behavioural system may in any particular individual be atypical and even inimical to survival.

In these chapters the adjective 'purposive' has sometimes been used to describe a system that has a set-goal. It carries with it, however, a risk that it will be interpreted as implying teleological causation (a risk that is even greater with the sister-adjective 'purposeful'). To meet these objections Pittendrigh (1958) has proposed the term 'teleonomic'. It can be used to denote any system, living or mechanical, that is so constructed that, when activated in its environment of adaptedness, it achieves a predictable outcome. All the behavioural systems with which these chapters are concerned can, therefore, be termed teleonomic.

To turn once again to the concept of set-goal it should be noted that the set-goal of a behavioural system, like that of any other control system, can be of two main types. One type of set-goal is the maintenance of some variable at a constant value. Thus some simple organisms are equipped with behavioural systems that have as a set-goal the task of maintaining the organism in an environment that is within certain narrow limits of temperature. The task of such behavioural systems is never finished: there is no climax to their performance and no drama. It is a drab routine task. The other type of set-goal is an event that is limited in time and that, once it has been brought about, is followed by a cessation of activity. An obvious example is sexual union, another is interception of prey. For some behavioural systems the set-goal lies somewhere between these extremes.

In the case of man there has been a marked tendency to give undue emphasis to behavioural systems that have finite set-goals, e.g. orgasm, and too little attention to systems that have continuing set-goals, e.g. proximity or accessibility to an object in the environment. Attachment behaviour, it is held, is the result of the activity of behavioural systems that have a continuing set-goal, the specification of which is a certain sort of relationship to another specified individual.

Chapter 9

Changes in Behaviour during the Life-cycle

THE behavioural development of an individual needs to be considered in two quite distinct ways:

a. the way in which the parts of the behavioural equipment in active use change from one phase of the life-cycle to the next;

b. the way in which each part of that equipment comes to take the particular form it does.

Both themes are of the greatest interest to psychoanalysts. The first is dealt with only briefly in this chapter but is referred to again at the end of Chapter 12. The second, which concerns the ontogeny of behavioural systems, is of much intricacy and importance and is discussed in the next chapter.

To ensure the survival of the individual and ultimately of his genes, it is necessary for an animal to be equipped with an appropriately balanced repertoire of instinctive behavioural systems at each stage of its life-cycle. Not only must an adult be so equipped but the young animal must also have a balanced and efficient equipment of its own. This is likely to differ in many respects from that of the adult. Furthermore, because in all but the simplest species survival is in greater or lesser degree dependent on the co-operation of individuals, much of the equipment of one individual is complementary to that of other individuals, usually of different age or sex. Behaviour patterns mediating attachment of young to adults are complementary to those mediating care of young by adults; in the same way, systems mediating adult masculine behaviour in one individual are complementary to those mediating adult feminine behaviour in another. This emphasises afresh that instinctive behaviour is never intelligible in terms of a single individual but in terms only of a greater or smaller number of individuals collaborating.

In all species of bird and mammal certain parts of the behavioural equipment that are operative during the immature phase of the life-cycle are different from certain parts that are operative during the adult phase. Such differences are of two main kinds:

i. The same biological function is fulfilled in both immature and adult, but the behavioural systems fulfilling it are not the same ones. An obvious example is the different means of food-intake used by immature and mature mammals: sucking in the young, biting and chewing in older individuals.

ii. The biological functions that are fulfilled differ in the young and in the adult. Because immature organisms are usually very vulnerable they are commonly endowed with behavioural equipment that produces behaviour specially likely to minimise risk, e.g. behaviour that maintains proximity to a parent. Because, on the other hand, immature organisms are unfitted to breed successfully, behaviour leading to reproduction and care of young is either not seen or seen only in an incomplete form.

It must, of course, be remembered that an absence of a particular sort of behaviour at a particular phase of the life-cycle can reflect one of several very different underlying states. First, the neural substrate of the behavioural systems responsible for that behaviour may not have developed and so the systems could not, in any circumstances, be activated. A second, and opposite, state is one in which the neural substrate of the behavioural systems is fully developed but the systems are lying dormant because some of the causal factors necessary to activate them are absent. A third state is where the behavioural equipment is developed only partially or where causal factors for only some of the component systems are present, so that, although bits of the behaviour are to be seen, the full functional pattern is still absent. The second and third of these states are more often present than is commonly realised.

Experiments entailing artificial changes in hormone level have shown that, in many species of vertebrate, behavioural systems responsible for both masculine and feminine behaviour are present in a full, or at least a potential, form in individuals of both sexes. Thus, when a domestic hen is injected with testosterone she will display a full range of masculine behaviour; similarly, when a male rat is castrated at birth and later injected with oestrogens he will display a full range of feminine behaviour. These findings make it plain that the behavioural systems appropriate to the opposite sex are potentially present in these animals and that the reason that the systems remain largely or totally inactive in the ordinary course of events is that hormone levels deviate from what are necessary for activation.[1]

Not infrequently the changes of behaviour that are shown at different phases of the life-cycle are due to shifts of hormone balance. In man there is good evidence that behavioural systems responsible for both masculine and feminine behaviour are present in both sexes long before puberty and that the much increased likelihood of one or other of them being active after puberty is due in large part to changes in hormone levels. Similarly, it may well be that changes of hormone level play some part in the disappearance of immature behaviour—by creating conditions such that the behavioural systems responsible for it, though themselves persisting, are no longer activated so readily.

Whilst some changes of behaviour during the life-cycle are due to changes occurring in hormone levels or their balance, other changes may be due to the fact that a new behavioural system has matured and that its activation takes precedence over a system active earlier. For example, the behavioural system responsible for sucking remains extant long after infancy but is less frequently activated. This might be because the behavioural systems responsible for biting and chewing have become operational and in most individuals are more readily activated than the system responsible for sucking.

Whatever the reason may be why behavioural systems specially characteristic of immatures are less often active in adult life, there is abundant evidence that the systems themselves persist. They are apt to become active in situations of three main sorts. First, juvenile patterns are often seen in adults when adult patterns prove ineffective or when, in conditions of conflict, adult patterns become disorganised. Secondly, they are sometimes seen when an adult is sick or incapacitated. On all such occasions activation of the immature system is usually referred to as 'regressive'. Thirdly, it may happen that an integrate of behavioural systems characteristic of an adult may include within itself a component derived from an earlier phase

---

[1] Some of the conditions that lead male and female mammals to show either masculine or feminine behaviour are described by Levine (1966). The hormone levels present at the period around birth are shown to be of great influence—an example of a sensitive phase, see p. 161. For instance, if a female monkey is treated with testosterone shortly before birth, though never again, her subsequent behaviour is typically masculine.

of life, perhaps one that originally served a different function. A specially clear example is the courtship feeding of birds in which the male feeds the female. Whilst the cock's behaviour is typical of an adult feeding young, the hen's is typical of young being fed by a parent. Here two patterns serving the nutrition of young, one an adult pattern and the other a juvenile one, are incorporated into a behavioural sequence serving reproduction. Psychoanalysts have long held that something analogous occurs in the sexual interchanges of adult humans.

In most mammalian species the shifts in behaviour exhibited from one phase of the life-cycle to the next occur in a remarkably regular and predictable way despite variations in the environment. They are, therefore, in high degree environmentally stable. Nevertheless, independence of the environment is never complete. In the human populations of Western countries, for instance, puberty has advanced appreciably during the past century, presumably owing to some environmental influence that affects the age at which the balance of sex hormones in the individual shifts. Little is yet known of the environmental factor responsible: a change in diet is a plausible suggestion, but the possibility that the shift could be due to a change in social environment should not be neglected. Nevertheless, in all mammals, variations in the pace at which changes occur in the behavioural systems in active use during the life-cycle are no more than marginal; and they pale into insignificance when compared with the enormous variation of form that any one behavioural system or integrate of systems may take in response to the environment in which an individual is reared. Non-adaptive variations in the form taken during development by man's behavioural systems are in fact the stuff of which psychopathology is made. A better understanding of the processes responsible for such variation has been a principal concern of psychoanalysts ever since Freud recognised that the way human sexual behaviour develops turns on happenings in years long before puberty. These processes are the main topic of the next chapter.

Chapter 10

Ontogeny of Instinctive Behaviour

The only scientific way to deal with adaptation is to get the facts for each case. Only after the facts are known is it possible to tell just how much of the adaptedness of a given phenomenon is due to inherited evolutionary prearrangements, and how much to direct adjustive interactions. The ratio varies greatly and unpredictably from species to species, from function to function, from unit to unit. PAUL WEISS (1949)

Changes that occur during the ontogeny of behavioural systems

Whereas, in some lower orders of animal, behavioural systems on first appearance in the life of an individual are, like Venus, already of almost perfect form, in higher orders they more usually take at first a primitive form and proceed thence to undergo an elaborate process of development. Although new-born birds and mammals are equipped with a few behavioural systems capable at once of fulfilling a vital function, e.g. food-intake, initially they are apt to fulfil it only very inefficiently. A number of other systems, moreover, on first manifesting themselves are so ill organised that not only is the behaviour for which they are responsible incomplete but the functional consequences that will later commonly follow it are conspicuous by their absence. In general, therefore, it is only as an individual bird or mammal grows older that its behavioural systems become complete and that the functional consequences of their activation come, as a rule, to follow with regularity and efficiency.

The behavioural equipment of newborn birds and mammals not only is limited in scope but is simple in form; and of no mammal is this more true than the human baby. Yet by the age of two years a human child is already talking, and soon afterwards he can use language as a means of ordering and controlling behaviour. Thus during this brief proportion of his life-span the sophistication of the behavioural systems operative within him grows out of all recognition. Very many processes are responsible for this transformation.

In this chapter a few of the more important of the processes mediating the behavioural development of higher vertebrates are outlined, and links made to what appears to occur in man.[1]

There are three main ways in which instinctive behaviour on its first appearance in immature members of higher species differs from that found in adults:

(a) a movement, though perhaps characteristic in form, is directed towards objects in the environment different from or more varied than those towards which the movement is directed in the adult; usually it is directed towards a much larger range of objects;

(b) behavioural systems that are functional in infancy tend to be simple in structure and to be superseded during development by systems of more complex structure; thus behaviour that in the neonate is little more than reflexive, e.g. sucking, comes to be replaced by behaviour regulated by feedback and, perhaps, organised so as to achieve set-goals;

(c) movements that are later seen as parts of complex sequences of behaviour with functional consequences are often exhibited at first only as non-functional fragments.

Each of these differences can cause instinctive behaviour in an immature either to fulfil its function inefficiently or to fail to fulfil it altogether. Each, moreover, can be a source from which a pathological form of behaviour can develop. It is no surprise, therefore, to find that each of these characteristics of instinctive behaviour in immatures has for long been given a central place in psychoanalytic theory. Within that tradition these three characteristics are reflected in the following propositions:

(a) the object towards which instinctive behaviour is directed, and a special relation with which terminates it, 'is what is most variable about an instinct' (Freud, 1915a, *S.E.*, **14**, p. 122);

(b) in the immature, behaviour is subject mainly to the pleasure principle; during healthy development regulation by pleasure principle becomes increasingly superseded by regulation by reality principle;

(c) instinctive behaviour is made up of a number of com-

[1] Much of what follows, including examples, is derived from Hinde's *Animal Behaviour* (1970), in which a comprehensive discussion of the principles of behavioural development will be found.

ponents (part-instincts) that, during development, come to be organised into integrates; the form these integrates take can vary greatly.

Thus not only in man but in many other species as well, great changes are found commonly to occur during the ontogeny of behavioural systems. In some species and for some behavioural systems these changes are environmentally stable, namely their course is not greatly influenced by variations of environment met with during development. In other species and for other behavioural systems the changes are environmentally labile and the form they take in the adult is much influenced by environmental variation. In such cases the period during which they are sensitive to change in the environment is often of only limited duration, and is termed a 'critical phase' or 'sensitive period'. Sensitive periods for different behavioural systems occur in different species at different points in the life-cycle. As a rule, however, these points occur relatively early in life and in some instances they occur before the system itself is functional (see p. 161).

The existence of sensitive periods in early life during which the form to be taken by an adult's instinctive behaviour is in great part determined is yet another characteristic of instinctive behaviour to which Freud drew attention. In the psychoanalytic tradition it is represented in the concepts of fixation and of stage in libidinal organisation.

Modern instinct theory, it is held, enables a number of time-honoured concepts derived from the psychoanalytic study of man to be aligned with similar concepts derived from observation and experiment with animals, to the clarification and enrichment of both.

Restriction of range of effective stimuli

The young of all species of bird and mammal show a certain number of complete movements that are, from the first, well executed and characteristic of the species. Examples in birds are pecking and preening, and in mammals sucking and urinating, and even complete prey-catching movements (e.g. in the polecat). Such movements appear without preceding practice and in their normal functional context. In man there is the rooting, sucking, and crying behaviour of the neonate and the patterns of smiling and walking exhibited at a rather later age. It seems likely, moreover, that some of the detailed components of adult masculine and feminine sexual behaviour, e.g. clasping and pelvic thrust, also fall into this category. Such movements, we may infer, are the expression of behavioural systems that, as regards motor pattern, are relatively little influenced during development by variations of environment and that, at a certain phase of the life-cycle, are ready to be activated by whatever causal factors they are structured to respond to. Some of them conform to Freud's concept of component instincts.

Such movements are organised and ready for execution as soon as an appropriate moment arrives, which shows that in motor form they are independent of learning. Whether or not on first appearance they are followed by their usual functional consequences, however, is an altogether different question. For pattern of movement is one thing and the object towards which it is directed is another.

Functional consequence follows only when a movement is directed at an appropriate object. For example, if a newly hatched chick happens to peck on ground that is strewn with seeds, food-intake results. But if it happens to peck on ground strewn with some other pale objects, e.g. wood chips or chalk, identical movements result in the chick receiving nothing of food value. In a similar way a newborn human baby may suck a suitably shaped object and receive, or not receive, nourishment. Thus, the behavioural systems responsible for pecking and for sucking are ready and become active the moment the necessary causal factors are present—and irrespective of whether the usual functional consequence follows or not.

Although the range of stimuli that may activate any one behavioural system in the immature is often very wide, it is not infinitely wide. From the first, stimuli tend to fall into categories and to elicit one or another different type of response. This has led Schneirla (1959, 1965) to suggest that many of the responses of very young animals are determined initially simply by quantitative differences in the intensity of stimulation received. Young animals, Schneirla points out, tend to approach with part or all of the body any source of stimulation whose neural effects are quantitatively low, regular, and limited in range of magnitude, and tend to withdraw from those whose neural inputs are high, irregular, and of extensive ranges. Although such discrimination is only rough and ready, more often than not its consequence is functional in that the young animal withdraws from a potentially dangerous part of the environment and approaches a potentially safe one. Whilst many observations of lower vertebrates support Schneirla's generalisation, the extent of its applicability remains unknown. Most students of higher vertebrates believe that the particular form of behaviour elicited is from an early stage of ontogeny determined, in part at least, also by stimulus pattern.[1]

The examples given show how, in higher vertebrates, the range of stimuli effective in activating a behavioural system in an immature and naïve animal is often very wide. With experience, however, comes restriction. Within a few days a chick has learned to peck mainly at seed and to disregard inedibles, and a human baby when hungry has come to prefer a milk-giving teat to another. Many other examples of restriction in range of effective stimuli can be given. Young birds of many species respond at first by following a wide range of visual stimuli, but within a few days do so only on seeing an object they have already followed. A human infant of a few weeks responds with a smile to any visual stimulus that has two black dots on a pale background; by three or four months a real human face is required; and by five months the effective stimulus may be confined to the face of a familiar person. That the range of effective stimuli commonly becomes restricted was well known to William James (1890) who expressed it as the 'Law of the inhibition of instinct by habits'.

What are the processes by which, first, the range of effective stimuli becomes so drastically narrowed, and, secondly, a particular response becomes as a rule linked to a functionally appropriate stimulus?

One such process is an improvement in the maturing individual's ability to discriminate sensory input. So long as vision and hearing are undiscriminating, a wide range of visual stimuli or of auditory stimuli may be treated as though they were alike. Whereas some sorts of improvement seem to be due to physiological development and cannot be attributed to

---

[1] There is evidence, reviewed by Bronson (1965), that in infancy the co-ordination of gross body movement, including orienting and defensive reactions, is mediated by the reticular system and motor nuclei of the brain-stem. So long as networks at this level of the CNS only are active, sensory discrimination is confined to change of intensity. Response to changes of pattern requires the contribution of neocortical systems. The fact that this contribution is of marginal importance during the early infancy of some mammalian species, including man, is in keeping with Schneirla's generalisation. It does not, however, support a view that responses to changes of pattern, when they appear, are necessarily a product of learning.

learning, other sorts are dependent on experience; the improvement is then referred to as 'perceptual learning' or 'exposure learning'.[1] For example, in mammals, there is evidence that the ability to perceive and respond to visual form, e.g. circle or square, is dependent on the animal's having first had experience of differing shapes. In some cases familiarity itself is enough— the animal does not have to have been rewarded by any of the conventional rewards. In other instances, visual experience alone is insufficient for improved discrimination to follow. Thus, for a kitten to develop efficient visually guided behaviour, it must not only have had visual experience of the environment, but have had the chance also to move actively in that environment.

Once stimuli can be discriminated, a number of processes can lead to restriction of the range of stimuli that are linked to any particular response. Through the opposing processes of reinforcement and of habituation, the consequences that follow a response can play a very large part in mediating restriction. Thus chicks continue to peck at objects that, after seizure, elicit swallowing, and cease to peck at those that do not. Young finches at first show only a limited degree of preference between different sorts of seed, but after experience take mostly those sorts that they can de-husk most efficiently.

A different class of processes that mould behaviour are those that result in familiar objects being approached and in unfamiliar ones being avoided. Unlike the processes of reinforcement and habituation, which have been the stock-in-trade of experimental psychologists for two generations, the importance of the dichotomy familiar–unfamiliar has been appreciated only in comparatively recent times, largely as a result of the work of Hebb (1946b).

In the development of young individuals of many species approach behaviour is exhibited early and precedes the appearance of avoidance and withdrawal behaviour. As a result, any stimulus to which the young animal is exposed initially, provided it falls within certain broad ranges, tends to elicit

[1] Sluckin (1965) points out that the term 'perceptual learning' is ambiguous and could well refer to several different processes. For this reason he advocates the term 'exposure learning', first proposed by Drever: 'It refers unambiguously to the perceptual registration by the organism of the environment to which it is exposed.' The effects appear to be due to the animal's having learned the properties of the stimulus, and not to its having formed any stimulus-response association.

approach. This phase lasts only a limited time, however, and is brought to an end by two closely related processes. On the one hand, experience of the environment enables the animal to learn the familiar and to discriminate it from the strange; on the other, avoidance and withdrawal responses become more readily elicited, and are then elicited especially by stimuli recognised as strange. In many species aggressive responses follow a course of development similar to that of withdrawal responses, maturing later than approach and being elicited especially by stimuli recognised as strange.

Thus, through the twin processes whereby different responses have differential maturing rates and the animal learns to discriminate between familiar and strange, the stimuli that elicit approach behaviour tend to become restricted to the familiar, whilst other stimuli tend to elicit withdrawal and/or aggression. (A balance of unfamiliar with familiar tends to elicit exploration.)

It will be evident that, comparatively simple in principle though these twin processes are, the effects they have on the way an animal's behaviour becomes organised are far-reaching. On the one hand, when the animal is reared in its environment of evolutionary adaptedness, the resulting organisation of behaviour tends to maintain it in proximity to animals that are friendly and to places that are safe and, in addition, tends to keep it away from predators and other dangers. By having these effects the resulting organisation has survival value. When an animal is reared in an environment other than its environment of evolutionary adaptedness, on the other hand, the resulting organisation of behaviour may be very different. Sometimes it is bizarre, sometimes inimical to survival.

One type of deviant, and often unadapted, behavioural organisation that follows rearing in an atypical environment is illustrated by the literature on unusual animal friendships. When young animals of different species are reared together, friendships between them can be produced, even when the two belong to species such as cat and mouse that in nature are 'hereditary enemies'. Another type of deviant organisation is seen in animals brought up in a severely restricted environment. Such animals are usually utterly undiscriminating in their behaviour, tending either to avoid all objects or to approach all objects. For example, experiments with two-year-old chimpanzees reared in a restricted environment show that they do not investigate or handle novel objects and that the more restricted the environment in which they are brought up the more timid they are. On the other hand, a series of experiments in which puppies were raised in confined conditions led to their approaching everything novel to a degree which was dangerous. In each case the resulting behaviour was undiscriminating and, as such, not well adapted to survival.

Much of the linking of particular stimuli with particular behavioural systems is achieved by a process of restriction, namely by reducing a wide range of potentially effective stimuli to a much narrower range; occasionally, however, such linking is achieved by an opposite process, namely by extending a narrow range to make it wider. An example is the way in which maternal behaviour in mice is elicited more readily and by more kinds of baby-like stimulus, e.g. dead babies, after the female has had experience of normal live babies than it can be before she has had that experience.

The phases of the life-cycle during which restriction of potentially eliciting stimuli (or extension of them) can occur are often brief. See the sections on sensitive periods (p. 161) and on imprinting (p. 166).

Elaboration of primitive behavioural systems and their supersession by sophisticated systems

In the neonate there are some behavioural systems, notably those mediating reproduction, that either are not active at all or, and more frequently, are active but are still insufficiently organised to achieve a functional consequence. Their ontogeny is considered in the next section. Here we are concerned with the development only of systems that are functional from the first.

In Chapter 5 an account is given of the many different ways in which a behavioural system can be organised—from the type responsible for the simplest of fixed action patterns to the type responsible for the most elaborate of goal-corrected sequences. In comparison with those of the mature animal, the behavioural systems functional in newborn mammals tend to be of the simpler types. In the course of development, behavioural systems of more complex types become operative, and not infrequently a function fulfilled at first by a system of simple type is fulfilled later by a system of more sophisticated type.

An example of a change of system occurring very early in life is seen in goslings. In their first twenty-four hours, following behaviour is elicited by any moving object. After another day or two, however, not only is it elicited by a familiar object only, but, when the object is absent, a gosling will *seek* the familiar object. Thus behaviour initially organised as a simple goal-corrected system quickly becomes reorganised as part of a plan. Similarly, the attachment behaviour of infant monkeys evolves from a simple reflexive grasping to complex sequences of following and clinging, organised also as components of a plan.

Change of control from a simple system to one organised on more sophisticated lines is commonly due to the simple system's becoming incorporated within the more sophisticated one. Once it is so incorporated, activation of the simpler system comes under more discriminating control than it was earlier. Instead of its being activated immediately on receipt of elementary stimuli (of a greater or narrower range), activation is inhibited until such time as certain very special conditions obtain. Realisation of such conditions may be awaited passively, or it may be actively promoted by behaviour of an altogether different but appropriate sort—for example, the gosling's seeking behaviour.

In adult carnivores and primates, behaviour appears sometimes to be structured in terms of simple plan hierarchies. For example, the ways in which lions hunt prey or a troop of baboons changes its formation to guard against predators are most easily understood on this assumption. Nevertheless such sophisticated ways of organising behaviour are exhibited only by relatively mature animals: young lions and young baboons are not capable of such organisation.

A change in the type of system controlling behaviour from a simple stimulus-response type to a goal-corrected type is often referred to as a change from behaviour governed by trial and error to behaviour governed by insight. By Piaget it is referred to as a change from behaviour organised on the basis of sensori-motor intelligence to behaviour organised on the basis of symbolic and preconceptual thought. To illustrate what he has in mind by this step in development Piaget (1947) writes: 'sensori-motor intelligence acts like a slow motion film, in which all the pictures are seen in succession but without fusion, and so without the continuous vision necessary for understanding the whole', whereas the more advanced mode of organisation resembles a film shown at the proper speed.

In human beings psychological development is characterised not only by simple systems' being superseded by goal-corrected systems, but also by the individual's becoming increasingly aware of the set-goals he has adopted, by his developing increasingly sophisticated plans for achieving them, and by his increasing ability to relate one plan to another, to detect incompatibility between plans and to order them in terms of priority. In psycho-analytic terminology these changes are described as being due to the supersession of id by ego.

The first steps in such development are illustrated by the change that takes place during a child's first two or three years of life in the types of system effecting bladder control, a process studied by McGraw(1943). During the first year of human life voiding of bladder contents is controlled by a reflex mechanism, sensitive during the first six months to a wide range of stimuli and becoming restricted during the second six months to a more limited range. Early in the second year the performance loses the automaticity of a reflex mechanism. The infant appears, however, still unaware both of the act itself and of its consequences, and for a brief spell he may become more co-operative and predictable in his performance. This phase also passes, however, and many children become especially unco-operative for a while. Finally, usually towards the end of the second year, control becomes vested in a far more complex behavioural system, a system organised to take account both of the child's posture and of his circumstances. In this phase voiding of contents is inhibited (usually) until he has found and positioned himself on a suitable receptacle. Such behaviour, it is evident, is structured to achieve a set-goal, namely void into receptacle, and is organised on the basis of a simple master plan. In the execution of the plan, shift from one phase of the required behavioural sequence to the next phase, e.g. seek pot to sit on pot, is dependent on a process of information feedback. Success in the first phase, seek pot, is moreover dependent on the child's having an adequate cognitive map of the family living accommodation.

Thus a simple response initially sensitive to a broad range of unpatterned stimuli becomes incorporated within a behavioural system organised as a plan hierarchy and sensitive to very specific percepts.

A comparable succession of increasingly sophisticated systems, it is believed, mediates human attachment behaviour. Whereas in the early months such behaviour consists only of reflexive and tracking movements, in the second and third years it is organised in terms of set-goals and plans. These plans become organised in increasingly complex ways and come ultimately to include sub-plans one set-goal of which may be to change the behavioural systems and set-goals of the mother-figure to whom the child is attached. These themes form the substance of Part IV.

Yet another example of the increasing sophistication of the systems that in a human being are successively employed to fulfil a single function is to be found in behaviour leading to food-intake. In the neonate, food-intake is a consequence of behaviour organised as a chain of simple fixed action patterns— rooting, sucking, swallowing: they are activated by relatively unspecific environmental stimuli, usually when the neonate's internal condition is of a certain sort. After a few months, feeding behaviour is initiated only when external conditions are perceived to conform to a certain expected pattern—mother ready with breast, bottle, or spoon. By the second year many new sorts of behaviour have been enlisted in the service of food-intake— seizing food, conveying to mouth, biting, chewing— and linkage between different sorts has become organised more as a plan than as a chain. As a child grows to be an adult the plan becomes more complex and the period of time over which it is to be executed grows longer—buying food, preparing it, cooking it, etc. Ultimately in adults of even undeveloped communities food-intake becomes a culminating point in a master plan that in execution may comprehend an agricultural year and contain as sub-plans a large array of cultivating, harvesting, storing, and cooking techniques.

Thus whereas during infancy and childhood humans are incapable of structuring their behaviour in any way more complex than the simplest of plans, in adolescence and adulthood behaviour is habitually structured on the basis of elaborate plan hierarchies. This tremendous development in the sophistication of the behavioural organisations employed is made possible, of course, by the increasing capacity of the growing human child to use symbols, especially language.

It is because, during human development, the behaviour employed to fulfil a function changes in its organisation from the simple and stereotyped to the complex and variable that it is customary to say that humans show no instinctive behaviour. An alternative way to put it is that systems responsible for instinctive behaviour usually become incorporated in sophisticated systems so that the typical and recognisable patterns expected of instinctive behaviour are no longer seen except when a set-goal is about to be reached.

Upgrading of control during individual development from

simple to more sophisticated systems is no doubt in large part a result of the growth of the central nervous system. A comparison by Bronson (1965) of what is known of the behavioural capabilities of different parts of the human brain and of their state of development during the early years of life with what is known of the increasing sophistication of the behavioural systems in operation at each age suggests that during human development brain structure and behavioural structure keep closely in step.

During the first month after birth the neocortex of the human baby is little developed and, in keeping with that, behaviour is at the level only of reflexive and tracking movements. During the third month some parts of the neocortex probably become functional and then responses become sensitive to pattern and for short periods can be delayed. For example, by three months a baby may be content to wait whilst his mother prepares to feed him, something he does not do in the early weeks. Nevertheless, throughout the first two years of life the development of the elaboration areas of the neocortex lags far behind that of the primary projection areas and, in correspondence with that lag, cognitive processes and plans do not develop beyond a comparatively primitive level.

Even by the time the second birthday is reached the prefrontal lobes remain very little developed. These parts of the brain, evidence suggests, are necessary if an individual is to inhibit immediate response so that a plan of action, dependent on factors not present in the immediate environment, can be carried to completion. Consistent with that, it is found that only towards the end of the preschool years are most children able to make a choice that gives substantial weight to factors not present in the here and now.

Thus it seems clear that throughout many years of childhood the sophistication of the behavioural systems that can be developed is strictly limited by the state of development of the brain. Without the necessary neural equipment, behavioural equipment cannot be elaborated; and, until it is elaborated, behaviour remains more in keeping with the pleasure principle than with the reality principle.

During ontogeny the supersession of simple behavioural systems by increasingly sophisticated ones, including plan hierarchies, is the rule. The advantages in terms of adaptedness and efficiency are obvious. So too are the dangers. The repeated supersession of one system by another provides countless opportunities for a faulty transition to occur and for the resulting behavioural system to prove less efficient and adapted instead of becoming more so.

Integration of behavioural systems into functional wholes

So far we have dealt with systems that are functional from the first and that during ontogeny are superseded by more sophisticated systems that continue to fulfil the same function. Other systems, however, start by being non-functional and become so only when they become integrated with other systems. When first activated, each component gives rise only to an isolated movement, or to a movement that occurs in an inappropriate context or in the wrong place in a sequence.

An example is the nut-burying behaviour of a squirrel. This is a complex sequence, including digging, depositing the nut, pushing it down with the snout, covering it over, and stamping. Though each bit of behaviour appears at a certain age and requires no practice, if the sequence as a whole is to be effective some practice is usually necessary. For example, an inexperienced animal may dig a hole and deposit a nut, but perform covering movements at the wrong place. Only with practice is the sequence so performed that the usual functional consequences follow.

The occurrence in young animals of instinctive behaviour that is so ineptly executed that it has no functional consequence is illustrated also in the development of reproductive behaviour. A great tit whilst still a fledgling may, for example, show isolated fragments of reproductive behaviour — snatches of sub-song, nest-building, and copulatory behaviour — but those fragments appear in contexts quite divorced from the context in which they appear in the adult. Young mammals of many species and of both sexes commonly mount each other, ineptly and without passage of semen into vagina. Studies of primates, of which there are now several, are of especial interest to psychoanalysis.

In the rhesus monkey sexual maturity is not reached until after four years of age. Nevertheless, fragments of sexual behaviour are seen from the earliest weeks. In young males penile erections have been observed in a number of infants from about six weeks of age and occur especially when the infant is being groomed by his mother. Pelvic thrusts are first seen a little later and not necessarily when two animals are in a mounting position. Not infrequently, the animal towards which the thrusts are directed is the infant's mother.

Erection and thrusting have been observed also in chimpanzee infants. In both rhesus monkey and chimpanzee they may be elicited in situations in which the general level of excitement is high; for example, upon rejoining a companion after brief separation, at feeding-time, when strangers are present, and when the animal is physically restrained. In a review of the subject, Mason (1965a) concludes that 'the various constituents [of male mating behaviour] seem to appear at different stages of ontogeny and are differentially related to experience and to eliciting conditions'.

Observations such as these make it plain that fragments of sexual behaviour of a non-functional kind occur in immature members of many, perhaps all, species of primate and are not infrequently first exhibited towards parents. The 'component sexual instincts' that are active in human infancy and childhood, and to which Freud called attention, are thus not confined to man: probably in all mammals infantile sexuality is the rule.

In human children systematic observation of non-functional fragments of sexual behaviour is not easily carried out. Recently, however, Lewis (1965) has reported on the incidence of pelvic thrust movements in human infants, starting at eight to ten months of age:

> It occurs only in conditions of maximum security. . . . In a moment of apparent delight, the child clasps the mother, perhaps while lying relaxed on her breast. Throwing his arms about her neck, nuzzling her chin, he begins rapid rotating pelvic thrusts at a frequency of about two per second. This does not last long (10–15 seconds). It is not usually accompanied by erection . . . and does not result in anything suggesting orgasm. . . . It is not restricted to boys. The mother of three girls observed it in all her daughters. . . . [It] decreases with the gradual decrease in intimate holding contact . . . [but] has been observed in children over three years of age. . . . It does not occur in connection with feeding, dressing or active play, although occasionally thrusting has been seen when the child is in relaxed ventral contact with a blanket or pillow.

Any observer of two- or three-year-old children playing together has noticed occasions when, with much excitement, a little boy and a little girl assume positions typical of adult coitus. Neither, it is evident, has more than the vaguest idea of the post-pubertal set-goal of the behavioural sequence one bit of which they are enacting.

Another example of typical items of instinctive behaviour occurring in the immature but in sequences insufficiently organised for the result to be functional is the maternal behaviour of little girls, and sometimes also of little boys. For a longish period a child of three may act in a typically maternal way towards a doll, or even towards a real baby. Then something distracts her, the maternal behaviour ends abruptly, and for a long stretch of time the doll, or baby, is left neglected.

The processes whereby these early-appearing fragments of instinctive behaviour come to be integrated into complete sequences with their normal functional consequences are probably multifarious. One sort are those, discussed already, that lead the stimulus objects that activate a behavioural system, and that terminate it or guide it, to become restricted. An interesting example is the way in which a number of responses in a newly hatched chick, initially discrete from one another, come as a rule all to be directed towards a mother hen. Experiment shows that in the early days after hatching a chick will (a) follow a moving object, (b) seek a haven of safety when it is alarmed, and (c) seek warmth when it is cold. Although in artificial conditions it is possible so to rear the chick that each of these behavioural systems is directed towards a different object, e.g. following towards a cardboard box, a haven of safety in a sack, and warmth at a radiator, in the natural environment all three become directed to the mother hen.

Processes of a closely related sort that result in behavioural fragments becoming functionally integrated are those that lead a behavioural system responsible for some simple item of behaviour to become a unit in one or more chains.

Yet another sort of process is one that integrates a piece of behaviour within a causal hierarchy. This can occur following a change in the causal relation between a pattern of behaviour and the internal state of the animal.

It might confidently be supposed that feeding behaviour would be most readily elicited when an animal is hungry, and the hungrier it is, it might be thought, the more readily would the behaviour be elicited. This is by no means always so, however, at least not in the very young. For example, when a fledgling great tit starts to peck it is most likely to do so when it is *not* hungry: when it is hungry it begs food from its parents. Similarly, experiment suggests that sucking behaviour in puppies is at first independent of both hunger and food-intake. Later in development pecking and sucking become elicited most readily in conditions of hunger and, by those means, are brought, together with other behaviour contributing to food-intake, within a system organised in terms of causal hierarchy.

If one effect of experience is that a particular response comes to be elicited only when the animal is in the appropriate physiological condition, e.g. hunger, another effect can be just the opposite. Thus the sexual behaviour of the male cat first becomes organised into a functional sequence when two conditions are met: (a) androgen level is high and (b) the cat has experience of mating. Once so organised, sexual behaviour may subsequently be exhibited even at times when androgen level is low. It is at least possible that the way in which the male cat's sexual behaviour is organised changes from a chain-linked system to a goal-corrected system. Whether or not this is so, a change of that sort is fairly common in higher mammals. The new behavioural system is then not only more efficient but likely to acquire some degree of autonomy from the conditions initially necessary to elicit it.

These examples illustrate a very general principle of behavioural development. This is that, once a sequence of behaviour has become organised, it tends to persist and does so even when it has developed on non-functional lines and even in the absence of the external stimuli and/or the internal conditions on which it first depended. The precise form that any particular piece of behaviour takes and the sequence within which it is first organised are thus of the greatest consequence for its future.

Because of a human's immense capacity to learn and to develop complex behavioural systems, it is usual for his instinctive behaviour to become incorporated into flexible behavioural sequences that vary from individual to individual. Thus once a human has had experience of reaching a consummatory situation the behaviour that leads to it is likely to become reorganised in terms of a set-goal and a plan hierarchy. That is what appears to occur in sexual behaviour.

Before intercourse and orgasm have been experienced human sexual behaviour appears to be organised largely as a chain. After experience it is reorganised more as a plan with a set-goal. Although such reorganisation leads the behavioural sequence for which a system is responsible to become more efficient in achieving predictable outcome, it may not be without drawbacks. For example, once the consummatory situation and act are foreseen, an individual may seek them precipitately, omitting intermediate steps, and the satisfaction experienced may be much less than was expected.

Whereas with experience the consummatory situation (or act) of an instinctive behavioural system comes often or always to be foreseen, whether or not its function is also foreseen before the behaviour is performed is much less certain. In the case of animals it presumably never is. In the case of man it sometimes is, but perhaps more often it is not. For example, though the functional consequences of sexual behaviour are no doubt usually known about before intercourse is practised, they may not be. The functional consequences of eating are likely to be only imperfectly understood even by adults, and the functional consequences of attachment behaviour, it is argued in later chapters, remain largely unknown even in sophisticated circles.

The fact that in man function is sometimes known about can lead to two sorts of aberrant behaviour. One is performing the behaviour but at the same time deliberately preventing the functional consequences from following, e.g. intercourse with contraception, eating food that is non-nutritious. The other is fulfilling the functions without performing the instinctive behaviour, e.g. artificial insemination, tube-feeding.

Sensitive periods of development

Enough has been said already to make it clear that the form taken by the behavioural equipment of an adult of many species of bird or mammal is to great extent dependent on the environment in which it is reared. For some systems in some species the degree of sensitivity to environment may change relatively little during the life-cycle; more often, probably, sensitivity to environment is greater at one phase than at another; and sometimes a behavioural system is highly sensitive at one phase and then ceases to be so.

The best-known examples of sensitive periods in the development of behavioural equipment are those in which the stimuli that activate or terminate a system become sharply and perhaps irreversibly restricted. Other examples concern the forms taken by motor patterns and by set-goals.

Earlier in this chapter it was pointed out that in young animals there is a marked tendency for stimuli identified as familiar to evoke approach behaviour and for stimuli identified as strange to evoke avoidance. A special case of this occurs during the development of following behaviour in ducklings and goslings. In the hours after hatching, young birds follow whatever moving object they first perceive. Not only this, but they very quickly reach a point when they will follow only the object already followed and will avoid all others. This rapid learning of the familiar and then following it is known as 'imprinting'. Something similar occurs in young mammals. Because these findings are highly relevant to any discussion of the human child's tie to his mother they are given the next section of the chapter to themselves (p. 166).

The range of objects towards which other behavioural systems are potentially directed may also be subject to sharp and apparently irreversible restriction at certain other phases of the life-cycle.

An example, which is of the greatest interest to psychoanalysts, concerns the mode of selection of objects towards which sexual behaviour is directed. Complete sequences of sexual behaviour are not usually seen in birds or mammals before they reach a certain age (though isolated fragments of such behaviour usually are). Nevertheless, the range of objects towards which such behaviour is later to be directed by a given individual is, in some species at least, determined long before the individual reaches sexual maturity. This is shown very plainly when an animal is brought up with animals of a different species and, as often happens, comes to direct all its sexual behaviour towards individuals of that species: in animals brought up in a human home sexual behaviour is sometimes directed towards men and women.

Exact information on the phase of immature development during which the nature of such sex objects is determined, or at least greatly influenced, in different species is still scarce. For this reason recent experiments with young mallard ducklings are of interest. Schutz (1965a) has found that the kind of bird towards which adult male mallards direct their sexual behaviour is much influenced by the kind of bird with which they spend the period of their lives that starts at about three weeks and ends at about eight weeks, namely long before complete sequences of sexual behaviour occur. When brought up with a foster-mother or with foster-siblings of their own species, male mallards always mate, as might be expected, with females of their own species; and the same is true when they are reared with birds of their own species and a few others of different, though related, species. When brought up with birds of related species only, however, two-thirds of them mate only with a female of that other species. Nevertheless, when they are reared with birds of a species quite unrelated to them, e.g. chicken or coot, the sexual preferences of male mallards are not directed to individuals of this other species.

These findings show that sexual preference in the mallard drake is biased from the start towards birds of his own species; that it is sufficiently labile environmentally to be directed towards birds of a closely related species; but that it is sufficiently stable environmentally never to be directed towards birds of an unrelated species.

Another finding of Schutz is that rearing with a foster-mother of another species is more likely to lead to a preference for a female of that species than is rearing with foster-siblings. Since, however, it is rare for birds brought up together to mate with each other, it is clear that the sexual preference established in these early weeks is for members of the species in general and not for any individual of it in particular.

Schutz (1965b) also reports the conditions which lead a mallard drake to select a homosexual partner. When reared with birds of both sexes male mallards select females. When brought up for not less than seventy-five days in a group comprising only males, however, they form homosexual pairs and are henceforward uninterested in females. Thenceforward preference for a homosexual partner is remarkably stable: it persists despite the fact that both members of the pair always take a masculine role and copulation is never achieved.

Stability in the class of object towards which sexual behaviour is directed, once a preference has been established, is indeed common in many species. Despite its inadequacy both for the sexual act and for functional consequences, once a preferred class of sexual object has been established a shift to a more adequate class is not usual even though the members of the more adequate class are available. In man the fetishist male is a case in point.

The objects towards which maternal behaviour may be directed are in many species of bird and mammal also environmentally labile. A notorious example is the devotion shown by small birds in caring for a young cuckoo that happens to have appeared in their nest. Many other species of bird will act as foster-parents to young of a strange species, and there are countless anecdotes of female mammals acting as foster-mothers to young of another species. In most cases, however, such perverse direction of maternal behaviour is plastic; that is to say, an experience of fostering young of a different species does not result in a permanent preference for young of that species.

There is, however, much evidence that in certain species of mammal the individual young creature towards which maternal behaviour is to be directed is sharply delimited during a sensitive phase occurring shortly after parturition. Shepherds have long known this fact through trying to get a ewe who has lost her lamb to adopt the orphaned lamb of another ewe. So fixated on the lost lamb is the ewe that only with difficulty is the shepherd able to persuade her to mother the orphan. This sharp restriction of objects towards which maternal behaviour is directed is strikingly illustrated in an experiment reported by Hersher, Moore, and Richmond (1958). Soon after twin kids had been born to a nanny-goat one of the twins was removed for two hours and then returned to the mother, whilst the other twin stayed with the mother throughout. Whereas the nanny-goat proceeded to mother the twin left with her, she refused to have anything to do with the twin that had been removed. A limiting of the objects towards which mothering behaviour is directed evidently occurs in this species in a matter of hours after parturition.

The forms that motor patterns take and the ways in which they become integrated into functional (or non-functional) sequences are known also in some cases to pass through sensitive phases. Examples are the stereotyped motor movements characteristic of many animals brought up alone in the confines of a small cage. Although non-adaptive, once established they tend to persist even when conditions are changed to those of the environment of evolutionary adaptedness. A similar perseveration of motor movements once established is familiar to all who play games entailing muscular co-ordination. If a person has acquired a particular version of a stroke at tennis, or similar game, he thenceforward finds it extremely difficult to abandon that version in favour of an improved one and he is apt constantly to regress to the version first acquired.

It is evidence of this kind, derived both from environmentally stable and from environmentally labile behaviour, that leads Hinde to conclude that the performance of any response is, *ipso facto*, likely to increase the probability that that response will be performed on subsequent occasions.

It has already been described how the class of object towards which sexual behaviour is to be directed tends, in some species at least, to pass through a sensitive phase occurring before puberty. In primates there is clear evidence that the motor patterns of sexual behaviour also pass through a sensitive phase of development. Following a long series of experiments in which Harlow and his colleagues have reared infant rhesus monkeys in a number of different social environments, all differing greatly from the environment of evolutionary adaptedness, Harlow concludes:

> A large body of observational data from the Wisconsin laboratories indicates that heterosexual behaviour is greatly influenced by early experience, and the failure of infants to form effective infant–infant affectional relations delays or destroys adequate adult heterosexual behaviour (Harlow and Harlow, 1965).

Although in earlier publications (e.g. 1962) Harlow and Harlow reported that behaviour develops normally provided the young monkey has play experience with his age-mates, even though he has no experience of being mothered by a monkey mother, more recent findings show that there are considerable individual differences and that not all such monkeys are heterosexually normal as adolescents and adults. In a personal communication Harlow writes: 'I am now quite convinced that there is no adequate substitute for monkey mothers early in the socialization process.'

Harlow and Harlow report that, in the rhesus monkey, male sexual behaviour is more labile environmentally than is female sexual behaviour. A difference of this kind, and one even more pronounced, is reported also for chimpanzees. In a comparative study of the development of male sexual behaviour in primates, Mason (1965a) observes:

> The integration of these responses into the adult mating pattern occurs much earlier in monkeys than in chimpanzees . . . If the male monkey is provided adequate social contacts [but not otherwise], it develops the sexual pattern characteristic of the adult well in advance of puberty, whereas under similar conditions the chimpanzee apparently does not. . . . On the other hand, the male monkey that has not achieved the adult pattern by adolescence is unlikely to do so later, whereas the chimpanzee is capable of such learning. . . . The male monkey whose opportunities for social learning have been curtailed until adolescence is probably handicapped in his sexual adjustment by the presence [in him] of strong playful and aggressive tendencies.

Mason's last sentence draws attention to the fact that, if social behaviour, including sexual and parental behaviour, is to be adaptive, certain responses have to be inhibited, or at least restrained. For example, in a male, intense aggressive behaviour that is adaptive when directed towards predators, and also sometimes when directed towards other adult or adolescent males, is likely to be maladaptive when directed towards females or young. Similarly, attachment behaviour and parental behaviour have to be exhibited on their proper occasions if they are to be adaptive. To perform an adaptive social role an adult mammal must, indeed, be extremely discriminating in the manifestation of his various social responses, and must preserve a nice balance between them.

Exactly what sensitive periods there may be in the development of adult social responses in non-human primates, and exactly what conditions and experiences are necessary in infancy, childhood, and adolescence if they are to develop adaptively, remain uncertain.[1] This is even more true of humans. That there are sensitive periods in human development seems more than likely. Until far more is known about them it is wise to be cautious and to assume that the more the social environment in which a human child is reared deviates from the environment of evolutionary adaptedness (which is probably father, mother, and siblings in a social environment comprising grandparents and a limited number of other known families) the greater will be the risk of his developing maladaptive patterns of social behaviour.

Imprinting

Usage of the Term

Since it is often asked whether imprinting occurs in the human infant it is as well to be clear what the term means and how it is at present applied.

The term 'imprinting' is used today in two distinct ways, both of which stem from Lorenz's pioneer studies of goslings and ducklings (Lorenz, 1935). One usage is narrow, the other broad.

In its narrow usage the term is tied tightly to Lorenz's original ideas about imprinting. In his early papers Lorenz not

[1] For example, new observations of the behaviour as adults of rhesus monkeys reared in isolation in another laboratory fail to confirm Harlow's finding that they show major impairment of heterosexual behaviour. Neither the research worker, Meier (1965), nor Harlow find it possible to account for the lack of agreement in their findings.

only called attention to the fact that in many species of bird attachment behaviour comes quickly to be focused on a particular object, or class of objects, but postulated also that the process whereby that occurred had unique properties: 'imprinting has a number of features which distinguish it fundamentally from a learning process. It has no equal in the psychology of any other animal, least of all a mammal' (Lorenz, 1935). The four distinctive properties that Lorenz attributed to imprinting are: (i) that it takes place *only* during a brief critical period in the life-cycle, (ii) that it is *irreversible*, (iii) that it is *supra-individual learning*, and (iv) that it *influences patterns of behaviour that have not yet developed* in the organism's repertoire, e.g. the selection of a sexual partner. Lorenz also identified imprinting as the learning that occurs in a young bird in the course of the particular activity of following a moving object.

During the thirty years since Lorenz made these claims the position has changed. On the one hand, more detailed knowledge of the phenomena to which Lorenz drew attention shows that neither the critical period nor the irreversibility is as clear-cut as he had supposed; and it shows further that learning of the same kind occurs even when the young creature is not engaged in following—when it is exposed to a stationary pattern, for instance. On the other hand, thanks largely to Lorenz's own work, it is now recognised that some of the features once thought to be distinctive of imprinting apply in some degree also to many other cases of learning, including learning in mammals. Thus what appeared at first to be a contrast of black and white is found on examination to be a graduated series of shades of grey.

These shifts of perspective have led the term imprinting to acquire a more generic meaning. So used, imprinting refers to whatever processes may be at work in leading the filial attachment behaviour of a young bird or mammal to become directed preferentially and stably towards one (or more) discriminated figure(s). By extension, it may also be used to refer to processes that lead other forms of behaviour to be directed preferentially towards particular objects, for example maternal behaviour towards particular young, and sexual behaviour towards particular mate(s). To quote Bateson (1966):

Although many responses become restricted to the stimuli which first elicited them, the development of social preferences in birds provides a particularly striking example; so much so, indeed, that the processes by which other preferences and habits are acquired are frequently classified by their likeness to it. This process which restricts social preferences to a specific class of objects is generally referred to as 'imprinting'.

Amongst other sorts of behaviour that have also been brought within the ambit of the term is the development of an animal's preference for a particular habitat or home (e.g. Thorpe, 1956).

In the late 1960s it has become almost academic to ask which is the better usage of the term, the narrow or the broad. For in two standard reviews of the subject both the authors, Sluckin (1965) and Bateson (1966), use it in its generic sense. The truth is that, although some of his initial hypotheses were mistaken, the phenomena to which Lorenz drew attention remain so striking and the term he introduced so telling that, whatever the exact processes may be, the term itself has come to stay.

Used in a generic sense the term always implies: (a) the development of a clearly defined preference, (b) a preference that develops fairly quickly, and usually during a limited phase of the life-cycle, and (c) a preference that, once formed, remains comparatively fixed. Whilst the responses that may be elicited specifically by the preferred figure may be of many sorts, and may change as an individual matures, they are all of an approach variety (including occasionally approach-attack).

Beyond these basic implications, however, current usage leaves much open. It leaves open in particular whether the processes underlying the phenomena in different species are all of a single sort or whether they differ from species to species, from order to order, or from class to class. This is important since, as Hinde is constantly emphasising, the lines of evolution that led to birds on the one hand and mammals on the other parted company as long ago as the days of the early reptiles. Since there was then no attachment behaviour, it follows that each higher branch of the animal kingdom has developed attachment behaviour independently of the other. Though the resulting forms of behaviour may look remarkably alike, that likeness is due only to convergent evolution; and it may therefore conceal utterly different underlying processes.

Why, then, bother with what occurs in birds? The reason is that, as a result of the extensive experimental work done with them during the past decade, issues have been sharpened and questions reformulated. For practical purposes, indeed, the present meaning of the term imprinting is the meaning it comes to have as a result of studies of the attachment behaviour of birds.

Imprinting in Birds

The following summary is derived from the reviews by Sluckin (1965) and Bateson (1966) and also owes much to Hinde (1961, 1963, 1966):

i. Within a short time of hatching young birds of many ground-nesting species show a clear preference for almost any object of which they have had experience, tending thenceforward to remain in visual and auditory contact with it. This commonly entails not only approaching it, staying near it, and following when it moves, but also searching for it when it is absent. It entails also changes of call according to whether the preferred object is present or absent. In the preferred object's absence the young bird is apt to give distress calls but, when the object is found, distress calling ceases and is replaced by contentment calling. Thus a wide variety of behaviour comes to be affected by the bird's becoming imprinted.

ii. Although by definition young birds are open to be imprinted to a broad range of stimulus objects, visual and auditory, they can be more effectively imprinted to some than to others. Thus, imprinting to something in movement or to something with conspicuous pattern is usually quicker and more lasting than to something stationary or of little patterning. Moreover, for some species at least, simultaneous exposure to auditory stimuli, such as quacking, much increases the effectiveness of visual stimuli. Thus, from the first, a young bird is strongly biased to become imprinted to some objects rather than to others.

iii. Although Lorenz suggested that the process of imprinting is more or less instantaneous, and perhaps an example of one-trial learning, it is now clear that the longer a bird is exposed to an object the stronger its preference for that object becomes.

iv. The process of imprinting seems to have much in common with the form of learning known as 'perceptual learning' or 'exposure learning', 'for in both cases the responsiveness to a stimulus is influenced by previous experience of that stimulus independently of its association with any reward' (Hinde, 1966). This view leads both Hinde and Sluckin to agree with Lorenz that imprinting is different from other forms of learning in that it is 'neither associative nor reinforced, at least, not in the same way as conditioning, whether classical or instrumental' (Sluckin, 1965).[1]

v. There is a sensitive period during which learning the properties of the preferred object is most readily initiated. Since some learning can occur both before and after the phase of maximum sensitivity, Lorenz's original suggestion of a critical period with an abrupt onset and end needs some modification, especially in regard to the end.

vi. The age of onset of the sensitive phase in birds, before which imprinting does not occur, is not greatly affected by experience after hatching. This means that the onset of the phase is due to developmental processes that are environmentally stable.

vii. The age at which readiness to imprint declines is much more labile. Conditions influencing it and the processes affecting it are still the subject of debate.

Many experiments show that if a young bird is kept in isolation in drab surroundings it remains unimprinted and still imprintable; whereas once it has become imprinted to an object it becomes increasingly difficult to imprint it to anything else. Thus keeping a bird in isolation can extend the sensitive period (though not indefinitely); but, once imprinting has occurred, the sensitive period ends. Were this the sole process at work no more need be said than that 'imprintability ends as a result of imprinting'.

Though Bateson (1966) is inclined to take this view, it seems likely that, in some species at least, a second process is at work independently of the first. The second process, postulated by Hinde (1963, 1966), is an increase with age in the ease with which fear, or escape, responses are elicited, with consequent decrease in the ease with which they can be habituated.

---

[1] It should be noted that Bateson (1966) is not in full agreement with Sluckin and Hinde. He regards associative learning and exposure learning as less different than they suppose. Nevertheless, none of these workers subscribes to a view, advanced by Moltz (1960), that imprinting to an object results from a young creature's associating the object with a state of low anxiety. As Sluckin (1965) points out, such an explanation is neither necessary nor parsimonious, and is likely to appeal only to those who are convinced that all learning must be reinforced by or associated with drive reduction.

Whether or not this is so, there is no doubt that, once a bird has become imprinted, it is apt to respond with fear to every other object it meets. If it is free to do so, therefore, it avoids any new object, so that exposure to it is brief and imprinting to it cannot take place. The stronger the original imprinting, moreover, the more persistent the avoidance of anything new.

If a young animal is forcibly kept in the presence of a new object, however, the fear response may be partially or wholly habituated. In such circumstances a new object may come in due course to be approached and even followed; and it may even come to be preferred to the original object. Whether or not that happens depends probably on many factors, of which the strength of the original imprinting is likely to be the most important. Since, however, an actual preference for a new object can sometimes be attained, it is evident that there are some conditions in which imprinting is reversible.

viii. There is no doubt that Lorenz overstated the case when he claimed that imprinting is irreversible. The stability of the preference may be high or low and turns on many factors: amongst them are the species of animal, the length of time a young creature has been exposed to the imprinting object, and the behaviour being considered, i.e. whether it be the filial attachment behaviour of the animal in the days or weeks after imprinting or its sexual behaviour in the months or years afterwards. Nevertheless, even if not always irreversible, preferences once firmly established tend to be much more stable than might be expected: many remarkable examples are known of strong preferences persisting in the absence of the imprinted object over long periods of time.

An area in which clarification is still needed is the relation between the learning of individual differences and the learning of species differences. In his original formulation, Lorenz held both that imprinting is supra-individual, namely learning the characteristics of a class of objects such as a species rather than those of a particular individual, and that imprinting influences patterns of behaviour that have not yet developed in the organism's repertoire, e.g. learning the class of object towards which sexual behaviour will later be directed. Now there is some evidence that in a number of species both those processes may occur. Nevertheless, when a young bird learns the characteristics of its parent and follows it, there can be no doubt that the learning is of a particular parent bird and is in no sense supra-individual. (As Hinde (1963) points out, a young bird that failed to discriminate its parent from others would soon be in trouble since a strange parent might well attack it.)

The theme of imprinting in mammals and the question whether anything similar occurs in man is taken up in subsequent chapters, especially Chapter 12.

Comparison of old and new theories of instinctive behaviour

In this and the preceding chapters an account has been given of the way in which many behavioural scientists today look at instinctive behaviour, of some of the problems they confront and some of the concepts they have introduced. In the course of this account there have been many opportunities to show that current instinct theory is grappling with the same problems that traditional psychoanalytic theory has grappled with and is advancing ideas that in a few cases are the same as those of psychoanalysis and in many others are closely related variants of them. Whether or not the new ideas will prove to have better explanatory power than the old, it cannot be said that they neglect either the empirical data of psychoanalysis or those generalisations that spring readily from the data. It is only at a more abstract metapsychological level that substantial differences exist between the two conceptual systems.

The kind of theory outlined is, as already noted, a direct descendant of the theory outlined by Darwin in *The Origin of Species*. It sees instinctive behaviour as the outcome of behavioural structures that are activated by certain conditions and terminated by other conditions. Complex sequences of behaviour are regarded as due to the sequential activation and termination of behavioural units, their sequential appearance being controlled by a superordinate behavioural structure organised as a chain, as a causal hierarchy, as a plan hierarchy, or as some integrate of them all. In a number of these respects the theory proposed incorporates ideas advanced by Freud in such works as *Three Essays on the Theory of Sexuality* (1905) and 'Instincts and their vicissitudes' (1915a), in which he postulates part-instincts, differentiates the aim of an instinct (namely the conditions that terminate instinctive behaviour) and its function, and notes how labile are the objects towards which any particular sort of instinctive behaviour is directed.

It is recognised, however, that the new ideas are the antithesis of certain other ideas that Freud advanced. One such is that of psychical energy that flows and can be discharged through different channels. Others are those to be found in *Beyond the Pleasure Principle* (1920a) and later works, in which Freud attempts to understand particular forms of behaviour as expressions of extremely generalised forces, the life and death instincts. Whereas Freud's later theories conceive of the organism as starting life with a quantum of unstructured energy that during development becomes progressively more structured—'where id is there shall ego be'—current theory, in keeping with many of Freud's earlier ideas, conceives of the organism as starting with, or developing, a large but finite number of structured behavioural systems (some of which are potentially active at birth and some of which become so later) which in the course of development become so elaborated through processes of learning and integration, and in man by imitation and the use of symbols, that the resulting behaviour is of amazing variety and plasticity. Whether or not it is also adapted turns on the many and diverse vicissitudes of ontogeny.

In the system of theory proposed, the belief that to understand the curious and often maladapted twists to which instinctive behaviour is subject requires a hypothesis of a general purpose psychical energy is rejected as redundant. When a behavioural structure is activated physical energy is, of course, employed; but there is no greater need to postulate psychical energy to account for the behaviour of an animal than there is to postulate it in order to account for the behaviour of a mechanical control system. The existence of maladapted behaviour and of behaviour that appears as though it is a substitute for some other behaviour can be accounted for in a number of ways none of which calls for the notion of a psychical energy that can be diverted from one channel to another. Similarly, variations in the intensity of a piece of behaviour are attributable to variations in the activating conditions present and to the developmental state of the behavioural systems activated, and not to a raised pressure of psychical energy. Freud's concept of *Trieb*, so unfortunately mistranslated as 'instinct', is therefore dispensed with; and with it, of course, the 'economic' approach.

The merits of a scientific theory are to be judged in terms of the range of phenomena it embraces, the internal consistency of its structure, the precision of the predictions it can make and the practicability of testing them. On each of these criteria, it is held, the new type of theory scores well. In particular, with concepts such as those advanced and with observational and experimental methods derived from ethology and comparative psychology, it is now possible to undertake a far-reaching programme of research into the social responses of man, from the preverbal period of infancy onwards. In that way the repertoire of behavioural systems mediating human instinctive behaviour may be catalogued and the mode of development of each identified. Each system can be studied to discover the nature of the conditions that activate it and of those that terminate it, and why in some individuals systems come to be activated and terminated by unusual objects. The conditions that lead to a manifestation of certain behaviour at abnormal levels of intensity, either too low or too high, and the conditions that lead to a perpetuation of such a state may be explored. Other main interests are to study the conflicts arising when two or more incompatible systems are activated at once and the modes by which conflict is regulated. Finally, it is of especial interest to investigate the sensitive periods during which processes for regulating conflict develop and the conditions that lead, in an individual, one mode of regulation to become dominant.

Even this brief sketch describes an extensive programme. Clinicians will differ in their evaluation of it and in how they perceive its relatedness to the traditional research method of reconstructing early phases of development from the investigation of later ones. Since, however, the fruits of this new approach are only beginning to be seen, it is perhaps premature to attempt to judge its likely value. For many, the approach carries with it the hope that, by introducing more precise concepts and more rigorous methods to the investigation of early emotional development, it may be initiating a phase when an increasing quantity of reliable data will be available in the light of which alternative theoretical formulations can be judged.

Part III

ATTACHMENT BEHAVIOUR

Chapter 11

The Child's Tie to his Mother: Attachment Behaviour

I began by stating the two facts which have struck me
as new: that a woman's strong dependence on her father
merely takes over the heritage of an equally strong
attachment to her mother, and that this earlier phase
has lasted for an unexpectedly long period of time.

Everything in the sphere of this first attachment to the
mother seemed to me so difficult to grasp in analysis . . .

SIGMUND FREUD (1931)

Alternative theories

Understanding of the response of a child to separation or loss
of his mother-figure turns on an understanding of the bond
that ties him to that figure. In psychoanalytic writings discussion of this theme has been conducted in terms of object
relations.[1] Thus in any description of traditional theory the
terminology of object relations must often be used; in the presentation of a new theory, however, terms such as 'attachment'
and 'attachment-figure' are preferred.

For long, psychoanalysts have been at one in recognising a
child's first human relationship as the foundation stone of his
personality; but there is as yet no agreement on the nature and
origin of that relationship. No doubt because of its very importance differences are sharp and feelings often run high.
Although it can now be taken for granted that all are agreed
on the empirical fact that within twelve months almost all
infants have developed a strong tie to a mother–figure,[2] there
is no consensus on how quickly this comes about, by what

[1] This terminology derives from Freud's theory of instinct in which
the object of an instinct is defined as 'the thing in regard to which or
through which the instinct is able to achieve its aim' (Freud, 1915a,
S.E., **14**, p. 122).

[2] It was explained in Chapter 2 that, although throughout this book
the text refers usually to mothers and not to mother-figures, it is to be
understood that in every case reference is to the person who mothers the

processes it is maintained, for how long it persists, or what function it fulfils.

Until 1958, which saw the publication of Harlow's first papers and of an early version of the views expressed here (Bowlby, 1958), four principal theories regarding the nature and origin of the child's tie were to be found in the psycho-analytical and other psychological literature. They are:

i. The child has a number of physiological needs which must be met, particularly for food and warmth. In so far as a baby becomes interested in and attached to a human figure, especially mother, this is the result of the mother's meeting the baby's physiological needs and the baby's learning in due course that she is the source of his gratification. I shall call this the theory of Secondary Drive, a term which is derived from Learning Theory. It has also been called the cupboard-love theory of object relations.

ii. There is in infants an in-built propensity to relate themselves to a human breast, to suck it and to possess it orally. In due course the infant learns that, attached to the breast, there is a mother and so relates to her also. I propose to term this the theory of Primary Object Sucking.[1]

iii. There is in infants an in-built propensity to be in touch with and to cling to a human being. In this sense there is a 'need' for an object independent of food which is as primary as the 'need' for food and warmth. It is proposed to term this the theory of Primary Object Clinging.

iv. Infants resent their extrusion from the womb and seek to return there. This is termed the theory of Primary Return-to-Womb Craving.

Of these four theories by far the most widely and strongly held has been the theory of secondary drive. From Freud onwards it has underlain much, though by no means all, psycho-analytic writing, and it has also been a common assumption of learning theorists. Representative statements are as follows:

---

child and to whom he becomes attached rather than to the natural mother.

[1] In this nomenclature, the terms 'primary' and 'secondary' refer to whether the response is regarded as developing autonomously or as being wholly derived, through a process of learning, from some more primitive system; throughout they will be used in this sense. The terms have no reference either to the period of life when the response appears or to the primary and secondary processes postulated by Freud.

love has its origin in attachment to the satisfied need for nourishment (Freud, 1940, *S.E.*, **23**, p. 188).

probably the feeding experience can be the occasion for the child to learn to like to be with others (Dollard and Miller, 1950).

My 1958 paper on this theme included a review of the psychoanalytical literature up to 1958, and with some additions this review was republished as an appendix to the first edition of this volume. For another review, especially strong on the learning theory literature, see Maccoby and Masters (1970).

The hypothesis to be advanced here is different from any of those listed above and is built on the theory of instinctive behaviour already outlined. It postulates that the child's tie to his mother is a product of the activity of a number of behavioural systems that have proximity to mother as a predictable outcome. Since in the human child ontogeny of these systems is slow and complex, and their rate of development varies greatly from child to child, no simple statement about progress during the first year of life can be made. Once a child has entered his second year, however, and is mobile, fairly typical attachment behaviour is almost always seen. By that age in most children the integrate of behavioural systems concerned is readily activated, especially by mother's departure or by anything frightening, and the stimuli that most effectively terminate the systems are sound, sight, or touch of mother. Until about the time a child reaches his third birthday the systems continue to be very readily activated. Thenceforward in most children they become less easily activated and they also undergo other changes that make proximity to mother less urgent. During adolescent and adult life yet further changes occur, including change of the figures towards whom the behaviour is directed.

Attachment behaviour is regarded as a class of social behaviour of an importance equivalent to that of mating behaviour and parental behaviour. It is held to have a biological function specific to itself and one that has hitherto been little considered.

In this formulation, it will be noticed, there is no reference to 'needs' or 'drives'. Instead, attachment behaviour is regarded as what occurs when certain behavioural systems are activated. The behavioural systems themselves are believed to develop within the infant as a result of his interaction with his environment of evolutionary adaptedness, and especially of his interaction with the principal figure in that environment, namely his mother. Food and eating are held to play no more than a minor part in their development.

Of the four principal theories found in the literature those of primary object sucking and primary object clinging come closest to the hypothesis now proposed: each postulates an autonomous propensity to behave in a certain kind of way towards objects with certain properties. Theories with which the present hypothesis has nothing in common are those of secondary drive and primary return-to-womb craving: the former is discussed; the latter is dismissed as both redundant and biologically implausible.

The hypothesis proposed represents a development of that advanced by me in 1958. The principal change is due to better understanding of control theory and to recognition of the very sophisticated forms that behavioural systems controlling instinctive behaviour may take. In the present version of the hypothesis it is postulated that, at some stage in the development of the behavioural systems responsible for attachment, proximity to mother becomes a set-goal. In the earlier version of the theory five patterns of behaviour—sucking, clinging, following, crying, and smiling—were described as contributing to attachment. In the new version these same five patterns are still held to be of great importance, but it is postulated that between the ages of about nine and eighteen months they usually become incorporated into far more sophisticated goal-corrected systems. These systems are so organised and activated that a child tends to be maintained in proximity to his mother.

The earlier version of the theory was described as a theory of component instinctual responses. The new version can be described as a control theory of attachment behaviour.

Before this theory is described in greater detail, with some of the evidence on which it rests (see Chapters 12 and 13), it is useful to compare the attachment behaviour seen in human children with that seen in young animals of other species and to consider what is known of the natural history of such behaviour.

Attachment behaviour and its place in nature

In the countryside in springtime there is no more familiar sight than mother animals with young. In the fields, cows and calves, mares and foals, ewes and lambs; in the ponds and rivers, ducks and ducklings, swans and cygnets. So familiar are these sights and so much do we take it for granted that lamb and ewe will remain together and that a flotilla of ducklings will remain with mother duck that the questions are rarely asked: What causes these animals to remain in each other's company? What function is fulfilled by their doing so?

In the species referred to, young are born in a state of development sufficiently advanced for them to be able to move freely within a few hours; and in each case it is observed that when mother moves off in some direction her young commonly follow her. In other species, including carnivores and rodents and including also man himself, development of the neonate is much less advanced. In these species weeks or even months may pass before the young acquire mobility; but once they have done so the same tendency to keep in the vicinity of the mother animal is evident. Admittedly there are times when the young animal strays and the mother may then herself behave in such a way that proximity is restored; but just as frequently the young animal, on finding itself alone, is itself the principal agent for restoring proximity.

The kind of behaviour described is characterised by two main features. The first is maintaining proximity to another animal, and restoring it when it has been impaired; the second is the specificity of the other animal. Often within hours of hatching eggs or giving birth to young, a parent can distinguish its own young from any others and then will behave parentally only to them; the young in their turn come soon to distinguish their own parents from all other adults and thenceforward behave in a special way towards them. Thus both parent and young usually behave towards each other in ways very different from the ways in which they behave towards all other animals. Individual recognition and highly differentiated behaviour are, then, the rule in the parent–young relations of birds and mammals.

Naturally, as with other forms of instinctive behaviour, the usual pattern of development may miscarry. In particular, a young animal may seek proximity to an animal other than its mother, or even to some inanimate object. But in natural conditions such anomalies of development are rare, and they need not detain us further at this point.

In most species there is more than one kind of behaviour shown by young that results in young and mother staying close to one another. For example, a young's vocal calls attract mother to it, and its locomotory movements take it to her. Since both kinds of behaviour, and others as well, have the same consequence, namely proximity, it is useful to have a general term to cover them all; and for this purpose 'attachment behaviour' is used. Any one form of juvenile behaviour that results in proximity can then be regarded as a component of attachment behaviour. This type of terminology follows established ethological tradition. Whenever several different sorts of behaviour commonly have the same consequence (or at least contribute to the same consequence) they are usually gathered into a category and labelled by reference to that consequence. Nest-building behaviour and mating behaviour are two well-known examples.

The behaviour of parents that is reciprocal to the attachment behaviour of juveniles is termed 'caregiving behaviour', and is discussed further in Chapter 13.

Attachment behaviour, and also caregiving behaviour, are common in ground-nesting birds which leave the nest soon after hatching, and both forms of behaviour are present in all species of mammal. Unless there is some mishap of development, attachment behaviour is initially always directed towards the mother. In species where the father plays a major role in upbringing it may come to be directed towards him as well. In humans it may be directed also towards a few other persons (see Chapter 15).

The proportion of the life-cycle during which attachment behaviour is manifested varies greatly from species to species. As a rule it continues until puberty though not necessarily until full sexual maturity is reached. For many species of bird the phase when attachment behaviour ceases is the same for both sexes, namely when the young are ready to pair, which may be at the end of their first winter or, as in geese and swans, at the end of their second or third winter. For many species of mammal, on the other hand, there is a marked difference between the sexes. In the female of ungulate species (sheep, deer, oxen, etc.), attachment to mother may continue until old age. As a result a flock of sheep, or a herd of deer, is built up of young following mother following grandmother following great-grandmother and so on. Young males of these species, by contrast, break away from mother when they reach adolescence. Thenceforward they become attached to older males and remain with them all their lives except during the few weeks each year of the rutting season.

Attachment behaviour in monkeys and apes is exhibited strongly during infancy and childhood, but during adolescence the bond to mother wears thin. Although in the past it has been tacitly assumed that it then ceases, recent evidence shows that, at least in some species, the bond persists into adult life; by so doing it produces sub-groups of animals all of which have the same mother. Reviewing the reports of Sade (1965) for rhesus monkeys and of Goodall (1965) for chimpanzees, Washburn, Jay, and Lancaster (1965) remark that these kinship sub-groups are 'determined by the necessarily close association of mother with newborn infant, which is extended through time and generations and allowed to ramify into close associations between siblings'; and they express their belief 'that this pattern of enduring social relations between a mother and her offspring will be found in other species of primates'.

Because the human infant is born so very immature and is so slow to develop, there is no species in which attachment behaviour takes so long to appear. This is probably one reason why until recent years the behaviour of the human child towards his mother seems not to have been recognised as belonging to the same general category of behaviour that is seen in so many animal species. Another probable reason is that it is only in the past two decades that attachment behaviour in animals has become the subject of systematic study. Whatever the reasons, that the child's tie to his mother is the human version of behaviour seen commonly in many other species of animal seems now indisputable; and it is in this perspective that the nature of the tie is examined.

Nevertheless caution is necessary. The two lines of animal evolution that led ultimately to birds and to mammals have been distinct since the days of the early reptiles, and it is therefore nearly certain that attachment behaviour has evolved independently in the two groups. That, and the fact that brain structure in birds is very different from what it is in mammals, make it more than probable that the behavioural mechanisms mediating attachment behaviour are also very different for the two groups. Any argument used here that is derived from what is known about bird behaviour must, therefore, be recognised as no more than argument from analogy. Argument from what is known about the attachment behaviour of young mammals, on the other hand, has a much better status. And whatever behaviour is found in non-human primates we can be confident is likely to be truly homologous with what obtains in man.

The growth of attachment behaviour in the human child and the course of its change over time are in fact still very poorly documented. Partly because of this but chiefly in order to provide a broader perspective in which to view the human case, the discussion starts with what is known about attachment behaviour in monkey, baboon, and great ape.

Attachment behaviour in non-human primates

At birth or soon after, all primate infants, bar the human, cling to their mothers. Throughout early childhood they are either in direct physical contact with mother or only a few feet or yards from her. Mother reciprocates and keeps the infant close to her. As the young grow older the proportion of the day when they are in direct contact with mother diminishes and the distance of their excursions increases; but they continue to sleep with her at night and to rush to her side at the least alarm. In higher species, it is probable that some attachment to mother is present until adolescence, and in some species the tie continues in weakened form into adult life.

Female young are less active and adventurous than males. During adolescence females are likely to be found in the centre of a group, often in proximity to adult males, whereas adolescent males are likely to be found at the periphery or even on their own.

Descriptions follow of the course of attachment behaviour in the young of four primate species—two Old World monkeys, the rhesus macaque and the baboon, and two great apes, the chimpanzee and the gorilla. Reasons for this selection are:

a. all four species, and especially baboon and gorilla, are adapted to a terrestrial existence;
b. good field studies are now available for all four;
c. for two species, rhesus and chimpanzee, experimental data are also available.

Although for the sake of brevity much of the description that follows is in the form of unqualified statements, it must be remembered not only that there is considerable variation of behaviour between different animals of the same species but that the behaviour typical in one social group of a species may differ in some respects from that typical in another group of the same species. Whilst some of these differences between groups can be accounted for by differences in the habitat that each is living in, some of them appear to be due to innovation started by an animal in one group and passed on to others in its group by social tradition.

Attachment Behaviour in Rhesus Monkeys

Rhesus monkeys have been observed in fairly natural conditions and have been the subjects of much laboratory observation and experiment.[1] They are common throughout Northern India where some still live in forest though many more live in villages and cultivated land. Although rather more of an arboreal than a terrestrial species, much of their day is spent on the ground; at night they resort to the tree tops or a roof. Bands, comprising adults of both sexes, juveniles, and young, are stable over long periods and spend their days and nights in a particular and quite limited locality. In size the bands vary from about fifteen to over a hundred members.

The rhesus monkey reaches puberty at about four years, is full-grown at about six years and may then live another twenty years. Until it is about three years of age a young rhesus monkey in the wild remains close to its mother. At that age 'most males leave their mothers and associate with other adolescents at the edge of the band or shift to other bands' (Koford, 1963a). Females, it is thought, probably remain with their mothers for longer. Sons of high-ranking females also sometimes remain with their mothers; as soon as they become adult these favoured sons are likely to assume a dominant position in the band.

Hinde and his associates have given a very detailed account of infant–mother interaction during the first two and a half years of life in small captive groups of animals (Hinde, Rowell, and Spencer-Booth, 1964; Hinde and Spencer-Booth, 1967).

As soon as they are born some infants immediately cling to their mother's fur, and they tend also to climb up her body. Other infants, however, at first hold arms and legs flexed and are then supported solely by their mother. By no infant was the nipple taken until several hours had elapsed, the longest interval being over nine hours. Once found, the nipple is gripped for

---

[1] For descriptions of behaviour, see Southwick, Beg, and Siddiqi (1965) on rhesus monkeys in Northern India; Koford (1963a and b) and Sade (1965) on the semi-wild colony on a small island off Puerto Rico; Hinde and his associates (1964, 1967) on monkeys living in captivity in small social groups (one adult male, three or four adult females and offspring); and a number of publications by Harlow and his colleagues (e.g. Harlow, 1961; Harlow and Harlow, 1965) on the results of rearing young monkeys in very atypical conditions.

long periods, though only a small proportion of that time is spent sucking.

During the first week or two of its life the infant is in continuous ventro-ventral contact with its mother, spending almost all the daytime hours gripping its mother with hands, feet, and mouth, and at night-time being held by her. Thereafter the infant begins to make short daytime excursions from mother and she from it; but until it is six weeks old virtually none of these excursions extends beyond a two-foot radius—close enough, in fact, for mother to gather the infant to her whenever she wishes. Thenceforward its excursions extend further and last longer. Not until it is about ten weeks old, however, is it spending half the daytime off its mother, and not until after its first birthday does the proportion rise above 70 per cent.

Although during their second year infants spend most of their daytime hours in sight of but out of physical contact with mother, most of them nonetheless are in actual contact with her for a substantial fraction of their day—usually from 10 to 20 per cent of it—and for the whole night. Only after their second birthday does amount of time in physical contact during the day become negligible.

Initiative for breaking and resuming contact lies partly with mother and partly with infant, and the balance changes in a complex way as the infant gets older. During the first few weeks the infants sometimes set out to explore 'in an apparently intrepid manner', and the mothers often restrain them. After the first two months the balance begins to shift. Mother restrains less and starts occasionally to hit or reject: 'From this time the infant comes to play an increasing role in the maintenance of proximity with its mother.' Nevertheless mother continues to take an important part—perhaps discouraging the infant from too close proximity when she is sitting quietly and no danger threatens but initiating quick contact when she is about to move or becomes alarmed.

When the mother moves any distance the infant usually travels under her belly, grasping mother's fur with hands and feet and a nipple with its mouth. During the first week or two some mothers give a little additional support with a hand. Babies quickly learn to adopt this carrying position and also to respond appropriately to a light touch of mother's hand on back of neck or shoulders, which seems to act as a signal that she is moving off. After they have reached three or four weeks of age babies may occasionally ride on mother's back.

During the weeks after the baby first leaves its mother, if it is on the ground and she moves away, it usually follows; and even though it can barely crawl it will still attempt to follow.

These early following attempts are often actively encouraged by the mother, who moves away only slowly and hesitantly, repeatedly looking back at the baby, or even pulling at it to encourage it to come.

Should mother move too fast or depart suddenly the baby 'geckers' and the mother responds by hugging it to her. On other occasions when it is away from its mother it may give a short, high squeaking call, and this too brings mother instantly to pick it up. A baby that loses its mother makes very long calls through protruded lips; and this may lead another female to pick it up. In the event of any sudden disturbance occurring when the baby is off its mother, each at once runs to the other; the baby clings to her in the ventro-ventral position and takes the nipple. Such behaviour continues for some years.

Though after the age of two and a half or three years juveniles usually move away from their mothers, evidence is accumulating that the bond may nevertheless persist and play a large part in determining adult social relationships. In a semi-wild colony that has been observed systematically over the course of many years and where the family history of individuals is known, it has become evident not only that in each band there are stable sub-groups, composed of several adult animals of both sexes and a number of juveniles and infants all of which remain in proximity to one another, but that all the members of such a sub-group may be the children and grandchildren of a single elderly female (Sade, 1965).[1]

Attachment Behaviour in Baboons

The chacma baboon, which is roughly twice the size of a rhesus monkey, has been observed in its natural habitat in several localities in Africa, where it is very common south of the Equator. Some troops live in forested ground but many occupy open savanna. In either case they spend most of their

[1] There seems to be a marked tendency for sons (half-brothers) to stay close to one another and for daughters (half-sisters) also to stay close together. Since in adolescent and adult life sons tend to leave their mother whereas daughters tend not to, a sub-group of relatives of several generations tends always to contain a higher proportion of females than males.

day on the ground, taking to trees or cliffs for sleeping and for refuge from predators. Like rhesus monkeys they live in stable bands, comprising adults of both sexes, juveniles, and young. Bands vary in size from about a dozen individuals to over a hundred. Each band keeps to a limited area of ground, though areas of adjacent bands overlap. Relations between bands are friendly.[1]

The maturation rate of young baboons is a little slower than that of rhesus monkeys. Puberty is reached at about four years and the female first gives birth at about six years. The male, however, who grows to be far larger than the female, is not fully grown until nine or ten years.

A baby baboon remains in close contact and association with its mother throughout its first year of life and, with some interruptions, during its second and third years also. Thereafter the development of males and females differs.

Almost the whole of its first month of life a baby baboon spends clinging to its mother in a ventro-ventral position, exactly like the rhesus monkey. After about five weeks of age the infant departs from its mother occasionally, and it is at this age too that it begins to ride on mother's back. By about four months of age its excursions from mother are more frequent and it may move as far as twenty yards from her. This is also the age when riding mother jockey-style becomes popular (except when she runs or climbs, when the infant resumes ventral clinging), and social play with peers begins. From six months onwards play with peers increases and absorbs a large part of the young baboon's time and energy. Nevertheless, until about twelve months it remains fairly close to mother and always sleeps with her. It rides her less and follows more often on foot.

The second year of a young baboon's life is spent mostly with peers and sees periods of intense conflict with its mother. As long as she is lactating a female baboon does not go through her normal sexual cycles; but when the infant is aged about one year and lactation is ceasing, cycles and mating are resumed. At these times the mother rebuffs her infant's attempts either to take the nipple or to ride on her back, and is rejecting even at night-time. Such rebuffs, DeVore reports, 'seem to make the

[1] See the two joint articles by Hall and DeVore in *Primate Behavior* (ed. DeVore, 1965) and the article by DeVore (1963) on mother–infant relations in free-ranging baboons. For more recent work see Altmann and others (1977) and the book by Altmann (1980) on mothers and infants.

infant more anxious than ever to be in her arms, to hold her nipple in its mouth, and to ride her back to the sleeping trees'. When the sexual swelling has subsided a mother 'often accepts the infant again'. Despite these rebuffs, when either mother or infant is alarmed, they seek each other out; and, when her infant is in trouble with peers or with adult males, mother tries to protect it.

By the end of its second year an infant's mother is likely to have a new baby but the youngster continues to spend time near her and frequently sleeps with her at night. When alarmed, a two-year-old often still runs to its mother though, if a familiar adult male is closer, it may run to him.

By the age of four years adolescent females tend to join adult females and to behave as adults. Males take another four or five years to mature and during this period they begin to show interest in other baboon troops; and by the time they are fully grown most males have transferred to another troop and have severed their ties with mother. A female baboon, by contrast, continues to maintain a close relationship with her mother throughout life, and in some cases does so as well with her female (maternal) siblings.

Attachment Behaviour in Chimpanzees

Chimpanzees have been observed in the forested regions and wooded uplands of Central Africa, which is their natural habitat; and they have for long been the subjects of laboratory experiment. Though they are skilled in arboreal locomotion and sleep in trees, when they travel distances of more than fifty yards they usually keep to the ground; and they always run from an intruder on the ground. Unlike most other primates studied, chimpanzees do not keep close together in stable social groups. Instead, the individuals belonging to what is believed to be a single social group of from sixty to eighty animals break into an ever-changing variety of temporary sub-groups. Each sub-group can comprise animals of any age, sex, or number; but two kinds of sub-group are specially common, one a party of several males together and the other a party of several females with infants.[1]

Chimpanzees are much slower to mature than are rhesus

[1] For descriptions of chimpanzees in the wild see Goodall (1965, 1975), Reynolds and Reynolds (1965) and Pusey (1978); for descriptions of their social behaviour in captivity see Yerkes's *Chimpanzees: A Laboratory Colony* (1943) and others of Yerkes's publications, and also Mason (1965b).

monkeys or baboons. Observations in Tanzania by Pusey (1978) show that female chimpanzees reach puberty at about nine years and first conceive two or three years later. Males also reach sexual maturity at about nine, but take several further years to reach full growth. Although animals are usually found in company with others, companions are constantly changing with the result that the only stable social unit is that of a mother with her infant and older offspring. Goodall (1975) reports that in most of the cases for which evidence is available close relationships between a mother and her offspring, and also between siblings, persist throughout the life-cycle.

Like all other primate infants, the baby chimpanzee spends the whole of its infancy in close proximity to its mother. During its first four months it clings to her in the ventral position and only very occasionally is seen apart from her, and usually then is sitting beside her. Should it venture more than a couple of feet from her, she pulls it back; and should she observe a predator approach she hugs it more closely.

Between the ages of about six and eighteen months the infant more often travels jockey-fashion on mother's back than on her belly, and the time it spends not actually clinging to mother increases. By the end of the period it is out of physical contact with her for as much as 25 per cent of the day, usually playing with age-mates; but it is never out of its mother's sight. Not infrequently it breaks off play to run back to her to sit on her lap or beside her. When mother is about to move off she signals her intention by reaching out to touch the infant, gesturing to it, or, when it is up a tree, tapping softly on the trunk. The infant at once obeys and assumes the carrying position.

The next eighteen months, until the age of three years, see increasing activity away from mother and play with companions, and the young chimpanzee is out of physical contact with mother for as much as 75 to 90 per cent of the day. Nevertheless it continues to be transported by her, jockey-fashion unless she is moving fast, and it still sleeps with her.

Between the ages of four and seven years infants are weaned but, despite being independent of mother for feeding, transport and sleeping, and spending much time playing with age-mates, a young animal continues to spend time with mother and to travel with her. For example, in a study at the Gombe Stream Reserve, Pusey (1978) observed that each of four juvenile females whose mothers were still alive spent at least four-fifths of their time in the company of her mother; and only after their first oestrous did they begin to spend less time with mother and more with adult males. Similarly, up to the time of reaching puberty males were still spending at least half their time with mother; and each of them continued to meet his mother occasionally up to the time of her death. Throughout these years of increasing independence the initiative for departure and return seems to lie with the young animal; no signs of a mother discouraging or rejecting one of her offspring have been observed.

Attachment Behaviour in Gorillas

Gorillas, like chimpanzees, inhabit the tropical rain forests and wooded uplands of Central Africa and have also been the subjects of systematic field observation in recent years. Though animals often sleep in trees and the young play in them, for the rest of the time gorillas are almost entirely terrestrial. Apart from a few adult males, they live in social groups made up of both sexes and all ages, the numbers in a group ranging from half a dozen to nearly thirty. Membership of groups is unstable over periods of years, more so in some groups than in others. Both males and females may leave the natal group at adolescence or later. Meetings between gorilla groups are not always peaceful: several instances of lone males, or males from other groups, attacking females and killing their infants have been observed. Relationships between different chimpanzee communities are also frequently hostile.[1]

Biological evidence suggests that gorillas and chimpanzees are man's nearest relatives.

The rate of maturation of gorillas is roughly the same as that of chimpanzees though, if anything, gorillas mature a little earlier. The course of the young's relation to mother is very similar to that seen in the chimpanzee.

During the first two or three months of life the young gorilla lacks the strength to clasp its mother's hair securely and receives support from its mother's arms. By the age of three months, however, it can cling efficiently and may begin to ride on mother's back. During the period from three to six months a young animal is occasionally on the ground beside mother and then she might, by walking slowly away, encourage it to follow

---

[1] For descriptions of gorillas in the wild, see the publications of Schaller (1963, 1965) and the recent studies of Fossey (1979) and Harcourt (1979).

her. An infant is rarely permitted to stray beyond a ten-foot radius, however, before its mother pulls it back. Until it is about eight months of age it is not aware when mother is about to move off and so has to be gathered by her. After that age it is clearly alive to her location and behaviour, and at the first sign of movement rushes back and climbs aboard.

By the age of a year infants may wander amongst the other animals whilst the group is resting and may be out of mother's sight for short periods. They also begin spending time sitting beside mother instead of on her lap. After they have reached eighteen months mothers are often reluctant to carry them.

A frequent sight was a female walking slowly with an infant toddling at her heels [sometimes with one or both hands grasping her rump hairs]. However, at the first sight of danger or the onset of rapid movement all infants up to the age of nearly three years rushed to their mothers and climbed aboard (Schaller, 1965).

The interaction of juveniles aged from three to seven years with their mothers is not unlike that seen in chimpanzees. The juvenile is no longer transported, and it feeds and sleeps on its own. Much of its day it spends with other juveniles. Nevertheless, the relationship with mother continues; and it does so even after another baby has been born, though thereafter the juvenile gets less attention than the baby. As maturity is approached, and the juvenile has become responsible for coming and going, the association with mother becomes less close; and by eight years almost all juveniles are spending most of their time with other adult animals.

Relations of Young Monkeys and Apes to other Animals in their Groups

During the period of infancy (up to one year in rhesus and baboon, and up to three years in the great apes) the infant spends little time with adults other than its mother. When away from her it is most likely to be playing with other infants or juveniles. Not infrequently, however, adult females without young of their own seek to mother a baby and sometimes they succeed in obtaining possession of it. In most species this is much disliked by the mother, who soon gets her infant back.[1] The Indian langur monkey, however, permits other adult females to cradle her infant; and Schaller (1965) describes how

[1] The intrusive behaviour of rhesus female 'aunts' is the subject of a paper by Hinde (1965a). The mothers of the infants concerned become extremely restrictive to prevent an 'aunt' from stealing their infant.

two infant gorillas were observed to have strong ties with females other than their mothers: one of six months would spend periods of up to an hour or more with the 'aunt', and another over a period of six months during its second year 'spent most of its time . . . with a female and small infant, returning to its mother only intermittently during the day and apparently at night'.

In most species adult males take considerable interest in mothers with babies and not only willingly permit mothers carrying young to remain close to them but may stay behind specially to escort them. As a rule, however, adult males never or only rarely carry young themselves. An exception to this is the Japanese macaque (a relative of the rhesus). In a few troops of that species adult males of high rank commonly 'adopt' a one-year-old infant after the mother has produced a new baby. For a period of limited duration their behaviour 'is quite similar to the behaviour of a mother toward her infant, except for the lack of suckling' (Itani, 1963). This paternal type of behaviour is not shown by the Indian rhesus male, who is either uninterested in young or hostile to them.

In many species, as the young grow older, association with adult males increases, but the age at which this occurs seems to vary greatly. Among savannah baboons a mother with a young infant usually associates with one (or sometimes two) particular male(s). Her infant is likely to become attached to this male and the relationship often continues after its mother has given birth to another baby (Altmann, 1980). It is therefore no surprise that as early as their second year juvenile baboons when alarmed begin to run to an adult male rather than to mother. Baby gorillas are attracted by the dominant male and when the group rests often sit by or play near him. On occasion they climb on to him or even hitch a lift. Provided the play is not too boisterous the male is remarkably tolerant. Juvenile gorillas also sometimes seek the company of an adult male and will leave the group to tag behind him. These amiable relationships are not reported for chimpanzees; when they become adolescent, however, chimpanzees of both sexes often associate with mature males. Since in all these species mating within a group is promiscuous, observers have hitherto assumed that there is no way for the animals to know which male has fathered which infant. But recent research indicates that, in at least some species, males spend more time with some infants than with others, and usually these infants are the offspring of females with whom the male mated when conception was most likely to have occurred (Berenstein and others, 1982; Altmann, 1980).

Roles of Infant and of Mother in the Relationship

From what has been said it is clear that during the earliest months of infancy mothers of all these species of non-human primate play a large part in ensuring that their infants remain close to them. If the infant is unable to grip efficiently the mother gives it support. If it strays too far she pulls it back. When a hawk flies overhead or a human approaches too closely she hugs it to her. Thus even if the infant were disposed to go far it is never allowed to do so.

But all the evidence is that the infant is not disposed to stray far. This is shown whenever an infant is brought up away from its mother, as infants of many different species of monkey and ape have been. In several cases in which an infant has been raised in a human home a biographical account is available. Good examples are those by Rowell (1965) of a young baboon, by Bolwig (1963) of a young patas monkey (also a terrestrial species, and with a maturation rate similar to that of a baboon), by Kellogg and Kellogg (1933) and by Hayes (1951) of young chimpanzees, and by Martini (1955) of a young gorilla. Of the cases in which an infant has been brought up on an experimental dummy the best-known reports are those of Harlow and his colleagues (Harlow, 1961; Harlow and Harlow, 1965).

All those brave scientists who have acted as a foster-parent to a young primate testify to the intensity and persistence with which it clings. Rowell writes of the little baboon she looked after (from the fifth to the eleventh week of age): 'when alarmed by a loud noise or a sudden movement he ran to me and clung desperately hard to my leg'. After she had had the infant ten days: 'he no longer allowed me out of his sight, and refused to accept dummy or apron, but clung the more fiercely'. Of the little patas monkey that Bolwig cared for from a few days old he writes that from the first 'he firmly gripped any object placed in his hand and protested by screaming if it was removed' and that 'his attachment quickly grew closer and closer until in the end it became almost unbreakable'. Hayes, describing Viki, the female chimpanzee she reared from three days of age, reports how, at four months old when Viki was walking well, 'from the moment she left her crib until she was tucked up at night, with time out for only an hour's nap, she clung to me like a papoose'. All the accounts contain similar passages.

Discrimination of Mother by Infant

Attachment behaviour has been defined as seeking and maintaining proximity to another individual. Whilst these reports leave no possible doubt that young primates of all species cling to objects with the utmost tenacity, it still remains to be considered how soon they come to discriminate, and to attach themselves to, a particular individual.

Harlow believes that a rhesus infant 'learns attachments to a specific mother (*the* mother)' during the first week or two of life (Harlow and Harlow, 1965). Hinde (personal communication) endorses that view: he points out that, within a few days of birth, a rhesus baby orients towards its mother in preference to other monkeys. For example, at the end of its first week it may leave mother briefly and crawl towards another female; but it soon about-turns and moves towards mother. A capacity so soon to recognise a particular individual is less surprising now that evidence suggests that non-human primates have some degree of pattern vision at birth (Fantz, 1965).

The reports of human foster-parents are also of interest in this connection.

Bolwig's little patas monkey began discriminating individual members of the household very soon after it arrived, then aged between five and fourteen days. This was shown only three days after its arrival when the monkey, which had been looked after mainly by Miss Bolwig, ran after her to the door, screaming, on being left with Dr Bolwig, and stopped crying when she returned and picked it up.

> During the following days the attachment shifted from my daughter to me, and it became so strong that I had to carry him on my shoulder wherever I went . . . right up to the age of $3\frac{1}{2}$ months he could be very troublesome if left in the care of some other member of the family.

Although at the end of five months the monkey was spending much time in the company of other humans and of other monkeys of its own species, its preference for Dr Bolwig continued, especially when it was in distress; and this same preference was again in evidence no less than four months later (when it was aged nine months) although Dr Bolwig had been absent throughout the intervening period.

Rowell's baboon was about five weeks old when she became its foster-mother. Already during its first week the little baboon could distinguish familiar people from strangers and could recognise its primary caregiver. At first, provided it was not hungry, it was content to stay alone with its dummy and its caregiver's apron. After ten days, however, 'he no longer allowed me out of his sight. . . . If he saw me move or even caught my eye he would drop the dummy and run to me.'

These reports leave no doubt, therefore, that in some species of Old World monkey attachment behaviour comes, within a week or so, to be directed especially towards a certain preferred individual, and that once it is so directed the preference is extremely strong and persistent.

In keeping with their slower rate of maturation, chimpanzee infants appear to be slower to show a clear preference for their caregiver. Once it has developed, however, the preference is no less strong than it is in monkey species. A reading of Hayes's account suggests that Viki was about three months old before she was greatly concerned about whom she was with. Around that age, however, her preference became unmistakable. For example, Hayes describes how Viki, when a little under four months, attended a party and how she alternately explored guests and retreated to be beside her foster-mother. When the guests moved to an adjacent room Viki inadvertently caught hold of another lady's dress; but when she happened to glance up and see her mistake she gave a short cry and transferred at once to climb up her foster-mother.[1]

Changes in Intensity of Attachment Behaviour

In every description of primate infants in the wild it is reported that at the least alarm an infant away from its mother will rush to her and that one already near her will cling more tightly. That attachment behaviour is exhibited without fail on such occasions is of much importance for our understanding of both cause and function.

Some other conditions that lead attachment behaviour to be shown, or shown more intensely, are reported in the accounts of infants raised by human foster-parents. Rowell reports that when her young baboon was hungry 'he was insistent in maintaining contact and screamed continually if left'. Both Rowell and Bolwig describe how, when the infant was a little older and was disposed to explore, the slightest sign that the caregiver

[1] Accounts by Yerkes also suggest that young chimps are some months old before they are very discriminating. A pair of twins brought up by their mother did not appear to 'recognise one another as social objects' until nearly five months old (Tomilin and Yerkes, 1935).

was moving off was noticed at once and brought the little animal quickly to cling. A short separation had the same effect. Bolwig records that when his little patas monkey was released from a cage in which it had been left for a few hours with other monkeys of its own kind,

> he would cling to me and refuse to leave me out of sight for the rest of the day. In the evening when asleep he would wake up with small shrieks and cling to me, showing all signs of terror when I tried to release his grip.

The Waning of Attachment Behaviour

In the accounts of the attachment behaviour of young primates in the wild it has been described how, as they get older, they spend a decreasing amount of time with mother and an increasing amount of time with peers and, later, with other adults, and how the change is mainly a result of their own initiative. The extent to which the mother herself promotes the change seems to vary much from species to species. A baboon mother does a good deal of rebuffing of her infant after it has reached ten months of age, especially if she is about to have another baby. The rhesus mother also does some rebuffing. Neither chimpanzee nor gorilla appears to do very much.

From such evidence as is available, however, it seems clear that, even with few or no maternal rebuffs, after a certain age attachment behaviour diminishes both in its intensity and in the frequency with which it is elicited. In all likelihood several different processes are at work. One probably is a change in form taken by the behavioural systems mediating attachment behaviour itself. Another is an increase of curiosity and of exploratory behaviour, on the effects of which Harlow (1961) and other workers lay much emphasis.

Bolwig's account of the waning of attachment behaviour as it occurred in his patas monkey is illuminating. He describes vividly how, from the first days, the monkey was inquisitive and liked to stare at hands and faces. Its interest in exploring inanimate objects, present from the start, increased steadily, and by the end of its second month in the household it spent much time climbing over the furniture. At the age of nearly four months it enjoyed itself so much with a crowd of students that it refused to come when called; subsequently such refusals became more numerous. Bolwig concludes that the young monkey's interest in play and exploration 'acted as an antagonist to the phase of attachment and gradually became dominant over it during his hour to hour activity'.

The rate at which attachment behaviour wanes is no doubt affected by many variables. One is the frequency of alarming events: all accounts agree that when alarmed even older juveniles instantly resume proximity to mother. Another is the frequency of enforced separation at too early an age. Bolwig describes the intense clinging shown by his little patas monkey after its caretaker had been persuaded (against his better judgement) to discipline it, for example by locking it out of the house or putting it in a cage. 'Every time I tried . . . it resulted in a setback in the monkey's development. He became more clinging, more mischievous and more difficult.'

Although in the natural course of events attachment behaviour directed towards the mother gradually wanes in non-human primates, it does not disappear altogether. There is, however, too little evidence from field studies for firm conclusions to be drawn regarding its role in adult life, and the same is true in respect of animals brought up in captivity.

All the human-raised monkeys and apes referred to in these reports have been placed in zoos or in laboratory colonies whilst still juvenile. The general experience with such animals is that, though they usually become reasonably sociable with members of their own species, they continue to show a much stronger interest in humans than do naturally raised animals. Some of them, moreover, become sexually aroused by, and direct sexual behaviour towards, humans. The nature of the figure towards whom attachment behaviour is directed during infancy has, therefore, a number of long-term effects.

Attachment behaviour in man

Differences from and Similarities to that seen in Non-human Primates

At first sight it might appear that there is a sharp break between attachment behaviour in man and that seen in non-human primates. In the latter, it might be emphasised, clinging by infant to mother is found from birth or very soon afterwards whereas in man the infant only very slowly becomes aware of his mother and only after he has become mobile does he seek her company. Though the difference is real, I believe it is easy to exaggerate its importance.

First, we have seen that in one at least of the great apes, gorilla, the infant at birth has not strength enough to support its own weight and that for two or three months its mother supports it. Secondly, it must be remembered that in the simpler human societies, especially those of hunters and gatherers, the infant is not placed in cot or pram but is carried by his mother on her back. Thus the difference in infant–mother relations in gorilla and in man is not so great. In fact, from lowest primates to Western man a continuum can be discerned. In the least advanced members of the primate order, for example lemur and marmoset, the infant must from birth forward do all the clinging; it receives no support whatever from its mother. In the more advanced Old World monkeys, such as baboon and rhesus, it must do most of the clinging but in the early days of its life its mother gives some assistance. In the most advanced, gorilla and man, the infant continues to cling but has not strength to support himself for long; in consequence, for some months the infant is kept in proximity to mother only by the mother's own actions; but keep in proximity mother and infant do. Only in more economically developed human societies, and especially in Western ones, are infants commonly out of contact with mother for many hours a day and often during the night as well.

This evolutionary shift in the balance from infant taking all the initiative in keeping contact to mother taking all the initiative has an important consequence. This is that, whereas a rhesus monkey is already clinging strongly before it learns to discriminate its mother from other monkeys (and inanimate objects), the human infant is able to distinguish his mother from other persons (or objects) before he can either cling to her or move actively towards her. This fact leads to a minor difficulty in deciding by what criteria to judge the beginning of attachment behaviour in man.

Growth of Attachment Behaviour during the First Year

There is good evidence that in a family setting most infants of about three months are already responding differently to mother as compared with other people. When he sees his mother an infant of this age will smile and vocalise more readily and follow her with his eyes for longer than he does when he sees anyone else. Perceptual discrimination, therefore, is present. Yet we can hardly say that there is attachment behaviour until there is evidence that the infant not only recognises his mother but tends also to behave in a way that maintains his proximity to her.

Proximity-maintaining behaviour is seen at its most obvious when mother leaves the room and the infant cries, or cries and also attempts to follow her. Ainsworth (1963, 1967) reports that, in one group of African infants, crying and attempts to follow occurred in one infant as early as fifteen and seventeen weeks respectively and that both sorts of behaviour were common at six months of age. All but four of these infants attempted to follow a departing mother as soon as they could crawl.[1]

In this study Ainsworth was observing infants of the Ganda tribe in Uganda by visiting their mothers for a couple of hours during the afternoon when the women were usually resting after a morning's work, and often receiving visitors. Any infant awake at this time either is held, propped in the lap, or is free to crawl about. Since a number of adults were always present, differential responses and attachment behaviour to mother were readily observed. Visits to twenty-five mothers with twenty-seven infants[2] were made at fortnightly intervals over a period of about seven months. By the end of the study the two youngest infants were still only six months of age but most of them had reached between ten and fifteen months; all but four were showing attachment behaviour.

Ainsworth's findings make it clear that in all but a small minority of Ganda children attachment behaviour is clearly present by six months of age, and is shown not only by the child's crying when mother leaves the room but also by his greeting her on her return with smiles, lifting of the arms, and crows of delight. The crying was more likely to occur when the child was left alone or with strangers, but at this age it did not occur on every such occasion. During the next three months, however, whilst the infant progressed from six to nine months of age, all these behaviours were exhibited more regularly and with more vigour 'as though the attachment to the mother was becoming stronger and more consolidated'. Children of this age followed mother when she left the room; after she had been

[1] The median age for crawling in this sample of Ganda children was twenty-five weeks, which compares with seven and a half months for white American children (Gesell, 1940). In this respect and many others the motor development of Ganda infants is much advanced compared with that of Caucasian infants (Géber, 1956).

[2] One other infant was observed but since she was only three and a half months old at the end of the study the case has been omitted from this abstract.

absent they first greeted her and then crawled as quickly as possible to her.

All these patterns of behaviour continued during the final quarter of the first year and throughout the second year of life. By nine months children could follow mother more efficiently when she left the room and thenceforward their crying on these occasions diminished. Clinging to mother, too, became especially evident after the age of nine months, particularly when a child was alarmed, e.g. by a stranger's presence.

Although attachment behaviour was shown by these children also towards other familiar adults, towards mother it was nearly always shown earlier, more strongly, and more consistently. Between the ages of six and nine months any child whose father came home regularly would greet him joyfully when he appeared; but the actual following of a familiar adult (other than mother) who departed was not observed until after the age of nine months. Thenceforward if his mother was not present a child tended to follow any familiar adult he happened to be with.

Whereas twenty-three of the twenty-seven Ganda children studied by Ainsworth showed unmistakable attachment behaviour, in four infants no attachment behaviour of any kind had been noted when observations ended. The ages of these four children were then eight and a half months (twins), eleven months, and twelve months. Possible reasons for their delayed development are discussed in Chapter 15.

The age at which attachment behaviour develops in the Ganda, as observed by Ainsworth, does not differ greatly from the age at which Schaffer and Emerson (1964a) found it to develop in Scottish children. Their study covered sixty infants from birth until twelve months of age. Information was obtained from parents at intervals of four weeks. Criteria of attachment were restricted to responses to being left by mother; seven possible situations, e.g. left alone in room, left in cot at night, were defined, and intensity of protest was scored. First-hand observations were limited, and greeting responses were not taken into account.

In the Scottish investigation one-third of the infants were showing attachment behaviour by six months of age and three-quarters by nine months. As in the case of the Ganda, a few infants were slow to show it: in two it was still not reported when the children were twelve months old.

Taken at their face value Schaffer and Emerson's findings

suggest that Scottish children are a little slower to develop attachment behaviour than are Ganda children. This may well be so and would be in keeping with the notably advanced motor development of the Ganda. An alternative explanation is that such differences as are reported are a result of the different criteria of attachment and methods of observation that were employed in the two studies. By being present and making the observations herself Ainsworth may be expected to have recorded the earliest signs of attachment, whereas Schaffer and Emerson in relying on mothers' reports may not have done so.[1] However that may be, the two reports agree well on many findings. These include the great range of age at which attachment behaviour is first shown by different children—from before four months to after twelve months. This wide individual variation must never be forgotten; possible reasons for it are discussed in Chapter 15.

There is also agreement regarding the frequency with which attachment behaviour is directed towards figures other than mother. Schaffer and Emerson found that, during the month after the children first showed attachment behaviour, one-quarter of them were directing it to other members of the family, and by the time they had reached eighteen months of age all but a handful of children were attached to at least one other figure and often to several others. Father was the most frequent of other figures to elicit attachment behaviour. Next in frequency were older children, 'not only very much older children, who might occasionally take over the mother's routine care activities, but also preschool children'. Schaffer and Emerson found no evidence that attachment to mother was less intense when attachment behaviour was directed to other figures also; on the contrary, in the early months of attachment the greater the number of figures to whom a child was attached the more intense was his attachment to mother as his principal figure likely to be.

Not only do both studies record great variation in speed of development between children, but both report also that in any one child the intensity and consistency with which attachment behaviour is shown can vary greatly from day to day or hour to hour. Variables responsible for short-term changes are

[1] The possibility that the earliest and less consistent instances of attachment behaviour were not reported to Schaffer and Emerson is suggested by their finding that, when first reported, protests at being left by mother were already at or near their maximum intensity.

of two kinds, organismic and environmental. Amongst the organismic Ainsworth lists hunger, fatigue, illness, and unhappiness as all leading to increased crying and following; Schaffer and Emerson likewise list fatigue, illness, and pain. As regards environmental factors both studies note that attachment behaviour is more intense when a child is alarmed. Ainsworth was particularly well placed to make such observations because, as a white-skinned stranger, she was especially apt to arouse alarm. No Ganda child showed alarm before forty weeks of age but in the subsequent weeks practically all those observed did so: 'Children whom we met for the first time in this [the fourth] quarter seemed to be terrified of me. . . . Clinging in fright was noticed in this context.' A further point noted by Schaffer and Emerson was that intensity of attachment was increased for a period after mother had been absent.[1]

It will be noticed that all the variables reported as influencing the intensity of attachment in human infants in the short term are the same as those reported as influencing its intensity in the short term in monkey and ape infants.

Although there is abundant evidence to show that the kind of care an infant receives from his mother plays a major part in determining the way in which his attachment behaviour develops, the extent to which an infant himself initiates interaction and influences the form it takes must never be forgotten. Both Ainsworth and Schaffer are among several observers who call attention to the very active role of the human infant.

Reviewing her observations of the Ganda, Ainsworth (1963) writes:

> One feature of attachment behaviour that struck me especially was the extent to which the infant himself takes the initiative in seeking an interaction. At least from two months of age onwards, and increasingly through the first year of life, these infants were not so much passive and recipient as active in seeking interaction.

Schaffer (1963) writes in the same vein about his Scottish infants:

[1] Schaffer and Emerson report that they were unable to identify the factors responsible for some fluctuations of intensity and that 'some appeared spontaneous in nature'. It is not unlikely, however, that more frequent and first-hand observation might have revealed events not reported by mothers at monthly interviews.

Children often seem to dictate their parents' behaviour by the insistence of their demands, for quite a number of the mothers we interviewed reported that they were forced to respond far more than they considered desirable . . .

Apart from crying, which is never easily ignored, an infant often calls persistently and, when attended to, orients to and smiles at his mother or other companion. Later, he greets and approaches her and seeks her attention in a thousand attractive ways. Not only does he by these means evoke responses from his companions but 'he maintains and shapes their responses by reinforcing some and not others' (Rheingold, 1966). The pattern of interaction that gradually develops between an infant and his mother can be understood only as a resultant of the contributions of each, and especially of the way in which each in turn influences the behaviour of the other. This theme is amplified in Chapter 16.

Subsequent Course of Attachment Behaviour in Man

Although the growth of attachment behaviour during the first year of life is reasonably well chronicled, the course it takes during subsequent years is not. Such information as there is strongly suggests that during the second and most of the third year attachment behaviour is shown neither at less intensity nor with less frequency than it is at the end of the first year. An increase in an infant's perceptual range and in his ability to understand events in the world around him leads, however, to changes in the circumstances that elicit attachment behaviour.

One change is that a child becomes increasingly aware of an *impending* departure. During his first year an infant protests especially when put down in his cot and, a little later, on seeing his mother disappear from sight. Subsequently a child who, when his mother leaves him, is otherwise engrossed, begins to notice that she is gone and then protests. Thenceforward he is keenly alert to his mother's whereabouts: he spends much time watching her or, if she is out of sight, listening for sound of her movements. During his eleventh or twelfth month he becomes able, by noting her behaviour, to anticipate her imminent departure, and starts to protest before she goes. Knowing this will happen, many a parent of a two-year-old hides preparations until the last minute in order to avoid a clamour.

By most children attachment behaviour is exhibited strongly and regularly until almost the end of the third year. Then a change occurs. This is well illustrated by the common experience of nursery school teachers. Until children have reached about two years and nine months most of them, when attending a nursery school, are upset when mother leaves. Though their crying may last only a short time, they are nonetheless apt to remain quiet and inactive and constantly to demand the attention of the teacher—in marked contrast to how they behave in the same setting should mother remain with them. After children have reached their third birthday, however, they are usually much better able to accept mother's temporary absence and to engage in play with other children. In many children the change seems to take place almost abruptly, suggesting that at this age some maturational threshold is passed.

A main change is that after their third birthday most children become increasingly able in a strange place to feel secure with subordinate attachment-figures, for example a relative or a school teacher. Even so, such feeling of security is conditional. First, the subordinate figures must be familiar people, preferably those whom the child has got to know whilst in the company of his mother. Secondly, the child must be healthy and not alarmed. Thirdly, he must be aware of where his mother is and confident that he can resume contact with her at short notice. In the absence of these conditions he is likely to become or to remain very 'mummyish', or to show other disturbances of behaviour.

The increase in confidence that comes with age is well illustrated in the account given by Murphy and her associates (1962) of the different ways in which children aged between two and a half and five and a half years respond to an invitation to come for a play session. During a preliminary visit to a child's family a plan was made for the researchers to call again a few days later to take the child by car to the session. Though the children were encouraged to go on their own, no obstacle was put in the way of mother coming too should child protest or mother prefer to do so. Though the mothers were familiar to the researchers, to the children they were strangers, except for a meeting during the researchers' preliminary visit.

Not unexpectedly, when the researchers called at the children's homes to take them to the centre, most of the young ones refused to go unless mother came too. Refusal was highly correlated with age: whereas all but two of seventeen four- and five-year-olds accepted mother's assurances and encouragement and were willing to go alone with the researchers, only a small

minority of the fifteen two- and three-year-olds would do so.[1]
Not only did most of the younger children insist that mother
came too, but during the first session they made sure also of
remaining in physical contact with her by sitting beside her,
clinging to her skirts, holding her hand, or pulling her along.
Given this support they became during later sessions steadily
more confident. A majority of the older children, by contrast,
went happily on their own to the first session and began soon
or at once to enjoy the toys and tests provided. None of those
older than four and a half years showed the clinging behaviour
so typical of the younger children. To illustrate these differences
Murphy gives a number of vivid sketches of the behaviour of
individual children.

The children Murphy describes in this study were all from
skilled artisan and professional white families and came mostly
of old American stock. Their upbringing had tended to be
conservative and strict. They had not, therefore, been molly-
coddled, and there is no reason to suppose that they were in
any way atypical.

English children are no different. The occurrence and incidence of attachment behaviour in a sample of 700 four-year-
olds in the English Midlands are well chronicled by Newson and
Newson (1966, 1968). To a question whether their four-year-old
'ever comes clinging round your skirts wanting to be babied a
bit', the mothers of 16 per cent answered 'often' and of 47 per
cent 'sometimes'. Though the mothers of the remaining third
answered 'never', in some cases it seemed likely that that was
wishful thinking. Common reasons for a child who was not
usually given to clinging behaviour to show it were his being
unwell and his being jealous of a younger sibling. Although almost all the mothers described themselves as responsive to their
child's demands, a quarter of them claimed that they responded
only reluctantly. In this connection the Newsons remark on
what proved to be a recurrent theme in their conversations
with mothers, namely the power that a child exerts, and exerts
successfully, to attain his own ends. This is a truth, the Newsons remark, 'which most parents come to realise, but of which
they are too seldom warned by manuals of child care'.

Thus, although most children after their third birthday show
attachment behaviour less urgently and frequently than before,
it nonetheless still constitutes a major part of behaviour.
Furthermore, though becoming attenuated, attachment be-

[1] Murphy does not give exact figures or correlation coefficients.

haviour of a kind not very different from that seen in four-year-olds persists throughout early school years. When out walking, children of five and six, and even older, like at times to hold, even grasp, a parent's hand, and resent it if the parent refuses. When playing with others, if anything goes badly wrong, they at once return to parent, or parent-substitute. If more than a little frightened, they seek immediate contact. Thus, throughout the latency of an ordinary child, attachment behaviour continues as a dominant strand in his life.

During adolescence a child's attachment to his parents changes. Other adults may come to assume an importance equal to or greater than that of the parents, and sexual attraction to age-mates begins to extend the picture. As a result individual variation, already great, becomes even greater. At one extreme are adolescents who cut themselves off from parents; at the other are those who remain intensely attached and are unable or unwilling to direct their attachment behaviour to others; between the extremes lie the great majority of adolescents whose attachment to parents persists but whose ties to others are of much importance also. For most individuals the bond to parents continues into adult life and affects behaviour in countless ways. In many societies the attachment of daughter to mother is more evident than that of son to mother. As Young and Willmott (1957) have shown, even in a Western urbanised society the bond between adult daughter and mother plays a great part in social life.

Finally, in old age, when attachment behaviour can no longer be directed towards members of an older generation, or even the same generation, it may come instead to be directed towards members of a younger one.

During adolescence and adult life a measure of attachment behaviour is commonly directed not only towards persons outside the family but also towards groups and institutions other than the family. A school or college, a work group, a religious group or a political group can come to constitute for many people a subordinate attachment-'figure', and for some people a principal attachment-'figure'. In such cases, it seems probable, the development of attachment to a group is mediated, at least initially, by attachment to a person holding a prominent position within that group. Thus, for many a citizen attachment to his state is a derivative of and initially dependent on his attachment to its sovereign or president.

That attachment behaviour in adult life is a straightforward continuation of attachment behaviour in childhood is shown by the circumstances that lead an adult's attachment behaviour to become more readily elicited. In sickness and calamity, adults often become demanding of others; in conditions of sudden danger or disaster a person will almost certainly seek proximity to another known and trusted person. In such circumstances an increase of attachment behaviour is recognised by all as natural.[1] It is therefore extremely misleading for the epithet 'regressive' to be applied to every manifestation of attachment behaviour in adult life, as is so often done in psychoanalytic writing where the term carries the connotation pathological or, at least, undesirable (e.g. Benedek, 1956). To dub attachment behaviour in adult life regressive is indeed to overlook the vital role that it plays in the life of man from the cradle to the grave.

Forms of Behaviour Mediating Attachment

In the earlier discussion of this theme (Bowlby, 1958) five responses were listed as leading to attachment behaviour. Two of them, crying and smiling, tend to bring mother to infant and to maintain her close to him. Two others, following and clinging, have the effect of bringing infant to mother and retaining him close to her. The role of the fifth, sucking, is less easily categorised, and requires close examination. A sixth, calling, is also important: at any time after four months an infant will hail his mother by short sharp calls and later, of course, by calling her by name.

Since the parts played by these responses and their characteristics are most conveniently discussed together with their development, further consideration of them is postponed until later chapters.

Use of Mother as Base from which to Explore

To describe the growth of attachment behaviour during the first year of life two main criteria were used: crying and following when mother leaves, and greeting and approach when mother returns. Other criteria are differential smiling at mother, usually observed during the fourth month, and movement to mother and clinging to her when the child is alarmed. A further indication is the different ways in which an attached child behaves in the presence of his mother and in her absence.

[1] R. S. Weiss has made a number of studies of attachment in adult life. For a review of his findings see Weiss (1982).

In her study of Ganda infants Ainsworth (1967) notes how, soon after an infant is able to crawl, he does not always remain close to his mother. On the contrary, he makes little excursions away from her, exploring other objects and people and, if allowed to do so, he may even go out of her sight. From time to time, however, he returns to her, as though to assure himself she is still there. Such confident exploration comes to an abrupt end if either of two conditions occurs: (a) if the child is frightened or hurt; (b) if the mother moves away. Then he returns to her as quickly as possible with greater or less signs of distress, or else cries helplessly. The youngest Ganda child in whom Ainsworth observed this pattern of behaviour was twenty-eight weeks. After eight months a majority of them showed it.

From about this age onwards a child behaves very differently in the presence of his mother compared with how he behaves in her absence, and this difference is especially marked if the child is confronted by a strange person or strange place. With mother present most children are clearly more confident and ready to explore; in her absence they are much more timid and not infrequently collapse in distress. Experiments demonstrating these reactions in children of about twelve months of age are reported by Ainsworth and Wittig (1969) and by Rheingold (1969). In each of these studies results are clear-cut and dramatic. This theme also is amplified in Chapter 16.

Feeling

No form of behaviour is accompanied by stronger feeling than is attachment behaviour. The figures towards whom it is directed are loved and their advent is greeted with joy.

So long as a child is in the unchallenged presence of a principal attachment-figure, or within easy reach, he feels secure. A threat of loss creates anxiety, and actual loss sorrow; both, moreover, are likely to arouse anger. All these themes are explored further in the second and third volumes of this work.

Chapter 12

Nature and Function of Attachment Behaviour

> You know—at least you *ought* to know,
> For I have often told you so—
> That Children never are allowed
> To leave their Nurses in a Crowd;
>
> Now this was Jim's especial Foible,
> He ran away when he was able,
> And on this inauspicious day
> He slipped his hand and ran away!
> He hadn't gone a yard when—Bang!
> With open jaws a lion sprang,
> And hungrily began to eat
> The Boy: beginning at his feet.
>
> *   *   *
>
> His Father, who was self-controlled,
> Bade all the children round attend
> To James' miserable end,
> And always keep a hold of Nurse
> For fear of finding something worse.
> 'Jim'—HILAIRE BELLOC

The theory of secondary drive: origin and present status

In the last chapter a sketch is given of the course taken by attachment behaviour in the life-cycle of five species of primate —from rhesus monkey to man. The task now is to consider how best to understand the nature of this kind of behaviour and the factors controlling it.

By far the most widely held theory has been that of secondary drive, so it is useful to begin by considering the origin and present status of that theory.[1]

The theory of secondary drive holds that a liking to be with

[1] For a comprehensive and up-to-date account of both the psychoanalytic and the social learning versions of this type of theory, see Maccoby and Masters (1970).

other members of the species is a result of being fed by them. As Dollard and Miller (1950) express it: ' . . . probably the feeding experience can be the occasion for the child to learn to like to be with others; that is, it can establish the basis of sociability'. Or, as Freud puts it: 'The reason why the infant in arms wants to perceive the presence of its mother is only because it already knows by experience that she satisfies all its needs without delay' (1926, *S.E.*, **20**, p. 137); and later, rather more specifically: 'love has its origin in attachment to the satisfied need for nourishment' (1940, *S.E.*, **23**, p. 188).

The first thing to note about this type of theory is that it arises from an assumption and not from observation or experiment. Hull adopted the position that there are only a limited number of primary drives—for food, liquid, warmth, and sex —and that all other behaviour is derived from them by a process of learning. Freud made much the same assumption. Both types of theory—learning theory and psychoanalysis— were then elaborated in the belief that the basic assumption was justified and without further discussion of it. Since no other theory was in the field, the theory of secondary drive came in time to be regarded almost as though it were a self-evident truth.

The theory was first called seriously in question by Lorenz's early work on imprinting. Although published in 1935, his findings were little known before 1950 and made a deep impact on psychological thinking only a decade or two later. What they showed beyond any possible doubt is that attachment behaviour can develop in ducklings and goslings without the young animals' receiving either food or any other conventional reward. In the hours after they have hatched, these young creatures tend to follow any moving object that they see, be it a mother bird, a man, a rubber balloon, or a cardboard box; once having followed a particular object, moreover, they come to prefer that object to others and after a time will follow no other. The process of learning the characteristics of the object followed is known as imprinting (see Chapter 10).

Once Lorenz's experiments were repeated and his findings verified, it was natural to consider whether attachment behaviour in mammals and in man himself develops in a comparable manner. There is now substantial evidence that it does so. Those who continue to favour a theory of secondary drive must, therefore, present some convincing evidence if they wish their theory to be taken seriously in future.

For mammals other than man, rigorous evidence that attachment behaviour can develop and be directed towards an object that provides none of the traditional rewards of food, warmth, or sex is available only for guinea-pig, dog, sheep, and rhesus monkey (see review by Cairns, 1966a).

In one series of experiments Shipley (1963) shows that guinea-pigs isolated within four hours of birth respond to the movement of a flat white wooden shape by following it. Responses include not only approach but a number of other typically social responses, e.g. sniffing, licking, and contact-seeking. In another experiment baby guinea-pigs remained with mother for five days in complete darkness. They were then removed from mother and exposed to the light and to the moving model. Once again they responded to the model by approach, following, and other social responses. Since they had been raised in darkness there was no possibility of visual generalisation from mother, and, since approach preceded contact with the model, any effect of previous contact with mother could be excluded.

Although the experiments of Scott and his associates with puppies (reviewed by Scott, 1963) are a little less rigorous, the results are nonetheless impressive. The puppies, whilst totally isolated from man, remained with their mother and litter-mates in the light until experiments began when they were two or three weeks of age or older. The questions asked were whether a puppy who had neither seen a man nor been fed by one would approach and follow one, and, if so, at what ages and in what conditions.

In one experiment, puppies were first exposed to a seated and inactive man when they were at one of several different ages; the exposure was for ten minutes each day for a week. All the puppies first exposed to a man when they were either three weeks or five weeks of age immediately approached the experimenter and spent the whole ten minutes with him. Those first exposed at older ages were more often afraid and none of those first exposed at fourteen weeks approached. Thus in the weeks after they can first crawl about puppies will approach a human being despite his being inactive and their having had no occasion whatever of associating food with him.

In another experiment one of Scott's associates (Fisher) kept puppies in complete isolation after they had reached three weeks of age and arranged for them to be fed by mechanical means. For a short time each day thenceforward they were let out and their response to a walking man was observed. All of them followed him. One group of puppies not only received no sort of reward but were punished each time they attempted to follow 'so that their only experience with human contact was painful'. After several weeks the experimenter stopped the punishment. The puppies soon ceased to run away from him and, furthermore, they actually spent more time with him than did control puppies whose approaches had been rewarded with uniform petting and kindness.

Cairn's experiments with lambs gave similar results (Cairns, 1966a and b; Cairns and Johnson, 1965). From about six weeks of age a lamb was kept isolated but in visual and auditory contact with an operating television set. Not only did the lamb maintain proximity to the set but when, after nine weeks of confinement, the lamb was separated from the set it immediately sought for it and approached it when found. In other experiments lambs were reared in visual, auditory, and olfactory contact with a dog; in some cases the pair were prevented from interacting with each other by a wire fence. After some weeks once again the lamb treated the dog as an attachment-figure, bleating on separation, searching for it, and, when it was found, accompanying it everywhere. Thus in lambs attachment can develop with nothing more than visual and auditory exposure to an object and without any physical interaction with it.

Furthermore, lambs, like puppies, will develop such attachments in spite of receiving punishing treatment from their companion. When a lamb and a dog are kept together in a cage without any restraint on their movements, the dog is apt to bite, maul, and otherwise ill-treat the lamb. Despite this, however, when the pair are separated, a lamb will immediately seek for its dog-companion and approach it. None of these findings is compatible with secondary drive theory.

Harlow's experiments with rhesus monkeys likewise give no support to the secondary drive type of theory. In a series of experiments in which infant monkeys were removed from mother at birth, they were provided with model mothers consisting either of a cylinder made of wire or of a similar cylinder covered by soft cloth. Feeding was from a bottle which could be placed in either model. This enabled separate assessments to be made of the effects of food and of something comfortable to cling to. All the experiments showed that 'contact comfort' led to attachment behaviour whereas food did not.

In one experiment eight infant monkeys were raised with the choice of a cloth model and a wire model. Four infants were fed (on demand) from the cloth model and four from the wire model and the time the infants spent on each model was measured. The results showed that, irrespective of which model provided the food, the infants came rapidly to spend most of their time on the cloth model. Whereas infants of both groups spent an average of fifteen hours a day clinging to the cloth model, no infants of either group spent more than an hour or two out of the twenty-four with the wire model. Some infants whose food came from the wire model managed to lean over and suck the teat whilst still maintaining a grip of the cloth model. Harlow and Zimmermann (1959) conclude:

> These data make it obvious that contact comfort is a variable of critical importance in the development of affectional responsiveness to the surrogate mother [i.e. model] and that nursing appears to play a negligible role. With increasing age and opportunity to learn an infant fed from a lactating wire mother does not become more responsive to her, as would be predicted from a drive-derived theory, but instead becomes increasingly more responsive to its non-lactating cloth mother. These findings are at complete variance with a drive-reduction theory of affectional development.

Several other of Harlow's experiments support this conclusion, especially those in which a comparison is made between the behaviour of infant monkeys brought up in company with a cloth model that does *not* feed them and that of other infants brought up in company with a wire model that *does* feed them. Two such experiments deal with a young monkey's behaviour (i) when it is alarmed and (ii) when it is in a strange setting.

When an infant monkey brought up with a non-feeding cloth model is alarmed it at once seeks the model and clings to it (just as the wild monkey in similar circumstances at once seeks its mother and clings to her). Having done so the infant becomes less afraid and may even start to explore the hitherto alarming object. When a similar experiment is done with an infant brought up with a 'lactating' wire model its behaviour is quite different: it does not seek the model, and instead remains scared and does not explore.

In the second experiment an infant monkey is placed in a strange test room (6' cube) in which are a variety of 'toys'. So long as its cloth model is present the young monkey explores the toys, using the model as a base to which to return from time to time. In the absence of the model, however, the infants

> would rush across the test room and throw themselves face down-ward, clutching their heads and bodies and screaming their distress. . . . The presence of the wire mother provided no more reassurance than no mother at all. Control tests on monkeys that from birth had known only a nursing wire mother revealed that even these infants showed no affection for her and obtained no comfort from her presence (Harlow, 1961).

In both these experiments typical attachment behaviour is directed to the non-feeding cloth model whereas no such behaviour is directed towards the feeding wire one.

In keeping with Harlow's findings for rhesus infants is Rowell's experience with the baby baboon she reared. The baboon was fed from a bottle; it also had a dummy to suck and its caretaker to cling to when it wanted to. In these circumstances the bottle was of interest only when the baboon was hungry. At these times the infant would grab wildly for it. At all other times it directed its behaviour towards the dummy or to its foster-mother: 'the bottle, though occasionally mouthed, seemed to have no more interest than any other object of comparable size' (Rowell, 1965).

In Harlow's experiments the only effect that food seems to have is to make one cloth model a little more attractive than another one. Thus, given the choice of two models both of cloth, say a green one that feeds it and a tan one that does not, the infant spends rather more time on the feeding model; at forty days of age it is about eleven hours a day on the feeding model against eight on the non-feeding one. But even this limited preference diminishes, so that at four months the two models are treated exactly the same (Harlow, 1961).

It is of interest that, just as Fisher found that puppies follow the more persistently despite punishment, and Cairns found the same in lambs, so Harlow found that an infant monkey clings the more intensely in the face of punishment. In this experiment a cloth model was fitted with nozzles through which blasts of compressed air could be forced. A buzzer served as a conditioned stimulus that warned the infant of an impending blast, known to be a strong aversive stimulus to monkeys. Although the infant monkeys soon learned what to expect, instead of taking evasive action they did just the opposite. They clasped the model with increased vigour and so received on face and belly a blast at maximum intensity (Harlow, 1961; Rosenblum and Harlow, 1963). Attachment behaviour of great intensity was shown also by infant monkeys whose mothers gravely maltreated them (Seay, Alexander, and Harlow, 1964). This paradoxical behaviour is, of course, an inevitable result of attachment behaviour's being elicited by anything alarming. This point is discussed further in the next chapter.

The Case of Man

Although all these experiments seem effectively to rule out a secondary drive theory for sub-human mammals, they still leave the human case unsettled. Inevitably the evidence for man is inconclusive. A number of observations, however, suggest that the factors that make for attachment behaviour in man are not greatly different from what they are in his mammalian relatives.

First, it is well known that a human infant is born with a capacity for clinging that enables him to support his own weight —a capacity that Freud observed and referred to as a 'grasping-instinct' (Freud, 1905, *S.E.*, **7**, p. 180). Secondly, babies enjoy human company. Even in the first days of life babies are quietened by social interaction such as being picked up, talked to, or caressed, and quite soon they seem to enjoy watching people moving about. Thirdly, the responses both of babbling and of smiling in infants are increased in intensity when they are responded to by an adult in a purely social way, namely by giving the baby a little attention (Brackbill, 1958; Rheingold, Gewirtz, and Ross, 1959). Neither food nor other bodily care is required, although their provision may well assist. Thus there is clear evidence that the human infant is so made that he responds readily to social stimuli and engages quickly in social interaction (see further discussion in Chapter 14).

So strongly are human infants disposed to respond to social stimuli, indeed, that they not infrequently become attached to other infants of their own age or only a little older, protesting and following when the other child departs, greeting and approaching when the other returns. Attachments of this type are reported by Schaffer and Emerson (1964a). They also form the subject of a paper by Anna Freud and Sophie Dann (1951), which describes a group of six children, aged between three and four years, who had been in a concentration camp and whose only persisting company in life had evidently been each other. The authors emphasise that 'the children's positive feelings were centred exclusively in their own group . . . they cared greatly for each other and not at all for anybody or anything else'.

That an infant can become attached to others of the same age, or only a little older, makes it plain that attachment behaviour can develop and be directed towards a figure who has done nothing to meet the infant's physiological needs. The same is true even when the attachment-figure is a grown-up. Amongst persons rated by Schaffer and Emerson (1964a) as principal or joint principal attachment-figures for the sixty Scottish children they studied, no less than one-fifth 'did not participate even to a minor degree in any aspect of the child's physical care. It appears that attachments may develop', they conclude, 'even when the individuals to whom they are formed have in no way been associated with physical satisfactions.' The variables that these researchers found determined most clearly the figures to whom the children would become attached were the speed with which a person responded to an infant and the intensity of the interaction in which he engaged with that infant.

Confidence in such findings is much increased by the results of recent experimental work which shows that one of the most potent ways of augmenting a child's performance of any task requiring discrimination or motor skill is to reward him with the greeting response of another human being. Bower (1966) describes how it is possible to explore the visual world of infants of two weeks of age and upwards by applying operant-conditioning techniques in which the reinforcing agent is simply an adult who appears before the infant in peek-a-boo style; and Stevenson (1965) reviews a number of studies in which children's skills in simple tasks are enhanced if each correct response is rewarded with a crumb of social approval.[1]

Thus such evidence as there is strongly supports the view that attachment behaviour in humans can develop, as it can

[1] A number of learning theorists, impressed by these results, have concluded that the development of attachment behaviour can be accounted for wholly in terms of the operant conditioning of an infant's social responses through social reinforcement coming from his attachment-figure (Gewirtz, 1961). Although nothing in that view contradicts the view advanced here, it tends to give too little attention to the strong innate biases that, it is held, each partner brings to the partnership. When innate biases are ignored, Ainsworth (1973) points out, there is danger that every behavioural system will be regarded as environmentally labile to an infinite degree, with potentially very adverse effects on practice.

in other species, without the traditional rewards of food and warmth. This means that, if the secondary drive theory is to be sustained for the human case when it has proved untenable for fairly closely related species, new and compelling positive evidence is required; and of that there seems no sign.[1] Why, then, hold on to the secondary drive theory?

Among several reasons why psychoanalysts are reluctant to abandon it is that some theory is needed to account for the high frequency of frankly oral symptoms in all kinds of neurotic and psychotic conditions.

On the basis of the secondary drive theory such symptoms are readily explained by being regarded simply as regressions to an earlier normal phase when object relations are nothing but oral. If that explanation is no longer acceptable, what alternative is offered? There are three ways in which this problem can be approached. In the first place, although on the hypothesis advanced attachment behaviour is conceived as developing independently of food, it does not develop independently of sucking—a paradox that is discussed fully in the next chapter. The theory of regression, therefore, is not wholly ruled out. In the second place, by means of a symbolic substitution oral symptoms may sometimes be regarded by a patient as the equivalent of a relationship with a person; for him the part represents the whole. In the third place, it seems probable that in many cases an oral activity is to be classed as a displacement activity, namely an activity that is evoked when another is frustrated and that seems to occur out of context. Possible ways in which such activities may arise in situations of conflict are discussed in Chapter 6. Since the processes postulated are at an infra-symbolic level, brief discussion of their role in human life may be useful.

In work with human beings we are so accustomed to seeing

---

[1] In recent times Murphy (1964) has advanced a modified form of secondary drive theory, but has presented no new evidence to support it. Thus, in the course of criticising my position, as expressed earlier (Bowlby, 1958), Murphy concedes that food may not be the only reward of significance. Nevertheless she postulates that an infant's attachment develops only because he learns that his mother-figure gratifies, protects, and sustains him: 'Clinging and following behaviour do not produce the attachment; they are an expression of the infant's reliance upon the need-gratifying, protecting, sustaining mother-figure.' Were that to be so, attachment would hardly develop towards young children or towards adults who do none of these things.

one activity take the place of another by means of a symbolic equivalence between the two that it may be difficult to imagine that superficially similar substitutions may also occur at an infra-symbolic level. Here are two examples. A child in disgrace sucks his thumb; a child separated from his mother over-eats. In such situations it is possible to think of the thumb and food as being symbolic of mother as a whole or at least of nipple and milk. An alternative is to regard such activities as substitutes produced by psychological processes operating at an infra-symbolic level, such for instance as underlie the nest-building behaviour of fighting gulls; in other words, to postulate that when a child's attachment to his mother is frustrated sucking or over-eating develops as a non-symbolic out-of-context activity. It is noteworthy that something of this sort almost certainly occurs in non-human primates. Both rhesus monkey and chimpanzee infants brought up without mothers to cling to show a great excess of auto-erotic sucking. Nissen reports that, though thumb-sucking is not seen in infant chimps reared with their mothers, it occurs in some 80 per cent of those reared in isolation. It is the same with rhesus monkeys. In Harlow's laboratory a full-grown rhesus female habitually sucked her own breast and a male sucked his penis. Both had been reared in isolation. In these cases what we should all describe as oral symptoms had developed as a result of the infant's being deprived of an attachment to a mother-figure and by means of processes which seem clearly infra-symbolic. May it not be the same for oral symptoms in human infants?

The observations of Anna Freud and Sophie Dann on the six children from a concentration camp are suggestive: 'Peter, Ruth, John and Leah were all inveterate thumbsuckers'. This the authors ascribe to the fact that for all of them 'the object world had proved disappointing'. They continue:

> That the excess of sucking was in direct proportion to the in-stability of their object relationships was confirmed at the end of the year, when the children knew that they were due to leave Bulldogs Bank and when sucking in the daytime once more became very prevalent with all of them. This persistence of oral gratification . . . fluctuated according to the children's relation-ship with the environment . . .

If this type of substitution can occur in human infants, may not a process occurring at an infra-symbolic level account also for some at least of the oral symptoms that appear in older subjects when whole object relations become difficult, for whatever reason?

Whether or not this way of looking at oral symptoms proves tenable, only further research will show. It is described here to demonstrate that the theory of attachment behaviour proposed can provide a reasonable alternative to the traditional explanations of oral symptoms based on secondary drive theory.

The question of imprinting

Once a theory of secondary drive is discarded and clues to a new theory are sought in the work of Lorenz and those inspired by him, the question is posed whether the way in which attachment behaviour develops in man is to be likened to imprinting.

In his earliest statements about imprinting Lorenz (1935) flatly denied that in mammals anything of the sort occurs. With time, however, viewpoints have changed. On the one hand, concepts of imprinting have broadened (see Chapter 10). On the other, experimental work with non-human mammals has shown that, in a few species at least, development is sufficiently like that of nidifugous birds to make comparison fruitful. Provided, therefore, that no facile assumptions are made of the sort that Hinde (1961, 1963) warns against,[1] it is useful to consider whether anything resembling imprinting occurs in man. This raises the prior question whether anything of the sort occurs in non-human mammals.

Non-human Mammals

Enough has been said in the preceding section to show that the way in which attachment behaviour develops in a number of mammalian species has much in common with the way in which it develops in nidifugous birds. Thus, at first, many responses that are appropriately directed to a mother can be elicited by a wide range of objects. Usually there is soon a narrowing down of effective objects, due, it seems, to exposure learning and to the reinforcing properties of certain perceptual features, such as contact, movement, and the sound of maternal

[1] In reviewing the usefulness of comparing mammals with birds Hinde warns that any 'similarities may be the result merely of similar selective forces, not of similar mechanisms' (1961). 'Seeing the problems in the one case', he continues elsewhere (1963), 'may highlight the problems in the other case but it won't provide the answers. We have got to analyse each case in detail in its own right.'

calls. Once the individual characteristics of an attachment-figure are learned, the responses are directed mainly or entirely towards it. Once a figure is selected, moreover, preference for that figure tends to be stable; and a shift of attachment behaviour from a familiar figure to a new and strange one becomes more and more difficult. A principal reason for this is that in mammals, as in birds, the reaction to any strange figure is, as the animal grows older, increasingly likely to be one of fear and withdrawal.

The role of fear responses in limiting the possibility that attachment will develop as the animal grows older is well illustrated by Scott's experiments with puppies, already referred to (Scott, 1963). So long as a puppy was no older than five weeks when first exposed to a man it approached at once. By contrast, puppies first exposed at seven weeks of age kept away during the first two days of the experiment and approached only on subsequent days. Others first exposed at nine weeks of age kept clear for the first three days. Yet others, first exposed at fourteen weeks of age, kept away on every single day of the experimental week. Only with careful and prolonged treatment, writes Scott (1963), did puppies in the last group overcome their fears; even so, in later life they continued to be timid of humans.[1]

The findings of Harlow and his associates with rhesus monkeys point in the same direction. Before six or seven weeks of age infant monkeys show only slight visually induced fear responses (Harlow and Zimmermann, 1959). Up to that age, therefore, an infant will readily approach any new animal or object; thenceforward, however, it becomes increasingly likely to withdraw. Thus an infant kept in social isolation for the first three months of its life shows such extreme disturbance on being moved to more varied surroundings with other monkeys that it remains rooted to where it is and may not eat. Even so, these infants show some degree of recovery in subsequent weeks, and a month or two later are playing fairly actively with other

---

[1] In a subsequent series of experiments Fuller and Clark (1966a and b) found that if previously isolated puppies were given a mild dose of chlorpromazine before a social test their fear responses to the strange situation could be reduced. As a result, puppies that had been kept isolated from the age of three weeks to fifteen weeks responded to the novel situation with much less fear than did comparable puppies that had not been drugged, they were not so reluctant as the latter to approach the experimenter, and they began to form attachments.

young monkeys (Griffin and Harlow, 1966). Those kept in social isolation for their first six months of life, however, do not show this recovery; and animals kept in isolation for as long as sixteen months do little more when taken to varied surroundings than crouch, hug themselves, and rock, and they continue thus for two or three years at least (Mason and Sponholz, 1963). It appears that this crippling of their behaviour is due to their extreme fear of all novelty, including, of course, other monkeys.

Thus in both puppies and rhesus monkeys the phase during which attachment can develop most easily is limited. Once that phase is passed, though it may still be possible for them to become attached to a new object, it becomes progressively more difficult.

In this respect, as in so many others to do with the development of attachment behaviour, there are clearly strong resemblances between mammals and birds. Indeed, considering that any similarities are a result, *not* of their having inherited some common mechanism, but of convergent evolution, the degree of resemblance is remarkable. No doubt, as Hinde (1961) points out, this is a consequence of the fact that the survival problem faced by each branch of the animal kingdom is the same.

Imprinting in Man

It will become apparent in subsequent chapters that, so far as can be seen at present, the development of attachment behaviour in human infants, though much slower, is of a piece with that seen in non-human mammals. Much evidence supports that conclusion and none contradicts it.

Present knowledge of the development of attachment behaviour in humans can be summarised briefly under the same eight heads that were used in Chapter 10 to describe present knowledge of imprinting in birds:

   i. In human infants social responses of every kind are first elicited by a wide array of stimuli and are later elicited by a much narrower array, confined after some months to stimuli arising from one or a few particular individuals.

  ii. There is evidence of a marked bias to respond socially to certain kinds of stimuli more than to others.

 iii. The more experience of social interaction an infant has with a person the stronger his attachment to that person becomes.

 iv. The fact that learning to discriminate different faces

commonly follows periods of attentive staring and listening suggests that exposure learning may be playing a part.

v. In most infants attachment behaviour to a preferred figure develops during the first year of life. It seems probable that there is a sensitive period in that year during which attachment behaviour develops most readily.

vi. It is unlikely that any sensitive phase begins before about six weeks and it may be some weeks later.

vii. After about six months, and markedly so after eight or nine months, babies are more likely to respond to strange figures with fear responses, and more likely also to respond to them with strong fear responses, than they are when they are younger. Because of the growing frequency and strength of such fear responses, the development of attachment to a new figure becomes increasingly difficult towards the end of the first year and subsequently.

viii. Once a child has become strongly attached to a particular figure, he tends to prefer that figure to all others, and such preference tends to persist despite separation.

Evidence in support of all these statements is presented in later chapters.

We may conclude, therefore, that, so far as is at present known, the way in which attachment behaviour develops in the human infant and becomes focused on a discriminated figure is sufficiently like the way in which it develops in other mammals, and in birds, for it to be included, legitimately, under the heading of imprinting—so long as that term is used in its current generic sense. Indeed, to do otherwise would be to create a wholly unwarranted gap between the human case and that of other species.

Function of attachment behaviour

In Chapter 8 a very sharp distinction was drawn between the causes of a particular sort of behaviour and the function that that behaviour fulfils. Given the structure of a behavioural system, variables that cause it to become active include such things as hormone level and stimuli of particular kinds from the environment. The function that the behaviour fulfils, on the other hand, is to be sought in the contribution it makes to survival. Male mating behaviour can serve as an example: amongst its usual causes are androgen level and presence of female; its function is the contribution it makes to reproduction.

In traditional discussions of the child's tie to his mother causation and function have not been clearly distinguished. As a result there is no systematic consideration of what the tie's function may be. Those who hold that the tie is a result of a secondary drive derived from hunger seem to assume that the tie is of use because it keeps the infant close to his food supply, though this is not discussed.

Though it might easily be supposed that Freud also held that the function of a child's tie to his mother is mainly to ensure food supply, Freud's position is in fact a little different. In his first systematic discussion of the problem (*Inhibitions, Symptoms and Anxiety*, 1926) he argues as follows: the basic danger confronting an infant is that his psychical apparatus may be thrown out of order by the presence of excessive stimulation arising from un-satisfied physiological need. This danger the infant is helpless to deal with alone. Mother, however, can put an end to that danger. Consequently the infant, knowing from 'experience that she satisfies all its needs without delay', . . . 'wants to perceive the presence of its mother'. The conclusion of this argument appears to be that the function fulfilled by the secondary drive that ties infant to mother is, by ensuring mother's presence, that of preventing the psychical apparatus from becoming deranged 'by an accumulation of amounts of stimulation which require to be disposed of' (*S.E.*, **20**, p. 137). On this view, food is of importance because it helps to dispose of excessive amounts of stimulation.

Since all the evidence suggests that, in whatever form it is held, the secondary drive theory of the child's tie is mistaken and that, even in mammals, food plays only a marginal part in the development and maintenance of attachment behaviour, the function of the child's tie to his mother must be considered afresh.

A view I have already proposed is that the function of attachment behaviour is protection from predators (Bowlby, 1964).[1] Another theory has also been advanced in recent years, namely, that it affords opportunity for the infant to learn from mother various activities necessary for survival. The latter suggestion is sometimes put forward in discussion and seems to be implied in a paper by Murphy (1964).[2]

[1] This hypothesis has also been advanced by King (1966).
[2] Murphy writes: '. . . the mother not only meets nutritional and other bodily needs . . . but also supports the development of the specific ego functions . . .'

Now these two suggestions do not contradict one another. Not only that: each is very plausible. If there are predators about, an infant's attachment behaviour no doubt contributes to its safety. In the company of mother, moreover, an infant is in a good position to learn activities and other things useful for its survival. Since each of these outcomes is a consequence of attachment behaviour, and a beneficial consequence at that, why cannot we agree that both of them are probably functions?

To settle the matter in that way, however, is to evade a problem. As was discussed in Chapter 8, the biological function of a particular bit of behaviour is not *any* favourable consequence that its performance may have. Biological function is defined more narrowly: it is that consequence that in the course of evolution has led the behaviour in question to become incorporated into the biological equipment of a species. Such incorporation occurs as a result of some advantage (in terms of survival and differential breeding success) that the behaviour confers on those possessed of it. Because individuals endowed with a ready ability to develop the behaviour in question leave more progeny than do those deficient in it and because, through heredity, their progeny are likely to be well endowed too, there comes a time when virtually all members of the species (or of some population of it) are well endowed with ability to develop the behaviour. In order to determine the biological function of that behaviour the question to be answered is: precisely what advantage does the behaviour being considered confer on individuals endowed with ability to develop it that leads them to achieve greater breeding success than is achieved by those who are deficient in that ability?

In the case of attachment behaviour there is too little evidence for anyone to be sure. What, then, are the arguments in favour of and against each suggestion?

The suggestion that the crucial advantage of attachment behaviour is that it affords opportunity for the infant to learn from mother various activities necessary for survival seems promising at first sight. The young of advanced species, especially mammals, are born with a plastic behavioural equipment. During development this equipment is greatly elaborated by processes of learning and much that is learned derives from imitating what mother does and from directing behaviour towards the same objects, e.g. food substances, that mother directs her behaviour towards. There is thus no doubt that one consequence of a young animal's remaining in proximity to mother is that it has ample opportunity to learn useful things from her.

Yet there are two reasons that make it unlikely that this is the essential advantage we are seeking. First, why should attachment behaviour persist into adult life long after learning is complete, as it does in many mammalian species? And why, moreover, should it be especially persistent in females? Second, why should attachment behaviour be elicited at such high intensity when an animal is alarmed? A theory of function that picks out the opportunity to learn seems to have no answer to these questions.

The suggestion that the cardinal advantage conferred on an animal by attachment behaviour is protection from predators introduces a line of reasoning that, familiar to all field naturalists, remains almost unknown to psychologists and psychoanalysts. Yet there can be no doubt that for animals of all species the danger of death from attack is fully as great as the danger of death from starvation. All animals are predators either of vegetable or of animal life, or of both. To survive, therefore, animals of every species must succeed in obtaining their own food supply and in breeding without, or at least before, becoming part of the food supply of an animal of some other species. Thus behavioural equipment that protects from predators is of an importance co-equal to that of equipment that leads to nutrition or reproduction. All too often this elementary fact of nature is forgotten in a laboratory or an urban environment.

That protection from predators is by far the most likely function of attachment behaviour is supported by three main facts. First, there is good evidence, derived from observations of many species of bird and mammal, that an isolated animal is much more likely to be attacked and seized by a predator than is an animal that stays bunched together with others of its kind. Secondly, attachment behaviour is elicited particularly easily and intensely in animals which, by reason of age, size, or condition, are especially vulnerable to predators, for example the young, pregnant females, the sick. Thirdly, attachment behaviour is always elicited at high intensity in situations of alarm, which are commonly situations when a predator is either sensed or suspected. No other theory fits these facts.

The paradoxical finding that the more punishment a juvenile receives the stronger becomes its attachment to the punishing figure, very difficult to explain on any other theory, is compatible with the view that the function of attachment behaviour is protection from predators. This is shown by the important observation that when a dominant male senses a predator or other danger he commonly threatens or even attacks a juvenile that unwarily approaches the danger spot (Hall and DeVore, 1965; Kawamura, 1963). The dominant male's behaviour, by frightening the juvenile, elicits the juvenile's attachment behaviour. As a result the juvenile seeks the proximity of an adult animal, as often as not that of the very male that frightened it; and by so doing the juvenile also removes itself from the danger.[1]

Though these arguments carry great weight, a measure of doubt may seem to be cast on their validity by the field studies of sub-human primates. Only very occasionally have attacks on monkeys been observed, and on chimpanzees or gorillas none at all. Indeed, it is even suggested that these two species of great ape live in a garden of Eden immune from enemies. Whether this is really so remains uncertain. Washburn and his colleagues question it. In a discussion of the problem (Washburn, Jay, and Lancaster, 1965) they write:

> The whole matter of predator–prey relations among primates has been difficult to study. Rare events, such as an attack by an eagle (Haddow, 1952 . . .) may be very important in the survival of primates, but such attacks are seldom observed because the presence of the human observer disturbs either the predator or the prey. We think that the present de-emphasis of the import-ance of predation on primates arises from these difficulties of observation and from the fact that even today most of the studies of free-ranging primates are made in areas where predators have been reduced or eliminated by man. Most predators are active at night, and there is still no adequate study of the nocturnal behaviour of any monkey or ape.[2]

[1] Kummer describes the behaviour of young monkeys that have left mother but are not yet mature. When severely threatened by an adult of its group a young monkey always seeks out the highest ranking animal available, usually a dominant male. Since this same animal is usually the one that threatened in the first place, it frequently happens that the animal that the juvenile approaches is the very animal that itself was the cause of its fear (quoted by Chance, 1959).

[2] In discussing further the methodological problems of measuring predation on primates, Washburn (1968) concludes that the only effective way of measuring it is to study the behaviour of potential predators. Thus, despite extensive field studies of langur monkeys, no observer has ever reported an attack on them by leopards. Nevertheless,

There the matter must be left. All in all, it is held, of the various suggestions advanced for the function of attachment behaviour, protection from predators seems by far the most likely. In what follows it is the function that is assumed.

A note on terminology : 'dependence'

It will be noticed that in this account the terms 'dependence' and 'dependency' are avoided, although they have for long been in common use by psychoanalysts and also by psychologists who favour a theory of secondary drive. The terms derive from the idea that a child becomes linked to his mother because he is dependent on her as the source of physiological gratification. Apart, however, from their deriving from a theory that is almost certainly false, there are other strong reasons for not using these terms.

The fact is that to be dependent on a mother-figure and to be attached to her are very different things. Thus, in the early weeks of life an infant is undoubtedly dependent on his mother's ministrations, but he is not yet attached to her. Conversely, a child of two or three years who is being looked after by strangers may show the clearest evidence that he continues to be strongly attached to his mother though he is not at that time dependent on her.

Logically, the word 'dependence' refers to the extent to which one individual relies on another for his existence, and so has a functional reference; whereas attachment as used here refers to a form of behaviour and is purely descriptive. As a consequence of these different meanings, we find that, whereas dependence is maximum at birth and diminishes more or less steadily until maturity is reached, attachment is altogether absent at birth and is not strongly in evidence until after an infant is past six months. The words are far from synonymous.

Despite these logical handicaps it might still be argued that a term like 'dependency behaviour' could continue to be employed in place of 'attachment behaviour', if only because so many psychologists are accustomed to the term dependency. But there is another reason for not using it even more weighty than that already given. It is that the value implications of the

---

a recent study by Schaller (1967) shows that 27 per cent of leopard scats contain evidence of the leopards' having eaten these monkeys. The recent evidence that predation is a major factor in determining both the morphology and the behaviour of primates is also discussed by Washburn.

term 'dependency' are the exact opposite of those that the term 'attachment' not only conveys but is intended to convey.

A common judgement is that for a person to be dependent is less good than for him to be independent: in fact, to call someone dependent in his personal relations is usually rather disparaging. But to call someone attached is far from disparaging. On the contrary, for members of a family to be attached to one another is regarded by many as admirable. Conversely, for a person to be detached in his personal relations is commonly regarded as less than admirable. Thus, whereas dependency in personal relations is a condition to be avoided or left behind, attachment is often a condition to be cherished.

For these reasons, it is contended, nothing but confusion can result from the continued use of the terms 'dependence' and 'dependency need' when what is referred to is behaviour that maintains proximity. It is not without interest that, despite their adherence to the theory of secondary drive, both Sigmund Freud and Anna Freud nonetheless employ the term 'attachment' (Freud, 1931; Burlingham and Freud, 1944).

Other terms that have been used are 'cathexis of object' and 'affiliation'.

'Cathexis' has two drawbacks. The first and principal one is that it derives from Freud's energy theory, the difficulties of which are discussed in Chapter 1. A subsidiary difficulty is that it does not permit of discussion of the differences between an object towards which attachment behaviour is directed and one towards which sexual behaviour is directed, a matter discussed later in this chapter.

'Affiliation' was introduced by Murray (1938): 'Under this heading are classed all manifestations of friendliness and goodwill, of the desire to do things in company with others.' As such it is a much broader concept than attachment and is not intended to cover behaviour that is directed towards one or a few particular figures, which is the hallmark of attachment behaviour. Murray himself recognises this difference by postulating an additional need – 'succorance'. In the Murray schema dependency is regarded as resulting from a fusion of affiliation and succorance.

Another drawback of 'affiliation' is that it is conceptualised in terms of 'needs', the ambiguities of which are discussed in Chapter 8. Since the term continues to be used in Murray's original sense (e.g. Schachter, 1959), it is clearly unsuitable as an alternative for attachment.

Attachment and other systems of social behaviour

In this chapter and the preceding one the child's tie to his mother has been discussed without any reference to sexual or any other sort of social behaviour. Instead, attachment is presented as a system of behaviour having its own form of internal organisation and serving its own function. Moreover, in so far as sexual behaviour has been discussed at all (see Chapter 10) it has been referred to as a system of behaviour distinct from attachment behaviour, and one having a different ontogeny and, of course, a different function. Does this mean, it may be asked, that in the new schema no links between attachment and sex are thought to exist? If so, does not this ignore one of Freud's greatest contributions?

The brief answer to these questions is that, although regarded as distinct behavioural systems, attachment behaviour and sexual behaviour are believed to have unusually close linkages. The new schema, therefore, clearly recognising the clinical phenomena to account for which Freud's theory was advanced, offers different explanations of them.

Some parts of Freud's theories regarding infantile sexuality were advanced to account for the finding that established sexual perversions usually (probably always) originate during childhood. In Chapter 10 reference is made to a number of developmental processes now known to be common in young animals that, should they go awry, could well lead to an atypical development of the organisation of sexual behaviour, and so may well be responsible for abnormal development in man.

Other parts of psychoanalytic theorising about infantile sexuality have been advanced to explain the finding that the form taken by an individual's sexual behaviour when he is adult is much influenced by the form taken by that individual's behaviour towards mother and/or father when he is young. In traditional psychoanalytic theory the existence of such a linkage is accounted for on the grounds that the two forms of behaviour, infantile and adult, are simply the different expressions of a single libidinal force. On this view, linkage and influence are taken for granted; what needs explanation is the differences between the two forms of behaviour. In the new theory, by contrast, it is the differences between the two forms of behaviour that are taken for granted, and what needs explanation is the linkage between them.

There are three main reasons why it is held wise to keep

attachment behaviour and sexual behaviour conceptually distinct. The first is that the activations of the two systems vary independently of one another. The second is that the class of objects towards which each is directed may be quite different. A third is that sensitive phases in the development of each are likely to occur at different ages. Let us consider the reasons serially.

Fully functional attachment behaviour always matures early in the life-cycle and is soon active at intense levels; whereas, in adulthood, attachment behaviour is usually active at lower levels of intensity or, in some species, hardly active at all. Sexual behaviour, by contrast, matures later; and, when seen in the immature, it is usually only in fragmentary and non-functional form.

A dramatic example of the distinctive ways in which attachment behaviour and sexual behaviour become active during the life-cycle is seen in the ungulates. Thus, a lamb follows its mother when it is young and, if female, continues to do so. As a result, as already noted, a flock of sheep is made up of lambs following mothers following grandmothers following great-grandmothers, etc., so that the flock is led by the oldest ewe of all. Thus in female sheep, and in females of many related species, attachment behaviour remains strongly in evidence from birth until death. Sexual behaviour in these creatures is, by contrast, episodic. As they approach maturity the young males leave the female flock and gather in bachelor bands. Once or twice a year only, at oestrus, the males invade the female flock and courtship and mating occur. Then the males leave again and individuals of both sexes resume a sexually non-active life until the next oestrus season. Thus not only do the actual patterns of attachment and sexual behaviour differ but the periods of the life-cycle when they are most active differ greatly also.

Again, the class of objects towards which these different patterns of behaviour are directed can in some cases be quite different. For example, a duckling that has directed all its attachment behaviour to a man may nonetheless direct all its sexual behaviour to birds of its own species. The reasons for this are, first, that the range of stimuli capable of eliciting each sort of behaviour may be very different and, second, that the sensitive periods during which the range of each becomes narrowed may differ as well. In mallard ducks experiment shows that the sensitive phase for following is the first forty-eight hours or so of life whereas that for sexual behaviour is from three to eight weeks (see Chapter 10). Although evidence is unsatisfactory for mammals, it seems not unlikely that in them also the sensitive phase for selection of sexual figure is later than that for selection of attachment figure. In man the reports of patients regarding the selection of a fetish seem often to centre on a period around the third birthday, namely at least two years later than the sensitive phase for selection of an attachment-figure.

Whether that is so or not, experimental work with non-human primates has led Harlow to the firm conclusion that in them as in other species attachment behaviour and sexual behaviour are best regarded as distinct systems.

In a recent review of their work, Harlow and Harlow (1965) distinguish five affectional systems[1]

which bind together various individuals within a [primate] species in coordinated and constructive social relations. . . . Each system develops through its own maturational stages and differs in the underlying variables which produce and control its particular response patterns. Typically the maturational stages overlap. . . . These five affectional systems, in order of development, are: (1) The infant–mother affectional system, which binds the infant to the mother [termed here attachment behaviour]; (2) the mother–infant or maternal affectional system; (3) the infant–infant, age-mate, or peer affectional system through which infants and children interrelate . . . and develop persisting affection for each other; (4) the sexual and heterosexual affectional system, culminating in adolescent sexuality and finally in those adult behaviours leading to procreation; and (5) the paternal affectional system, broadly defined in terms of positive responsiveness of adult males toward infants, juveniles, and other members of their particular social groups.

The reasons given by the Harlows for distinguishing these systems from each other are, it will be noted, the same as those already given here, namely that 'Each system develops through its own maturational stages and differs in the underlying variables which produce and control its particular response patterns'. The experimental evidence that leads them to these conclusions is contained in their scientific papers.

[1] In the terminology used in this book each affectional system is an integrate of behavioural systems mediating socially directed instinctive behaviour of a particular kind.

Thus there is good evidence that in primates as well as in other orders and classes of animal the properties of attachment behaviour and of sexual behaviour are distinct; nor is there reason to suppose that man is any exception. Nevertheless, distinct though the two systems are, there is good evidence also that they are apt to impinge on each other and to influence the development of each other. This occurs in other species as well as in man.

Attachment behaviour is made up of a number of component patterns and the same is true of sexual behaviour. Some components are shared. They are thus seen as elements in both sorts of behaviour, though usually more typically in one than in the other. For example, movements seen typically during courtship in some species of duck are seen also in newly hatched ducklings, in which case the movements are directed towards whatever object elicits their following response (Fabricius, 1962). In man, clinging and kissing are examples of patterns common to both types of behaviour.

Other evidence of a linkage between attachment behaviour and sexual behaviour is reported by Andrew (1964). Young male birds of several species and also young male guinea-pigs, when treated with testosterone to accelerate sexual development, show sexual behaviour towards any object on which their attachment behaviour is already imprinted. Control animals similarly injected but not yet imprinted show no sexual behaviour when presented with similar objects. A likely explanation is that in these species attachment behaviour and sexual behaviour share certain eliciting and controlling mechanisms.

It may in fact be that not only do attachment and sexual behaviour share certain components and causal mechanisms but that parental behaviour shares some of them as well. An example, cited earlier, of overlap between sexual behaviour and parental behaviour in birds is courtship feeding, in which the cock treats the hen in the same way as both treat young, whilst the hen begs from the cock with a posture used otherwise only by young begging food from parents (Hinde, 1966).

In man, overlaps between attachment behaviour, parental behaviour, and sexual behaviour are commonplace. For example, it is not uncommon for one individual to treat a sexual partner as though the partner were a parent, and the partner may reciprocate by adopting a parental attitude in return. A possible, indeed probable, explanation of the behaviour of the partner who takes the juvenile role is that, in that partner, not only has attachment behaviour persisted into adult life, which is usual, but it has, for some reason, continued to be almost as readily elicited as it is in a young child, which is not usual.

Plainly a great research effort is required to unravel all these overlaps and the influences of one class of behaviour on another. Enough has been said, it is hoped, to show that recognition of attachment behaviour, sexual behaviour, and parental behaviour as distinct systems in no way imperils the fruits of psychoanalytic insight.

Chapter 13

A Control Systems Approach to Attachment Behaviour

They must go free
Like fishes in the sea
Or starlings in the skies
Whilst you remain
The shore where casually they come again.
FRANCES CORNFORD

Introduction

For a secondary drive type of theory the facts of attachment behaviour prove awkward and obdurate. For a control type of theory, by contrast, they present an interesting challenge. Once an approach of this sort is brought to bear, indeed, the broad outlines of possible solutions are not too difficult to see.

In Chapter 5 it was pointed out that much instinctive behaviour maintains an animal for long periods of time in a certain sort of relationship to certain features of the environment. Examples are brooding behaviour, which results in the maintenance of proximity to eggs and nest over a period of weeks, and territorial behaviour, which results in the maintenance of location within a certain bit of the environment over months and sometimes over years. It was pointed out also that behaviour having this kind of predictable outcome could be organised on less or on more sophisticated lines. A less sophisticated version, for example, could be organised so that movement towards a specified goal-object would become increasingly probable the greater the distance from the goal-object. A main proposition of this chapter is that attachment behaviour is organised in this kind of way.

The above formulation is, of course, no more than the bare bones of the theory to be proposed. To account for the behaviour that is actually seen much elaboration is required. In the first place, the intensity with which attachment behaviour is shown by a young child varies not only from day to day but from hour to hour and from minute to minute; thus it is

235

necessary to examine the conditions that activate and terminate attachment behaviour, or that alter the intensity at which it is activated. Secondly, great changes occur during the course of infancy and childhood in the way in which the different systems mediating attachment behaviour are organised. Before these matters are discussed, however, the role of the mother as partner must be considered. For not only may increased distance be caused by movement either of mother or of child, but decreased distance likewise can result from movement of either of the two parties.

The roles of child and of mother in mother–child interaction

Interaction a Resultant of Several Classes of Behaviour

Anyone who observes how a mother and her one- or two-year-old child behave over a period of time will see that each exhibits very many different patterns. Whilst some of the behaviour of each partner has the effect of increasing or maintaining proximity between the pair, much of it is of a completely other sort. Some is irrelevant to the question of proximity: mother cooks or sews; child plays with a ball or empties mother's handbag. Other behaviour is antithetic to maintenance of proximity: mother goes to another room or child leaves to climb the stairs. Other behaviour again may be a negation of proximity-seeking: on occasion, usually rare, either mother or child may feel so provoked and angry as to act in a way that increases distance from the other. Maintenance of proximity, therefore, is only one of many outcomes that the behaviour of the two partners may have.

Nevertheless it is most unlikely that on an ordinary day distance between the two will ever exceed a certain maximum. Whenever it does so, either one or other member of the pair is likely soon to act in such a way that distance is reduced. On some occasions it is mother who takes the initiative—she calls, or goes to see where the child has got to; on others the child may take the initiative either by scampering back to mother or by crying.

Thus there is a dynamic equilibrium between the mother–child pair. Despite much irrelevant behaviour by each, and some competing and some incompatible or contrary behaviour, distance between them is as a rule maintained within certain stable limits. To understand how this comes about it is useful to regard the spatial relationship between the two as the resultant of behaviour of the following four classes:

    a. the child's attachment behaviour;

    b. behaviour of the child that is antithetic to attachment, notably exploratory behaviour and play;

    c. the mother's caregiving behaviour;

    d. behaviour of the mother that is antithetic to parental care.

Forms of behaviour classified in (a) or in (c) are homogeneous in regard to function; those classified in (b) or in (d) are heterogeneous.

Behaviour of each of these four classes varies greatly in intensity from moment to moment, and behaviour of any one class may for a time be absent altogether. Each class of behaviour, moreover, is likely to be affected by the presence or absence of the others, because the consequences of behaviour of any one class are likely either to elicit or to inhibit behaviour of the other three classes. Thus, when mother is called away a child's attachment behaviour is likely to be elicited and his exploratory behaviour inhibited; conversely, when a child explores too far, a mother's care behaviour is likely to be elicited and whatever else she is doing to be inhibited. In a happy couple these four classes of behaviour occur and progress together in harmony. But risk of conflict is ever-present.

This analysis shows that a child's attachment behaviour is one class only of four separate classes of behaviour—two intrinsic to the child and two to the mother—that go to make up mother-child interaction. Before discussing attachment behaviour further it is useful to consider briefly each of the other three classes. We begin with that class of behaviour which, by taking a child away from his mother, is the very antithesis of attachment behaviour.

Exploratory Behaviour and Play

During the past decade a view long held by Piaget has become widely accepted: exploration and investigation constitute a class of behaviour that is as distinct and important as are such recognised classes as feeding and mating.

Exploratory behaviour takes three main forms: first, an orienting response of head and body that brings sense organs into a better position for sampling the stimulus object and alerts musculature and the cardiovascular system for ready action; secondly, bodily approach to the stimulus object, which enables all the sense organs to obtain more and better information about it; thirdly, investigation of the object by manipulating it or experimenting with it in other ways. Such behaviour is common in all species of bird and mammal and especially so in certain species, notably the crows among birds, and the primates among mammals. Young creatures show more of it than do older ones.[1]

Exploratory behaviour is elicited typically by stimuli that are novel and/or complex, characteristics that often go together. Any novel object left in the cage of an animal, be it monkey, rat or rhinoceros, sooner or later is inspected and investigated. After a time interest wanes: 'the novelty has worn off'. But each new object presented arouses fresh interest, and so does an old one introduced again after an interval.

An animal may work for long periods pushing levers or opening shutters when the reward of its labours is no more than a novel object to play with or a novel scene to look at. Food is unnecessary. Furthermore, when both food and something novel are present together, exploration of the novel usually takes precedence over feeding—even when the animal is hungry.

Humans, especially young ones, behave in the same way. Every mother knows that a baby loves to watch a changing scene and, as Rheingold (1963a) has shown experimentally, a baby even as young as four months soon learns to touch repeatedly a little ball when the consequence of doing so is a brief movie-show. Every mother knows also that a baby will at once cease eating when something or someone new enters his range of vision. Such is the effect of novelty on a human child, indeed, that the phrase 'like a child with a new toy' has come to express the epitome of concentrated absorption in some one item of the environment.

Exploratory behaviour is thus no appendage of feeding behaviour or of sexual behaviour. Instead, it is a class of behaviour in its own right. It is best conceived as mediated by a set of behavioural systems evolved for the special function of extracting information from the environment. Like other behavioural systems, these systems are activated by stimuli that have certain characteristic properties and are terminated by stimuli that have other characteristic properties. In this case activation results from novelty and termination from familiarity. It is the special prop-

[1] A useful review of empirical work on exploratory behaviour in animals and man is to be found in Chapters 4, 5, and 6 of Berlyne's *Conflict, Arousal and Curiosity* (1960). See also Flavell's *The Developmental Psychology of Jean Piaget* (1963).

erty of exploratory behaviour that it transforms the novel into the familiar and by this process turns an activating stimulus into a terminating one.

A paradoxical feature of exploratory behaviour is that almost the very same properties that elicit exploration elicit alarm and withdrawal also. Because of this, an interested approach and an alarmed withdrawal are often shown by an animal or child either simultaneously or in rapid succession. As a rule the balance between the two shifts from alarm to interest. At first, something wholly strange elicits only withdrawal. Next comes inspection from a distance—often intense and prolonged. Then, sooner or later, provided the object remains stationary and emits no startling sounds or sights, the object is likely to be approached and explored—at first cautiously, later with more confidence. In most creatures such a process is greatly speeded up in the presence of a friend; and in a young creature especially it is notably accelerated by the presence of mother.

Play with peers seems to begin as an extension of exploration and play with inanimate objects. What Harlow and Harlow (1965) write of young monkeys probably applies equally to human children:

> The variables that elicit object exploration and social exploration are doubtless similar in kind. . . . Mobile physical objects afford a monkey an opportunity for interactive responsiveness, but no mobile object can give to an infant primate the enormous opportunity for stimulative feedback that can be achieved by contact with a social partner or partners. . . . The stage of play probably starts as individual activity involving very complex use of physical objects. . . . These individual play patterns . . . are undoubtedly the precursors of the multiple and complex interactive play responses that subsequently appear.

Through taking him away from mother, a child's exploratory behaviour and play are antithetic to his attachment behaviour. Conversely, by taking a mother towards her child, a mother's maternal behaviour is reciprocal to his attachment behaviour.

Maternal Caregiving

In all mammals, including man, maternal behaviour is of more than one kind. In a number of species it is useful to distinguish, as a start, nursing, nest-building, and retrieving. Each kind is vital if young are to survive, but for present purposes retrieving is the one of special interest.

Retrieving can be defined as any behaviour of a parent a predictable outcome of which is that the young are brought either into the nest or close to mother, or both. Whereas rodents and carnivores use mouth, primates use hands and arms. In addition, animals of most species use a characteristic call—often a rather soft, low note—that by eliciting attachment behaviour has the effect of bringing young towards them.[1]

In humans, retrieval behaviour has been included under many heads: 'mothering', 'maternal care', and 'nurturance' are among them. In some contexts the more general term 'maternal care' is to be preferred; in others 'retrieval' is better. In particular, 'retrieval' calls attention to the fact that much maternal behaviour is concerned with reducing the distance between infant and mother, and with retaining the infant in close physical contact with her. This critical fact can easily be lost to sight when other terms are used.

The retrieving behaviour of a primate mother gathers the infant into her arms and holds him there. Having a similar outcome to the attachment behaviour of young, it is probably best understood in similar terms—namely, as being mediated by a number of behavioural systems the predictable outcome of which is maintenance of proximity to the infant. Conditions that activate and terminate the systems can be studied. Amongst organismic variables that affect activation, the hormone levels of the mother almost certainly play a part. Amongst environmental variables are the whereabouts and behaviour of the infant: for example, when an infant strays beyond a certain distance or when he cries, a mother is likely to take action. And should she have occasion for alarm or see her infant carried off by others, she makes the most immediate and strenuous efforts to recover him. Only when the infant is safely in her arms does this type of behaviour cease. At other times, especially when her infant is playing contentedly with other known individuals in the vicinity, a mother may let things be. Yet her tendency to retrieve him is not wholly dormant: she is likely to keep a watchful eye on him and to be alert to any cry, ready to act at shortest notice.

Just as the predictable outcome of maternal retrieving behaviour is similar to that of a child's attachment behaviour, so do similar processes lead to the selection of the figures towards whom retrieving behaviour and attachment behaviour are

[1] For a review of maternal behaviour in mammals, see Rheingold (1963b).

directed. In the same way that an infant's attachment behaviour comes to be directed towards a particular mother-figure, so does a mother's retrieving behaviour come to be directed towards a particular infant. Evidence shows that, in all species of mammal, recognition of the infant occurs within hours or days of his birth and that, once he is recognised, only that particular infant is mothered.

Yet a third respect in which a mother's retrieving behaviour resembles a child's attachment behaviour is in its biological function. For a mother to remain in proximity to an infant and to gather him to her in conditions of alarm clearly serves a protective function. In the wild the main danger from which the infant is thus protected is probably that of predators. Other dangers are those of falling from a height and of drowning.

Whilst maternal retrieving behaviour is to be seen in its most elementary forms in non-human species, it is evident also in human mothers. In primitive societies a mother is likely to remain very near her infant, and almost always within eyeshot or earshot of him. The mother's alarm or the infant's distress will at once elicit action. In more developed communities the scene becomes more complex, partly because not infrequently a mother appoints someone to deputise for her for a shorter or longer part of the day. Even so, most mothers experience a strong pull to be close to their babies and young children. Whether they submit to the pull or stand out against it depends on a hundred variables, personal, cultural, and economic.

Maternal Behaviour Antithetic to Care of Infant

When a mother cares for a child she is always behaving in many other ways as well. Some of these other ways, while not inherently incompatible with the giving of care, nevertheless compete with it in greater or less degree. Other sorts of behaviour, however, are the very opposite of care and so are inherently incompatible with it.

Behaviour that in some degree competes with infant care includes all the usual household duties. Most of these, however, can usually be dropped at short notice and so are quite consistent with mothering. Other activities are less easily shelved; some of the most intractable are the demands of other family members, especially of husband and other young children. Inevitably, therefore, a mother experiences conflict, and her care of the baby may suffer.

Nonetheless a mother's activities that merely compete for

time and energy with her caring for a child are in a quite different category from behaviour that is inherently incompatible with care. Such are dislike of contact with the infant, or dislike of his screaming, either of which may lead a mother to withdraw from him. In an ordinary mother, withdrawing behaviour, though occurring on occasion, is likely to be neither frequent nor prolonged, and is quickly replaced by care behaviour when events require it. In an emotionally disturbed mother, on the other hand, it may interfere greatly with care.

Thus, just as an infant's attachment behaviour is counterbalanced by his exploratory behaviour and play, so a mother's retrieving behaviour is counterbalanced by a number of competing and a few incompatible activities.

This completes a brief review of some of the several classes of behaviour of child and mother that, in concert with the child's attachment behaviour, go to make up mother–child interaction.

All such interaction, it is well to remember, is accompanied by the strongest of feelings and emotions, happy or the reverse. When interaction between a couple runs smoothly, each party manifests intense pleasure in the other's company, and especially in the other's expressions of affection. Conversely, whenever interaction results in persistent conflict each party is likely on occasion to exhibit intense anxiety or unhappiness, especially when the other is rejecting.

When cast in terms of the theory sketched in Chapter 7 this amounts to saying that the internal standards against which the consequences of behaviour are appraised by both mother and child are such as strongly to favour the development of attachment: for proximity and affectionate interchange are appraised and felt as pleasurable by both whereas distance and expressions of rejection are appraised and felt as disagreeable or painful by both. For no other behavioural consequences, perhaps, are standards of appraisal in man more clear-cut from the start, or more environmentally stable. So stable indeed are they as a rule that for babies to love mothers and mothers to love babies is taken for granted as intrinsic to human nature. As a result, whenever during the development of some individual these standards become markedly different from the norm, as occasionally they do, all are disposed to judge the condition as pathological.

Shift in Responsibility for Maintaining Proximity

During the course of infancy and childhood in all higher primate species responsibility for maintaining proximity between mother and young shifts progressively from the mother to the young.

In all these species, man included, initially the infant's attachment behaviour is absent or very inefficient. Either he is not strong enough to grip or he is not mobile; and, even when he is mobile, he may stray imprudently far. As a result there is a phase of infancy during which maintenance of proximity to mother is achieved mainly by mother's own behaviour. At first she holds the infant to her, a condition that obtains in non-human species and in primitive man alike; in more advanced human societies this phase is represented by the period during which a mother lays her baby in a cradle or straps him to a cradle-board. In either case the mother takes full responsibility for her infant and she is most unlikely to move far from him without appointing someone to deputise for her.

The next phase is one in which the infant has become mobile—in rhesus monkeys after a week or two, in gorilla after a month or two, and in man from six months forward. In all these species, though the infant is often showing a very strong tendency to maintain proximity to his mother-figure, his competence to do so consistently is low. When his mother is stationary he is inclined not only to explore but to do so without much discrimination or judgement, with the result that he may go beyond the range acceptable to mother. When his mother is walking along his capacity to follow her is still woefully inadequate. Hence, during this phase also, proximity is maintained by the behaviour of the mother as much as, or more than, by that of the infant. In man this phase continues until about the end of the third year. Throughout these two and a half years (six months to third birthday) attachment behaviour, though strong, is not consistently efficient.

In the subsequent phase the balance shifts. By now the infant's attachment behaviour is becoming much more efficient and his judgement of when proximity is essential and when not is improved; proximity is then maintained as much by him as by mother. At times, indeed, mother may rebuff him and encourage him to stay further from her. Yet should mother become alarmed the first thing she does is to seek her child and clutch him to her. And whenever the pair are in strange surroundings mother keeps a close eye on child to make sure he is not imprudently curious. In man this transitional phase lasts many years, the length of time depending on the conditions in which the family is living. In modern urban society, for instance, few children are allowed to go far from home on their own until they are ten years old.

Imperceptibly this transitional phase passes into a final phase in which mother increasingly leaves maintenance of proximity almost entirely to the growing juvenile. Thenceforward, except in conditions of emergency, she plays only a minor role.

Forms of behaviour mediating attachment and their organisation

In man attachment is mediated by several different sorts of behaviour of which the most obvious are crying and calling, babbling and smiling, clinging, non-nutritional sucking, and locomotion as used in approach, following, and seeking. From an early phase of development each sort has proximity to mother as a predictable outcome. Later, each becomes organised within one or more superordinate and often goal-corrected systems.

All forms of attachment behaviour tend to be directed towards a particular object in space, usually the special attachment-figure. In order that they should be so directed it is necessary for the infant to orient towards that figure; this he does in various ways. For example, by the age of six months most infants are already adept at discriminating mother from other figures and at tracking her movements visually and aurally. By these means an infant is kept well informed of mother's whereabouts so that whatever form or forms of attachment behaviour become activated are directed towards her. Orientational behaviour is thus an essential requirement for attachment behaviour (as it is, of course, for very many other sorts of behaviour).

The more specific forms of behaviour making for attachment can be grouped into two main classes:

i. signalling behaviour, the effect of which is to bring mother to child;
ii. approach behaviour, the effect of which is to bring child to mother.

Signalling Behaviour

Crying, smiling, and babbling, and later calling and certain gestures, are all readily classifiable as social signals, and all have as a predictable outcome increased proximity of mother to child. Nevertheless the circumstances in which each kind of signal is emitted and the effects each has on the different components of maternal behaviour are very different. Even a single form of signalling behaviour, crying, is of several different kinds, each kind being elicited by a different set of conditions and having a rather different effect from the others. Thus, close examination reveals that the different signalling components of attachment behaviour are far from being interchangeable; rather, each is found to be distinctive and to be complementary to each of the others.

Crying is elicited by a number of quite different conditions, and takes one of several different forms.[1] Examples are crying from hunger and crying from pain. Crying from hunger builds up slowly. When first heard it is of low intensity and arrhythmical; as time passes it becomes louder and rhythmical, an expiratory cry alternating with an inspiratory whistle. Crying from pain, on the other hand, is loud from the start. A sudden long and strong initial cry is followed by a long period of absolute silence, due to apnoea; ultimately this gives way, and short gasping inhalations alternate with expiratory coughs.

Both sorts of cry are likely to affect a mother's behaviour, but each is likely to affect it differently. The pain-type of cry, Wolff found, is among the most powerful of all stimuli for bringing a mother hurrying to her child. To a cry that starts at low intensity, on the other hand, her response is likely to be more leisurely. In the one case she is prepared to take emergency action on the baby's behalf; in the other to rock him or to feed him.

Smiling and *babbling* occur in quite different circumstances from those in which crying occurs, and have effects of a quite different sort as well.[2]

Unlike crying, which is effective from birth onwards, neither smiling nor babbling is effective in influencing a mother's behaviour much before four weeks have elapsed. Also unlike crying, smiling and babbling are elicited when a baby is awake and content, namely, is not hungry, lonely, or in pain. Finally,

[1] My information derives from Wolff's study of the natural history of crying in babies in fourteen families (Wolff, 1969) and from personal communications from my colleague, Dr Anthony Ambrose.

[2] For the early development of smiling and babbling, see Wolff (1963). For a discussion of the effects of smiling on maternal behaviour, see Ambrose (1960).

whereas crying leads a mother to take action to protect, feed, or comfort her baby, smiling and babbling elicit behaviour of a very different kind. When her baby smiles and babbles a mother smiles back, 'talks' to him, strokes and pats him, and perhaps picks him up. In all this each partner seems to be expressing joy in the other's presence and the effect is certainly one of prolonging their social interaction. It is not easy to find a term to describe this very important component of maternal behaviour: perhaps 'maternal loving behaviour' would be appropriate.

Not only do her infant's smiles have this immediate effect on a mother's behaviour, but they probably exert a long-term influence on it as well. Ambrose (1960) has described the electrifying effects on a mother of seeing her baby's first social smile, and how it seems to make her thenceforward altogether more responsive to him. When she is tired and irritated with her infant, his smile disarms her; when she is feeding or otherwise caring for him, his smile is a reward and encouragement to her. In strict scientific terms, her infant's smile so affects a mother that the future likelihood of her responding to his signals promptly and in a way favouring his survival is increased. Hearing the contented babbling of her infant probably has the same long-term effect.

Initially, neither crying, nor smiling, nor babbling is goal-corrected. Instead, a signal is emitted and either is responded to by the partner or is not responded to. When it is responded to by the partner, crying and smiling commonly cease. Thus, as is well known, a good way to stop a baby crying is to pick him up and rock him, or perhaps to talk to him. Less well known is that when a baby is picked up he ceases also to smile (Ambrose, 1960).

Babbling is organised on rather different lines. Babbling by a baby usually elicits babbling back by the mother and a more or less long chain of interchange. Nevertheless, here again, picking the baby up tends to stop it.

When a signal is not responded to the resulting behaviour varies. In some instances, for example crying, the signal may continue to be emitted for a long while. In other instances it may cease, or else be replaced by a different signal. When, for example, smiling is not responded to, it does not continue indefinitely; not infrequently it is replaced by crying. Similarly, a rather older child who starts by calling for his mother may change to crying if she does not come.

A very different sort of signal from those so far considered, and one of considerable interest, is the *gesture of raised arms* that can be seen in an infant of about six months[1] when his mother appears near his cot and that often occurs in the crawling and toddling child both when he approaches his mother and when she approaches him. By the mother the gesture is always interpreted as a wish to be picked up and she usually responds accordingly.

In form the human gesture of raised arms is strikingly similar to the monkey movement of stretching arms to grip mother's flanks, which occurs in non-human primate babies as a part of the sequence leading to their clinging to mother. It seems not improbable, therefore, that the arms-raised gesture of human infants is a homologous movement which has become ritualised to serve a signal function.

Yet another form of behaviour that seems best understood as a form of signalling behaviour, but which is goal-corrected from the start, is that of *trying to catch and hold mother's attention*. Amongst the twenty-three infants studied by Shirley (1933), the first to exhibit this form of behaviour was thirty-two weeks old, and half were showing it a fortnight later.

The intensity with which babies and young children from about eight months onwards seek to elicit a parent's attention and are not content until they have obtained it is well known and sometimes a source of much irritation. Indeed it is sometimes regarded, in the same way as much other attachment behaviour, as a tiresome feature of young children and one of which they need to be cured as soon as possible. Once it is regarded as an integral part of attachment behaviour, however, it becomes intelligible, and it can then be looked upon more sympathetically. In man's environment of evolutionary adaptedness it is clearly vital that the mother of a child of under three or four years should know exactly where he is and what he is doing, and be ready to intervene should danger threaten; for him to keep advertising his whereabouts and activities to her and to continue doing so until she signals 'message received' is therefore adaptive.

Approach Behaviour

The two best-known examples of behaviour that brings infant to mother and/or keeps him there are, first, approach itself,

[1] The first occurrence of this response in a baby may be as early as fourteen weeks and as late as thirty-seven weeks (Shirley, 1933).

including seeking and following, in each case using whatever means of locomotion are available, and, secondly, clinging. A third not so readily recognised is non-nutritional sucking or nipple-grasping.

Approaching mother and *following* her are usually apparent as soon as a human child is mobile. Soon, moreover, and commonly during the final quarter of the first year, this behaviour becomes organised on a goal-corrected basis. This means that should his mother change her position, the child's own movement changes direction accordingly. Furthermore, once a child's cognitive apparatus has matured to a condition in which he can begin to conceive of absent objects and search for them, a phase which Piaget (1936) holds starts at about nine months, a child can be expected not only to approach and/or follow a mother whom he can see or hear but also to *seek* her in familiar places when she is absent.

To achieve his set-goal of proximity to mother any and all locomotory skills at a child's disposal are likely to be called upon. He will crawl, shuffle, walk, or run. If he is grossly deficient in locomotory equipment, for example as a result of thalidomide, he will still achieve his end, even if it means rolling (Décarie, 1969). These observations indicate that the behavioural systems concerned not only are goal-corrected but are organised in terms of a plan: the overall objective is constant; the techniques for obtaining it are flexible.

Though the human infant is much less adept at *clinging* than are his monkey cousins, he is nonetheless able to cling even at birth. And during the next four weeks he can do so with increasing efficiency. At thirty days of age, McGraw (1943) found, he can suspend himself by hands from a rod for all of half a minute. Subsequently, in Western countries, the ability declines, though this may be in part a result of disuse. After about eighteen months of age the ability improves again, though by then it is organised on more sophisticated lines.

Amongst conditions that elicit clinging in a baby during his early weeks and later are: being naked, e.g. undressed on his mother's knee, and being subjected to changes of 'g', e.g. when his mother jumps or stumbles.[1] Later he clings tightly, especially when alarmed. For example, at the age of nine months a baby in a stranger's arms will cling so tightly if she tries to put him down in a strange setting that it is only with great

[1] I am indebted to my daughter, Mary, for drawing my attention to the eliciting properties of nakedness.

difficulty that she can 'peel him off' (Rheingold, personal communication).

Although at one time it was imagined that the human infant's clinging is a relic of the days when men lived in the trees, there is no reason to doubt that it is in fact no other than the human version of the infant clinging found in all monkeys and apes, and that, less efficiently, it serves the same function. In terms of its organisation, clinging appears initially to be a fairly simple reflex response. Only later does it become goal-corrected.

Though *sucking* is usually thought of as a means simply of ingesting food, it has a further function. All primate infants, human and sub-human alike, spend a great deal of time grasping and/or sucking a nipple or nipple-like object, although for most of that time they are obtaining no food. In human babies sucking of thumb or comforter is extremely common. In monkey babies brought up without a mother it is universal. When they are brought up with a mother, however, it is the mother's nipple that young monkeys suck or grasp. As a result, in natural conditions a principal consequence of non-nutritional sucking and nipple-grasping is that the infant maintains close contact with mother. This is emphasised by Hinde, Rowell, and Spencer-Booth (1964) who point out that, when a rhesus infant is clinging to its running or climbing mother, it is usually attached not only by its two hands and its two feet but also by its mouth, which grasps one or even both nipples—in fact, a five-point hold. In such circumstances, then, nipple-grasping fulfils the same function as clinging.

Such observations make it clear that, in primates, nipple-grasping and sucking have two separate functions, one for nutrition and a second for attachment. Each of these functions is of importance in its own right, and to suppose that nutrition is in some way of primary significance and that attachment is only secondary would be a mistake. In fact, far more time is spent in non-nutritional sucking than in nutritional.

In view of the two separate functions of sucking it is not surprising to discover that the movements used in the two forms of this behaviour are different, the movements of non-nutritional sucking being shallower than those of nutritional sucking, a point to which Rowell (1965) has drawn attention. In the infant baboon she reared, the two forms of sucking were, in fact, especially easily distinguished because nutritional sucking was always directed towards a feeding-bottle whereas attachment sucking was directed to a comforter. When hungry, the baby baboon always sucked the bottle; when alarmed, always the comforter: 'the food provider had very little value as a security provider', and of course, vice versa. On sucking the comforter when it was alarmed, the baby baboon quickly became relaxed and content.

These findings go far to account for the time spent in non-nutritional sucking by the human infant. In primitive communities a baby's non-nutritional sucking is usually directed towards his mother's breast. In other communities it is usually directed towards a nipple-substitute, thumb or comforter. Towards whatever object it is directed, however, the baby able to engage in non-nutritional sucking is likely to become more content and relaxed than one not able to. Furthermore, just as in monkeys, it is especially when he is upset or alarmed that a human child engages in non-nutritional sucking. Both these findings are consistent with the conclusions that the non-nutritional sucking of human infants is an activity in its own right and separate from nutritional sucking; and that, in man's environment of evolutionary adaptedness, non-nutritional sucking is an integral part of attachment behaviour and has proximity to mother as a predictable outcome.

This ends a brief sketch of some of the main forms of behaviour that mediate attachment to a mother-figure. In the next chapters, dealing with ontogeny, these forms and others are discussed in greater detail.

Intensity of Attachment Behaviour

Because of the many forms and sequences of behaviour that can mediate attachment no simple scale of intensity exists. Instead, each form of behaviour mediating attachment can vary in intensity, and, as overall intensity rises, more and different forms of behaviour may come to be evoked. Thus the forms of behaviour commonly evoked when overall intensity of attachment is low are smiling, relaxed locomotion, watching, and touching. Forms of behaviour likely to be evoked when intensity of attachment is high are rapid locomotion and clinging. Crying is always present when intensity is high, and is sometimes present also when intensity is low.

Organisation of Behavioural Systems Mediating Attachment

In a section of Chapter 5 an account is given of some of the principles that underlie the different ways in which behavioural systems can be organised. A basic distinction lies between those that are goal-corrected and those that are not goal-corrected. Whilst both sorts, when activated in the environment of evolutionary adaptedness, commonly lead to a specified and predictable outcome, they do so in two quite distinct ways. In the case of a goal-corrected system the predictable outcome follows activation because the system is so structured that it takes continuous account of discrepancies between a set-goal and performance. The peregrine's stoop is an example. In the case of other systems there is no set-goal and therefore no calculation of discrepancy. Instead, the predictable outcome is a result simply of certain actions being performed in a certain sequence in a certain setting. An example of this type of system is restoration of egg to nest by the egg-rolling behaviour of a goose.

In the case of systems mediating attachment, some are organised as goal-corrected systems and others on simpler lines. The earliest systems to develop are certainly not goal-corrected, but later in infancy, especially after the first birthday, goal-corrected systems come to play an increasing and ultimately a dominant role.

Let us consider two examples of behavioural systems that have proximity to mother as a predictable outcome but are not goal-corrected. When a baby of four months or so sees his mother after a brief absence he is likely to smile. In response to this his mother is likely to approach closer, to smile and to talk to him, and perhaps to pat him or pick him up. Thus a predictable outcome of a baby's smile is his greater proximity to mother; but in the achieving of this result there appears to be no tendency for the smile to vary in a regular way according to whether mother is seen to be coming or not. Instead, at this age the baby's smile appears to be a fixed action pattern elicited mainly by sight of his mother's face (full face, not profile), to be intensified by social interaction, and to be terminated when he is picked up.

A second example of a system that when activated commonly leads to proximity but is not goal-corrected is crying. When a young baby cries in his environment of evolutionary adaptedness, namely within earshot of a responsive mother, a predictable outcome is that mother goes to him. Here again, however, in the early months there appears to be no tendency for the cry to vary according to whether mother is far or near, or is coming or going, as would occur in a goal-corrected system.

After about eight months of age, and more especially after the first birthday, the existence of more sophisticated systems mediating attachment becomes increasingly evident. Not infrequently a child keeps a close eye on his mother, content to play whilst she is present but insisting on following her whenever she moves. In such circumstances the child's behaviour can be understood by postulating that it is governed by a system that remains inactive as long as mother is in sight or in touch but that is apt to become activated when those conditions change. Once it is activated, approach continues, with appropriate goal-correction, until such time as the child is again within sight or touch of his mother, whereupon the system is terminated.

Another type of goal-corrected behaviour mediating attachment is calling. At some time during the second year of life a child commonly begins calling in a new kind of way for his mother. Then the way he calls varies according to his estimate of her whereabouts and current movements, increasing if he estimates her far away or departing, decreasing if he estimates her close by or coming to him.

A goal-corrected sequence of behaviour such as locomotion or calling is not infrequently succeeded by some other form of attachment behaviour such as an arms-up gesture or a handgrasp, the predictable outcome of which is that physical contact between child and mother ensues. In such a case the succession appears to be organised as a chain. Only when the distance between child and mother has narrowed to be within certain limits is the second type of movement elicited.

Behaviour typical of two-year-olds in different situations

The particular forms of behaviour mediating attachment and the particular combinations in which they may be organised and appear at different ages and in different situations are almost infinitely variable. Nevertheless, after a certain age, say fifteen months, certain forms and combinations of behaviour tend to occur fairly frequently, and certain of them tend typically to occur when a child is in one of a limited number of situations. A principal way of defining these situations is in terms of mother's whereabouts and movements; another way is in terms of whether the situation in which the child finds himself is familiar or strange.

In what follows an attempt is made to describe behaviour typical of a few common situations. In view of the many variables affecting behaviour, the great variation between different children, and the paucity of careful studies, no more than a sketch map is possible.

Behaviour when Mother is Present and Stationary

Not infrequently a child of one or two years in a familiar situation is content for half an hour or more to play and to explore using his stationary mother as a base. In maintaining proximity in such situations he relies on orienting towards her, keeping her whereabouts in mind, and locomotion. Clinging, sucking, and crying are all absent. Exchange of glances and of an occasional smile or touch assures each that the other is aware of his (or her) whereabouts.

Observations of how young children behave whilst with mother in a secluded part of a park are reported by Anderson (1972). Selecting children estimated to be between fifteen months and two and a half years, whose mothers were sitting quietly allowing them to run about in what was presumably a fairly familiar place, Anderson noted the movements of each child relative to mother over a period of fifteen minutes. Of the thirty-five children observed, twenty-four remained throughout within a distance of about 200 feet of mother, travelling away from her and back again without her taking any action to ensure proximity. Anderson comments on the ability of the children to remain mother-oriented while establishing a distance which takes them out of her immediate control. Of the remaining eleven children, eight sallied further, attracted by swings or similar interests; in each case mother followed to escort her child. Only three children had to be retrieved because they wandered too far or remained out of mother's sight.

Typically, the mother-oriented children moved either directly away from mother or directly towards her, moving in short bouts punctuated constantly by halts. Return towards mother seemed to be accomplished in longer hops and at a faster rate than the outward journey. Halts near mother were infrequent but of relatively long duration; those at a distance were more frequent and much briefer.

Anderson emphasises that only very occasionally did the sallies out or the returns bear any obvious relationship to ongoing events: 'With no evident motive other than a wish to be on his feet at a distance from her he wriggles free and moves some paces off, there to stand until the next bout of activity begins'; as often as not the return journey starts without his having cast even a glance at his mother. Of forty-nine return moves made by seven infants, only two seemed to have been elicited by anything to do with mother: on each occasion she had been joined by a friend.

Return moves can halt at some distance from mother, within a few feet of her, or touching her. In about a quarter the child made contact by climbing on to her lap, leaning against her knee, or pulling her hand. In just as many he came close but made no actual contact. In half he halted at a distance.

Neither children nor mothers engaged in vocal communication with each other except when close together. When more distant a child vocalised little, and then only to himself. Mothers on their part made few efforts to retrieve their child by calling him, and such efforts as they made were, with rare exceptions, of no avail.

Though not reported systematically by Anderson, we know from other sources that, when playing near a stationary mother, a child often seeks to attract her attention and is dissatisfied until he obtains it. In an account of the way in which children of thirteen months interact with mother within the home setting, Appell and David (1965) describe one couple who comparatively rarely came into contact and whose interaction was very largely a matter of watching each other. After recording how mother watched her son and provided him with many things to play with, they continue:

> Bob himself watches his mother a lot. . . . He needs to be looked at and cannot bear it when mother gets too absorbed in her work. . . . He then becomes whiny and frustrated, very much as he does when his mother goes away. . . .

In contrast to this pair, Appell and David found other couples who interacted as much by tactile as by visual interchange.

Behaviour when Mother is Present and Moving

There comes a time in a child's life when he is capable of maintaining proximity to a moving figure by means of goal-corrected locomotion. This age lies probably around the third birthday and is therefore considerably later than is commonly supposed. Though a child of two and a half years may be an excellent walker and capable of long and well-oriented excursions whilst mother remains stationary, once she rises to move he becomes singularly incompetent. This fact of child development is little known, and ignorance of it gives rise to much parental exasperation. Once again it is to Anderson's observations that we look for detailed information.

As a rule, when a mother of one of the two-year-old children Anderson was observing rose at the end of the outing, she signalled to her child. If offered it, he would then willingly climb into his push-chair. But if mother preferred him to walk, difficulties quickly arose unless she walked very slowly and held his hand. More often than not, Anderson reports, mother lost patience, lifted her child by his arm and dragged him away.

Were mother to rise unexpectedly without a signal, perhaps to fetch something, the child was most likely to remain rooted to the spot where he was standing. If she then wished him to join her, she needed to be very patient and encouraging; otherwise he was likely to remain immobile.

Observations by Anderson of a further dozen children of the same age who were out of a pram and whose mothers were walking in the park confirmed the extreme inefficiency of their following behaviour. Again and again a child would stop, often at some distance from mother, so that over the course of some five to eight minutes every one of these mothers spent more time waiting for her child than walking. Eight of the children wandered off course and had to be retrieved. No less than half of them were being transported by the time these brief observations ended, three of them on the initiative of the child and three on that of the mother.

Anderson's evidence strongly suggests that children of under about three years are not equipped with efficient goal-corrected systems that enable them to maintain proximity to a figure when it is moving, and that up to this age transport by mother is the arrangement for which man is adapted. This likelihood is supported by the alacrity with which children of this age accept the offer of transport, by the contented and efficient way in which they poise themselves to be carried, and also by the determined and often abrupt ways they have of demanding it. Anderson reports how a child walking by his mother's side was apt suddenly to move round to face her, with arms uplifted. So sudden was the manœuvre that it was easy for her to stumble over him and even to knock him over. The fact that a child is not discouraged by this untoward result suggests that the manœuvre is an instinctive one and is elicited by his seeing his mother in movement.

Evidence available suggests that, in both developed and undeveloped communities, whenever parents are going places children of under three years are almost always transported by their parents. In Western communities such transport is commonly in some sort of baby carriage; nevertheless, carrying by a parent is not uncommon. In a study by Rheingold and Keene (1965), of over five hundred children being carried by adults (mostly parents) in public places in Washington, D.C., some 89 per cent were under three years of age, distributed fairly equally between each of the three years. Children who had passed their third birthday comprised only a small proportion of those observed being carried: 8 per cent were in their fourth year and only 2 per cent beyond it.

After about their third birthday, it seems likely, most children have become equipped with reasonably efficient goal-corrected systems that enable them to maintain proximity even when the parent-figure is moving. Even so, for a couple of years or more many such children insist on holding a parent's hand or garment or grasping the handle of a pram. Only after they have reached and passed their seventh birthday are most children likely to forgo holding a parent's hand, but in this as in all else there are great individual differences.

Behaviour when Mother Departs

After twelve months of age and often before, children commonly protest when they see mother depart. The protest may be anything from a whimper to a full-blooded cry. They often also attempt to follow her. The exact behaviour shown, however, depends on very many factors. For example, the younger the child the more likely is he to cry and the less likely is he to attempt to follow. Another factor is the way a mother moves when she departs: a slow quiet withdrawal is likely to elicit little protest and following, a quick bustling exit loud protest and strenuous effort to follow. Yet another factor concerns the familiarity or strangeness of the setting. Left in a familiar setting a child may be relatively content; left in an unfamiliar one he is certain either to cry or to attempt to follow.

Seeing mother depart elicits very different behaviour from simply being alone. Many a child who protests and tries to follow when he sees his mother depart is quite content to play on his own in her absence provided always he knows where she is and can reach her should he wish. He may then play for periods of up to an hour or two before he exhibits one or another form of attachment behaviour—as a rule either seeking her or crying, depending on his age and other factors.

Behaviour when Mother Returns

How a child behaves on his mother's return depends on the length of time she has been absent and on his emotional state when she reappears, which in turn depends on how his relationship to his mother has become patterned (see Chapter 16).

After a short routine absence, a child is almost certain to orient towards his mother and approach her. He may smile. If he is crying he is likely to stop, especially if she picks him up. When there has been much crying he is likely to clutch her and to cling tightly when picked up.

After a longer and less routine absence a child may be much distressed at the time when his mother ultimately returns. In such a condition he may be less responsive on first seeing her and may even withdraw. If he is not crying he may remain silent for a time and then start to cry. Once he is in physical contact with his mother crying is likely to diminish and finally to cease. He is then likely to cling tightly and to resist being put down. There may also be much non-nutritional sucking.

After a separation lasting some days or longer, especially when it involves strange surroundings, a child's attachment behaviour is likely to take unusual forms, differing from the norm either by its excessive intensity or by its apparent absence.

Whichever of these different ways of responding to mother's return is shown, some of the behaviour is evidently goal-corrected whilst other parts of it probably are not.

Activation and termination of systems mediating attachment behaviour

Observation of any one child during his second and third years of life, when attachment behaviour is most evident, shows that such behaviour varies enormously in activation, form, and intensity. At one moment the child is content to explore his surroundings, his mother out of sight and apparently out of mind; at the next he is searching for her desperately or bawling for her. One day he is cheerful and undemanding of his mother; on the next whiny and 'mummyish'.

To consider the conditions responsible for such variations in the attachment behaviour of a single child is, in terms of the theory advanced, the same as to consider the conditions that activate and those that terminate the systems mediating such behaviour.

In this chapter we consider only goal-corrected systems and

the conditions that affect them. A discussion of conditions leading to the activation and termination of systems that are not goal-corrected is postponed until the next chapter, when their ontogeny is considered. Variables that may account for differences in the behaviour of a single child over months or years and those that may account for differences between individual children are discussed briefly in Chapter 16.

In the first edition of this work the model proposed was a fairly simple start-stop one, but further study, notably by Bretherton (1980), has shown that that, although a good beginning, is inadequate. In chapter 19, therefore, the model is elaborated; meanwhile we begin with the simple version.

As in the case of most behavioural systems when activated, systems mediating attachment behaviour can vary in intensity of activation from low to very high. A principal feature of the model proposed is that the terminating conditions vary greatly according to the intensity of activation. When systems are intensely active nothing but physical contact with mother herself will serve to terminate them. When systems are less intensely active sight of mother or even sound of her may do; and proximity to some subordinate attachment-figure may then be sufficient as an alternative to mother. Such variations in terminating conditions can be said to range from stringent to relaxed.

Many conditions activate attachment behaviour. The simplest, perhaps, is sheer distance from mother. The part it plays is shown by Anderson's observations. All but a few of the children he observed remained within a 200-foot radius of mother; at that distance they returned to her instead of going further. Another condition of the same sort may be elapse of time. Though there are only a few systematic observations relevant to it, ordinary nursery experience suggests elapsed time may play a part. For example, a two-year-old child contentedly occupied will, as a rule, from time to time check to see where his mother is. Such checks can be conceived as examples of attachment behaviour activated periodically and at low intensity.

Other conditions well known to activate attachment behaviour and to influence the form it takes and the intensity with which it is exhibited fall under three main heads:

1. Condition of child:

fatigue	pain	ill health
hunger	cold	

2. Whereabouts and behaviour of mother:
   mother absent
   mother departing
   mother discouraging of proximity

3. Other environmental conditions:
   occurrence of alarming events
   rebuffs by other adults or children.

Let us consider first the effects of those listed in the category 'condition of child'.

Every mother knows that a child who is tired, hungry, cold, in ill health or in pain is likely to be especially 'mummyish'. Not only is he reluctant for his mother to be out of sight but often he demands to sit on her knee or to be carried by her. At this intensity, attachment behaviour is terminated only by bodily contact, and any breaking of contact produced by mother's movements evokes intense attachment behaviour afresh—crying, following, clinging—until such time as the two of them are in contact again. When, by contrast, a child is no longer tired, hungry, cold, in ill health or in pain, his behaviour is quite different: once again he is content even when mother is at some distance from him or is perhaps only within earshot. Thus the effect of these five conditions can be understood in terms of their causing attachment behaviour to be exhibited at high intensity and thereby causing the terminating conditions to become correspondingly stringent.

Similar changes occur when a child is alarmed or has received a rebuff from another adult or child—conditions categorised under 'other environmental conditions'.

Events especially likely to alarm a child are, first, those that lead to a big, especially a sudden, change of stimulus level, such as bright light, sudden darkness, loud noise; and, secondly, objects that either are themselves strange or appear in an unexpected context. Almost always a child of two years or older much frightened in one of these ways rushes to his mother; in other words, attachment behaviour is elicited at high intensity and terminating conditions become correspondingly stringent. In addition to approach, crying or clinging may be elicited. When, on the other hand, a child is only a little frightened, intensity of attachment behaviour is low and terminating conditions remain relaxed. Then he may move to be just a little nearer his mother, or even may do no more than turn his head, check his mother's whereabouts and note her expression and gesture.[1]

Finally, the way a mother is herself behaving towards her child can affect the intensity with which his attachment behaviour is shown. Maternal behaviour that commonly elicits it at high intensity, with correspondingly stringent terminating conditions, is any that seems to discourage proximity or to threaten it. When a mother rebuffs her child for wishing to be near her or to sit on her knee it not infrequently has an effect exactly the opposite of what is intended—he becomes more clinging than ever. Similarly, when a child suspects his mother is about to leave him behind, he insists remorselessly on remaining by her side. When, on the other hand, a child observes that his mother is attending to him and is ready to respond whenever he may desire greater proximity to her, he is likely to be content and may explore some distance away. Although such behaviour may appear perverse, it is in fact what is to be expected on the hypothesis that attachment behaviour fulfils a protective function. Whenever mother seems unlikely to play her part in maintaining proximity a child is alerted and by his own behaviour ensures that proximity is maintained. When, on the other hand, mother shows herself ready to maintain proximity her child can relax his own efforts.

In most young children the mere sight of mother holding another baby in her arms is enough to elicit strong attachment behaviour. The older child insists on remaining close to his mother, or on climbing on to her lap. Often he behaves as though he were a baby. It is possible that this well-known behaviour is only a special case of a child reacting to mother's lack of attention and lack of responsiveness to him. The fact, however, that an older child often reacts in this way even when his mother makes a point of being attentive and responsive suggests that more is involved; and the pioneer experiments of Levy (1937) also indicate that the mere presence of a baby on mother's lap is sufficient to make an older child much more clinging.

[1] Rosenthal (1967), in an experiment with little girls aged from three and a half to four and a half years, found that, when alarmed, her subjects tended to keep close to whomever was available in the test room (sometimes mother, sometimes a stranger). Thus, mean scores for proximity-keeping were 50 per cent higher when conditions were alarming than when conditions were not so. By contrast, the mean scores for seeking attention and help did not differ for the two situations.

Changes with Age

In Chapter 11 it is described how after their third birthday most children show attachment behaviour less urgently and less frequently than before, and how this trend continues for some years, although attachment behaviour never disappears completely. In terms of the theory proposed these changes can be understood to come about largely because the behaviour itself becomes less readily activated and because, in any given conditions, the intensity at which it is activated is lower. As a result, terminating conditions tend to become more relaxed. Thus in an older child conditions that would earlier have elicited attachment behaviour at high intensity now elicit it at less intensity; so that, whereas earlier it would have been terminated only by close bodily contact, now it is terminated, perhaps, by a light touch or even by a reassuring glance.

What causes attachment behaviour to become less readily and less intensely activated is not known. Experience no doubt plays some part: for example, much that was formerly strange becomes more familiar and consequently less alarming. Yet it seems unlikely that, in effecting the changes that come with age, experience is the sole influence. In the case of the major systems of instinctive behaviour, for example sexual behaviour and maternal behaviour, changes of endocrine balance are well known to be of great importance. In the case of attachment behaviour it seems likely that changes of endocrine balance are playing a principal role also. Evidence that attachment behaviour continues to be rather more easily elicited in females than in males would, if confirmed, support such a conclusion.

In addition to attachment behaviour's becoming less frequently and less intensely activated, another change that occurs with age is that attachment behaviour can be terminated by an increasingly large range of conditions, some of which are purely symbolic. Thus, photographs, letters, and telephone conversations can become more or less effective means of 'keeping contact' so long as intensity is not too high.

These and other changes in the form taken by attachment behaviour are discussed further in the final chapters.

Such, then, is a sketch of a control theory of attachment behaviour. It is advanced with two purposes in mind. The first is to demonstrate that a theory of this type is able reasonably well to encompass what is at present known about attachment behaviour during the early years of human life. The second is to encourage research. With a model of this kind, behaviour can be predicted with some precision and the predictions tested.

Part IV

ONTOGENY OF
HUMAN ATTACHMENT

Chapter 14

Beginnings of Attachment Behaviour

Heredity proposes . . . development disposes.
P. B. MEDAWAR (1967)

Phases in the development of attachment

In a given child the complex of behavioural systems mediating attachment comes into being because in the ordinary family environment in which the vast majority of children are raised these systems grow and develop in a certain comparatively stable way. What do we know of this growth and of the variables that affect it?

When he is born, an infant is far from being a *tabula rasa*. On the contrary, not only is he equipped with a number of behavioural systems ready to be activated, but each system is already biased so that it is activated by stimuli falling within one or more broad ranges, is terminated by stimuli falling within other broad ranges, and is strengthened or weakened by stimuli of yet other kinds. Amongst these systems there are already some that provide the building-bricks for the later development of attachment. Such, for example, are the primitive systems that mediate neonatal crying, sucking, clinging, and orientation. To these are added, only a few weeks later, smiling and babbling, and some months later still, crawling and walking.

When first exhibited each of these forms of behaviour is simply structured. Some of the motor patterns themselves are organised on lines little more elaborate than those of a fixed action pattern, and the stimuli that activate and terminate them are discriminated in only the roughest and readiest of ways. Even so, some discrimination is present from the start; and also from the start there is a marked bias to respond in special ways to several kinds of stimuli that commonly emanate from a human being—the auditory stimuli arising from a human voice, the visual stimuli arising from a human face, and the tactile and kinaesthetic stimuli arising from human arms and body. From these small beginnings spring all the highly discriminating and sophisticated systems that in later infancy and childhood—indeed for the rest of life—mediate attachment to particular figures.

In Chapter 11 a rough sketch is given of the way in which attachment behaviour develops in the human infant. For purposes of further analysis it is convenient to divide this development into a number of phases, though it must be recognised that there are no sharp boundaries between them. In the following paragraphs four such phases are briefly described; their fuller discussion forms the substance of this and subsequent chapters.

Phase 1 : Orientation and Signals with Limited Discrimination of Figure

During this phase an infant behaves in certain characteristic ways towards people but his ability to discriminate one person from another is limited to olfactory and auditory stimuli. The phase lasts from birth to not less than eight weeks of age, and more usually to about twelve weeks; it may continue much longer in unfavourable conditions.

The ways in which a baby behaves towards any person in his vicinity include orientation towards that person, tracking movements of the eyes, grasping and reaching, smiling and babbling. Often a baby ceases to cry on hearing a voice or seeing a face. Each of these sorts of infantile behaviour, by influencing his companion's behaviour, is likely to increase the time the baby is in proximity to that companion. After about twelve weeks the intensity of these friendly responses rises. Thenceforward he gives 'the full social response in all its spontaneity, vivacity and delight' (Rheingold, 1961).

Phase 2: Orientation and Signals Directed towards One (or More) Discriminated Figure(s)

During this phase an infant continues to behave towards people in the same friendly way as in Phase 1, but he does so in more marked fashion towards his mother-figure than towards others. To auditory stimuli, differential responsiveness is unlikely to be readily observable before about four weeks of age, and to visual stimuli before about ten weeks. In most babies brought up in families, however, both are plainly evident from twelve weeks of age onwards. The phase lasts until about six months of age, or much later according to the circumstances.

Phase 3: Maintenance of Proximity to a Discriminated Figure by means of Locomotion as well as Signals

During this phase not only is an infant increasingly discriminating in the way he treats people but his repertoire of responses extends to include following a departing mother, greeting her on her return, and using her as a base from which to explore. Concurrently, the friendly and rather undiscriminating responses to everyone else wane. Certain other people are selected to become subsidiary attachment-figures; others are not so selected. Strangers become treated with increasing caution, and sooner or later are likely to evoke alarm and withdrawal.

During this phase some of the systems mediating a child's behaviour to his mother become organised on a goal-corrected basis. And then his attachment to his mother-figure is evident for all to see.

Phase 3 commonly begins between six and seven months of age but may be delayed until after the first birthday, especially in infants who have had little contact with a main figure. It probably continues throughout the second year and into the third.

Phase 4: Formation of a Goal-corrected Partnership

During Phase 3 proximity to an attachment-figure begins to be maintained by infant and young child by means of simply organised goal-corrected systems utilising a more or less primitive cognitive map. Within that map the mother-figure herself comes sooner or later to be conceived as an independent object, persistent in time and space and moving more or less predictably in a space-time continuum. Even when that concept has been attained, however, we cannot suppose that a child has any understanding of what is influencing his mother's movements to or away from him, or of what measures he can take that will change her behaviour. That her behaviour is organised about her own set-goals, which are both numerous and in some degree conflicting, and that it may be possible to infer what they are and to act accordingly, are likely to be still far beyond his competence to grasp.

Sooner or later, however, this changes. By observing her behaviour and what influences it, a child comes to infer something of his mother's set-goals and something of the plans she is adopting to achieve them. From that point onwards his picture of the world becomes far more sophisticated and his behaviour is potentially more flexible. To use another language, it can be said that a child is acquiring insight into his mother's feelings and motives. Once that is so, the groundwork is laid for the pair to develop a much more complex relationship with each other, one that I term a partnership.

This is clearly a new phase. Although evidence is still scanty, what is available, e.g. Bretherton and Becghly-Smith (1981), suggests that for some children it is already well started by the middle of the third year. The matter is discussed further in chapter 18.

It is of course entirely arbitrary to say by what phase a child can be said to have become attached. Plainly he is not attached in Phase 1, whereas equally plainly he is so in Phase 3. Whether and to what extent a child can be said to be attached during Phase 2 is a matter of how we define attachment.

In the remainder of this chapter and in the next ones an attempt is made to describe some of the internal processes and external conditions that lead the behavioural equipment of an infant to develop through these successive phases. In tracing its growth we shall continually be referring to principles of ontogeny already set forth in Chapter 10, namely:

a. a tendency for the range of effective stimuli to become restricted;

b. a tendency for primitive behavioural systems to become elaborated and to be superseded by more sophisticated ones;

c. a tendency for behavioural systems to start by being non-functional and later to become integrated into functional wholes.

But before embarking on this ontogenetic journey, let us pause to examine our point of departure, namely the behavioural equipment with which a human infant comes into the world.

Behavioural equipment of the human neonate

Much nonsense has been written about the behavioural equipment of a human baby during his first months of life. On the one hand, the neonate has been described as though his reactions were completely undifferentiated and inchoate; on the other, ideation and behaviour of the kinds that are categorised here as typical of Phase 4 have been attributed to a small baby. The capacity to learn with which he has been credited has varied from virtually none to the equivalent of that of a child of perhaps three years of age.

Even during the sixties there was no excuse for these myths. Now, in the early eighties, thanks to the painstaking research of an army of developmental psychologists, there is available a wealth of knowledge of much that was formerly only guessed at. The reader wishing to know more is referred to the impressive collection of articles compiled by Osofsky (1979). Rheingold's generalisation of a decade ago has proved prophetic: 'Careful probing with improved techniques almost always yields evidence of keener sensitivity than had been suspected' (1968).

Experiment shows that at a baby's birth, or very soon after it, every sensory system is working. Not only that, but within a few days he is already capable of distinguishing the smells and voices of different individuals. By turning his head or by sucking more often, he shows that he prefers both the smell and the voice of his mother (Macfarlane 1975; DeCasper and Fifer, 1980). Visually he is less expert, though he can soon fixate a light and track it briefly, and within a few weeks he can perceive pattern.

The extent to which an infant is able to discriminate between stimuli is elucidated by observing whether or not he responds differently either when given a choice or when stimuli are changed. By noting how he responds to different stimuli, therefore, it is possible to obtain valuable information about an infant's preferences. Thus, some sounds make him cry whereas others quieten him; to some things seen he pays much attention and to others far less. Some tastes elicit sucking and a happy expression, others aversive movements and a disgusted expression. By means of these differential responses, it is evident, a child exerts a not inconsiderable influence over the sensory input he receives, greatly increasing some sorts and reducing others to zero. Again and again, it is found, these inbuilt biases favour the development of social interaction.

In one of the earliest of such experimental enquiries Hetzer and Tudor-Hart (1927) exposed infants to a large variety of sounds—some loud, some soft; some from a human voice, others from rattles, whistles, or crockery. From the first days infants responded very differently to the loud and the soft sounds. To the loud ones they flinched and frowned in ways suggestive of displeasure, but to the soft ones they looked up calmly, slowly stretched their arms and made sounds suggestive of pleasure. From the third week onwards the sound of a human voice was responded to in quite specific ways. When the voice was heard, the infant began to suck and gurgle and wore an expression suggestive of pleasure. When the voice ceased the baby started to cry and showed other signs of displeasure.[1]

Much work has been done to investigate the rate at which an infant's visual capacities develop and, in particular, what he prefers to look at; for a review, see Cohen and others (1979). Although the findings of many experiments have led to the belief that an infant has not the visual ability to discriminate a human face from any other equivalent stimulus before about four months of age, Thomas (1973) has faulted this conclusion. When the preferences of individual infants are examined (instead of averaging the preferences of many), he points out that a preference for face-like stimuli is found as early as five weeks. In one of his studies (Thomas and Jones-Molfese, 1977) infants aged from 2 to 9 months were presented with four pictures—a blank oval, a scrambled schematic face, a regular schematic face and a black and white photograph of a real face. From the youngest infant onwards the more face-like the picture the more it was preferred.

Discrimination of individual faces, however, seems not to be present before about fourteen weeks. Thenceforward, recognition of the face of his mother-figure is clearly present in a baby brought up at home, manifested by his greeting her with a more immediate and more generous smile than he gives anyone else.

Thus, owing to the selective sensitivity with which a baby is born, different sorts of behaviour are elicited by different sorts of stimuli and much more attention is paid to some parts of the environment than to other parts (Sameroff and Cavenagh, 1979). Not only that but, because the consequences of a piece of behaviour when fed back centrally have differential effects on future behaviour, some sorts of behavioural sequence are rapidly augmented (reinforced) whilst other sequences are as rapidly diminished (habituated). Changes of both these kinds can be demonstrated in infants as young as two or three days and it is evident that their effects, accumulating over the early

---

[1] Hetzer and Tudor-Hart are inclined to regard these differential responses to a female voice at three weeks as being due to the baby's having come to associate the voice with food. This, however, is an unnecessary assumption. Moreover, it is not supported by their finding that, at the same age, noises arising from preparation of a feeding-bottle elicit no such special responses.

weeks and months of life, can be far-reaching.

In the past it has been imagined that the main way in which a baby's behaviour is modified is by his receiving or not receiving food as a consequence of his behaviour. This pre-occupation with food as a reward had two bad effects: it led to much speculative theorising of a sort that is almost certainly mistaken and it has led also to a sad neglect of all other rewards, some of which play a far larger part than food in the develop-ment of social attachment. Even in the case of sucking, for which, not surprisingly, reception of food is shown to act as a reinforcer, it is not the only consequence that can augment the response: as Lipsitt (1966) has shown, the shape of the object sucked is also of importance.

In the rest of this chapter attention is given to the various forms of behaviour that mediate attachment. First, there is the infant's perceptual equipment and the way it tends to orient him towards his mother-figure and thereby enables him to become familiar with her. Secondly, there is his effector equip-ment, notably hands and feet, head and mouth, which, when given a chance, tend to latch him in contact with her. Thirdly, his signalling equipment, crying and smiling, babbling and arm gestures, which have so striking an effect on his mother's movements and treatment of him. In considering each we concentrate especially on the course its development takes during the early months of life, during which an infant is still in the first phase of the development of attachment, the phase of 'Orientation and signals with limited discrimination of figure'. Discussion of factors that are known or suspected to influence those courses is postponed to a later chapter.

Early responses to people

Orientation

Newborns do not respond to people as people. Nevertheless, as we have seen, their perceptual equipment is well designed to pick up and process stimuli emanating from people and their reactive equipment is biased to respond to such stimuli in certain typical ways. Very frequently, it is found, babies behave in such a way that they maximise the kinds of stimuli that emanate from humans. Examples already given include a tend-ency to look at pattern, or at least contour, especially when it resembles a human face, and a tendency to listen to a human voice, especially a female one, and to cry when it ceases. An-other bias, present from very early days, is a tendency to look at anything that moves in preference to something static.

Not only are babies biased to behave in special ways towards humans but mothers also are biased to behave in special ways towards babies. By bringing her baby into a face-to-face orientation to herself a mother gives him opportunity to look at her. By cradling him to herself in a ventro-ventral position she is likely to elicit reflex responses that not only orient him more precisely to her but also give him the chance to use mouth, hands, and feet to grasp parts of her. And the more each experiences the other in these interactions the stronger do the relevant responses of each tend to become. In this reciprocal way early interaction between mother and baby is begun.

Let us consider further an infant's visual behaviour and the way it tends to promote interaction with the mother-figure. Whilst being breast-fed, a newborn who happens to be alert and to have his eyes open will often fixate his mother's face (Gough, 1962; Spitz, 1965). This is hardly surprising when we recall a baby's preference for certain sorts of pattern, and learn, in addition, first, that in the early weeks of life an infant is able to focus clearly only objects that are eight or nine inches from his eyes (Haynes, quoted by Fantz, 1966), and, second, that once he has fixated an object he tends to track it with his eyes and head, at first only occasionally and inefficiently but, by two or three weeks, more often and more efficiently (Wolff, 1959). The face of a mother feeding her baby, it will be found, is ideally positioned to be so fixated and tracked.

By the time he is four weeks old a baby's inclination to look at a human face in preference to other objects is becoming well established (Wolff, 1963). This is emphasised also by McGraw (1943), who studied the development of visual convergence and who notes how very much more readily a face appropriately placed evokes convergence than does an inanimate object. It may be that the preference she recorded can be explained simply on the ground that the human face contains more contour than any other object she tried, since Berlyne (1958) found that, at least from three months onwards, infants tend to look especially at anything that contains a relatively large amount of contour. Another factor of great and increasing importance is the movement of a face with all its changing expressions. Wolff (1963) holds that 'up to two months the crucial factor is movement'.

Not only is there an early preference for looking at a human face but, from about fourteen weeks onwards, there is a clear preference, at least in certain conditions, for looking at mother's face rather than at the faces of others. From the age of about eighteen weeks, moreover, Ainsworth observed that Ganda infants, when held by someone else, keep oriented towards mother even when she is a little distance from them:

> The baby, when apart from his mother but able to see her, keeps his eyes more or less continuously oriented towards her. He may look away for a few moments, but he repeatedly glances towards her. When held by someone else, he can be sensed to be maintaining a motor orientation towards his mother, for he is ready neither to interact with the adult holding him nor to relax in her arms (Ainsworth, 1964).

In determining this course of development at least four processes are likely to be at work:

a. an in-built bias towards looking at certain patterns in preference to others and at things that move;

b. exposure learning, by which the familiar comes to be distinguished from the strange;

c. an in-built bias to approach the familiar (and later to withdraw from the strange);

d. feedback of results, by which a behavioural sequence is augmented when it is followed by certain results and diminished when it is followed by others.

Traditionally, the result that has been assumed to play a major role in augmenting infant behaviour is food. There is, however, no evidence that food in fact reinforces visual orientation to mother. Instead, it is now clear that the more a baby watches his mother the more likely is she to move towards him and to gesture, to talk or sing to him, to pat him or hug him. A feedback to the controlling systems of these results of his behaviour is evidently what augments his visual orientation and watching.

Not only is mother an interesting and rewarding object to watch but she is an interesting and rewarding object to listen to. The very special quietening properties of a female voice on a three-week-old infant have already been described. In addition to having a quietening effect, hearing a voice is likely to elicit head-turning and also comfort sounds from a baby. Wolff (1959), indeed, has found that differential responses of these kinds are present even during the first twenty-four hours after birth:

> When a sharp clear noise was presented to the alert inactive baby in a quiet nursery, he turned his head and eyes to the left and right as if to discover the source of the sound . . . a soft noise evoked more clear-cut pursuit movement than a loud one.

More recent study, moreover, has shown that by the third day he is already able to discriminate his mother's voice.

Furthermore, just as in the case of visual attention and tracking, a baby's auditory attention and pursuit are encouraged and augmented by processes of feedback and learning. On the one hand, her infant's interest in her voice is likely to lead a mother to talk to him more; on the other, the very fact that his attention to her has the effect of increasing mother's vocalisations and other baby-oriented behaviour is likely to lead the baby to pay even more attention to the sounds she makes. In this mutually reinforcing way the vocal and auditory interaction between the pair increases.[1]

Head-turning and Sucking

The main organs with which an infant makes physical contact with another human being are head and mouth, hands and feet.

The movements of the head by which a neonate's mouth is brought into contact with a nipple have been studied in detail by Prechtl (1958). He distinguishes two main forms of behaviour. Both have been termed 'rooting', though perhaps the term is best reserved for the first form.

The first, an alternating side-to-side movement, appears to be a fixed action pattern. It can be evoked by tactile stimuli of many sorts when applied anywhere within a large zone surrounding the mouth. It may also be exhibited as a 'vacuum

[1]Recent studies, notably those of Klaus and Kennell (1976), Brazelton and colleagues (1974), Sander (1977), Stern (1977), and Schaffer (1977) have shown the strong potential of the healthy neonate to enter into an elemental form of social interaction and the potential of the ordinary sensitive mother to participate successfully in it. Already by two or three weeks after birth phases of lively social interaction are alternating with phases of disengagement. At first, an infant's initiations of, and withdrawals from, interaction follow his own autonomous rhythm, whilst a sensitive mother regulates her behaviour so that it meshes with his. Subsequently, the infant's rhythms shift to suit his mother's interventions. The speed and efficiency with which these dialogues develop and the mutual enjoyment they give point clearly to each participant being preadapted to engage in them. For an excellent review of these studies, see Schaffer (1979).

activity' when an infant is hungry. Though it varies in frequency and amplitude, the movement is stereotyped in form and is not influenced by the particular whereabouts of the stimulation.

The second form of behaviour, a directed head-turning movement, is organised on much more sophisticated lines. When a tactile stimulus is given on the skin immediately adjacent to the lips, the head turns in the direction from which the stimulus is coming. Moreover, if the stimulus is kept constant on one point of the skin for a longer time and then moved around, the head follows. This shows not only that the movement is elicited by tactile stimuli but that its form and direction are continuously regulated by the precise location of those stimuli.

Whereas the side-to-side fixed action pattern can easily be elicited in premature babies of twenty-eight weeks and older, the directed head-turning behaviour is much later to develop. Even at full term only about two-thirds of babies show directed head-turning. Of those that do not, a majority go through a phase during which both sorts of movement are exhibited; in a minority, however, there is a gap of one or more days between the disappearance of the fixed action pattern and the appearance of the regulated movement.

Whichever of these two movements is in use is likely to lead, in the infant's environment of evolutionary adaptedness, to the same predictable outcome, namely food-intake. In each case the sequence of behaviour, organised as a chain, appears to be as follows (Prechtl, 1958):

a. movement of head leads a baby's mouth to come into contact with mother's nipple;
b. a tactile stimulus occurring on his lips or the immediately adjacent areas leads a baby's mouth to open and his lips to grasp the nipple;
c. tactile stimulation anywhere in his mouth area, and especially probably on his hard palate (Gunther, 1961), elicits sucking movements;
d. presence of milk in his mouth elicits swallowing movements.

Observe the sequence: moving head, grasping nipple, sucking —all before food is obtained. As Gunther emphasises:

The ordinary concept that the baby feeds because it is hungry does not hold. If you put an empty bottle into a baby's mouth, even immediately after birth, the baby is driven to try to feed. This is in marked contrast to [what happens when he is given] a teaspoonful of milk which merely seeps away at the back of the mouth.

No sooner has feeding behaviour been initiated in the new-born by means of a chain-linked sequence of this sort than the behaviour starts to undergo change and development. For example, during the earliest days of life, it has been shown (Lipsitt, 1966), the strength of a baby's sucking can readily be either augmented or diminished. In increasing it food, not sur-prisingly, is one factor of importance. Thus an ill-shapen object that yields food is sucked more than the same object when it does not yield food. Nevertheless, food is very far from being the only factor that augments sucking: the shape of the object sucked is also of great relevance. When the shape is a traditional one, e.g. a rubber nipple, it is not only sucked readily but to an increasing degree even when it yields no food; when the shape differs markedly from the traditional one, e.g. a rubber tube, and still yields no food, it is sucked less and to a decreasing degree.

Another sort of development that occurs during the early days of life is that an infant comes to orient towards the breast or bottle in anticipation of his face and mouth coming into contact with it. Call (1964) observed this anticipatory orienta-tion to occur as early as the fourth feed; and by the twelfth it was usual. Once it is developed, an infant opens his mouth and brings his free arm up to the region of his mouth and of his mother's approaching breast as soon as he is placed in a nursing position, namely when his body is in contact with his mother's though his face is not. A few of the babies observed were slow to develop such orientation. These were babies who, whilst being fed, were having minimal bodily contact with their mothers.

At first, a baby's anticipatory movements are elicited not by sight of breast or bottle but by the tactile and/or proprioceptive stimuli that he receives when he is placed in the nursing position. Not until his third month are his anticipatory move-ments guided by what he sees (Hetzer and Ripin, 1930).

Since the directed head-turning movement described by Prechtl is specially easily elicited when a baby is hungry and since it commonly brings mouth to nipple, it is evidently an integral part of feeding. In addition to that, however, directed head-turning has the effect of orienting the baby towards mother even when there is no feeding. This point has been made by Blauvelt. Using time and motion study techniques,

Blauvelt and McKenna (1961) demonstrate with what precision an infant rotates his head in response to stimuli. Thus when a tactile stimulus is moving from his ear towards his mouth an infant rotates his head to meet it; conversely, when the stimulus is moving in the opposite direction he rotates his mouth to follow it. In both circumstances the result is the same: he is brought to face the stimulus.

Grasping, Clinging, and Reaching

The human neonate's ability to cling and to suspend his own weight has already been described; and it has, further, been postulated that this behaviour is homologous with the clinging behaviour of non-human primates. Research of recent years has supported this view and has also cast much light on how the directed clinging of later human infancy develops from certain primitive responses with which the human neonate is equipped. Two of these primitive responses are the Moro response and the grasp response.

In 1918 a German paediatrician, E. Moro, first described the *Umklammerungs–Reflex* (embracing reflex), now usually known as Moro's response. According to Prechtl (1965), it is 'a very complex pattern built up of several components'; it is elicited when a baby is suddenly shaken, tilted, raised, or dropped. Eliciting stimulation is certainly vestibular and may also be proprioceptive from the baby's neck.

Not a little controversy has arisen both over the nature and sequence of the movement and over the place and function of the response in an infant's behavioural repertoire. It is significant that much of the perplexity and controversy has arisen because the response has usually been studied in an environment other than the human infant's environment of evolutionary adaptedness. Once the movements are studied in a biologically appropriate setting, problems are seen in a new light and the solution becomes clear.

Traditionally, the Moro response has been elicited when a baby's hands are not grasping anything. Then the response is usually in two phases, during the first of which there is abduction and extension of arms and also of certain fingers, and during the second, adduction of arms; meanwhile legs are extended and flexed in no very consistent order. Prechtl shows, however, that the Moro response is very different when it is elicited whilst an infant is held in such a way that traction is exerted on his hands and arms, thereby eliciting the palmar grasp reflex. Then, when he is subjected to a sudden drop, little or no extension is elicited but, instead, strong flexion and considerably strengthened clinging. Prechtl concludes that to elicit the Moro response when the baby's arms are free is to do so in conditions that are biologically inadequate and that lead to a strange motor pattern that is difficult to understand. Once the human Moro response is seen in the context of primate clinging, however, it becomes explicable. The new findings, Prechtl continues, are 'in agreement with observations on young rhesus monkeys. . . . A rapid movement of the mother animal elicits an increase in the clasp and grasp of the young, preventing the young animal from falling off the mother's body.' In other words, Moro was right in believing that the function of the response is to 'embrace' the mother.

The grasping response of human infants has been studied by Halverson (1937) and by Denny-Brown (1950, 1958). The latter distinguishes three different types of response, each organised at a different level of sophistication.

The simplest is the *traction response*, which consists of flexion of hands and feet in response to traction when the suspended infant is suddenly lowered in space. The next in order of sophistication is the *true grasp reflex*, which is a double-phase response. The first phase, which is a weak closure of the hand or foot, is elicited by tactile stimuli in the palm. The second phase, which is strong flexion, is elicited by proprioceptive stimuli arising in the muscles engaged in the initial closure.

Neither the traction response nor the grasp reflex is oriented in space. The *instinctive grasp response*, on the other hand, which develops some weeks later, is so oriented. Like the grasp reflex, it has two phases. The first phase, which is elicited when tactile contact is broken, consists of a movement of the hand at right angles to the last point of contact, and gives the impression of groping. The second phase is a snap closure elicited as soon as the palm again receives tactile stimulation.

At a later stage again all these forms of response are superseded by still more sophisticated ones. In particular, grasping comes under the control of visual stimuli. No longer does an infant grasp involuntarily the first thing that enters his palm, but instead he is able to grip selectively some object that he sees and prefers.

The steps by which reaching and grasping come under visual control have been studied by White, Castle, and Held (1964). These investigators found that it is not until after two months of age that a human infant is able to integrate movements of arm and hand with what he sees. During his second and third months an infant reaches out towards a patterned moving object, swipes at it with his fist, but makes no attempt to grasp it. By four months, however, his approaching hand is open, he glances alternately at object and hand as his hand comes closer, and finally he grasps the object. Although at first his performance is clumsy, a few weeks later all these movements have become integrated so that he reaches and grasps the object in one quick direct motion.

By now the infant is five months old. Not only is he able to recognise his mother but he is likely also to direct most of his social behaviour towards her. He is therefore likely to reach for and grasp parts of her anatomy, especially her hair. It is not until a month or two later, however, that he starts really to cling to her, which he does especially when he is alarmed or unwell. Six months was the earliest age at which Ainsworth observed clinging in the Ganda infants and some did not show it until they were nine months old. After that age clinging was pronounced at sight of a stranger and especially so when mother attempted to hand the baby to the stranger.

In examining the results of their experiments on the growth of visually directed grasping, White, Castle, and Held conclude that a number of relatively distinct motor systems each make a contribution:

> These include the visual motor systems of eye–arm and eye–hand, as well as the tactual motor system of the hands. These systems seem to develop at different times . . . and may remain in relative isolation from one another . . . gradually they become co-ordinated into a complex superordinate system which integrates their separate capacities.

The authors postulate that this development is dependent on a number of spontaneous activities in which an infant in his family environment commonly engages. An example is an infant's spontaneous grasping and manipulating of his two hands: when these movements are visually monitored, vision and touch are linked 'by means of a double feedback system. For the eyes not only see what the hands feel, namely each other, but each hand simultaneously touches and is being actively touched.' Were a baby to have no opportunity for active experience of this type, on the other hand, it is probable that the usual integration of systems to permit of visually directed reaching would never take place, or would take place late and only imperfectly. This is yet another illustration of the general principle that, heavily biased to develop in certain directions though behavioural equipment usually is, it does not develop so unless the infant animal is being cared for in the species' environment of evolutionary adaptedness.

Smiling

The smile of a human infant is so endearing and has so strong an effect on his parents that it is no surprise to find that it has engaged the attention of a great many workers from Darwin (1872) onwards. The extensive literature is reviewed briefly by Freedman (1964) and subjected to a detailed critical appraisal by Ambrose (1960).

In the past it has been suggested that the motor pattern of an infant's smile is learned and also that a main factor leading a baby to smile at a human is having been fed by one. Neither view is supported by evidence. Today the views best supported are: (i) that the motor pattern of a smile belongs to the category termed in this book instinctive; (ii) that, although smiles can be elicited by a range of stimuli, the organism is so biased that from the first some stimuli are more effective than are others; (iii) that in the environment of evolutionary adaptedness the effective stimuli are far more likely to come from a baby's mother-figure and from other people in his family than from any other source, animate or inanimate; (iv) that, by processes of learning, the effective stimuli become restricted to those of human origin, notably human voice and face; (v) that, by further processes of learning, smiles become elicited more promptly and more intensely by a familiar voice (at about four weeks) and a familiar face (at about fourteen weeks) than by others. To these widely accepted views regarding causation we may add (vi) that a baby's smile acts as a social releaser, the predictable outcome of which is that the baby's mother (or other figure smiled at) responds in a loving way that prolongs social interaction between them and increases the likelihood of her exhibiting maternal behaviour in future (see Chapter 13); and (vii) that the function of a baby's smile is that of increasing interaction between mother and baby and maintaining them in proximity to each other.

During the first year of life an infant's smiling develops through four main phases:

(i) A phase of *spontaneous and reflex smiling* during which an occasional response is elicited by any of a great variety of stimuli, but is fleeting and incomplete when it comes. The phase starts at birth and usually lasts about five weeks. During the first three weeks the response is so incomplete that it leaves the spectator wholly unmoved: in other words, it has no functional consequence. During the fourth and fifth weeks, sometimes earlier, it is still very brief, but it is more nearly complete and it begins to have social effects. These two weeks, therefore, are transitional to the second phase.

(ii) The second phase is one of *unselective social smiling* during which the eliciting stimuli become increasingly restricted, and those that are effective are mostly derived from human voice and face. The response itself, though still difficult to elicit, is now complete and sustained, and has the full functional consequence of leading the baby's companion to respond to him in a playful and loving way. In most babies the phase is clearly present by the end of the fifth week of life.

(iii) The third phase is one of *selective social smiling* during which the infant becomes increasingly discriminating. Already by the fourth week of life he is not only discriminating voices but is smiling more readily to a familiar one. Some ten weeks later the face of the familiar caregiver also comes to elicit a more immediate and generous smile than do the faces of less familiar people, or painted masks. Such differential smiling to faces starts earlier in babies cared for at home (fourteen weeks) than in babies cared for in an institution (about twenty weeks). Nevertheless, until a baby is six or seven months old, strange faces and even masks are still likely to elicit smiling, albeit sometimes reluctant and weak.

(iv) Finally comes a phase of *differential social responsiveness* that will last for the rest of life. Now, whereas familiar figures are smiled at freely, especially during play or in greeting, strangers are treated in one of many different ways that range from a frightened withdrawal through reluctant greeting and on to an almost self-consciously sociable smile, usually given from a safe distance.

Phase of spontaneous and reflex smiling. Our knowledge of the earliest steps in the ontogeny of smiling is derived very largely from the thorough observations made by Wolff (1963) of the behaviour of some eight infants during their first weeks of life, at first in obstetric hospital and later in their families. On five days a week for four hours, and on one day a week for ten hours, Wolff made both systematic and anecdotal observations, and also conducted planned experiments on all forms of socially relevant behaviour. Another valuable study is by Freedman who, with a colleague, studied the development of social responses in twenty pairs of same-sexed twins (Freedman and Keller, 1963; Freedman, 1965).

Within twelve hours of birth all eight infants observed by Wolff occasionally grimaced with their mouths in a way suggestive of smiling. When it came, however, the movement was brief and was not accompanied by the typical smiling expression of the eyes (caused by a contraction of the muscles around the eyes in a way that produces a crinkling at their corners). Often the movement was unilateral. These very early, incomplete and non-functional smiles occur spontaneously from time to time and can also be elicited. When occurring spontaneously during the first weeks of life they do so usually 'at the precise moment during drowsiness when the eyes close' (Wolff, *ibid.*). There is no reason to suppose that they are caused by wind and, pending further information, they are best regarded as 'vacuum activities'. In most infants these occasional spontaneous smile-grimaces are not seen after the first month of life (Freedman, 1965).

During the first fortnight of life, Wolff reports, almost the only condition in which a smile can be elicited is when a baby is in a state of undisturbed but irregular sleep. During the second of these two weeks, however, a smile can also be elicited when a baby is well fed with eyes open, but staring into space in a vapid glassy way. In both such states a brief smiling movement can sometimes be elicited by gentle stroking of the baby's cheek or belly, by a soft light shone into his eyes, and by a soft sound; but the response is uncertain and its latency long, and once it has been elicited no further response can be produced for some time. During the first week, sounds of several different sorts appear to be equally effective, but during the second week a human voice seems rather more effective than others, e.g. a bell, a bird whistle, or a rattle.

Since during the first fortnight all smiles, both elicited and spontaneous, are fleeting and incomplete, they have little effect on spectators. In other words, they are non-functional.

Phase of unselective social smiling. Wolff found that the start of a new phase occurs commonly at about the fourteenth day and that the phase itself is usually well established by the end of the fifth week. It is ushered in by two great changes: (a) the smile occurs now in an alert, bright-eyed baby; (b) the movements of his mouth are broader than formerly and his eyes crinkle. In addition, it is now evident that his smile is most readily elicited by a distinctively human stimulus. Nevertheless, the response remains slow to come and of brief duration.

During the third week of life the stimulus that most regularly produces this primitive social smile is auditory, and by far the most effective is the human voice, especially a high-pitched one. By the end of the fourth week, Wolff found, the sound of a female voice has become so efficacious that it can elicit a smile even when a baby is crying or sucking. When a baby is crying, 'the first phrase of her talking usually arrests the cry; the second phrase alerts the baby; and the third phrase may produce a full-fledged smile'. When a baby is sucking his bottle, even during his first minute of it, on hearing a voice he may interrupt his sucking, give a broad smile, and then return to his food.

Until the end of the fourth week visual stimuli still play practically no part in smiling. All they do is to make the sound of a human voice a little more effective. For example, the sight of a nodding head augments the effectiveness of a voice; but by itself it is entirely without visible effect.

During the fifth week the voice, hitherto much the most effective stimulus, loses most of its power to elicit smiles. Thenceforward the most usual and effective stimulus for eliciting them is a human face, and thereafter it is in happy visual interchanges that the baby's smile comes into its own.

At about the same age that visual stimuli come to play so central a part, proprioceptive and tactile stimuli come also to be of much importance. Thus, during the fourth and fifth weeks, Wolff found, the proprioceptive-tactile stimuli arising from a game of pat-a-cake become suddenly and remarkably effective in eliciting smiles, even when the baby can neither see nor hear his human companion.

Before a baby starts to smile at what he sees, he commonly goes through a phase lasting several days or a week during which he stares intently at faces. During the first three weeks of his life a baby may look at a face and track it, but he seems not to focus on it. After he has reached about three and a half weeks, however, the impression given to an observer is radically different. Thenceforward, Wolff reports, the baby seems to focus on his companion's face and to engage her in eye-to-eye contact. Exactly what change has taken place is difficult to define, but its effect on the baby's companion is unmistakable. Within two or three days of Wolff's having noted this change in a baby's gaze the baby's mother began remarking 'Now he can see me' or 'Now he is fun to play with'. And simultaneously she began suddenly to spend much more time playing with her baby.[1]

During the fourth week intent gazing is the rule, and in a few babies also the first visually elicited smiles are to be seen. In a majority, however, they do not occur until the fifth week. From the first the companion's eyes are all-important:

> First the child searches the face, looking at the hairline, the mouth, and the rest of the face, and then as soon as eye-to-eye contact is made he grins. Other infants who showed the same behaviour later all followed the same pattern of inspecting the rest of the face before focusing on the eyes and smiling (Wolff, 1963).

By the end of the fifth week almost all babies are engaging in visual smiling and their smiles become sustained for increasing lengths of time. They are accompanied moreover by babbling, waving of arms, and kicking. Henceforward a mother experiences her baby in a new way.

Although social smiling is present in almost all babies throughout the second and third months, smiles tend still to be slow to come, of low intensity, and of relatively short duration. After about fourteen weeks, however, most babies become much more smiley—smiling more readily, more broadly, and for longer (Ambrose, 1961).

From the time that smiling to visual stimuli is first established, the most effective visual stimulus is a human face in movement; and a face is made even more effective when it is well lit and approaching the infant, and still more so when it is accompanied by touch and voice. In other words, a baby smiles most and best when he sees a moving figure who looks at him, approaches him, talks to him, and pats him (Polak, Emde, and Spitz, 1964).

The extent to which a baby smiles at visual stimuli other than a face is uncertain. Several experimenters, including Spitz, report that babies do not smile at their feeding-bottle. On the other hand, smiling at familiar toys—little balls of wool or celluloid—has been observed in infants of from ten to sixteen weeks by Piaget (1936). In reviewing his results, Piaget lays special emphasis on the point that the objects are familiar to

---

[1] The same sequence of events is described by Robson (1967). The shift, Bronson points out (personal communication), may well signal the inception of neocortical control.

the infant, and he concludes: 'the smile is primarily a reaction to familiar images, to what has already been seen'. From this conclusion he moves to another: the reason that gradually the smile comes to be elicited only by people is because people 'constitute [the] familiar objects most inclined to this kind of reappearance and repetition'.

In laying great emphasis on the role of familiarity Piaget's views are in keeping with much recent work (see Chapter 10). His belief that familiarity is the main or only factor that leads smiling to become confined to people is, however, unlikely to be true. As already discussed, it seems more probable that a baby arrives in this world with certain in-built biases, one of which is a bias to look at a human face in preference to other objects. Another appears to be to smile at a human face more readily than at anything else, especially at a human face in movement.

Since the classic work of Kaila (1932) and of Spitz and Wolf (1946), many experimenters have striven to discover what it is about a human face that makes it so powerful an elicitor of infant smiles. In the interpretation of this work it is necessary to distinguish between a sufficient stimulus and an optimum stimulus. Any stimulus capable of producing even an occasional smile can be termed sufficient, but it may be clear on many criteria that it is far from optimum. In general, a good stimulus elicits a smile that is quick to come, long, and strong; a weak stimulus elicits one that is slow to come, brief, and of low intensity (Polak et al., 1964).

Although the moving human face soon becomes the optimum visual stimulus, during the whole half-year from two to seven months of age certain schematic renderings of the face are sufficient sometimes to elicit some sort of smile. Almost from the first all these schemata have in common a pair of eye-like dots. This very consistent finding is in keeping with Wolff's natural-istic observations that an infant's sight of his companion's eyes plays a major part in eliciting his smile. It is also consistent with the well-attested finding that a face in profile is ineffective.

In one series of experiments using masks of different sorts, Ahrens (1954) found that during his second month an infant will smile at a pair of black dots on a face-sized card, and that a six-dotted model is more effective than a two-dotted one. He found also that even during the third month an infant will smile at a mask that comprises only eyes and brows with no mouth or chin. As he gets older the mask is sufficient to elicit a smile only when it provides greater and greater detail, until by eight months nothing short of an actual human face will do.

Though these experiments show that until he is about seven months of age a baby is not too discerning upon whom he bestows his smiles, it must not be concluded that he lacks all discrimination. On the contrary, Polak *et al.*, using as criteria latency, intensity, and duration, found that already by the end of the third month a baby discriminates a real face from a life-sized coloured photo and that, though the photo continues to be a sufficient stimulus for him to smile at, it is far from an optimum one. To a human face his smiles are quicker, longer, and stronger.

Blind babies smile, and observations on the way in which smiling develops in them cast light on some of the processes at work in sighted babies (see Freedman (1964) for observations and a review of literature).

In blind babies, voice and touch are the main stimuli that elicit smiling, and voice alone is fairly effective. Nevertheless, until they are six months old blind babies do not smile normally. In place of the sustained smile of sighted babies, the smiles of blind babies remain for long extremely fleeting, as they are in half-asleep babies during the first weeks of life. Before their smiles become sustained, at about six months of age, blind babies go through a phase during which their smiles are made up of a succession of rapid reflex smiles.

Thus in blind babies the human voice, a stimulus that in sighted babies plays the main role only during the early weeks, continues to carry that role also during later infancy. In doing so, however, the voice is insufficient to elicit the sustained smiling seen in sighted babies until the blind baby is six months of age. This supports the view, derived from observation of sighted babies, that what sustains the smile of a sighted baby after he has reached five weeks of age is his continuing perception of the eliciting visual patterns. For example, a sighted baby may show sustained smiling so long as he sees his companion full-face but sober immediately the face is turned to profile.

Phase of selective social smiling. Already by his fourth week a baby is smiling more consistently when he hears his mother's voice than when he hears any other (Wolff, 1963). To visual stimuli, however, he remains undiscriminating far longer. Until the end of his third month, indeed, a baby smiles as freely at sight of a stranger as he does at that of his mother. Babies in institutions fail to respond differently to a familiar face as opposed to a strange one until the end of their fifth month (Ambrose, 1961).

Once a baby starts discriminating stranger from familiar, he smiles less at the stranger than he did earlier. For example, whereas at thirteen weeks of age a baby may have smiled freely even at a stranger's immobile face, a fortnight later he may not smile at it at all. At his mother, on the other hand, he smiles as freely as before and probably more so. Ambrose (1961) has discussed some of the many possible explanations for this change of responsiveness. Whereas alarm at a stranger undoubtedly plays a part during the third and fourth quarters of the first year, during the second quarter it seems unlikely to be a main factor. Instead, mother's loving behaviour on seeing her baby smile, or even simply her familiar presence, seem likely to be the principal influences.

There is good evidence that when a baby's smile is responded to in a loving sociable way he smiles thereafter more strongly. Experimenting with eight three-month-old babies, Brackbill (1958) elicited a smile by presenting her face to a baby. Every time the baby smiled she smiled back, cooed, picked him up, and cuddled him. As a result of a few experiences of this sort all the babies became more smiley (measured in terms of their rate of responding). Conversely, when the experimenter ceased to respond, the rate of smiling gradually declined until eventually it died out. Her results fall neatly into the pattern of operant conditioning. They are consistent also with many other observations regarding what leads a baby to become attached to a particular figure: these are discussed in the next chapter (pp. 313–18).

When a baby smiles much else happens as well. Not only does he look at the approaching figure but he orients his head and body, waves his arms and kicks his legs. He also babbles. This leads on to the second of the two powerful and characteristic responses with which the human infant is endowed and the possession of which results in his entering into social communication with his companions.

Babbling

The role of babbling in social interchange is rather similar to that of smiling. Both occur when a baby is awake and contented, and both have as a predictable outcome that the baby's companion responds in a sociable way and engages with him in a chain of interaction. Both, moreover, become effective as social releasers at about the same age, namely five weeks, and, because both are elicited by the same stimuli, both are apt to occur together. The main difference, obviously, is that, whereas smiles and their associated limb movements are visual signals, babbling is an auditory one.

When a baby first gurgles and coos, which he does at about four weeks of age, he does so mainly in response to a voice, which at that age elicits also smiles. Although for a week or so a voice elicits both babbling and smiling, it then ceases to elicit much smiling and thenceforward elicits mainly babbling (Wolff, 1963). This it does very effectively. From about the sixth week onwards, Wolff reports, 'by imitating the baby's sounds it is possible to engage in an exchange of between ten and fifteen vocalisations'. Already by that age, Wolff found, mother's voice was more effective than his own.

Babbling, however, is elicited also by visual stimuli. No sooner has an infant begun to smile at sight of a moving human face than he babbles at it also, though he does not babble quite as regularly as he smiles. When he both sees a moving face and hears a voice he babbles most of all.

Thus babbling, like smiling, tends to occur most frequently in a social context. Nevertheless, also like smiling, it can occur as well in other situations. Rheingold (1961) has emphasised how a baby of three months may smile and gurgle on sight and sound of a rattle, whereas a baby of five months will not. The reason he discontinues to respond so, it seems probable, is that an inanimate object fails to be influenced by his smiles and babbles—in marked contrast to his human companions.

Just as Brackbill succeeded in reinforcing a baby's smile by responding to it every time by smiling, cooing, and picking him up, so were Rheingold, Gewirtz, and Ross (1959) successful in increasing the frequency of babbling in babies by similar social rewards. Their experiment was done with twenty-one infants aged three months. The experimenter elicited babbling by leaning over the baby and looking at him with an expression-less face for a period of three minutes. On days one and two the experimenter remained unresponsive to the ensuing babbles. On days three and four she made an immediate response each time the infant vocalised: each of her responses was threefold —a broad smile, three 'tsk' sounds, and a light squeeze of the infant's abdomen. On days five and six she was again unrespon-sive. Results were unambiguous. When the infants' vocalisations were responded to the infants vocalised more: on the second of the two rewarded days vocalisations had almost doubled. When the infants' vocalisations were no longer responded to, they diminished again.

Whether an infant's babbling can be increased by other means, and, if so, by what sort, remains unknown. The sounding of door chimes every time an infant babbled was, however, unsuccessful in producing any increase (Weisberg, 1963).

So far as they go, it is clear, these results are in keeping with the view that babbling, like smiling, is a social releaser, and that it has the function of maintaining a mother-figure in proximity to an infant by promoting social interchange between them.

As in the case of other social responses, infants come sooner or later to vocalise more in interaction with their familiar mother-figure than in interaction with anyone else. Wolff (1963) noticed this as early as five or six weeks. Ainsworth (1964) did not notice it before twenty weeks but remarks that her observations of this particular feature of behaviour were not systematic.

By the fourth month an infant is capable of making a very large variety of sounds. Thenceforward he uses some sounds more frequently than others, and during the second half of the first year he shows a marked tendency to select the intonations and inflections of his companions. It seems likely that in this development important parts are played both by an infant's tendency to imitate the particular sounds made by his companions and by his companions' tendency selectively to reinforce the same sounds when they are made by the infant.

Crying

All the infantile responses so far considered are welcomed by a baby's companions, who are usually more than happy to elicit and encourage them. Crying, by contrast, is not welcomed by those companions, and they are likely to do their best not only to stop it when it occurs but to reduce the likelihood of its occurring. The role of social stimuli for crying, therefore, is almost the reverse of what it is for the friendly responses. For the friendly responses, social stimuli are the main elicitors and the main reinforcers; for crying, social stimuli are amongst the main terminators and also amongst the main agents for reducing the likelihood of its further occurrence.

In the preceding chapter it was pointed out that there is more than one sort of crying. Each sort tends to have its own pitch and pattern, its own causal stimuli, its own terminating stimuli, and its own effects on a baby's companions. As a rule, crying leads a mother to take steps to arrest it; this she does either instantly, as when she hears a sudden pain cry, or in her own time, as when rhythmic crying builds up gradually. A baby's cry, indeed, is not easily overlooked or tolerated. A main reason for this, Ambrose points out, is that the variations in rhythm and range of the cries of any one baby are large; this means that it is not easy to become habituated to them.

As every mother knows, each baby cries in his own individual way. Sound spectrograms show, indeed, that 'cry-prints' are as distinctive as finger-prints for identifying newborn babies (Wolff, 1969). A mother soon comes to recognise the crying of her own baby. In a sample of twenty-three mothers studied by Formby (1967), half were proficient within forty-eight hours of the baby's birth, and thenceforward, of eight tested, none made a mistake. Wolff, too, found that most mothers soon become adept in this respect. Thenceforward they respond selectively, mothering their own infant but not necessarily others.

Two sorts of cry have already been described—crying from hunger, which starts gradually and becomes rhythmical, and crying from pain, which starts suddenly and is arrhythmical. A third type, described briefly by Wolff (*ibid.*), has a characteristic braying sound and is said usually to be interpreted as a signal of anger. A fourth type, given mainly or only by infants with brain damage, is reported by Wolff to be especially disagreeable to the baby's companions who tend to become agitated and to wish to get out of earshot of it.

The commonest cry of a young baby is rhythmical, but it may be due to much else besides hunger. It may, for instance, start fairly suddenly, in which case it is probably caused by an external stimulus; or it may start with fussing and build up slowly, in which case it is likely to be caused either by some change internal to the child or by chilling.

The external stimuli that elicit rhythmic crying include sudden noises, and sharp changes of illumination and posture. They include also nakedness: Wolff (*ibid.*) reports that, especially during the second, third, and fourth weeks of life, many infants begin crying as soon as their clothes are removed and cease as soon as they are reclothed or covered with a heavy blanket.

Babies that are hungry or chilled are likely to signal their condition by rhythmic crying that slowly builds up and that is terminated respectively by food or warmth. A similar build-up of rhythmic crying occurs also, however, in babies that have been recently fed and are kept warm. The causes of such crying, which is common, have proved a little perplexing.

There are several means by which a mother identifies the cause of her baby's crying. When it is pain, the type of crying is likely to provide a clue. When it is an external stimulus, she may herself have noticed the offending event. When it is hunger or cold, the circumstances are suggestive, and the provision of food or warmth is an effective test of the accuracy of her guess. When it is none of these things a mother may be flummoxed.

The striking thing about crying that is not due to the causes so far considered is that it is effectively terminated by stimuli that, in a natural environment, are almost certain to be of human origin. These include sounds, especially the human voice, and the tactile and proprioceptive stimuli that arise from non-nutritive sucking and from being rocked. Let us consider what is known of the efficacy of each of these socially derived terminators of an infant's crying.

During his study of the early social responses of fourteen infants cared for in their own families in Boston, Wolff made many natural history observations on crying and carried out many experiments (Wolff, 1969). He notes that, from birth, *sounds* of several different sorts are effective, at least temporarily, in arresting crying. During the first week of life the sound of a rattle or a bell seems as effective as a human voice, or even more so. This balance of effectiveness does not last long, however, and, whilst it does last, it may be because the sound of bell or rattle is heard more readily by the baby above his own cries. However that may be, during a baby's second week of life the sound of a human voice becomes the most effective stimulus for arresting his cries, and during the third week a female voice is more effective than a male one. A couple of weeks later it is specifically mother's voice that is usually most effective—so effective, indeed, that her voice may not only terminate crying but, if continued, may come also to elicit smiling (Wolff, 1963).

Most mothers know that the mere act of *sucking* quietens a baby, and in Western countries rubber comforters have been on the market for years. One large-scale study of child care in the Midlands of England (Newson and Newson, 1963) showed that 50 per cent of the mothers who were rated as satisfactory gave a dummy to their baby—with no obvious ill effects. In less developed countries a mother commonly puts a crying baby to her breast, without much concern whether milk is available there or not.

The efficacy of *non-nutritive sucking* for quietening an infant has been the subject of experiment by Kessen and Leutzendorff (1963), who observed thirty infants aged between twenty-four and sixty hours. Their object was to determine the efficacy for quietening a baby of short periods of sucking a rubber dummy compared with similar periods of being gently stroked on the forehead. Both the amount of movement of the baby's hands and feet and also the amount of his crying were measured. Results were clear-cut. After half a minute of sucking, a baby's movements were on average reduced by a half and his crying by four-fifths. After the same period of being stroked, not only a baby's movements but also his crying had on average increased slightly (though not significantly). The authors comment that, because the babies had already on other occasions received some food by means of sucking, it is still possible to maintain that the quietening effect is 'the result of secondary reinforcement learned from the association of nipple and sucking with food'. Evidence that this is probably not the case, however, is reported by Wolff (1969). Babies born with atresia of the oesophagus, who therefore are unable to receive any food by mouth, still cease to cry when given something to suck.

Wolff (*ibid.*) notes also that the presence of a comforter between the lips has an effect even when it is not sucked. He points to the fact that, if a baby has gone off to sleep whilst sucking a comforter but has not yet reached deep sleep, removal of the comforter may result in his awaking again and crying.

That *rocking* a baby is commonly also a good way to quieten him has long been part of nursery lore. Since in recent years its value has been obscured by a misplaced insistence on the primacy of feeding, there is reason to reflect on the fruits of practical experience obtained with infants during their first three months of life, in two very different settings.

The first account is by a British paediatrician:

A most important cause of crying in this period is loneliness or a desire to be picked up. At least, it seems as if this is the cause of the crying, for the crying promptly stops when the baby is picked up and cuddled. It is remarkable how many mothers fail to realise that babies want and need cuddling, and so make the mistake of thinking that all baby's crying is due to hunger. The basic feature which differentiates crying from hunger from that of loneliness is the fact that crying from hunger or any other cause of discomfort is not stopped by picking the baby up (Illingworth, 1955).

The second account refers to the practices of a Bantu-speaking community of East Africa:

> Mothers recognise a kind of crying during the first three months that cannot be satisfied by nursing. . . . Most often at night . . . the mother puts on a light, binds the infant to her back and walks about in the house, shaking him up and down. With the side of his face pressed tightly against her back, the infant is frequently silenced by jostling in this position. In the daytime, child nurses also use shaking, either on the back or in the arms, as a means of calming a small infant who cries but refuses food (Levine and Levine, 1963).

A few years ago Ambrose (1969 and personal communication) began an experimental analysis of the stimuli that are effective in such conditions. He observed one full-term baby, aged five days, per afternoon session, starting soon after the baby has been fed and changed. Each baby lies in his crib, which is placed on a device that acts both as a rocker and as a stabilimeter. The device is initially immobile and the baby is studied for about an hour during which behavioural and physiological variables are recorded polygraphically.

In these circumstances a baby may lie quietly, awake or asleep, without crying throughout the session. Not infrequently, however, he starts sooner or later to cry, usually for no apparent reason. Sometimes the crying ceases soon after it has begun; at other times it continues. When crying continues for as long as two minutes, the baby is rocked. The motion is applied at varying rates to see whether, for terminating crying, certain rates are more effective than others.

Preliminary findings show that in such circumstances every baby stops crying when he receives vestibular stimulation from the rocker. The movement is a vertical one with a traverse of three inches. Rocking at slow speeds, such as thirty cycles per minute, is not effective in arresting crying. Once the speed is increased to fifty cycles a minute, however, crying diminishes; and at speeds of sixty cycles a minute and above every baby stops crying and, almost always, remains quiet. Furthermore, once that speed is reached there is a sharp decline in heart-rate (which during crying may reach 200 per minute and higher), breathing becomes more regular, and the baby becomes relaxed. A remarkable feature of this observation is the specificity of rate: at sixty cycles most babies stop crying though a few require seventy; below fifty cycles is ineffective. It is also to be noted that day in day out rocking continues to be an effective means of stopping a baby crying (personal observation); in other words, rocking is a stimulus to which a baby appears never to habituate.

In the course of his experiments Ambrose studied the comparative efficacy of other classes of stimuli for terminating crying. For non-nutritive sucking his observations confirm and extend those of Kessen and Leutzendorff.

Slipping an ordinary comforter into a baby's mouth, Ambrose found, soon quietens a baby. Its efficacy, however, is not as great as that of rocking. This is shown by their respective effects on heart-rate. When a baby is rocked his heart-rate usually returns to near the resting level. During non-nutritive sucking, on the other hand, though crying may cease as completely as when he is rocked and heart-rate slacken, the rate nevertheless remains above the resting level.

The conclusions to be drawn from the observations and experiments described are that, when a baby is not hungry, cold, or in pain, the most effective terminators of crying are, in ascending order, sound of voice, non-nutritive sucking, and rocking. These findings readily explain why babies are said to cry from loneliness and to have a desire to be picked up. Although to attribute such sentiments to babies in the early months of life is almost certainly not warranted, the statements nonetheless contain more than a grain of truth. When they are not rocked and not spoken to infants are apt to cry; when they are rocked and spoken to they cease crying and are content. And by far the most probable agent to rock and talk to a baby is his mother-figure.

In this connection the apparently unfailing and complete efficacy of rocking a baby in a certain way is especially striking. The fact that, if it is to terminate crying, rocking must be at sixty cycles a minute or above may perhaps be related to the rate at which an adult walks. Sixty steps a minute is in fact a very slow walk and is almost always exceeded. This means that, when carried on his mother's back or hip, a young baby is rocked at not less than sixty cycles a minute and so does not cry—unless he is hungry or in pain. This happy consequence might be due to chance: more likely, it seems, it is a result of selective pressures that have been operating during the course of man's evolution.

It is clear, therefore, that as a terminator of rhythmic crying rocking is on a par with feeding. When a baby is hungry, feeding is the effective terminator; when he is not hungry, rocking is the most effective one. In the opposite set of conditions neither is effective for more than a short while.

Rocking a baby, it is found, is effective not only in terminating rhythmic crying but in delaying its onset. This is shown by an experiment of Gordon and Foss (1966). As a part of the routine of an obstetric hospital the babies, ranging in age from a few hours to ten days, are placed in the nursery for an hour or so every afternoon. Since they have recently been fed, all but one or two are quiet. Each day for eighteen days one of the quiet babies was selected (at random) to be rocked, and was rocked in its cot for half an hour. Then for another half-hour the experimenter remained in the nursery to note which, if any, of the quiet babies began to cry. Results showed that the baby who had been rocked was less likely to cry during the period of observation than were the babies who had not been rocked.

As a baby grows older the situations that elicit and terminate crying change. What a baby can see comes to have special importance. As early as the fifth week, Wolff (1969) found, many babies otherwise content start crying when a person at whom they are looking leaves their visual field, and they cease to cry each time the person reappears. At this age and until a few months later the particular figure seen is of little or no significance; and the departure and reappearance even of a pet animal may have the same effect as that of a person. From the age of about five months, however, the particular figure who comes and goes matters a great deal.

In her account of Ganda babies Ainsworth (1967) reports that, from about five months, with much variation between children, a baby was apt to start crying when his mother left the room even though he still had some other companion with him. After about nine months he often cried less because he could then follow his mother more effectively. The incidence of such crying varies not only from child to child but also with the particular conditions that obtain. For example, an observation that can be made in any household is that how a twelve-month-old behaves when his mother leaves the room turns a great deal on how she moves. A slow quiet withdrawal is likely to elicit little protest; a quick bustling exit a loud and noisy one.

Towards the end of the first year of life infants become increasingly aware of and alarmed by strange faces and strange circumstances. Thenceforward strangeness becomes a common cause of crying and of turning to mother. Because of its important and intimate connection with attachment behaviour, fear of strange faces and strange places is discussed more fully in the next chapter.

At about the same age that a baby starts to cry at sight of a stranger he may start crying also in anticipation of the occurrence of something unpleasant. An example, recorded by Levy (1951), is crying when at a clinic a baby catches sight of the doctor preparing to repeat an injection that was given a few weeks earlier. Before eleven months of age only a very occasional infant was observed to react in this way. At ages eleven and twelve months, on the other hand, one-quarter of the sample did so. Such behaviour is part and parcel of the rapidly increasing grasp of the world about him that a child of twelve months is acquiring.

Nature and nurture

In the development of attachment behaviour, as in the development of every biological character, nature and nurture play continually interacting parts. So long as the environment is kept within certain limits, it seems likely that much of the variation in the behaviour of different children is attributable to genetic differences. Once environmental variation is increased, however, the effects to which such variation gives rise are plain to see.

An example of variation that seems almost certain to be due to genetic variation is the differences in the visual attention of boys and girls (Lewis, Kagan, and Kalafat, 1966; Lewis and Kagan, 1965). These workers studied babies aged twenty-four weeks and found that girl babies showed a pronounced preference for looking at faces rather than at non-facial patterns whereas boy babies showed no such preference.

Evidence suggesting that the first appearance of orientation and smiling is also affected by genetic variables comes from a comparative study of identical and fraternal twins by Freedman (Freedman and Keller, 1963; Freedman, 1965). This showed that the ages at which orientation and smiling appear in pairs of identical twins tend to be closer than are the ages at which they appear in pairs of same-sex fraternal twins. Since in every pair in this study both twins were reared together in the same family, environmental variation was minimised.

Once the environment of different children is made more different, the effects on development of environment soon become evident. Many such studies have been done comparing children reared in families with children reared in institutions. Thus, in the experimental situation used by Ambrose (1961), smiling was seen some weeks earlier in family infants than in institution ones (between six and ten weeks for family infants and between nine and fourteen for institution infants). Provence and Lipton (1962) report that, already at three months, institution infants babble less than do family ones. Thenceforward the development of infants in a depriving institution deviates progressively from that of family babies. Provence and Lipton report that institution infants are later to discriminate between face and mask, and between different faces (also reported by Ambrose), they make fewer attempts to initiate social contact, their repertoire of expressive movements is smaller, and as late as twelve months they still show no sign of attachment to any particular person. This absence of attachment is especially noticeable when they are distressed: even then they rarely turn to an adult.

There has been much discussion of what it is about an institution that is responsible for these retarding effects. Some, e.g. Casler (1961), have argued that the main retarding agent is a reduction of stimulus input, and that those who have implicated absence of mother-figure are mistaken. To this argument Ainsworth (1962) has replied by emphasising that during the early months of life an infant's mother-figure is by far the main source of whatever stimulation he receives. In addition to providing stimulation, moreover, a mother in the ordinary course of interacting with her baby provides him with opportunities for actively exploring his world both visually and manually. That such opportunities are of much importance for sensori-motor development was first suggested by Piaget (1936) and is supported by recent experimental studies by White and Held (1966). The deprivations to which an infant reared in a depriving institution is exposed are therefore multiple—lack of stimulus input, lack of opportunity for exposure learning, and lack of opportunity for 'self-induced movement in dependably structured environments', to name some.

In all that follows, therefore, the tremendous differences in development that can result from variations of environment must constantly be borne in mind. The topic is discussed further in Chapter 16.

Chapter 15

Focusing on a Figure

'Ah', said the Cat, listening, 'but what is the Baby fond of?'

'He is fond of things that are soft and tickle' said the Bat. 'He is fond of warm things to hold in his arms when he goes to sleep. He is fond of being played with. He is fond of all these things.'

Just So Stories—RUDYARD KIPLING

Introduction

In the previous chapter our account of the development of attachment is carried only a little beyond the first of four phases, that of 'Orientation and signals with only limited discrimination of figure'. In this chapter the second and third phases are described as they occur in infants brought up in an ordinary family setting. These phases are:

Phase 2—'Orientation and signals directed towards one (or more) discriminated figure(s)';

Phase 3—'Maintenance of proximity to a discriminated figure by means of locomotion as well as signals'.

The issues that arise in understanding development during Phase 4, 'Formation of a goal-corrected partnership', are discussed in chapters 17 and 18.

For the development of behaviour that takes place during Phase 2, main sources of data are the very detailed observations made of Irish American infants in Boston by Wolff (1963), of infants in Washington, D.C. by Yarrow (1967) and of Ganda infants by Ainsworth (1967). For developments during Phase 3, main sources are observations of Ganda infants by Ainsworth and of Scottish infants in Glasgow by Schaffer and Emerson (1964a).

It is particularly fortunate that, with regard to development in Phase 3, reasonably comparable data are available for infants being brought up in such very different circumstances as rural Africa and urban Scotland, since whatever behavioural changes are common to infants in both these settings are likely to hold for infants in other settings also. One difficulty in comparing the two sets of data has, however, continually to be borne in mind. In the study of Schaffer and Emerson, the sole criterion of attachment behaviour is a child's protest on being left by someone. In Ainsworth's study of the Ganda, by contrast, the criteria are more broadly based: in addition to protest at separation, an infant's greeting of a figure and use of a figure as a base from which to explore are included as criteria of attachment.

Patterns of differentially directed behaviour

As already described, a principal change that habitually takes place during the ontogeny of behaviour is for the range of stimuli that are effective in eliciting and in terminating a response to become restricted. This is conspicuously true of the friendly responses and crying of infancy.

An ability to discriminate his mother by smell and voice, shown by his tendency to orient more markedly towards her than towards others or to suck more often when it leads to hearing her voice, is developing rapidly during the earliest days of life. By the fifth week, moreover, the mother's voice is consistently more effective in eliciting smiles in some infants than is the father's voice or the observer's (Wolff, 1963). Yarrow (1967) also observed differences in response to mother when compared to a stranger at the end of the first month, though only in a minority of the infants he studied. Based on a sample of not less than 40 infants at each age level, and using as a criterion an infant's selective attention to voice or sight of mother in preference to voice or sight of a stranger, with excitement and positive affect exhibited towards mother and not towards stranger, Yarrow found a clear preference for mother in 20 per cent of infants at one month of age. By three months 80 per cent were showing it, and by five months all infants observed did so.

Ainsworth (1967) lists more than a dozen different kinds of behaviour that are shown by an infant during his first year and that, during it, come in most family infants to be elicited especially by and to be directed especially towards a particular figure. What follows is abstracted mainly from Ainsworth's account. As she herself emphasizes, there is reason to believe that, with more systematic and more sensitive observation, instances of each kind of discrimination would be seen weeks or even months earlier than any she was able to observe in the naturally occurring situations in which her observations were made. Since there is great variation from infant to infant, and also according to the precise conditions in which any one infant is observed, it is possible to give only a rough indication of the ages at which these discriminations first appear.

Differential Vocalisation

The criterion is that a baby vocalises more readily and more frequently in interaction with his mother than in interaction with others. Wolff (1963) noticed it as early as five or six weeks.

Differential Stopping of Crying on being Held

The criterion is that a baby continues to cry when held by someone other than his mother and stops crying when taken by her. The earliest occurrence noted by Ainsworth was in a child aged nine weeks.

Differential Crying on Mother's Departure

The criterion is that a baby cries promptly when mother leaves the room but not when others do so. The earliest occurrence noted by Ainsworth was in a child aged fifteen weeks.

Differential Smiling at Visual Stimuli

The criterion is that a baby smiles more frequently, more readily, and more fully at sight of his mother than at sight of anyone else. The earliest instance noticed in the Ganda was in a child of ten weeks. In a number of London infants on whom Ambrose (1961) conducted experiments, the age at which smiling at a stranger was at its peak was about thirteen weeks; thereafter infants tended to smile mainly or only at mother.

Differential Visual–Postural Orientation

The criterion is that when a child is held by someone else he keeps his eyes on mother in preference to others and is tensely oriented towards her. This was noted by Ainsworth in one child aged eighteen weeks.

Differential Greeting Response

The criterion is that an infant greets his mother in certain typical ways when he sees her after an absence. At first a full greeting usually combines smiling, vocalising, and general bodily excitement; later it includes also lifting the arms. The full response was noted by Ainsworth in a child of twenty-one weeks, but she has little doubt that parts of it could have been observed some weeks earlier. As soon as a child can crawl, crawling towards mother also occurs as part of the greeting response.

Two other greeting responses are fairly common, but both appear to be culturally determined. These are clapping the hands, which Ainsworth notes was fairly common in Ganda infants after about thirty weeks of age but which was not observed in a sample of white American infants, and kissing and hugging, which were not observed in the Ganda infants but which are shown by infants of Western cultures towards the end of their first year of life.

Differential Approach

The criterion is that, when in a room with mother and others, a child selects his mother to crawl towards. Sometimes this occurs also after mother has reappeared and has been greeted. This behaviour was noted by Ainsworth in one child aged twenty-eight weeks.

Differential Following

The criterion is attempting to follow mother when she leaves the room, but not to follow others. Ainsworth notes that infants tended to do this as soon as they were able to crawl, which occurred in most of the Ganda infants at about twenty-four weeks. The younger infants tended to cry as well as follow. After about nine months they often followed without crying, provided mother did not move too fast.

Differential Climbing and Exploring

The criterion is that an infant climbs over his mother, explores her person, and plays with her face, her hair, or her clothes, and does so less, if at all, with other people. Such behaviour was first noted by Ainsworth in a child of twenty-two weeks.

Differential Burying of Face

The criterion is that, either in the course of climbing and exploring or on return after an excursion, an infant buries his face in his mother's lap, or elsewhere in her person. Ainsworth observed that the behaviour was directed only towards a child's mother and never towards anyone else. It was seen in one child aged twenty-eight weeks and in others a few weeks older.

Use of Mother as Base from which to Explore

The criterion is that a child makes exploratory excursions from mother and returns to her from time to time, but does not use others in this way to the same extent. It was observed by

Ainsworth in one child of twenty-eight weeks and was common at eight months.

Flight to Mother as Haven of Safety

The criterion is that when alarmed a child moves as fast as possible away from the alarming stimulus and towards mother, rather than towards others. Such behaviour was noted by Ainsworth at about eight months. In the case of Yarrow's study about half the infants as young as three months, when distressed, looked towards mother in expectation of being soothed.

Differential Clinging

Differential clinging to mother is especially evident when a child is alarmed, tired, hungry, or unwell. Though Ainsworth did not make a special study of its occurrence, she reports that it was especially evident during the final quarter of the first year.

To summarise these and other findings: it can be said that before sixteen weeks differential responses are relatively few and are seen only when methods of observation are sensitive; that between sixteen and twenty-six weeks differential responses are both more numerous and more apparent; and that in the great majority of family infants of six months and over they are plain for all to see.

Figures towards whom attachment behaviour is directed

In the discussion so far it has been implied that a child directs his attachment behaviour towards one particular figure, referred to either as his mother-figure or even simply as his mother. This usage, which for the sake of brevity is unavoidable, has nonetheless given rise on occasion to misunderstanding.[1] Questions that arise and to which answers are required include the following:

a. Do children commonly direct their attachment behaviour towards more than one person?

b. If they do so, do attachments to a number of figures

---

[1] For example, it has sometimes been alleged that I have expressed the view that mothering should always be provided by a child's natural mother, and also that mothering 'cannot be safely distributed among several figures' (Mead, 1962). No such views have been expressed by me.

develop simultaneously, or does one attachment always precede the others?

c. When a child has more than one figure to whom he is attached, does he treat all figures alike or does he show a preference for one of them?

d. Can a woman other than a child's natural mother fill adequately the role of principal attachment-figure?

Since the answers to these questions are interrelated, it is convenient before discussing each separately to give a brief answer to the set: almost from the first many children have more than one figure towards whom they direct attachment behaviour; these figures are not treated alike; the role of a child's principal attachment-figure can be filled by others than the natural mother.

Principal and Subsidiary Attachment-Figures

During their second year of life a great majority of infants are directing their attachment behaviour towards more than one discriminated figure, and often towards several. Some infants select more than one attachment-figure almost as soon as they begin to show discrimination; but probably most come to do so rather later.

Of fifty-eight Scottish infants studied by Schaffer and Emerson (1964a), 17 (29 per cent) are reported to have been directing attachment behaviour towards more than one figure almost from the time they started showing it to anyone. After another four months not only had half the children more than one attachment-figure but a number of them had as many as five or more different attachment-figures. By the time these children had reached eighteen months of age, those who still restricted their attachment behaviour to only one figure had fallen to 13 per cent of the sample; which means that for a child of eighteen months still to have only one attachment-figure is quite exceptional. Ainsworth's findings for the Ganda show a comparable state of affairs: all but a tiny minority were showing multiple attachments by nine or ten months of age.

Nevertheless, although by twelve months a plurality of attachment-figures is probably the rule, these attachment-figures are not treated as the equivalents of one another. In each of the two cultures considered the infants show clear discrimination. In the case of the Scottish sample a scale was devised for measuring the intensity of protest that a child exhibited on being left by each figure. Results showed that for most children there was regularly more protest when he was left by one figure than by another, and that a child's attachment-figures could be arranged in hierarchical order. Using a broader range of criteria Ainsworth found that Ganda children tended to focus most of their attachment behaviour on one special person. Up till about nine months of age, she observed, a child with more than one attachment-figure nevertheless tended to confine actual following to a single figure. Moreover, when a child was hungry, tired, or ill he usually turned specifically to that figure. Other figures, on the other hand, were sought when a child was in good spirits: such a figure might be an older child who was in the habit of playing with him.

These findings suggest that from an early age different figures may elicit different patterns of social behaviour, and that it may be confusing to refer to them all as attachment-figures and to all the behaviour as attachment behaviour. In future studies it will be necessary to give more attention to these differences: approach to a playmate and approach to an attachment-figure as defined here may well prove to have quite different characteristics. This is a question to which further consideration is given later (see p. 307). Meanwhile we may note Ainsworth's conclusion:

> there is nothing in my observations to contradict the hypothesis that, given an opportunity to do so, an infant will seek attachment with one figure, . . . even though there are several persons available as caretakers (Ainsworth, 1964).

The Principal Attachment-Figure

It is evident that whom a child selects as his principal attachment-figure, and to how many other figures he becomes attached, turn in large part on who cares for him and on the composition of the household in which he is living. As a matter of empirical fact there can be no doubt that in virtually every culture the people in question are most likely to be his natural mother, father, older siblings, and perhaps grandparents, and that it is from amongst these figures that a child is most likely to select both his principal attachment-figure and his subsidiary figures.

In both the Scottish study and the Ganda study only those children who were living with their natural mother were selected for observation. In those circumstances it is not surprising that in an overwhelming proportion of cases a child's principal attachment-figure was his natural mother. There were, however, a few exceptions. Two Ganda children of about nine months, one a boy and one a girl, were said to be attached to both mother and father but to prefer father, in the boy's case even when he was tired or ill. A third Ganda child, a girl, showed no attachment to her mother even at twelve months, but instead was attached to her father and a half-sister.

Amongst the Scottish infants mother was almost always principal attachment-figure throughout the first year of life, but in some cases came to share the role, usually with father, during the second year. There were, however, three out of fifty-eight Scottish infants whose first attachment-figure was said to have been someone other than mother: two chose father and a third, whose mother was in full-time work, chose grand-mother who looked after him most of the day. (Owing to the restricted criterion of attachment used by Schaffer and Emerson it is not easy to be sure how some of their other data should be interpreted.)

Observations such as these and many others make it abundantly clear that, although it is usual for a child's natural mother to be his principal attachment-figure, the role can be taken effectively by others. Such evidence as we have is that, provided a mother-substitute behaves in a mothering way towards a child, he will treat her as another child would treat his natural mother. Just what comprises a 'mothering way' of treating a child is discussed in the next section. Briefly, it appears to be engaging in lively social interaction with him, and responding readily to his signals and approaches.

Though there can be no doubt that a substitute mother can behave in a completely mothering way to a child, and that many do so, it may well be less easy for a substitute mother than for a natural mother to do so. For example, knowledge of what elicits mothering behaviour in other species suggests that hormonal levels following parturition and stimuli emanating from the newborn baby himself may both be of great import-ance. If this is so for human mothers also, a substitute mother must be at a disadvantage compared with a natural mother. On the one hand, a substitute cannot be exposed to the same hormonal levels as the natural mother; on the other, a sub-stitute may have little or nothing to do with the baby to be mothered until he is weeks or months old. In consequence of both these limitations, a substitute's mothering responses may well be less strong and less consistently elicited than those of a natural mother.

Subsidiary Figures

It has already been remarked that we may need to distinguish more carefully than has hitherto been done between attachment-figures and playmates. A child seeks his attachment-figure when he is tired, hungry, ill, or alarmed and also when he is uncertain of that figure's whereabouts; when the attachment-figure is found he wants to remain in proximity to him or her and may want also to be held or cuddled. By contrast, a child seeks a playmate when he is in good spirits and confident of the whereabouts of his attachment-figure; when the playmate is found, moreover, the child wants to engage in playful interaction with him or her.

If this analysis is right, the roles of attachment-figure and playmate are distinct. Since, however, the two roles are not incompatible, it is possible for any one figure at different times to fill both roles: thus a child's mother may at times act both as playmate and as principal attachment-figure, and another person, for example an older child, who acts mainly as playmate may on occasion act also as a subsidiary attachment-figure.

Unfortunately the two pioneer studies on which we are drawing for our data do not make these distinctions. As a result it is not easy to be clear whether the various figures described in them as 'subsidiary attachment-figures' should always be so categorised. In this account of their findings, therefore, all these other figures are referred to simply as 'subsidiary figures', in the supposition that some are truly subsidiary attachment-figures, others are principally playmates, and a few are both.

For both the Ganda and the Scottish infants the commonest subsidiary figures to be reported were father and older siblings. Others included a grandparent or other persons staying in the house, and occasionally a neighbour. Both studies agree that each of these additional favoured figures is clearly discriminated from those not favoured. Ainsworth (1967) remarks that 'the specificity . . . and the sharpness of preferences among familiar people is very striking'; for example, whereas one sibling may always be greeted joyously, others are not.

Inevitably, for each child both the number and the identity of these additional figures change over time. Schaffer and Emerson record how, for a particular child, there might be a sudden increase in the number of additional figures and later perhaps a decrease. As a rule, though not always, such changes reflected clearly who happened to be available in the household at the time.

It is uncertain whether social behaviour begins to be directed towards discriminated subsidiary figures at the same time as it is first directed towards a principal attachment-figure or whether it is directed towards subsidiary figures a little later. Using as their criterion protest at being left, Schaffer and Emerson present their findings as supporting the first view. Ainsworth, on the other hand, inclines to the belief that the direction of attachment behaviour towards subsidiary figures occurs a little later than it does to a principal figure. Neither of these studies, however, used methods sufficiently refined to enable the issue to be settled.[1]

When a child has more than one attachment-figure it might well be supposed that his attachment to his principal figure would be weak, and, conversely, that when he has only one figure his attachment to that one would be specially intense. This, however, is not so: indeed, precisely the opposite is reported for both the Scots infants and the Ganda. In the case of the Scots, the infant who begins by showing an intense attachment to a principal figure is reported as significantly more likely to direct his social behaviour to other discriminated figures as well, whereas an infant who is weakly attached is more likely to confine all his social behaviour to a single figure. Ainsworth notes the same correlation in the Ganda infants. She offers as a possible explanation that the more insecure a child's attachment to his principal figure is the more inhibited is he likely to be in developing attachments to other figures. Another explanation that can be advanced, either as an addition to Ainsworth's or as an alternative to it, is that the more insecure a child the more inhibited is he in developing play relations with other figures.

Whatever the true explanation of the correlation may prove to be, one conclusion seems clear: it is a mistake to suppose that a young child diffuses his attachment over many figures in such a way that he gets along with no strong attachment to anyone, and consequently without missing any particular person when that person is away. On the contrary, both the older evidence and that more recently available (Rutter, 1981, Ainsworth, 1982) supports a hypothesis advanced in an earlier paper (Bowlby, 1958), namely that there is a strong bias for attachment behaviour to become directed mainly towards one particular person. In support of that view attention was drawn to

[1] Ainsworth's observations were made at intervals of about a fortnight; the reports from parents on which Schaffer and Emerson's study is mainly based were obtained at intervals of four weeks.

the way in which young children in a residential nursery tend, when given any opportunity, to latch themselves on to a particular nurse. In their *Infants without Families* (1944) Burlingham and Anna Freud give many illustrations of this. For example:

Bridget (2–2½ years) belonged to the family of Nurse Jean of whom she was extremely fond. When Jean had been ill for a few days and returned to the nursery, she constantly repeated: 'My Jean, my Jean'. Lilian (2½ years) once said 'my Jean' too, but Bridget objected and explained: 'It's my Jean, it's Lilian's Ruth and Keith's very own Ilsa.'

Because the bias of a child to attach himself especially to one figure seems to be well established and also to have far-reaching implications for psychopathology, I believe it merits a special term. In the earlier paper I referred to it as 'monotropy'.

The Role of Inanimate Objects

So far we have been concerned only with the different human figures towards whom attachment behaviour may be directed. It is well known, however, that certain components of attachment behaviour are sometimes directed towards inanimate objects. Non-nutritive sucking and clinging are examples.

It is also very common, of course, for nutritive sucking to be directed towards an inanimate object, namely a feeding-bottle. Since, however, feeding behaviour is regarded as a category of behaviour distinct from attachment, the direction of nutritive sucking to objects other than the mother's breast lies outside the scope of this book.

In the simplest societies, in which an infant may spend most of the twenty-four hours in contact with his mother, non-nutritive sucking and also clinging are directed towards the mother's body, as they are in all species of non-human primate. In other societies, on the other hand, including our own, non-nutritive sucking may come during the early weeks of life to be directed towards a dummy or a thumb, and some time later, usually not much before the end of the first year, a child may become attached to some particular bit of cloth or blanket, or to a cuddly toy. This he insists on taking to bed with him, and he may also demand its company at other times of day, especially if he is upset or tired. Often these soft articles are sucked as well as clasped, but this is not invariable.

Following the attention drawn to first treasured possessions by Winnicott (1953), more than one investigator has collected reports about them from parents. These show that in the United Kingdom at present the incidence of such attachments is fairly high. Of twenty-eight Scottish children aged eighteen months, Schaffer and Emerson (1964b) found that eleven, over a third, were or had been attached to a special cuddly object. Moreover, a third were said also to be given (or to have been given) to thumb-sucking. It is of some interest that almost all the children who had had cuddlies and who sucked their thumb were reported also to be children who much enjoyed being cuddled by their mothers.

Whereas sucking of thumb or dummy usually starts in the earliest weeks, attachment to a *particular* soft cuddly object is rarely present before nine months of age and often starts considerably later. In a series of forty-three children who had been or still were attached to such possessions, nine were reported by their mothers to have become attached before twelve months, twenty-two between their first and second birthdays, and a dozen after their second birthday (Stevenson, 1954).

There is no evidence that in any of these respects boys differ from girls.

The tremendous importance for a child's peace of mind of the particular cuddly object to which he has become accustomed is well known to mothers. Provided it is available a child is content to go to bed and relinquish his mother. When the object is lost, however, a child may be inconsolable until it is found. Sometimes a child becomes attached to more than one object. Mark, the eldest of three children, who was reported always to have had his mother's undivided attention, is an example:

> Mark sucked his thumb up to the age of four and a half, especially at times of stress and at night-time. Before he was fourteen months old he drew up his topmost blanket with his left hand and sucking his right thumb he entwined the blanket round his left fist. Then he beat his forehead with his muffled fist until he fell asleep. This blanket became known as his 'cloak' and accompanied him everywhere—in bed, on holidays, and so on. From the age of three he had as well a wooden squirrel, which at night he swathed in the end of 'cloak' and tucked beneath him (report by mother, quoted by Stevenson, 1954).

There is no reason to think that attachment to an inanimate object bodes ill for a child; on the contrary, there is plenty of evidence that such an attachment can be combined with satisfactory relations with people. With some children, indeed, an absence of interest in soft objects may give grounds for concern. For example, Provence and Lipton (1962) report that none of the infants they observed who had been cared for during their first year in a depriving institution became attached to a favourite cuddly object. Other infants sometimes show a positive dislike of soft objects, and here again there is reason to think that their social development may have gone astray. Stevenson (1954) describes such a child: he had been notable since early infancy for his strong dislike of soft toys. From the first he had been rejected by his mother and was later deserted by her, and it was plausible to suppose that in some way his dislike of soft objects reflected a dislike of his mother.

Not only is attachment to a cuddly object consistent with satisfactory relations with people but prolongation of an attachment to an inanimate object into later childhood may well be much commoner than is generally supposed: not a few children retain such attachments well into their school years. Though it would be easy to assume that a prolongation of these attachments suggests that a child is insecure, this is far from certain. The position may be different, however, when a child prefers an inanimate object to a person. Stevenson gives some examples:

> Roy's mother told me that if Roy fell down he would always ask for 'Say', his duster, rather than ask her for comfort. Two mothers told me that their sons' first requests on coming round from operations were for the objects.

One of these two was Mark who, when he was aged six, had his tonsils out. On coming round from the anaesthetic he asked for 'Squirrel' and, once he had it, went to sleep peacefully.

Presumably it would be possible for the whole of a child's attachment behaviour to be directed towards an inanimate object and none towards a person. Such a condition, were it to last any time, would almost certainly be inimical to future mental health. This 'common-sense' view is strongly supported by the observations of Harlow and Harlow (1965) on rhesus monkeys whose attachment behaviour during infancy had been directed exclusively to a dummy-figure. When later they were placed with other monkeys these infants proved grossly disturbed in all their social relationships.

The theoretical significance of a child's attachment to inanimate objects has been discussed by clinicians, notably by Winnicott (1953) who termed them 'transitional objects'. Within the theoretical schema he advances these objects are held to occupy a special place in the development of object relations; they belong, he believes, to a phase during which an infant, whilst barely capable of the use of symbolism, is nonetheless progressing towards it: hence the term 'transitional'.[1] Though Winnicott's terminology is now widely adopted, the theory on which it is based is open to question.

A much more parsimonious way of looking at the role of these inanimate objects is to regard them simply as objects towards which certain components of attachment behaviour come to be directed or redirected because the 'natural' object is unavailable. Instead of to the breast, non-nutritive sucking is directed to a dummy; and instead of to mother's body, hair, or clothing, clinging is directed to a blanket or cuddly toy. The cognitive status of such objects, it is reasonable to assume, is equivalent at each stage of a child's development to that of his principal attachment-figure—at first something little more elaborate than an isolated stimulus, later something recognisable and expectable, and ultimately a figure persisting in time and space. Since, pending more evidence, there is no reason to suppose that the so-called transitional objects play any special role in a child's development, cognitive or other, a more appropriate term for them would be simply 'substitute objects'.

The more parsimonious type of theory is strongly supported by the findings of studies made since the first edition of this volume (Boniface and Graham, 1979) and also by observations of the behaviour of non-human primate infants brought up away from mother. As in the case of human infants, monkey and ape infants take readily to bottle for food, and to comforter and thumb for non-nutritive sucking. Non-nutritive sucking may also be directed to a variety of other parts of their body: to toes commonly, and occasionally in a female to her own

---

[1] Because Winnicott's position is not easy to describe it is best presented in his own words:

. . . the piece of blanket (or whatever it is) is symbolical of some part-object, such as the breast. Nevertheless the point of it is not its symbolic value so much as its actuality. It's not being the breast (or the mother) is as important as the fact that it stands for the breast (or mother). . . . I think there is use for a term for the root of symbolism in time, a term that describes the infant's journey from the purely subjective to objectivity; and it seems to me that the transitional object (piece of blanket, etc.) is what we see of this journey of progress towards experiencing.

nipple and in a male to his own penis. As something to cling
to, Harlow has shown, baby monkeys take quickly to a dummy
mother-figure provided it is soft.

When cared for by a human foster-mother, monkeys and
apes at once take her for mother and cling with great tenacity.
Because their clinging is so unremitting it is fortunate that it is
sometimes possible to fob them off temporarily with a piece of
cloth. Such redirected behaviour is described vividly by Hayes
(1951) who brought up an infant chimpanzee. Reporting the
behaviour of Viki at about nine months of age, she writes:

> Although Viki and I were staunch friends, I was not her only
> solace in times of distress. We discovered that Viki could be
> comforted . . . by giving her a towel to hold. . . . Everywhere
> Viki went a towel trailed behind, clutched in one hand, or fist,
> or draped over her back . . . [When] she tired of [a] toy and
> decided to move on, she always reached behind her confidently
> for her towel. If she could not feel it, she looked, and if it was not
> in sight either, she ran frantically around the room searching for
> it. Then she grabbed my skirt and bounded up and down until
> I gave her a towel in self-defence.

Many other examples of such behaviour in primate infants
brought up in atypical surroundings could be given.

Thus it seems clear that, whether in human infants or monkey
infants, whenever the 'natural' object of attachment behaviour
is unavailable, the behaviour can become directed towards
some substitute object. Even though it is inanimate, such an
object frequently appears capable of filling the role of an
important, though subsidiary, attachment-'figure'. Like a principal attachment-figure, the inanimate substitute is sought
especially when a child is tired, ill, or distressed.

Processes leading to selection of figures

In the previous chapter it is postulated (p. 273) that the
development of an infant's attachment behaviour towards particular figures is the product of at least four processes at work in
him. The first three of these processes, together with the
consequences to which they almost inevitably lead when an
infant is cared for in an ordinary family, are listed below:

    a. an in-built bias to orient towards, to look at, and to listen
       to certain classes of stimuli in preference to others, which
       results in a very young infant's coming to pay special
       attention to the humans caring for him;

b. exposure learning, which results in an infant's learning the perceptual attributes of whoever is caring for him and discriminating that person from all other persons and things;

c. an in-built bias to approach whatever is familiar, which leads an infant, as soon as his motor equipment permits, to approach such familiar figure(s) as he has learned to discriminate.

The fourth process at work is that well-known form of learning through which, as a result of feedback of certain of the consequences of a piece of behaviour, that behaviour can become augmented (reinforced). Which, it may now be asked, are the particular consequences to which primitive forms of attachment behaviour lead that, when fed back centrally, have the effect of augmenting that behaviour?

It has already been remarked in Chapter 12 that no evidence has ever been presented that supports the traditional theory that the crucial reinforcer of attachment behaviour is food and that the reason a child becomes attached to a particular figure is because she feeds him and satisfies his other bodily needs. Conversely, evidence is now weighty that amongst the most effective reinforcers of attachment behaviour is the way a baby's companions respond to his social advances. This evidence can now be presented more fully. It derives from two sources—natural observation and experiment.

Amongst studies using natural observations are those of Schaffer and Emerson for Scottish children and of Ainsworth for Ganda children, and also some less systematic studies of children reared in Israeli kibbutzim. Findings all point in the same direction.

Schaffer and Emerson (1964a) were concerned to identify conditions that are associated with whether a baby of eighteen months becomes attached to mother at a high or a low degree of intensity, as measured by protests at her departure. Their conclusions are based on data for thirty-six children.

A number of conditions that have traditionally been thought to be relevant to intensity of attachment showed no significant association. These included several variables connected with methods of feeding, weaning, and toilet-training. Other variables that proved unrelated were sex of child, birth order, and developmental quotient. By contrast, two variables relating to mother's social interactions with her infant stood out as clearly significant. These were the readiness with which a mother responded to her infant's crying and the extent to which she herself initiated social interaction with her baby: the more readily she responded to his cries and the more interaction she initiated the stronger did her eighteen-month-old infant tend to be attached to her (as measured by his protests at her departure). Though these two variables showed some overlap, their degree of association was not statistically significant:

> ... some of the mothers ... who responded quickly to the infant's crying rarely interacted with him spontaneously, and, conversely, some of those who discouraged crying nevertheless interacted a great deal with the child.

The conclusion that responsiveness to crying and readiness to interact socially are amongst the most relevant variables was supported by the data that Schaffer and Emerson obtained on subsidiary figures. Individuals who responded readily to an infant's crying but who might give him no physical care tended to be those whom infants selected as subsidiary figures; whereas those who sometimes gave him physical care but were socially unresponsive were unlikely to be selected.

Naturally, quite often figures who were readily responsive to crying and who frequently interacted socially were also those who were most frequently available. But this was not always so: for example, some mothers who were available all day were not responsive to or sociable with their infants, whereas some fathers who were not frequently available interacted strongly with their infants whenever they were with them. In such families, Schaffer and Emerson found, a child tended to become more intensely attached to father than to mother.

> Several of the mothers ... indeed complained that their policy of not 'spoiling' was being ruined by their husbands and that the infant who was quite undemanding as long as only the mother was about would make intense demands for his father's presence and attention during holiday periods, weekends and evenings.

In analysing her data on the Ganda children Ainsworth is inclined to draw similar conclusions, though the deficiencies of her observations make her cautious. Her experiences in Africa, however, led her in a subsequent study (of white infants in Maryland) to make much more systematic records of the speed, frequency, and form of the social responses a mother tends to show her baby. The results of that study (Ainsworth and others, 1978) show clearly that two variables are significantly related to development of attachment behaviour: (i) sensitivity of mother in responding to her baby's signals, and (ii) the amount and nature of interaction between mother and baby. The mothers whose infants are most securely attached to them are mothers who respond to their babies' signals promptly and appropriately, and who engage in much social interchange with them—to the delight of each party.

Certain well-attested observations of the development of attachment behaviour in infants brought up in Israeli kibbutzim are not easily understood in terms of traditional theory; with a theory that emphasises the role of social interaction in the development of attachments, on the other hand, they square well.

In some Israeli kibbutzim a child is cared for most of the time by a nurse in a communal nursery; his parents look after him for only an hour or two a day, except on the Sabbath when they have him all day.[1] Thus by far the most of his feeding and other routine care is provided by the nurse. Despite this, however, the principal attachment-figures of a kibbutz child are his parents—a matter on which all observers seem agreed. For example, after studying the development of children in one particular kibbutz, Spiro (1954) writes:

> Although the parents do not play an outstanding role in the socialization of their children, or in providing for their physical needs . . . parents are of crucial importance in the psychological development of the child. . . . They provide him with a certain security and love that he obtains from no one else. If anything the attachment of the young children to their parents is greater than it is in our own society.

This generalisation is repeated by Pelled (1964) who bases her conclusions on twenty years of psychotherapeutic work with individuals brought up in kibbutzim:

> . . . the main object-relationships of the Kibbutz child are his relations to his family—parents and siblings. . . . In none of my cases could I find a strong and lasting tie to a metapeleth. . . . The metapeloth who belong to the past are usually mentioned only in passing, in a tone of emotional indifference, sometimes with much resentment. . . . In retrospect, the relationship to the

---

[1] By 1981 this regime had become less common than formerly.

metapeleth appears as a kind of transient, interchangeable, need-satisfying object-relationship which stops when the need-situation comes to an end.

These findings, it is clear, are the reverse of what the traditional theory would predict. It is not difficult, on the other hand, to understand them in terms of the theory now advanced. In the communal nursery the metapeleth always has several children to care for and must also prepare their food, change their clothes, and so on. Consequently she may have relatively little time to respond to an infant's signals or to engage in play with him. When, by contrast, a mother is in charge of her child, she is usually not otherwise engaged and so is free to respond to his advances and to initiate social play. It seems not unlikely therefore that in the course of a week a child engages both in more social interaction and in more appropriately timed interaction with his mother than ever he does with his metapeleth. Whether or not this is really so can, of course, be checked by systematic observation.[1] If it proves a true picture of what obtains in a kibbutz, it would be a counterpart of what is reported by Schaffer and Emerson of some families, namely that a child becomes more attached to father, of whom he sees little but who responds to him freely, than to mother, who cares for him all day but interacts with him rarely.

The observations so far reported were all made in the every-day settings in which children are cared for—with all the advantages of being made in the course of real life and all the difficulties of interpreting the findings that such settings present. It will be noticed, however, that the conclusions drawn from these studies are wholly consistent with the results of the few experiments so far done (and reported in the previous chapter). Thus Brackbill (1958) was able to increase the smiling of three-month-old babies by the simple expedient of responding socially every time a baby smiled—namely, by smiling back, cooing, picking him up, and cuddling him; and Rheingold, Gewirtz, and Ross (1959) were able to increase the babbling of babies of the same age by rather similar methods—each time the baby

---

[1] This suggestion is strongly supported by the findings of Gewirtz and Gewirtz (1968) who, in a study using direct observation, found that during the first eight months of his life an infant in a kibbutz sees his mother each day for at least twice as much time as he sees the metapeleth. This is largely because the metapeleth is out of the infant's actual presence for much of the time that he is in her care.

babbled the experimenter responded with a broad smile and three 'tsk' sounds, and lightly squeezed the infant's abdomen.

Delay in becoming Attached

The data on infants who are slow to develop an attachment are also consistent with the theory being advanced. Whereas most children show very clear signs of differentially directed attachment behaviour by nine months of age, in a few the appearance of such behaviour is delayed, sometimes until well into the second year. The evidence suggests that these are usually infants who for one reason or another have experienced much less social stimulation from a mother-figure than have those whose development has been faster.

Infants brought up in an impersonal institution are cases in point. The findings of Provence and Lipton (1962) have already been noted: at the age of twelve months, they report, there was no sign of differentially directed attachment behaviour in any of the seventy-five infants they studied. (All had been in the institution from the age of five weeks or earlier.)

The findings of Ainsworth (1963, 1967) in regard to Ganda infants brought up within a family setting are of a piece with those of Provence and Lipton. Of the twenty-seven Ganda children she observed, four were deviant in that they were markedly delayed in showing attachment. Two of them were half-sisters (by different mothers) and showed hardly any discrimination or attachment at eleven months and twelve months respectively. The other two were twins (boy and girl) who showed virtually no attachment behaviour at thirty-seven weeks when observations ended.

When the mothers of each of these twenty-seven children were rated on a seven-point scale in regard to the amount of care each gave her baby, the only mothers to be rated in the lowest two categories were the mothers of the non-attached infants. These mothers regularly left their babies for long periods, and shared mothering with others even when they themselves were available. When the total amount of care each baby received, whether from mother or someone else, was considered, these babies remained in a very low category in comparison with all but one of the infants who became attached.

In discussing her results Ainsworth points out that the dimension of 'motherly care' she used in that study is altogether too unspecific. As already stated, the component of mothering care that she believes to be most important is social interaction, not routine care.

The Roles of Receptors of Different Kinds

Both in these experiments and in the everyday settings the social stimulation reported as being effective in promoting attachment behaviour comprises a mixture of visual, auditory, and tactile, and usually kinaesthetic and olfactory stimulation as well. Questions thus posed are: which, if any, of these modes of interaction are indispensable for attachment to develop, and which are the most powerful for the purpose?

In discussions of the subject two trends are noticeable. In much of the earlier literature, which assumed that attachment developed as a result of a child's being fed, emphasis was placed on tactile, and particularly oral, stimulation. Later on, this supposition was challenged, especially by those such as Rheingold (1961) and Walters and Parke (1965) whose theoretical position is similar to that adopted here. These workers emphasise that, from quite early weeks, an infant's eyes and ears are active in mediating social interchange, and they call in question the special role hitherto attributed to tactile and kinaesthetic stimulation. Not only smiling and babbling, but eye-to-eye contact also seems to play a very special part in developing a bond between infant and mother (Robson, 1967).

That visual contact is of great importance is further supported by the fact that, during routine caregiving, a mother tends to hold her infant in such a way that face-to-face contact occurs only rarely; whereas when she is feeling sociable she habitually holds him facing towards herself (Watson, 1965). This observation is in accord with the finding that an infant becomes attached to figures who interact socially with him rather than with figures who do little more than attend to his bodily requirements.

At first reading it might be thought that the view that visual rather than tactile and kinaesthetic stimuli are prepotent receives support also from a study of the development of attachment in infants who are averse to being cuddled, reported by Schaffer and Emerson (1964b). Such a conclusion would, however, hardly be warranted.

In this study, which is a part of their larger study of the development of attachment (Schaffer and Emerson, 1964a), the researchers identified a group of nine infants, out of a sample of thirty-seven, who at the age of twelve months were reported by their mothers to be actively resistant to being cuddled: as one mother put it, 'He won't allow it; he fights to get away.' Another nineteen infants were reported to enjoy being cuddled, while the remaining nine occupied an intermediate position.[1] Differences found in the development of attachment as between non-cuddlers and cuddlers were few: the only significant difference was that, at the age of twelve months, intensity of attachment was rated as higher in the cuddlers than in the non-cuddlers. At eighteen months, however, this difference, though still present, was no longer significant; nor was there at that age any difference between the children in the number of persons to whom attachment behaviour was directed.

Although the finding of so little difference between the two groups might be interpreted to mean that experience of physical contact plays little part in the development of attachment, caution is necessary. For it would be a serious mistake to suppose that a baby described by Schaffer and Emerson as a non-cuddler receives no tactile or kinaesthetic stimulation. On the contrary, non-cuddly infants enjoyed being swung around and romped with; moreover, they were content to sit on mother's knee when being fed; and, when alarmed, liked to hold mother's skirt or hide their face against her knee. The only thing that led them to be regarded as different from other children, indeed, was that they resented being restrained: whenever being cuddled entailed restriction of their movement, they protested. Thus, although these infants probably received rather less tactile stimulation than the cuddlers received, what they received was very far from negligible.

Studies of the development of attachment in blind infants also give rather ambiguous results. On the one hand are statements that the tie of a blind infant to his mother, in terms of

[1] Schaffer and Emerson state that all their non-cuddlers were described by their mothers as having shown their peculiarities from the early weeks. Dr Mary Ainsworth (personal communication), however, is sceptical of any retrospective report that 'he never was a cuddly baby'. Work with her Maryland sample suggests to her that at least some non-cuddlers are babies whose mothers hold them little during the first few months:

My assistants and I have made a special point of picking up tiny babies who their mothers say are not cuddly. With us they are cuddly. The fact is that the mother does not like to cuddle a baby. Later on, we find, these babies become non-cuddlers and squirm when held. Of course, some brain-damaged babies are hypertonic and may be non-cuddlers from the beginning.

both specificity and intensity, is significantly weaker than is that of a sighted infant (quoted by Robson (1967) as personal statements from Daniel Freedman, Selma Fraiburg, and Dorothy Burlingham); on the other is the view that the impression sometimes given by blind children that they readily exchange a familiar attachment-figure for an unfamiliar one is false and arises from the fact that a blind child, like a sighted child who is alarmed, tends, when the familiar figure is temporarily missing, to cling to whoever may be available(Nagera and Colonna, 1965). A possible solution to these apparently opposing views is that blind infants develop an attachment to a particular figure more slowly than do sighted ones but, once an attachment has developed, it is more intense in blind infants and persists so for longer than it does in sighted children.

The truth is that data do not yet exist for answering the questions posed. That the distance receptors play a far more important part than they have hitherto been accorded seems indubitable, but this is far from concluding that tactile and kinaesthetic receptors are unimportant. On the contrary, when an infant is much distressed, bodily contact seems vital, whether it is in soothing a crying infant during his early months or, a little later, in comforting him when he is frightened. The wisest position to take at present is that in all likelihood all modes of social interaction play a major role, but that, thanks to considerable redundancy in the organisation of attachment behaviour, a shortfall in one mode can, perhaps within wide limits, be made good through some other mode. A plethora of alternative means by which the requirements of survival can be met is, it is known, very common in the animal kingdom.

Sensitive phases and the fear of strangers

Since in other species it is now well established that there is a phase during which attachment behaviour to a preferred figure is most readily developed, the question is naturally raised whether the same holds for man. Most workers with an ethological orientation tend to think it probably does. What is the evidence?

Evidence for a Phase of Increasing Sensitivity

Several students of the subject, e.g. Gray (1958), Ambrose (1963), Scott (1963), Bronson (1965), suspect that during the first five or six weeks of life an infant is not yet ready to develop attachment behaviour towards a discriminated figure. Neither perceptual capacities nor the level at which behaviour is organised are such that he can interact socially in any but very primitive ways.[1]

After about six weeks of age an infant becomes increasingly able to discriminate what he sees, hears, and feels, and in addition his behaviour becomes much better organised. As a result, by the third month, differences in the social behaviour of infants brought up in families and in institutions are becoming apparent. From evidence such as this, and from consideration of the rapid growth of an infant's neurological equipment, it is tentatively concluded that, whilst readiness to develop attachment is low in the weeks after birth, it increases during the second and third months. The fact that by the end of a half-year the elements of attachment behaviour are clearly established in many infants suggests that during the preceding months—fourth, fifth, and sixth—most infants are in a high state of sensitivity for developing attachment behaviour.

Beyond a general statement of this kind it is not possible to go. In particular, there is no evidence whether sensitivity is greater during any one of these months than during another.

Without further evidence, for example, it is not possible to accept a suggestion by Ambrose (1963) that the period from about six to fourteen weeks, during which an infant is learning the characteristics of human faces (supra-individual learning) and before he can discriminate particular faces, may be a specially sensitive one. The evidence he presents is inconclusive; moreover, a theory on which part of his argument is based— that imprinting is a product of anxiety reduction (Moltz, 1960) —is not generally accepted (see Chapter 10, p. 170n).

Evidence that a Degree of Sensitivity Persists for some Months

Although by six months of age a majority of family-reared infants are showing attachment behaviour, some are not; neither are most of those raised in institutions. Since it seems certain that a majority of such children do develop attachment later, it is evident that some degree of sensitivity persists for a time at least.

One of Schaffer's studies casts some light on the question. In this, Schaffer (1963) aimed to discover the effect on the onset of attachment behaviour of longish separations occurring dur-

[1] An argument, used by Gray (1958), that during his first six weeks a human infant cannot learn is, however, certainly mistaken (see Chapter 14).

ing the middle of the first year of life. All the twenty infants in the study spent periods of ten weeks or more in one of two institutional settings, in neither of which had they any opportunity of making a discriminated attachment; and all of them returned to their homes somewhere between thirty and fifty-two weeks of age. Since on return they were all at an age when discriminated attachment behaviour could be expected, the interest was to discover how much delayed by the preceding period of separation they might be in showing it.

Schaffer found that, by twelve months of age, all but one of these children had developed attachment behaviour. Delay in doing so varied enormously—from three days to fourteen weeks. Eight children were showing attachment by the end of two weeks at home; another eight took between four and seven weeks; the remaining three took from twelve to fourteen weeks.

Of the many factors that probably accounted for the variation two were fairly easy to identify: (i) conditions in the institution, and (ii) experience after return home. Surprisingly, neither length of time away nor age on return seemed significant.

The infants fell into two groups. One group of eleven were cared for in hospital where they received little stimulation, either of a social or of other kinds. Mother was able to visit, however; but most were visited only once weekly, a few four or five times a week. The second group of nine infants were cared for in a baby home in order to avoid contact with active tuberculosis. Although these nine were never visited by mother, they experienced a considerable amount of social interaction from a relatively large staff of nurses.

After return home the infants who had been in the baby home developed attachment to mother far sooner than did those who had been in hospital. Whereas all but one of the hospital infants took four weeks or longer to show attachment, all but two of the baby-home infants were showing attachment within fourteen days. One baby-home child, discharged aged twelve months after no fewer than thirty-seven weeks away, was already showing attachment behaviour on his third day home.

From these findings it seems safe to conclude that, given plenty of social interaction during the middle and latter half of the first year of life, an infant will quickly develop a discriminated attachment once he is given the opportunity to do so; whereas, without such social stimulation, he will be much slower to develop it. When the general level of social stimulation is low, it is clear, the occasional visit of mother is insufficient to make good the position (though it may be better than nothing).

Undoubtedly the most interesting part of Schaffer's study concerns the speed with which attachment developed in the infants who had been cared for in the baby home. Seven of the nine showed it within a fortnight of returning home; and in one of the other two the reason for delay was almost certainly that the infant received very little social attention after his return. This was a boy who was thirty-six weeks old when he went back to his family after twelve weeks away in the baby home. His father was an invalid and his mother worked, which meant that the child was cared for by father and saw little of mother. Though both parents were fond of him, during this time neither gave him much attention, and attachment behaviour was not seen. Two and a half months later, however, mother gave up work and devoted herself to her family. Within a few days of her doing so the child, now nearly a year old, had developed a strong and specific attachment to her.

These data indicate that, provided social conditions are above a minimum, readiness to develop attachment can be maintained in some infants at least until the end of the first year. Many questions remain unanswered, however. First, what are minimal conditions? Secondly, is an attachment that develops late as stable and secure as one that develops earlier? Thirdly, for how long into the second year can readiness to develop an attachment be maintained? Whatever the safety margin may be it is certain that after the age of about six months conditions for developing attachment tend to become more complicated. A main reason for this is the growing ease and strength with which fear responses are aroused.

Fear of Strangers and Reduced Sensitivity

As they grow older human infants, like young creatures of other species, come to show fear at sight of anything strange, including strange people. Once such responses are common and/or strong, an infant tends to withdraw instead of to approach. As a result he becomes less likely to make an attachment to a new figure.

Before an infant shows fear he goes through three other phases in his response to sight of a stranger (Freedman, 1961; Schaffer, 1966; Ainsworth, 1967). These are:

a. a phase during which he shows no visual discrimination between strangers and familiars;

b. a phase, usually lasting six to ten weeks, during which he responds to strangers positively and fairly readily, though not as readily as to familiars;

c. a phase, usually lasting four to six weeks, during which he sobers at sight of a stranger and stares.

Only after that does he show behaviour typical of fear, for example, orientation and movement away from the stranger, whimpering or crying, and a facial expression of dislike.[1]

The age at which unmistakable fear on sight of strangers first occurs varies greatly from infant to infant, and varies too according to the criteria used. In a few infants it is seen as early as twenty-six weeks; in a majority it is present by eight months; and in a small minority its onset is delayed until the second year (Freedman, 1961; Schaffer, 1966; Ainsworth, 1967).[2] Fear on being touched or picked up by a stranger occurs earlier than fear on sight (Tennes and Lampl, 1964).

In accounting for the late appearance in some babies of fear on sight of strangers, different workers point to different variables. Both Freedman (1961) and Ainsworth (1967) report that the later attachment develops the later also does fear of strangers develop; whereas Schaffer (1966) reports that the more people an infant habitually encounters the later the onset of fear. No doubt there are other variables besides these two.

As infants grow older their fear of strangers is usually more evident. Tennes and Lampl (1964) give seven to nine months as the age of peak intensity, whereas Morgan and Ricciuti (1969) believe the peak to be in the second year. Ainsworth (1967) notes that there tends to be a marked increase at nine or ten months. She notes also, however, that there is great variation from infant to infant, and that for any one infant there tend to be inexplicable variations from month to month.

A principal difficulty in determining both onset of fear and

[1] Ambrose (1963) suggests that fear responses may be present before such overt behaviour is seen. He bases his view on the sharp reduction in an infant's smiling response to a stranger, observed in infants of fourteen to sixteen weeks, and due, he believes, to a 'massive inhibition by a newly interfering response ... probably fear'. It is by no means certain, however, that this conclusion is justified; furthermore, if it is, it seems that the response is at low strength and is quickly habituated.

[2] Yarrow (1967) reports the following incidence for his sample: at three months, 12 per cent; at six months, 40 per cent; at eight months, 46 per cent.

peak of intensity is that, in any one infant, the occurrence of fear of strangers varies greatly according to conditions. For example, both occurrence and intensity depend in large measure on how far distant the stranger is, whether he approaches the infant and what else he does; they probably depend also on whether the infant is in familiar or strange surroundings and on whether he is ill or well, fatigued or fresh. Yet another variable, studied especially by Morgan and Ricciuti (1969), is whether an infant is on his mother's knee or away from her. From the age of eight months onwards this makes a big difference, an infant sitting four feet from his mother showing much more fear than when sitting on her knee; this finding is no doubt related to the fact that from eight months onwards an infant begins to use his mother as a secure base from which to explore.

Other evidence that points to an increased tendency to respond adversely to strangers is found in the way infants of different ages react to being moved from one mother-figure to another. The preliminary results of a study of seventy-five infants, each of whom was shifted from a temporary foster-home to an adoptive home at an age between six weeks and twelve months, have been reported by Yarrow (1963).

Of the infants shifted between the ages of six and twelve weeks none was observed to be upset; but of those transferred at the age of three months a few were so. Thenceforward, with increasing age, not only were a larger proportion recorded as disturbed but the severity and pervasiveness of their disturbance were greater. Of those aged six months 86 per cent showed some disturbance; and every one of those aged seven months or older 'reacted with marked disturbance'. Disturbed behaviour included a reduction in such social responses as smiling and babbling, and an increase in crying and clinging. It included also unusual apathy, disturbed eating and sleeping, and a loss of abilities previously present.

Conclusion

As Caldwell (1962) has emphasised, the problem of sensitive periods is complex. Hinde (1963) suggests, for instance, that each separate response probably has its own sensitive period. Much turns, of course, on whether we are concerned with the development of a discriminated attachment or with the effects of disrupting an attachment once made. There can be no doubt, for example, that an established attachment is in a specially vulnerable condition for several years after the first birthday.

As regards development of the first attachment, it is plain that during the second quarter of the first year of life infants are sensitive and ready to make a discriminated attachment. After six months of age they can still do so; but as the months pass difficulties increase. By the second year, it seems clear, these difficulties are already great; and they do not diminish. In Chapter 18 further evidence is presented.

Spitz's position: a critique

Anyone familiar with René Spitz's theories regarding the development of object relations during the first year of life will realise that they are very different from those presented here. Since Spitz's views are widely accepted there is reason to discuss them in detail.

First outlined in earlier papers (Spitz, 1950, 1955), Spitz's views are restated unchanged in his book, *The First Year of Life* (1965). The main feature of his position is that true object relations are held not to be established before eight months.

In reaching this conclusion Spitz anchors his argument to what he terms 'eight-months anxiety' (termed here 'fear of strangers'). His position can be summarised under four heads:

a. *Observations* regarding the age at which withdrawal from strangers commonly occurs: Spitz holds that this behaviour begins in most infants at about eight months.

b. *An assumption that withdrawal from strangers cannot be due to fear*: since the stranger can have caused the infant no pain or unpleasure, the infant, in Spitz's view, can have no reason to fear him.

c. *A theory that withdrawal from strangers is, therefore, not a withdrawal from something frightening, but instead a form of separation anxiety*: 'what [an infant] reacts to when confronted with a stranger is that this is not his mother; his mother "has left him" . . .' (1965, p. 155).

d. *An inference*, drawn from data and theory, *regarding the age at which a child discriminates his mother-figure and develops 'a true object relation'*. Spitz writes (1965, p. 156):

We assume that this capacity [to identify strangers] in the eight-month-old child reflects the fact that he has now established a true object relation, and that the mother has become his libidinal object, his love object. Before this we can hardly speak of love, for there is no love until the loved one can be distinguished from all others. . . .

It will be evident from observations already detailed in this chapter that the position taken by Spitz is not tenable.

First, and most crucially, Spitz is mistaken in supposing that a child's fear of a person or thing develops only as a result of his or its having caused him pain or unpleasure. Strangeness *per se* is a common cause of fear. There is thus no reason to look for any explanation of why an infant withdraws from strangers other than that he is alarmed by their strangeness.

Secondly, there is clear evidence that fear of strangers is a response quite distinct from separation anxiety: even when his mother is simultaneously in sight an infant may continue to show fear of a stranger. When this objection was first pointed out, Spitz (1955) replied that a child who behaved in this way was a rare exception. But that view can no longer be sustained. In their careful experimental study Morgan and Ricciuti (1969) observed that, in infants of from ten to twelve months of age, this behaviour occurred in nearly half of them (thirteen out of thirty-two).

Finally, there is abundant evidence that an infant can discriminate familiar from unfamiliar long before he shows overt fear of strangers.

An examination of Spitz's position shows that the central flaw in it is his supposition that, when confronted by a stranger, an infant cannot be possessed of 'realistic fear', a supposition based on the assumption that 'realistic fear' is elicited only by people and objects that a child associates 'with a previous experience of unpleasure'.

Spitz's theory has had certain ill effects. One is that, by regarding 'eight-months anxiety' as the first indicator of a true object relation, it has distracted attention from observations showing unmistakably that both discrimination of a familiar figure and attachment behaviour occur in a majority of infants long before they reach eight months. A second is that, by identifying fear of strangers with separation anxiety, it has confounded two responses that it is vital to keep distinct.[1]

---

[1] Spitz's terminology 'eight-months anxiety' is unsatisfactory on two grounds: (a) since fear of strangers begins at different ages, follows different courses in different infants, and is influenced by many variables, it is misleading to label it by reference to any particular month of life; (b) following Freud's usage (1926), the term 'anxiety' is best restricted to situations of 'missing someone who is loved and longed for' (*S.E.*, **20**, p. 136).

FOCUSING ON A FIGURE

Fear of Strangers, Separation Anxiety, and Attachment Behaviour

The position advanced here, namely that separation anxiety and fear of strangers are two distinct, though related, forms of behaviour, has been advocated by nearly all those who have presented data and considered the issue. They include Meili (1955), Freedman (1961), Ainsworth (1963, 1967), Schaffer (1963, 1966; Schaffer and Emerson, 1964a), Tennes and Lampl (1964), and Yarrow (1967).

Although there is much disagreement over detail, all these workers hold that, during a child's development, fear of strangers and separation anxiety appear independently of one another. For example, Schaffer (in a personal communication) reports, for a sample of twenty-three infants, that in twelve infants separation anxiety developed before fear of strangers; in eight, both developed simultaneously; and in three, fear of strangers developed before separation anxiety. By contrast, Benjamin (1963) reports that in his sample the mean ages for both onset and peak intensity of separation anxiety are *later* by some months than they are for fear of strangers.[1]

Although there is thus diversity of opinion regarding the relationship of fear of strangers and separation anxiety, owing no doubt to the many variables at work and the differing criteria used, there is general agreement that the relationship is no simple one. None of the reports gives evidence that the two responses have a simultaneous origin or run a parallel course.

That separation anxiety and fear of strangers are distinct responses is in keeping with Freud's position. From the first Freud held that anxiety is not the same thing as being afraid of some alarming object in the environment and considered that there is need for two distinct terms. Most psychoanalysts have sensed that the distinction is valid, though their formulations of it have been extremely varied. In earlier papers

---

[1] Whilst Benjamin's data and those of his colleagues (Tennes and Lampl, 1964) strongly support the view that there are two distinct patterns of behaviour, his theorising is something of a compromise. On the one hand, following Spitz, Benjamin (1963) holds that 'stranger anxiety' and separation anxiety have a main determinant in common, namely fear of object loss. On the other, unlike Spitz, Benjamin believes that the two are not identical: whereas fear of object loss is 'the sole *immediate dynamic* determinant of separation anxiety', it is 'only a major co-determinant of stranger anxiety ...'. The other co-determinant, Benjamin holds, is fear of the strange as such.

(Bowlby, 1960a, 1961a) I have discussed some of these problems with special reference to separation anxiety and have advocated a schema in many ways similar to that adopted by Freud in his later years.

The simplest form in which the distinction can be stated is that, on the one hand, we try at times to *withdraw* or *escape from* a situation or object that we find alarming, and, on the other, we try to *go towards* or *remain with* some person or in some place that makes us feel secure. The first type of behaviour is commonly accompanied by a sense of fright or alarm, and is not far from what Freud had in mind when he spoke of 'realistic fear' (Freud, 1926, *S.E.*, **20**, p. 108). The second type of behaviour is, of course, what is termed here attachment behaviour. So long as the required proximity to the attachment-figure can be maintained, no unpleasant feeling is experienced. When, however, proximity cannot be maintained because either the figure is lost or some barrier intervenes, the consequent searching and striving are accompanied by a sense of disquiet, more or less acute; and the same is true when loss is threatened. In this disquiet at separation and at threat of separation Freud in his later work came to see 'the key to an understanding of anxiety' (Freud, 1926, *S.E.*, **20**, p. 137).

These are matters to which attention is given in the second volume of this work, in which revised versions of earlier papers appear. Meanwhile there is more to be said about the development of attachment behaviour.

Chapter 16

Patterns of Attachment and Contributing Conditions

We are moulded and remoulded by those who have loved us; and though the love may pass, we are nevertheless their work, for good or ill.

FRANÇOIS MAURIAC

Problems to be solved

If the satisfactory development of attachment is as important for mental health as is claimed, there is urgent need to be able to distinguish favourable development from unfavourable and also to know what conditions promote the one or the other. There are, in fact, four separate classes of problem to be solved:

a. What, descriptively, is the range of variation in attachment behaviour at any particular age, and in terms of what dimensions are variations best described?

b. What antecedent conditions influence the development of each variety of pattern?

c. How stable is each pattern at each age?

d. How is each pattern related to subsequent personality development and mental health?

Although there is a wealth of studies aimed to answer these and related questions, conclusions are difficult to draw. The truth is that the issues are extremely complex, and no one investigation can expect to throw light on more than a fraction of them. Hardly any of the studies undertaken before 1970, moreover, were in any way adequate to the tasks they set themselves—whether at a theoretical or an empirical level.

At a theoretical level, the old concept of 'dependency' failed to fill the role expected of it. For example, the various measures of dependency that Sears used in a long programme of research, and that were based on the assumption that 'overt dependency behaviour' in young children reflects 'a unitary drive or habit structure', were found to show practically no intercorrelation. As a consequence, Sears concluded that 'the notion of a generalized trait of dependency is indefensible' (Sears and others, 1965). Subsequently, he emphasised that attachment conceived as governed by a behavioural system bears little relation to dependency conceived as the expression of a drive (Sears, 1972).

At an empirical level many of the antecedent variables formerly selected for study, for example the techniques of feeding, weaning and toilet training, are now known to bear only an indirect relation to attachment; furthermore, information about those variables and others was obtained retrospectively from the parents themselves, with all the inaccuracies and misinterpretations that are born of such methods. It has therefore been necessary to start afresh.

In the previous chapter the conditions described as probably contributing to whether or not attachment develops towards any one figure include (i) the sensitivity of that figure in responding to the baby's signals, and (ii) the amount and nature of interaction between the couple. If that is so, the basic data required to answer our questions can be obtained only from detailed first-hand reports of mothers and children interacting. In recent years a number of such studies have been undertaken and findings, mostly confined to the first and second years of life, reported. They constitute a great advance. There is difficulty in drawing upon some of them, however, because data regarding a child's attachment behaviour and data regarding the amount and pattern of interaction that a child has with his mother are not always kept distinct. Yet, as we saw in Chapter 13, a child's attachment behaviour is only one component in the bigger system of a mother and child in interaction.

Nevertheless the studies in question are far from being valueless for our purpose. For, if we are to understand patterns of attachment behaviour and the conditions that give rise to variations between children, it is necessary to bear constantly in mind the larger system of which attachment behaviour is a part, and the variations in patterns of interaction that occur between one mother-child couple and another. Here some of the early first-hand accounts of mothers and infants interacting, for example those of David and Appell, are most instructive. First, these studies document in an impressive way the extraordinary range of variation in amount and kind of interaction that is seen when a series of couples are compared. Secondly, they confirm that by the time a child has reached his first birthday each mother–child couple has usually already developed a highly characteristic pattern of interaction. Thirdly, they show that the patterns persist in recognisable form over at least two or three years (Appell and David, 1965; David and Appell, 1966, 1969).[1] The accounts given of a number of contrasting couples make lively reading.

Perhaps what most forcibly strikes the reader of these and other portraits of interacting couples is the degree of fit that so many mothers and infants have achieved after twelve months of getting to know one another. During the process, it is evident, each has changed in very many ways, small and large. With few exceptions, whatever child provides in the way of behaviour, mother has come to expect and to respond to in a typical way; conversely, whatever mother provides, child has come to expect and to respond to, usually also in a typical way. Each has shaped the other.

Because of this, in considering patterns of attachment that characterise different children, it is constantly necessary to refer also to patterns of mothering that characterise different mothers.

Criteria for describing patterns of attachment

One of the most obvious criteria in terms of which to describe a child's attachment behaviour is whether or not he protests when his mother leaves him for a brief time and how strongly he does so. This has been the criterion of strength of attachment used by Schaffer (Schaffer and Emerson, 1964a). Ainsworth, however, found this criterion alone to be insufficient, indeed misleading. Reflecting on her observations of the Ganda infants, she writes (1963):

> some of the infants . . . who seemed most solidly attached to their mothers displayed little protest behaviour or separation anxiety, but rather showed the strength of their attachment to the mother through their readiness to use her as a secure base from which they could both explore the world and expand their horizons to

---

[1] Amongst many differences of interaction pattern they note are differences of the following sort: the habitual quantity of interaction between a child and his mother, expressed as a percentage of waking time that he is interacting with her; the lengths of their chains of interaction, and who initiates and who terminates them; the couple's habitual mode of interacting, e.g. by looking, touching, or holding, and the typical distances maintained between them; the child's reactions to separation; his reactions to a stranger, both when with and when without his mother; and mother's reactions when her child explores or makes friends with others.

include other attachments. The anxious, insecure child may appear to be more strongly attached to his mother than does the happy, secure child who seems to take her more for granted. But is the child who clings to his mother—who is afraid of the world and the people in it, and who will not move off to explore other things or other people—more strongly attached, or merely more insecure?

It seems clear that strength of attachment to one or more discriminated figures is itself altogether too simple a concept to be useful (just as the concept of a unitary dependency drive has proved to be). New concepts are needed. To develop them it is necessary to record a child's attachment in terms of a number of different forms of behaviour as they occur in a number of specified conditions. Forms of behaviour should include:

a. behaviour, including greeting, that initiates interaction with mother: for example, approaching, touching, embracing, scrambling over her, burying face in her lap, calling, talking, the hands-up gesture, and smiling;

b. behaviour in response to mother's interactional initiatives and that maintains interaction: it includes all the above, and also watching;

c. behaviour aimed to avoid separations: for example, following, clinging, crying;

d. behaviour on reunion with mother after a stressful separation, to include not only greeting responses, but also avoidant, rejecting and ambivalent ones;

e. exploratory behaviour, especially how it is oriented with reference to the mother-figure and how intense and persistent his attention to items in the environment.

f. withdrawal (fear) behaviour, also especially how it is oriented with reference to the mother-figure.

The conditions in which a child's behaviour is to be observed must include, as a minimum, mother's whereabouts and movements, presence or absence of other persons, the state of the non-human environment, and the state of the child himself. The following list gives some idea of the variety of conditions to be taken into account:

A. Mother's whereabouts and movements:
    mother present
    mother departing
    mother absent
    mother returning

B. Other persons:
   familiar person(s) present or absent
   stranger(s) present or absent

C. Non-human situation:
   familiar
   a little strange
   very strange

D. Condition of child:
   healthy, sick, or in pain
   fresh or fatigued
   hungry or fed

It is worth emphasis that how a child behaves when fatigued or in pain is often especially revealing. Whereas an ordinary child on such occasions will almost certainly go to his mother, neither a child who has become detached as a result of long deprivation of maternal care nor an autistic child is likely to do so. Robertson has reported a case of how a detached child behaved when in severe pain (see Ainsworth and Boston, 1952), and Bettelheim (1967) the case of an autistic child.

In practice, perhaps a fairly limited selection from such a theoretically complete range of conditions might give an adequate picture of a given child. If that proves to be so, a child's attachment behaviour could be described by a profile showing his behaviour in each of that number of selected conditions. Ainsworth has herself used this kind of thinking both in her naturalistic observations and in planning her experiments.

To complete the picture it would, of course, be necessary also to construct a complementary profile of how the child's mother behaves, including both how she responds to his attachment behaviour in each of a comparable series of situations and how and when she herself initiates interaction. For only when this has been done can the pattern of interaction between them be seen and the child's part in it understood.

Some patterns of attachment seen at the first birthday

In this section the aim is to give brief attention to some of the common variations in pattern of attachment seen around the first birthday. Only patterns that occur with children brought up at home with a stable mother-figure are considered; patterns, including deviant patterns, that occur in separated or deprived children constitute a large and specialised problem which is considered briefly in the penultimate chapter.

In the first edition of this volume it was possible to give only preliminary findings of the short longitudinal study that Mary Ainsworth and her colleagues were engaged upon, in Baltimore, Maryland, in which they were observing the development of a child's attachment behaviour during his first twelve months of life in a sample of white middle class families. Since then the study has been carried a long way forward, by increasing the numbers in the sample followed from birth to twelve months and by subjecting the data to a great deal of detailed analysis. They have also obtained further evidence regarding typical patterns of attachment to be observed at twelve months by assessing additional samples totalling 83 mother-infant pairs by means of the Strange Situation procedure devised for the purpose. Full details of this important study are now available in monograph form (Ainsworth and others, 1978). Since the procedures adopted and also the principal findings are already presented in the second volume of this work (Chapters 3 and 21), only an outline need be given here. Results of recent short longitudinal studies, using similar or related methods, which follow children through their second and subsequent years, are described in Chapter 18.

The strange situation procedure was designed to assess individual differences in the organisation of attachment behaviour towards mother in infants of twelve months. In brief, the procedure consists of a series of three minute episodes, lasting in all twenty minutes, during which a one-year-old is observed in a small and comfortable but strange playroom, equipped with a generous supply of toys, first with his mother, then without her and subsequently after her return. The procedure presents a cumulative stress situation in which there is opportunity to study individual differences in an infant's use of his caregiver as a base for exploration, his ability to derive comfort from her and the attachment-exploration balance as it changes during the series of changing situations.

Although during each episode of the series there is much variation in the patterns of behaviour shown by infants, the similarities between a majority of them are as striking as any differences. These are described in detail, with an illustrative example, in Chapter 3 of Volume 2. During the initial three minutes, when infant is alone with mother, almost all infants spend their time busily exploring the novel situation whilst at the same time keeping an eye on mother: there is virtually no crying. Although advent of the stranger reduces the exploring of almost all children, there is still virtually no crying. When mother withdraws leaving child with stranger, however, the behaviour of over half the children changes abruptly, and differential responses become much more evident.

In discussing her results Ainsworth draws attention to the absurdity of trying to arrange the children in simple linear order of strength of attachment: plainly, to do justice to the data a number of scales are required.

The dimension that Ainsworth has found especially useful is that of the security of a child's attachment. Thus a child of twelve months who can explore fairly freely in a strange situation using his mother as a secure base, who is not distressed by the advent of a stranger, who shows awareness of his mother's whereabouts during her absence, and who greets her on her return, Ainsworth rates as securely attached, whether he is distressed by his mother's temporary absence or can weather brief periods of it without upset. At an opposite pole, and rated as insecurely attached in extreme degree, are infants who do not explore even when mother is present, who are much alarmed by a stranger, who crumple into helpless and unoriented distress in mother's absence, and who when she returns may not greet her.

A particularly valuable index of the security of a child's attachment to his mother has proved in fact to be the way in which he responds to her on her return from a brief absence. A secure child shows an organised sequence of goal-corrected behaviour: after welcoming mother and approaching her, he either seeks to be picked up and to cling or else remains close to her. Responses shown by other children are of two main sorts: one is an apparent disinterest in mother's return and/or avoidance of her, the other an ambivalent response, half wanting and half resisting her.

Applying these criteria to the way infants perform on this procedure has resulted in the emergence of three main patterns of attachment. These, having first been identified by clinical judgment, have since been examined by sophisticated statistical techniques which have established their validity (Ainsworth and others 1978). The patterns, termed by Ainsworth B, A and C respectively, are as follows:—

Pattern B

A main characteristic of infants classified as *securely attached to mother*, in most samples a majority, is that they are active in play and also in seeking contact when distressed after a brief separation, they are readily comforted and soon return to absorbed play.

Pattern A

Infants classified as *anxiously attached to mother and avoidant*, about 20 per cent in most samples, avoid her during reunion, especially after her second brief absence. Many of them treat a stranger in more friendly a manner than their own mother.

Pattern C

Infants classified as *anxiously attached to mother and resistant*, about 10 per cent, oscillate between seeking proximity and contact with her and resisting contact and interaction with her. Some are markedly more angry than other infants; a few more passive.

Evidence that this classification, derived entirely from an infant's performance on the strange situation procedure, may be tapping variables having general psychological significance comes from the finding that the behaviour of an infant when observed with his mother at home not only resembles in most respects that seen in the strange situation but differs systematically according to which of the groups he is classified in. Differences in this behaviour are most striking when infants classified as securely attached (Group B) are compared with those classified as anxiously attached, whether as anxious and avoidant (Group A) or as anxious and resistant (Group C).

The main characteristics of the Group B infants, when their behaviour at home during the final quarter of the first year was compared to that of infants in Group A and C, were as follows. When exploring and playing a group B infant was likely to use his mother as a secure base. Content to move away from her, he would nonetheless keep track of her movements and from time to time gravitate back to her. The picture was that of a happy balance between exploration and attachment. None of the anxiously attached infants showed such balance. Some tended to be passive, exploring little and/or rarely initiating contact; it was among these infants that stereotyped movements were most often observed. Others of the anxiously attached engaged in exploration, but they did so more briefly than the securely attached; and they seemed constantly concerned about mother's whereabouts. Although often eager to keep close to her and to make contact with her, doing so seemed nevertheless to give them no pleasure.

PATTERNS OF ATTACHMENT

A Group B infant cried less than one in Group A or C. When mother left the room a Group B infant was unlikely to be upset and when she returned he greeted her promptly and cheerfully. When picked up he enjoyed it and, later, when put down again he was content to resume play. By the end of the first year not only did he cry less than the anxiously attached, but he had developed more varied and more subtle means of communicating with his mother. Furthermore, he was more co-operative in meeting her spoken wishes and commands, and less likely to express anger when crossed.

When observed at home there were various differences found between the behaviour of infants in Group A, the anxious and avoidant, and that of those in Group C, the anxious and resistant, though the differences were less striking than those just considered. A principal feature of infants in Group A was evidence of a typical approach–avoidance conflict in regard to close bodily contact with mother. For example, an infant of Group A might approach mother, but then halt and either retreat or veer away in another direction. When near mother he tended not to touch her and, if he did so, was likely to touch only a peripheral part, such as her foot. When picked up he was unlikely to relax comfortably in his mother's body, but when put down was more likely than other infants to protest and want to be picked up again. He was also more likely than other infants to follow his mother when she left the room.

An infant of Group A was also more prone to angry behaviour than infants in either of the other groups. Such anger when aroused was rarely directed towards his mother, however; more usually it was redirected towards some physical object. Nonetheless, there were occasions when he might be seen hitting or biting his mother for no apparent reason and without any show of emotion.*

Infants in Group C, the anxious and resistant, also showed much conflict. Instead of avoiding contact with mother, however, an infant of this group seemed to want more of it, and to be especially resistant and angry when his mother was attempting to get him interested in playing apart from her. In keeping with this, he was likely to be notably passive in situations in which other children would be actively playing.

* This type of behaviour appears to be an example in very early life of the disconnection of a response from the situation that elicited it, which occurs in many psychopathological conditions. See Volume 3, Chapters 4 and 14.

Findings such as these give confidence in the criteria used by Ainsworth to classify patterns of attachment; and this confidence is enormously increased by the results of the many studies undertaken since the first edition of this volume and to be reported in Chapter 18. Meanwhile, we note that the dimension security-insecurity makes much sense to a clinician. It seems clearly to refer to the same feature of infancy that Benedek (1938) refers to as a 'relationship of confidence', that Klein (1948) refers to as 'introjection of the good object', and that Erikson (1950) refers to as 'basic trust'. As such it assesses an aspect of personality of immediate relevance to mental health.

Conditions of the first year contributing to variation

It is evident that the particular pattern taken by any one child's attachment behaviour turns partly on the initial biases that infant and mother each bring to their partnership and partly on the way that each affects the other during the course of it. In practice, a constant problem is to determine to what extent the behaviour of each partner is a result of his or her initial bias and to what extent it has resulted from the influence of the other. Because there is an almost infinite range of possibilities and systematic research has still far to go, only a few examples can be given.

Bias of Baby and Influence on Mother

Moss (1967) has shown the great variations from one infant to another in time spent sleeping and crying during the early months, and how this affects the way a mother behaves. In these respects boys and girls differ. On balance, Moss found boy babies tend to sleep less and to cry more than do girl babies. Probably as a result of this, Moss believes, boy babies up to three months of age receive on average more social attention and more contact (holding or rocking) from their mothers than do girls. How this affects future interaction is unknown, but it would be surprising were it to have no effect.

Another source of bias in babies is neurophysiological damage arising from prenatal and perinatal hazards: there is good evidence that infants with such trouble show a number of unfavourable tendencies that may directly or indirectly affect the pattern of attachment behaviour that later develops. In a study in which the behaviour during their first five years of twenty-nine boys recorded at birth as suffering from asphyxia was compared with that of a control group, Ucko (1965) found a number of significant differences. Boys who had suffered from asphyxia were from the first more sensitive to noise and more disturbed in their sleep than were the controls. Changes of environment were much more apt to upset them: for example, the change entailed during a family holiday or in moving house, or by a brief separation from a member of the family. Both on starting nursery school and on starting regular school significantly more of them than the controls were apprehensive and clinging. When all the information available on their behaviour over the first five years was assessed, those who had suffered asphyxia were far more frequently rated as 'very difficult' or 'difficult much of the time' than were the controls (thirteen of the asphyxia group against two of the controls). Moreover, the distribution on this scale of the damaged children was significantly correlated with the degree of asphyxia originally recorded.

Plainly, the kind of behavioural bias present in these infants at birth is not only apt to persist in its own right, at least in some degree, but apt also to influence the way a mother responds. Prechtl (1963) gives some evidence of this. He describes two syndromes as occurring commonly in infants with minimal brain damage: (i) a hypokinetic apathetic baby who responds weakly and cries little; (ii) an excitable baby who is not only over-reactive to slight stimulation and cries readily, but tends to show sudden and unpredictable shifts from a state of being drowsy and difficult to arouse to the opposite condition of being wide awake and difficult to pacify. Although both syndromes improve during the first year, a baby showing either presents his mother with problems much greater than those faced by the mother of a normally reactive baby. Thus an apathetic baby initiates less and rewards his mother less, and thereby tends to be neglected, whereas an over-reactive and unpredictable baby can drive his mother to exasperation. She may then become either over-anxious in her efforts to mother him or else despairing of ever doing the right thing and hence inclined to reject him. In either case a mother's pattern of behaviour can be significantly changed from what it might otherwise have been; though, as Sander (1969) has shown, given an equable mother that need not happen.

Other evidence of the differential effect on maternal behaviour of babies with different initial, or at least very early, biases comes from the work of Yarrow (1963), who has studied babies in foster-homes and adoptive homes. Even when infants of the same age and sex are from earliest weeks in the same foster-home together, he found, an actively disposed infant may receive far more social attention than a passively disposed one for the simple reason that he both demands it and rewards it when it comes.

As an illustration Yarrow contrasts the behaviour and social experience of two boys at the age of six months, both of whom had been cared for from early weeks by the same foster-mother. From the first, one of them, Jack, had been relatively passive and the other, George, relatively active. Jack 'showed no initiative in social interaction. He did not reach out toward people or make approach responses . . . when awake [he] spent much of his time in a state of passive contentment, sucking his fingers or thumb.' George, by contrast, was at the same age 'very forceful in demanding what he wanted, and persisted in his demands until he was satisfied . . . [he] was highly responsive to social stimulation and took the initiative in seeking social response from others'. Not unexpectedly, these two boys were receiving quite different amounts and forms of social experience. Whereas George 'was held and played with a great deal by the foster-mother, the foster-father, and all the children', Jack 'spent much of his time lying on the floor of the playpen . . . in an isolated corner of the dining room, outside the main stream of family traffic'. Only in regard to the amounts of physical care that each received was there much resemblance.

Examples of this sort bring home the degree to which an infant himself plays a part in determining his own environment. There is, however, no reason to suppose that all initial behavioural biases are apparent at birth, as those described are. On the contrary, it is very probable that some declare themselves only months or years later. Until methods are available for determining the existence of such biases, however, discussion of them tends to degenerate into speculation.

Bias of Mother and Influence on Baby

Just as the initial characteristics of a baby can influence the way his mother cares for him, so the initial characteristics of a mother can influence the way her baby responds to her. What a mother brings to the situation is, however, far more complex: it derives not only from her native endowment but from a long history of interpersonal relations within her family of origin (and perhaps also within other families) and also from long absorption of the values and practices of her culture. An examination of these many interacting variables, and of how together they produce the varieties of maternal behaviour we see, lies beyond the scope of this work.

It is no surprise to find that how a mother will treat her baby is to some extent predictable before the baby is born. Thus, Moss (1967), in the project already referred to, was able to discover whether and to what extent the way a mother responded to her baby's crying during the first three months of his life was correlated with ideas and feelings she had expressed two years earlier—ideas about domesticity and caring for infants in general and also about what sorts of pleasures and frustrations she imagined that having a baby of her own would bring. In a study of twenty-three mothers and babies he found that a woman rated two years earlier as 'accepting of a nurturant role' and as dwelling on the rewarding aspects of having a baby of her own was more likely after her baby had arrived to be responsive to his crying than was a woman who had earlier been rated lower on these scales.

Another type of evidence, namely a mother's experience in her family of origin, has also been shown to predict the way a mother will treat her baby. Firm evidence of this is reported by Wolkind and others (1977).

Though neither Moss's study nor Wolkind's gives data on the point, it can be expected that those babies who had the more responsive mothers would tend to develop differently from those babies who had the less responsive mothers, and that such differential development would, in turn, further influence the way the mothers themselves behaved. In these ways circular processes with far-reaching effects can be set going.

Evidence of this is presented by those who have made longitudinal records of mothers and babies interacting, starting in some instances before the baby himself is born. In the gallery of portraits of interacting couples presented by David and Appell (1969), by Sander (1964, 1969), and by Ainsworth (Ainsworth and Wittig, 1969), mothers initially biased in many different ways appear. Each mother, of course, is shown to be influenced in greater or less degree by the particular baby she has. Nevertheless, each mother reacts in her own idiosyncratic way, one being encouraged by her baby's social advances and another evading them, one being made more solicitous by his crying and another more impatient. How any one mother treats any one child, therefore, is a complex product reflecting how her own initial biases have been confirmed, modified, or amplified by her experience with him.

It has already been noted how, by the time the first birthday is reached, each mother–child couple has already developed a highly characteristic pattern of interacting. The magnitude of the differences between one couple and another can, moreover, hardly be exaggerated. David and Appell (1966, 1969), for example, in reporting their findings, emphasise what an immense range of variation there is between couples simply in the amount of interaction that occurs—altogether apart from differences in its quality.[1] They describe, at one extreme of their series, a couple who are interacting almost continuously throughout their little girl's waking hours, and, at an opposite extreme, a couple who are hardly ever together, mother occupying herself with housework and largely ignoring her daughter. In a third pair mother and son spend much time silently watching each other whilst at the same time each is engaged in some private activity. In a fourth pair there are long spells of non-interaction, interrupted occasionally and unpredictably by a longish period of close interaction initiated by mother.

Although David and Appell have published too few data for us to be sure what mainly accounts for these great differences between couples, there is no doubt that, in the extent to which one partner responded to the other's initiatives, the mothers varied far more than did the infants. Thus every infant in the study was observed to respond on almost every occasion that his mother initiated interaction, so that variance in incidence of response amongst the infants was near to zero. By contrast, variance in incidence of response amongst the mothers was very great. Every mother ignored some of her infant's initiatives; yet, whereas one mother responded regularly to well over half of them, there were others who responded hardly ever. As might be expected, responsive mothers seemed to enjoy their infant's company, whereas the unresponsive ones seemed to

[1] David and Appell have made visits, lasting three hours, at fortnightly (or more frequent) intervals, to the families of twenty-five infants in Paris. During these visits they have compiled detailed moment-to-moment records of how infant and mother interact in their natural home setting during the first year of life. These records have been extended upwards in age by monthly visits until each infant is thirty months old, and have also been amplified by laboratory sessions occurring at the ages of thirteen, eighteen, and thirty months. Only limited data have been published, however, and those are mostly confined to the first thirteen months.

find it a burden, except on the occasions when they themselves began interaction.

These findings strongly suggest that at the time of the first birthday mothers play a much larger part than do infants in determining how much interaction takes place. A similar conclusion seems to emerge from the study by Bishop (1951) of a series of nursery school children who were observed spending a couple of half-hours together with mother in a playroom. Patterns of interaction between mother and child varied from almost continuous interaction to very little, a principal variable being, it would appear, the extent to which a mother responded to her child's initiatives or ignored them.

Whatever the causes of a mother's behaving in one way or another towards her infant, there is much evidence suggesting that whatever that way is plays a leading part in determining the pattern of attachment he ultimately develops. Indirect evidence of this is provided by Yarrow (1963) from his study of the development of forty infants during their first six months of life, spent either in a foster-home or in an adoptive home. Assessments of their respective capacities to cope with frustration and stress at six months were found to correlate with the following characteristics of maternal behaviour:

the amount of physical contact a mother gave her infant;

the extent to which a mother's way of holding her infant was adapted to his characteristics and rhythms;

the degree to which her soothing techniques were effective;

the extent to which she stimulated and encouraged him, whether to respond socially, to express his needs, or to make developmental progress;

the extent to which materials and experiences given an infant were suited to his individual capacities;

the frequency and intensity of expression of positive feelings towards him by mother, father, and others.

In each case correlation coefficients were $+0.50$ or higher, the two highest being indices of the extent to which a mother adapted herself to her infant's rhythms and to his development.

In recent years Ainsworth, and other workers using the same and related methods, have presented extensive evidence of a strong correlation between the pattern of attachment observed in an infant or older child and the pattern of mothering he is receiving at the time. (For a review of this evidence, see Chapter 21 Volume 2.) Not only that, but there are also clear indications that the pattern of attachment a child is showing towards his mother figure is to a high degree the consequence of the pattern of mothering he is receiving. Further discussion of this central issue will be found in Chapter 18. Recent findings, indeed, strongly support the validity of the indices of maternal behaviour believed to contribute to secure attachment that were first outlined by Ainsworth after reflecting on her longitudinal data.[1] Her list includes: (a) frequent and sustained physical contact between infant and mother, especially during the first six months, together with mother's ability to soothe a distressed baby by holding him; (b) a mother's sensitivity to her baby's signals, and especially her ability to time her interventions in harmony with his rhythms; (c) an environment so regulated that the baby can derive a sense of the consequences of his own actions. Another condition she lists, which is perhaps as much a result of those given above as a condition in its own right, is the mutual delight that a mother and infant find in each other's company.

A number of other workers with clinical experience (e.g. David and Appell, 1966, 1969; Sander, 1962, 1964; Bettelheim 1967) have come also to regard several of these conditions as of the greatest significance for a child's development. Conditions especially referred to are, on the one hand, a mother's sensitivity to signals, and her timing of interventions, and, on the other, whether a child experiences that his social initiatives lead to predictable results, and the degree to which his initiatives are in fact successful in establishing a reciprocal interchange with his mother. When all these conditions are met, it seems likely, active and happy interchange between the couple ensues and a secure attachment develops. When the conditions are met only in part, there is some measure of friction and discontent in the exchanges, and the attachment that develops is less secure. Finally, when the conditions are met hardly at all, grave deficiencies of interchange and attachment may result. Amongst these are, certainly, major delay in the development of attachment due to insufficiency of interaction, and, probably, some forms of autism, owing to a child's finding the social

---

[1] The passage following is a slightly abbreviated and paraphrased quotation from Ainsworth and Wittig (1969). Data supporting the conclusions are in Ainsworth and others (1978).

responses of his mother-figure too difficult to predict.[1]

In view of the nature of the variables that now seem of importance in determining patterns of attachment behaviour, it is small wonder that studies of the effects of one or another child-rearing technique have produced so many negative results (see Caldwell, 1964). Data regarding breast- versus bottle-feeding, self-demand versus schedule, or early weaning versus late, even if accurate, are seen to tell us little of relevance. As Brody (1956) demonstrated some years ago, the practice of breast-feeding offers no guarantee of maternal sensitivity to a baby's signals, nor does holding an infant during a feed ensure either rapport or intimacy.

Nevertheless, there is no reason to dismiss what happens during feeding as wholly irrelevant. During the early months, especially, the feeding situation constitutes a principal occasion for mother–infant interaction; it thus provides an excellent opportunity to gauge a mother's sensitivity to her baby's signals, her ability to time her interventions to suit his rhythms, and her willingness to pay heed to his social initiatives—each of which plays a major part in determining how their social interaction will develop. Thus the way a mother feeds her baby, when considered in these terms, may well prove predictive of how his attachment behaviour is going to develop. Ainsworth and others (1978) give data in support of this thesis; and Sander (1969) illustrates it with case material.

Admittedly the hypotheses advanced regarding conditions likely to be relevant to the development of attachment behaviour during the first year remain inadequately tested. Yet, as a reading of chapter 18 shows, much new data supports them and they are more firmly established to-day than when first formulated during the late sixties. May they continue to be subjected to rigorous inquiry.

---

[1] This view is expressed by two clinicians with much experience of autistic children. Bettelheim (1967) holds that autistic children have lacked the experience that what they do in social interaction has any predictable effect and that, as a result, in their dealings with people they have 'given up goal-directed action ... [and] also prediction'; this he contrasts with their behaviour towards impersonal objects which, he states, commonly becomes and remains goal-directed. Mahler (1965) also holds that 'retreat into secondary autism' can result from finding mother unpredictable. See also Tinbergen and Tinbergen (1982).

Persistence and stability of patterns

By the time the first birthday is reached both mother and infant have commonly made so many adjustments in response to one another that the resulting pattern of interaction has already become highly characteristic. What, it may be asked, is the degree of stability of the pattern and of its two components, the child's attachment behaviour and the mother's caregiving behaviour? The answers to these questions are complex.

Plainly, the more satisfaction the interactional pattern adopted by a couple gives to each partner the more stable it is bound to be. When, on the other hand, the pattern adopted leads to dissatisfaction in one or both partners there must be less stability, since the dissatisfied partner is, either always or intermittently, seeking to change the current pattern. An example of an unstable pattern, arising from personality disturbance in the mother, is described by Sander (1964).

Nevertheless, whether satisfying or unsatisfying to the partners, whatever interactional pattern a couple has worked out during the first year tends to persist, at least during the next two or three (David and Appell, 1966). This is in part because each member expects the other to behave in a certain way and each, as a rule, cannot avoid eliciting in the other whatever behaviour is expected, if only because that behaviour is the customary response of the other. Expectations tend, therefore, to be confirmed. As a result of processes of this sort, and whether for good or for ill, the interacting couple develops in a way of its own and achieves a stability independent of each partner considered separately.

Even so, there is abundant evidence that persistent and apparently stable patterns of interaction between mother and child can be materially changed by events occurring in subsequent years. An accident or a chronic illness may make a child more demanding and/or his mother more protective; distraction or depression in mother will make her less responsive; whilst, should anything lead a mother to reject her child or to use threats of separation or loss of love as sanctions, he is almost certain to become more clinging. Either the advent of a new baby or a period of separation of child from mother will create its own disequilibrium, and either event may on occasion so alter the behaviour of one or other that the interactional pattern between them becomes radically changed for the worse. Conversely, more perceptive treatment of child by mother and more acceptance of his attachment behaviour may greatly reduce the intensity of such behaviour and thereby make it easier for his mother to meet.

Thus, too much of prognostic significance must not be read into the statement that at the first birthday a couple is likely to have established a characteristic pattern of interaction. All that it means is that for most couples a pattern that is likely to persist is by that time present.

All recent evidence shows that any statement about a child of twelve months himself showing a characteristic pattern of attachment behaviour, distinct from the interactional pattern of the couple of which he is a partner, and implying some degree of autonomous stability, is certainly mistaken, and that the behavioural organisation of a child of that age is much less stable than is that of the couple of which he is a partner. The truth is that at the present time extremely little is known about the stability or lability of the behavioural organisation of young children considered as individuals. All that can safely be said is that, as the years pass, lability diminishes; whether it be favourable or unfavourable, whatever organisation exists becomes progressively less easily changed.

Between couples, interactional patterns probably stabilise much faster, if only because whatever interactional pattern is established has come into being as a result of mutual adaptation. The pressure to maintain it, therefore, comes increasingly from two sides. This stability is both the strength and the weakness of the arrangement. When the pattern is favourable for the future of both, its stability is its strength. When the pattern is unfavourable for one or both partners, its stability poses a major problem; for any change in the pattern as a whole requires a change in the behavioural organisation of both.

Nothing in child psychiatry has been more significant in recent years than the increasing recognition that the problems its practitioners are called upon to treat are not often problems confined to individuals but are usually problems arising from stable interactional patterns that have developed between two, and more often several, members of a family. Diagnostic skill lies in the assessment of these interactional patterns, and of the current biases in each family member that help to perpetuate them; therapeutic skill lies in techniques that enable changes to occur more or less concurrently in all members of a family so that a new pattern of interaction can come into being and become stabilised.

Chapter 17

Developments in the Organisation of Attachment Behaviour

IT has been said repeatedly that attachment behaviour does not disappear with childhood but persists throughout life. Either old or new figures are selected and proximity and/or communication maintained with them. Whereas outcome of behaviour continues much as before, means for achieving it become increasingly diverse.

When an older child or adult maintains an attachment to another person he does so by diversifying his behaviour so that it includes not only the basic elements of attachment behaviour present at the first birthday but, in addition, an increasingly varied array of more sophisticated elements. Compare, for example, the degree of behavioural organisation underlying the actions of a schoolboy when he seeks and finds his mother in a neighbour's house, or pleads with her to include him on a visit she intends to pay to relatives the following week, with that of the same individual when as an infant he first attempted to follow his mother out of the room.

All these more sophisticated elements of attachment behaviour are organised as plans with set-goals. Let us consider what these set-goals are.

During the first three-quarters of his first year, it seems probable that a child makes no planned attempt to bring into being whatever the conditions may be that would in fact terminate his attachment behaviour. Either the necessary conditions obtain, in which case he is content, or they do not, in which case he is distressed. Whatever attachment behaviour he may then exhibit is not yet goal-corrected; though in the ordinary home it is very likely to have proximity to mother amongst its predictable outcomes.

As a child passes eight months and nears his first birthday,[1]

---

[1] Piaget's experiments, which have been repeated with French-speaking Canadian children, and with similar results, by Décarie (1965), show that it is a very exceptional child who can make a plan before he is seven months old: the great majority of children are already eight or

however, he becomes more skilful. Thenceforward, it seems, he discovers what the conditions are that terminate his distress and that make him feel secure; and from that phase onward he begins to be able to plan his behaviour so that these conditions are achieved. As a consequence, during his second year he develops a will of his own.

Since the terminating conditions for each child vary according to the intensity with which his attachment behaviour happens from time to time to be elicited, the set-goals he selects vary also from occasion to occasion. At one moment he is determined to sit on his mother's knee and nothing else will do; at another he is content to watch her through the doorway. In ordinary circumstances, it seems clear, whatever conditions are at any one time necessary to terminate his attachment behaviour become the set-goal of whatever attachment plan he adopts.

Goal-corrected attachment plans can vary in structure from being simple and swiftly executed to being something far more elaborate. The particular degree of complexity of a plan turns partly on the set-goal selected, partly on the subject's estimate of the situation obtaining between himself and his attachment-figure, and partly on his skill in devising a plan to meet that situation. Whether the plan be simple or elaborate, however, it cannot be devised except by reference to working models of environment and organism (see Chapter 5). We may infer, therefore, that the construction and elaboration of working models are occurring contemporaneously with the birth and development of a child's ability to plan.

A principal way in which a child's attachment plans vary is in whether and in the extent to which they entail influencing the behaviour of his attachment-figure. When an attachment goal is simply sight of mother or greater proximity to her, no planned action to change her behaviour may be necessary. At other times, an attachment goal may require that mother responds only in a friendly way, and again no planned action by the child may be necessary. At yet other times, however, a child's attachment goal may demand from his mother much

---

nine months, and some are older still. At these ages, moreover, and for some months longer, the ability to make plans is embryonic and confined to the simplest of situations (Piaget, 1936, 1937). Flavell (1963) has written a comprehensive exposition of and guide to the Piagetian literature. Piaget himself does not use the terms 'plan' or 'goal', but 'intention' and 'intentionality'.

more activity; and then his plan will almost certainly have to include measures designed to ensure that she behaves in the way desired.

Inevitably, the earliest attempts that a child makes to change his partner's behaviour are primitive. Examples might be pulling and pushing, and such simple requests or commands as 'Come here' or 'Go away'. As he grows older, however, and it dawns upon him that his mother may have her own set-goals and, moreover, that his mother's set-goals may perhaps be changed, his behaviour becomes more sophisticated. Even so, the plans he makes may be sadly misconceived, owing to the inadequate working model he yet has of his mother. An example is a little boy, just short of two years, who, having been deprived of a knife by his mother, attempted to get her to return it by offering her his teddy bear.

The truth is that to frame a plan the set-goal of which is to change the set-goal of another's behaviour requires a good deal of cognitive and model-building competence. It requires, first, a capacity to attribute to another a capacity to have goals and plans; secondly, an ability to infer from such clues as are given what the other's goals may be; and, thirdly, skill in framing a plan that is likely to effect the desired change in the other's set-goal.

Although to be able to picture others as being goal-directed may perhaps be fairly well-established by the second birthday, a child's competence in grasping what another's goals actually are is still only embryonic. A main reason for this is that, in order to grasp what another's goals and plans are, it is usually necessary to see things through the other's eyes. And this is an ability that develops only slowly.

Since a child's inadequacies in this regard limit his social relationships and may lead him to be misjudged, a brief digression may be useful.

The Handicap of Egocentrism

Piaget was first to call attention to the difficulties a young child has in seeing things from a viewpoint other than his own and to give the condition a name: 'egocentrism'. Yet the conclusion he drew from his experiments using a three dimensional model of an alpine scene—that it is not until a child reaches seven years of age that he is capable of seeing things from another's viewpoint (Piaget, 1924; Piaget and Inhelder, 1948) —is too pessimistic, as the findings of more recent studies of the problem, presented in the next chapter, go to show. Even so, in their dealings with other people, whether at a verbal or non-verbal level, young children certainly are at some disadvantage compared to adults, as the following examples make plain.

In his verbal communications to others, it is found, a child of under six years makes only limited attempts to suit what he has to say, or the way he says it, to the needs of his listener. His assumption seems to be that any and every listener is as fully cognisant as he is himself of both the context and the actors in any incident he wishes to relate, and that only the details that are novel and interesting to him need be described. As a result, whenever the listener is not familiar with context and characters, the account is apt to be incomprehensible.

In a purely practical sphere the same kind of difficulty in picturing how the world looks to others, and what their goals may be, is to be seen. Thus, Flavell (1961) reports the results of giving children ranging in age from three years to six some very simple little tasks. One was to select from an array of objects, varying from a toy truck to a lipstick, one suitable to give to mother on her birthday; another was to show a picture so that it appeared upside down to someone seated opposite; a third concerned a stick, soft one end and pointed the other: when the soft end was in child's hand and the pointed end in experimenter's, the child was asked whether the stick felt soft to him (Yes), and then whether the stick felt soft also to the experimenter. Of the three-year-olds, not more than a half were successful on any of these tasks and on some of them only a quarter were. Of the six-year-olds, either all or a great majority were successful on every one.

One rather typical example of three-year-old failure in these tasks was a child who selected the toy truck to give his mother as a birthday present. That is a replica at the age of three of the little boy who attempted to get his mother to return the knife to him by offering her his teddy bear.

Evidently these are the years during which a child is elaborating his 'picture' of his mother. Only gradually, therefore, does his working model of her become fitted for its role of helping him to frame plans to influence the way she behaves towards him.

A recent study by Light (1979) shows that the rate of development of a child's capacity to grasp the viewpoint of another is probably much influenced by whether or not his mother takes account of his viewpoint in her dealings with him: details are presented in the next chapter.

It is, of course, vital to realise that Piaget's concept of egocentrism refers solely to the cognitive equipment a child has available when building his models of other people and has nothing whatever to do with egotism. There is, in fact, no reason to think that a child is any more egotistical than an adult. As recent studies (e.g. Zahn-Waxler and others, 1979) have confirmed, he may indeed express much concern about the welfare of another and genuinely do all he can for that other. But, as anyone knows who has had experience of being ministered to by a young child, the results are not always welcome. Where a child fails is not in his lack of will to benefit the recipient of his care but in his grasp of what would, from the recipient's point of view, be beneficial.

To follow this theme further would be to broach the large, difficult, and profound questions of how a child gradually builds up his own 'internal world'. Starting, we may suppose, towards the end of his first year, and probably especially actively during his second and third when he acquires the powerful and extraordinary gift of language, a child is busy constructing working models of how the physical world may be expected to behave, how his mother and other significant persons may be expected to behave, how he himself may be expected to behave, and how each interacts with all the others. Within the framework of these working models he evaluates his situation and makes his plans. And within the framework of the working models of his mother and himself he evaluates special aspects of his situation and makes his attachment plans.

How these models are built up and thenceforward bias perception and evaluation, how adequate and effective for planning they become, how valid or distorted as representations they are, and what conditions help or hinder their development, all these are matters of great consequence for understanding the different ways in which attachment behaviour becomes organised as children grow older. Since, however, they are matters that raise giant problems as well as giant controversies, consideration of them is postponed. In volumes 2 and 3 of this work relevant evidence is reviewed and a conceptual framework designed to accommodate it outlined.

Collaboration and Conflict

Once his attachment behaviour has become organised mainly on a goal-corrected basis, the relationship developing between a child and his mother becomes much more complex. Whilst true collaboration between the two then becomes possible, so also does intractable conflict.[1]

When any two people are interacting together and each is capable of making plans, a prospect arises of their sharing a common goal and a common plan. When they so do, the interaction resulting takes on new properties, properties altogether different from those of an interaction based, say, on chains of interdigitating fixed action patterns. The new style of interaction is best spoken of as a partnership. By sharing a common set-goal and participating in a joint plan to achieve it, partners have a rewarding sense of common purpose; and they are likely also to identify with one another.

Nevertheless partnership is bought at a price. Since each partner has his own personal set-goals to attain, collaboration between them is possible only so long as one is prepared, when necessary, to relinquish, or at least adjust, his own set-goals to suit the other's.

Which of any two partners does the adjusting turns, of course, on many factors. In the case of an ordinary mother–child couple, each is likely to make very many adjustments so as to suit the other, though each at times is likely also to dig in heels and demand his own way. Yet in a happy partnership there is constant give and take.

Even in a happy partnership, however, there is likely also to be constant minor conflict until such time as set-goals are aligned. Thus, whilst a mother may usually fall in with her child's demands, there are nevertheless occasions when she does not. At times, indeed, especially with a small child and when time is pressing, she may use a strong right arm. Far more often, however, if she is wise she will strive to achieve her ends by reason or a mini-bargain, namely, by seeking to alter his set-goals.

In the case of attachment demands, it is evident that during the course of any ordinary day the mother of a two-year-old is likely many times to attempt to change the set-goals of his behaviour. Sometimes she may be trying to get him to stay

[1] Some of the problems that arise when one individual seeks to change his environment by inducing changes in the goals of another individual have been discussed in terms of control theory by MacKay (1964). When two individuals are each attempting to alter the goals of the other 'it may become logically impossible to dissociate the two goal-complexes. The individuals have then acquired a relationship in which their individualities have partly merged.' See also Hinde (1979).

away, as for example when he comes through to his parents' bedroom during the early hours, or hangs round his mother's skirts when friends visit. At other times she may be trying to get him to keep close, as when they are in the street or a shop together. By encouragement or discouragement, and sometimes by nagging, punishment, or bribes, a mother is intermittently striving to regulate her child's proximity to herself by attempting to change the set-goals of his attachment behaviour.

In complementary fashion a child is intermittently striving to change his mother's behaviour and her proximity to him, and in doing so is almost certain to adopt some, at least, of the methods she herself employs. Therein lies both hope and a warning.

As a child gets older, and especially when he is past his third birthday, his demands tend to ease. Other interests and activities attract him and occupy his time, and there is less that alarms him. Not only is his attachment behaviour less frequently and less intensely activated, but it can be terminated in novel ways, thanks to his increasing cognitive competence, especially a greatly improved capacity to think in terms of space and time. Thus, for spells of increasing duration, a child may feel content and secure even in his mother's absence, simply by knowing where she is and when she will return, or by being assured that she is available whenever he really wants her.

To most children at their fourth birthday information that mother is readily available is likely to be of great significance. At their second birthday, by contrast, it is likely to carry little meaning (Marvin, 1977).

The Regulation of Mothering

A question that is constantly raised both by mothers and by professional people is whether it is wise for a mother always to meet her child's demands for her presence and attention. Will giving in to him lead to his becoming 'spoilt'? If she gives in to him over mothering, may he not demand that she give in to him over everything else, and expect her to do so? And will he ever become independent? How much mothering, in fact, is good for a child?

The question is perhaps best seen in the same perspective as the question 'How much food is good for a child?' The answer to that is now well known. From the earliest months forward it is best to follow a child's lead. When he wants more food, it will probably benefit him; when he refuses, he will probably come to no harm. Provided his metabolism is not deranged, a child is so made that, if left to decide, he can regulate his own food-intake in regard to both quantity and quality. With few exceptions, therefore, a mother can safely leave the initiative to him.

The same is true of attachment behaviour, especially during the early years. In an ordinary family in which a mother is caring for her child, no harm comes to him when she gives him as much of her presence and attention as he seems to want. Thus, in regard to mothering—as to food—a young child seems to be so made that, if from the first permitted to decide, he can satisfactorily regulate his own 'intake'. Only after he reaches school years is there occasion for gentle discouragement.

Just how much pressure towards greater self-reliance a parent is thenceforward wise to exert, and especially at what age and in what circumstances, is difficult to know and calls, therefore, for research. In Western cultures there is probably too much pressure too early; in Eastern cultures perhaps the reverse may be true.[1] During the earlier years the pattern that seems happiest for both child and mother is that illustrated by the portraits of interacting couples referred to in the previous chapter. When a mother is perceptive of her child's signals and responds promptly and appropriately to them her child thrives and the relationship develops happily. It is when she is not perceptive or not responsive, or when she gives him not what he wants but something else instead, that things go wrong.

Disturbances of attachment behaviour are of many kinds. In the Western world much the commonest, in my view, are the results of too little mothering, or of mothering coming from a succession of different people. Disturbances arising from too much mothering are less common: they arise, not because a child is insatiable for love and attention, but because his mother has a compulsion to shower them on him. Instead of taking her cue from her child, a mother who overmothers is found, when observed closely, to be herself taking all the initiative. She is insisting on being close to her child and occupying his attention or guarding him from danger—just as the mother of a child who is overfed is found to be insisting on filling him with food. In later volumes much attention is given to the ill-effects

[1] Current evolution theory, using gene survival as the criterion (see Chapter 3), points to some degree of conflict becoming inevitable between mother and young as the young grow older (Trivers, 1974). What the implications would be of applying these ideas to the special case of the human family are yet to be determined.

of a parent acting in this way, which commonly results in the attachment-caregiving relationship becoming inverted (see Volume 2, Chapters 16, 18; Volume 3, Chapters 11, 12, 19).

Other disturbances of attachment behaviour, of which there are a multitude of kinds, can best be regarded as due, not to too much or too little mothering, but to distortions in the pattern of mothering that a child has received or is receiving. This, however, is not the place to pursue further the psychopathology of attachment behaviour; in a few paragraphs it would be easy to oversimplify.

This is a brief chapter and one totally inadequate to its theme. The developmental processes touched upon are not only of great intrinsic interest but they are the very processes that make man different from other species. Man's capacity to use language and other symbols, his capacities to plan and build models, his capacities for long-lasting collaboration with others and for interminable strife, these make man what he is. All these processes have their origin during the first three years of life, and all, moreover, are from their earliest days enlisted in the organisation of attachment behaviour. Is there, then, no more to say than this about developments in the organisation of attachment behaviour that occur during the second and third years of life?

In the first edition of this work I answered my question by hazarding that there was probably not much more, and remarking also that the least studied phase of human development remained the phase during which a child is acquiring all that makes him most distinctively human. In concluding the volume, I pointed to the continent of ignorance still to be conquered. Since then explorers, both numerous and gifted, have been active. In the chapters that follow I attempt to outline a few of their discoveries.

Part V

OLD CONTROVERSIES AND NEW FINDINGS

Chapter 18

Stability and change in patterns of attachment

The best introduction to astronomy is to think of the nightly heavens as a little lot of stars belonging to one's own homestead.

GEORGE ELIOT

Further development of infants assessed as securely or anxiously attached

In Chapter 16 an account is given of the procedure devised by Mary Ainsworth by which the pattern of attachment to mother presented by an infant of 12 months can be assessed. Confidence that the procedure is assessing socio-emotional characteristics of significance rested originally on the finding that infants showing each of these patterns behave in a closely related way at home and also that the principal dimension used in the classification, security-insecurity, is clearly related to a dimension, variously described as trust-distrust or as quality of object-relations, long used by clinicians. The fact, moreover, that the pattern of attachment shown by a child correlates strongly with the way his mother treats him not only squares with the experience of many child psychiatrists but suggests a causal relationship of practical consequence.

Today our confidence in the value of this classification is enormously enhanced by the finding that, provided family environment remains stable, these patterns are not only likely to persist during the second year of life but, during both the second and subsequent years, they correlate, as predicted, with patterns of social and play behaviour with adults and children other than mother. Thus a means for assessing those aspects of personality that show developmental continuity, hitherto so elusive, is at last available.

Evidence that Ainsworth's classificatory system gives stable assessments for most infants between 12 and 18 months comes from studies by Connell (1976, quoted by Ainsworth and others, 1978) and Waters (1978). Connell assessed 47 infants at 12 months and again at 18 months and found that the pattern assessed at the two ages was the same for 81 per cent of the infants. In the study by Waters of 50 infants 96 per cent were found to show the same pattern.

Evidence that the pattern which an infant shows at twelve months predicts his social and exploratory behaviour many months later comes first from an early study in Baltimore (Main, 1973; Main and Townsend, 1982) in which it was found that, when infants classified on the strange situation at 12 months were given an opportunity nine months later to engage in free play and in play with an adult stranger, those classified earlier as securely attached engaged for a longer time in each episode of play, showed more intense interest in toys and gave more attention to detail, and they laughed or smiled more frequently than did those earlier classified as avoidant or ambivalent. In addition, the secure infants were more co-operative, both with mother and with other persons (Londerville and Main, 1981), a finding confirmed in another sample, in Minnesota, by Matas, Arend and Sroufe (1978). In yet a third sample, in Berkeley, Main and Weston (1981) examined the responses of infants to an adult who first attempted to engage the infant in play and later showed distress. Not only did the infants earlier classified as secure respond with an evident readiness to interact but some also showed concern at the adult's distress. Infants earlier classified as insecure, by contrast, showed little readiness to interact. In a further study of this kind (Waters, Wippman and Sroufe, 1979) infants classified as securely or as anxiously attached at 15 months, using videotapes made by W. Bronson, were subsequently observed at $3\frac{1}{2}$ years in nursery school. In this setting, with mothers absent, children classified at 15 months as securely attached showed themselves to be more competent socially, more effective in play and more curious, and also more sympathetic to other children's distress, than those earlier classified as insecurely attached. Thus by preschool age the favourable patterns of behaviour of the securely attached children have become a function of the child himself and, as the theory predicts, are no longer dependent on mother's presence.

Although the findings so far described span only the period from 12 to 42 months their significance is greatly amplified by the finding, reported by Arend, Gove and Sroufe (1979) that similar sorts of difference between children, classified earlier as either secure or anxious, continue to be present during their fifth and sixth years. Since as a child's personality develops it is necessary to employ different procedures and scales to obtain relevant information, a brief description of those used is called for: they were devised by Jack and Jeanne Block (1980).

Using data amassed during the thirty years covered by the two well-known Berkeley longitudinal studies and also from a number of studies of their own, the Blocks have elaborated two dimensions of personality which they believe to be of social and clinical value and also to be stable over time. One they term ego-control, the other ego-resilience. Ego-control varies from over-control, through moderate-control to under-control, with the optimum in the middle. Ego-resilience varies from high to low, or brittle, with the optimum at the high end.

Among characteristics of the over-controlled person are constrained and inhibited responses, reduced expression of emotion, and narrow restriction of the information processed. Among characteristics of the under-controlled person are impulsiveness, distractability, open expression of emotion, and too little restriction on the information processed.

Ego-resilience refers to a person's capacity to modify his level of control according to circumstances. Among characteristics of the highly resilient person is resourcefulness in adapting to changing situations, a flexible use of his behavioural repertoire, and an ability to process competing and conflicting information. By contrast, a brittle person shows little flexibility and responds to changing and stressful situations either by persevering rigidly in his original response or else by becoming disorganised. Competing and conflicting information makes him unduly anxious.

In devising their procedures to assess ego-control and ego-resilience the Blocks draw on data from two main sources: (a) the observations of teachers who have known the children well in nursery school, recorded by means of a Q-sort, (b) the performance of the children in a large battery of laboratory tests. For both classes of data the Blocks derive their indices from as many different sources as possible and pool data of a similar type. By these means their indices are made more representative and valid than any single measure derived from a single source.

The Blocks demonstrate the applicability and usefulness of the two concepts in studies that cover both sexes, a range of ages, different samples, and a variety of methods of data gathering: by observation, by testing and by self-report (Block and

Block, 1980). In a longitudinal study of a sample of over 100 children of a fairly wide ethnic and socio-economic range, starting at three years and still in progress, the Blocks report good predictive powers for assessments made at the age of three years with those made four years later when the children were seven.

The longitudinal study of Arend and others (1979) bridges the period 18 months to 5 years. Of a sample of white middle class infants classified at 18 months by the Ainsworth procedure, 26 were traced when between the ages of $4\frac{1}{2}$ and $5\frac{1}{2}$ years: 12 had been classified as securely attached and 14 as anxiously attached. Now, three or four years later, all these children were attending nursery school or a day-care centre. Two procedures to assess their ego-resilience and ego-control were employed: one a Q-sort by a teacher who had known the child for at least 8 months, the other a sub-set of the Blocks' laboratory procedures. Results were in accordance with predictions. Mean scores for ego-resilience, derived from each source separately, were in each case significantly higher for the 12 children earlier classified as securely attached than for the 14 anxiously attached. For ego-control mean scores from the Q-sorts showed the securely attached children to be moderately controlled, those of the 8 anxious and avoidant children to be over controlled and those for the 6 anxious and resistant children to be under-controlled. (Mean scores for ego-control from the laboratory procedures showed no differences.) Another finding that accords with prediction was that, on three separate measures of curiosity, the securely attached children scored significantly higher than did the anxiously attached.

A point to be emphasised is that these five-year-olds were assessed on performances in settings, school and laboratory, from which mother was absent. Thus, here again, the performance of the securely attached children was shown to have become independent of mother's presence. For a review of these and related studies see Sroufe (1979).

Results of a further longitudinal study strongly confirmatory of these findings, and with a valuable discussion of their clinical and educational implications, are recently reported, also by Sroufe (1982).

The organisation of attachment: from lability to stability

There is ample evidence that during the first year or two the stability of attachment pattern thus far described is a property more of the couple in which the child is a partner than of the behavioural organisation within the child himself. As the months pass, however, the inner organisation of attachment, with its working model of attachment figure, becomes ever more stable. As a consequence not only does it resist change but it does so increasingly.

Evidence that the organisation of attachment is initially labile comes from several sources. In the studies described in the previous section in which stability of pattern is reported the subjects have been of white middle class origin, the parents' marriages intact, and a high degree of continuity found in the way each mother treats her child. Such continuity of parental care is much less common, however, in disadvantaged families. In a study of 100 subjects drawn from such a population (Vaughn and others, 1979), a sample in which only half the mothers were married and most were under twenty, no less than one third of the patterns assessed at twelve months had changed six months later, some for the better and some for the worse. In the case of ten children who had changed from showing secure attachment at twelve months to anxious attachment at eighteen, the mothers reported having experienced significantly more stressful life events during the period of change than did the mothers of the 45 children whose pattern had continued to be secure. In several cases in which change had been in the opposite direction, from anxious to secure, the advent of a grandmother seemed likely to have played a beneficial part (Egeland and Sroufe, 1981).

In another study, by Main and Weston (1981), it was found that during the first eighteen months a child may show different patterns with each of his two parents. Some sixty infants were observed, first at twelve months with one parent and then, six months later, with the other. It was found that, when looked at as a group, the patterns of attachment shown with a father resembled closely the patterns shown with a mother, with roughly the same percentage distribution of patterns. But, when the patterns shown by each child individually were examined, no correlation was found between the pattern shown with one parent and that shown with the other. In a child's approach to new people and new tasks his relationship with each parent was found to be playing a part. Children with a secure relationship with both parents were most confident and most competent; children with a secure relationship with neither were least so;

and those with a secure relationship with one parent but not with the other came in between.

Clearly such evidence as we have regarding the pattern of attachment a child develops confirms the influential role of the caregiver, already emphasised in Chapter 16. Among much other evidence pointing in that direction is Ainsworth's comparison of the amount of crying of the 23 infants in her sample during the last quarter of their first year with what it had been during the first quarter (Ainsworth and others, 1978). Whereas at the beginning there had been no correlation between the amount of crying a baby did and the way his mother was treating him, by the end of the year mothers who had attended promptly to their crying babies had babies who cried much less than did the babies of mothers who had left them to cry. Thus, whilst the behaviour of the mothers continued as it had started, that of the infants changed.

Similar findings of a close relationship between maternal sensitivity in the early months and pattern of attachment at twelve are reported from a new longitudinal study by Egeland, Deinard and Sroufe (see Sroufe, 1982). In this study, moreover, several measures of infant temperament were made during the neonatal period; but they did not account for the profoundly different patterns of attachment seen at a year.

The powerful effects on pattern of attachment, and thereby on personality development, of a child's early experiences are nowhere more evident than in the deeply disturbed social behaviour of children who have been physically abused by a parent or who have spent their early years in an institution.

George and Main (1979) report observations of ten toddlers aged between one and three years known to have been physically abused and compare their behaviour in day care centres with that of ten closely matched toddlers from families experiencing stress. Behaviour seen significantly more frequently in the abused children included assaulting peers, harassing and threatening to assault caregivers, and responding to friendly overtures either by avoiding interaction or by mixed movements of avoidance and approach. In these ways the children tend to isolate themselves and also to alienate adults who might help them, leading thus to a self-perpetuating cycle. Similar types of behaviour but on a lesser scale have been observed in avoidant infants in normal samples and are correlated with a mother's aversion to physical contact with her infant and angry behaviour towards him (Main and Weston, 1982). These findings illustrate well how each partner is in varying degree influencing the other and how their current pattern of interaction is the product of an historical, transactional process.

Tizard and Hodges (1978) report on the behaviour at the age of eight years of 51 children all of whom had spent their first two years in an institution. Half had been adopted, 20 before they reached four years and another 5 subsequently. (Of the other 26, 13 had been restored to their parents, 6 had been fostered and 7 had remained in the institution.) Of the 25 adopted children, 20 seemed to have formed a close mutually affectionate relationship with their new parents; but 5, a significant minority, had failed to do so. At school at least half of all these late-adopted children were proving extremely troublesome. They were restless, quarrelsome and disobedient, resented criticism, and seemed to have 'an almost insatiable desire for adult attention', from teachers and strangers alike.

Whether or not a child became attached (in some form) to his adoptive parents turned mainly on how they treated him. The more readily they accepted his desire for attention and care, and the more time they gave him, the more evident the attachment. The development of the children who were not adopted showed the same clear correlation. As is to be expected, the unattached children were more likely to be 'over-friendly' than were the attached. Even so, many of the children who were said to be closely attached to mother-figure were nonetheless undiscriminatingly friendly. The quality of their attachment remains seriously in question, therefore. Findings from this and other studies (see Rutter, 1981) support the hypothesis that there is a sensitive phase in early life after which development of the capacity to make secure and discriminating attachments becomes progressively more difficult; or, put another way, that the pattern in which a child's attachment behaviour is already organised tends to persist and as he grows older to be modified less and less easily and less and less completely by his current experience. This is not only an issue of the greatest practical consequence but, as so much recent work is showing, is one now yielding to systematic research.

The finding that the quality of care received influences the pattern of attachment developing excludes in no way the infant playing a part too. The way a mother treats her infant turns in part on her personality and her initial ideas about babies, and on the experiences she had in her family of origin (Frommer and O'Shea, 1973; Wolkind and others, 1977), and in part on what she is experiencing in the present, including amongst much else the type of behaviour shown by her infant (Korner, 1979). An easy newborn may assist an uncertain mother to develop a favourable pattern of care. Conversely, a difficult unpredictable newborn may tip the balance the other way. Yet all the evidence shows that a potentially easy baby is still likely to develop unfavourably if given unfavourable care and also, more fortunately, that with only few exceptions a potentially difficult baby can develop favourably if given sensitive care (Sameroff and Chandler, 1975; Dunn, 1979). The capacity of a sensitive mother to adapt to even a difficult unpredictable baby and thereby enable him to develop favourably is perhaps the most heartening of all recent findings in this field.

Development of conceptual perspective taking

The development of what in Chapters 14 and 17 I term a goal-corrected partnership turns on a child's capacity both to conceive of his mother as having her own goals and interests separate from his own and to take them into account. Recent studies (e.g. Marvin and others, 1976) provide evidence about this development. At the third birthday it is only a very small minority of children who are capable of this feat. By the fifth birthday, however, the great majority can probably do it. The period during which this transformation is most likely to occur is the fourth and fifth years of life.

Light (1979) provides a useful review of current thinking. Piaget's work on egocentrism, he points out, has serious limitations. For example, his findings are concerned only with visual perspectives and even these are confined to impersonal scenes; and in his conclusions Piaget relied on group-differences found in cross-sectional studies of children of different ages.

Light himself studied a sample of 56 children (equal boys and girls) immediately after reaching their fourth birthday and thus near the middle of the transition period. Each child, who was seen in his own home, was given eight tasks. The most striking finding is the very great range of scores. Thus, with a maximum possible of 40, scores ranged from 9 to 37, with a mean of 22, indicating that some children of four are fully capable of conceptual perspective taking whereas others have little idea of it. The grave limitations of basing conclusions on group means are apparent.

Since the sample of children tested is part of a longitudinal study (being undertaken in Cambridge, England), there is a great deal of other information about the children and their families. This enabled Light to discover whether scores on conceptual perspective taking are correlated either with other characteristics of the children or with characteristics of their families. No relation to sex of child emerged nor was there one with social class of father. Nor did children who spent the most time with peers score higher than the others. When the children's scores were correlated with the way a mother described herself as perceiving and treating her child, by contrast, strong and consistent correlations emerged.

Each mother was given an extended interview, lasting one or two hours, in which open-ended questions, mainly related to fairly specific situations, were asked in a flexible sequence, ending with some rather general questions regarding her ideas about children and how best to bring them up. Mothers of children scoring high on conceptual perspective taking differed from mothers of children who scored low in the following ways. Mothers of high scorers were as much concerned with a child's feelings and intentions as with his actual behaviour and were prepared to make reasonable concessions when the situation warranted it, whereas mothers of low scorers took a more authoritarian line. This difference was clearly exposed in the answers mothers gave to the question: 'What happens if you ask him to do something for you and he says he can't because he's busy, in the middle of a game or something?' To this a mother of a high scorer might reply: 'If he says he's doing something, I'll say "do it when you've finished" and he will'; whereas a mother of a low scorer is more likely to reply that she would say: 'you'll do it now—I've told you to do it'. Thus, mothers of high scorers tend to make concessions and to propose bargains whereas mother's of low scorers are more likely to resort to punishment. Children given physical punishment were notably low on conceptual perspective taking. It is clear, therefore, that a mother who usually takes account of her child's perspective and interests is likely to have a child who reciprocates by taking account of his mother's perspective and interests—yet another example of the powerful influence of a parent and also, we may assume, of learning from a model.

Reflecting on his findings, Light concludes that the variance in children's scores is probably a reflection principally of 'the child's general level of *awareness* of perspective differences and of the need to adapt to them', rather than of variations between children of genetic origin. In judging an adult's behaviour as being egocentric, Light points out, it is rarely implied that he is ignorant that another person's perspective may differ from his own or that he is incapable of taking it into account. Rather we assume that he has the mental capacity but either has never become accustomed to using it or simply is not bothering.

Since Light and other workers find many children who at their fourth birthday are fully capable of conceptual perspective taking, it is natural to ask what is the youngest age at which it begins to develop in children whose mothers treat them propitiously. Findings from a longitudinal study of symbol development in a sample of 30 children from middle class families by Bretherton and Beeghly-Smith (in press) provide clues. About a week before her child reached two years and four months (when a home visit was due) a mother was asked to note whether her child used any of the words on a special word list and, if so, in what context and to whom they referred. The words concerned the perceptions of the child himself and of others, their physiological states, their affects, positive and negative, their desires and abilities, their cognitions, and their moral judgements and obligations. Mothers' observations were recorded in the subsequent interview.

Words used by a majority of the children included 'see' and 'hear', a number of affect words—in order of frequency 'cry' (=distress), 'mad' (=angry), 'scared', 'fun', 'happy', and 'sad'—and 'know'. Eighty per cent of the children used causal statements, the majority of which referred to actions designed to alleviate discomfort or promote comfort. Almost sixty per cent of all words used were applied to others as well as self. 'These children,' the researchers found, 'interpret their own and other people's mental states, comment on their own and others' expected and past experiences, and discuss how their own or someone else's state might be changed or what gave rise to it.' The data, they conclude, 'suggest that the ability to analyse the goals and motives of others, as these interlock with the child's own, is already fairly well developed in the third year', although, we should probably add, only in children whose mothers treat them sensitively. These findings encourage speculation that for humans, as well perhaps as for other primates (Premack and Wodruff, 1978), it is as natural to attribute internal states of mind to self and to others as it is to attribute spatial qualities to the world around us.

Chapter 19

Objections, misconceptions
and clarifications

> ... without the making of theories I am convinced
> there would be no observation.
>
> CHARLES DARWIN

Attachment as an organisational concept

During the dozen years that have passed since the first edition of this work was published, the theory of attachment outlined has been at the centre of much debate. By some it has been found wanting. By others it has not only been welcomed but has been clarified and amplified. Above all, as we have seen, it has been used to good effect to guide further empirical research. The aim of this chapter is to indicate some of the points of controversy, to clear up misunderstandings and to draw attention to contributions I value.

One source of misunderstanding has been due to my failure in the first edition to make clear the distinction to be drawn between an attachment and attachment behaviour. Fortunately this omission has already been made good by a number of colleagues, notably Mary Ainsworth in several of her publications (1969, 1972 and in Chapters 1 and 14 of her jointly authored monograph of 1978). Others who have made valuable contributions include Bischof (1975), Sroufe and Waters (1977) and Bretherton (1980).

To say of a child that he is attached to, or has an attachment to, someone means that he is strongly disposed to seek proximity to and contact with a specific figure and to do so in certain situations, notably when he is frightened, tired or ill. The disposition to behave in this way is an attribute of the child, an attribute which changes only slowly over time and which is unaffected by the situation of the moment. Attachment behaviour, by contrast, refers to any of the various forms of behaviour that a child commonly engages in to attain and/or maintain a desired proximity. At any one time some form of such behaviour may be either present or absent and which

371

it is is, to a high degree, dependent on the conditions obtaining at the time.

The theory of attachment advanced is an attempt to explain both attachment behaviour, with its episodic appearance and disappearance, and also the enduring attachments that children and older individuals make to particular figures. In this theory the key concept is that of a behavioural system, to the explication of which chapters 3 to 8 of this volume are already devoted.

When it was first proposed as a plausible way for understanding the behaviour of a child in relation to his mother, the concept of behavioural control system, or behavioural system, was an unfamiliar one amongst developmental psychologists and clinicians alike. There can be no surprise, therefore, that many already steeped in theories of other sorts have either failed to understand it or have recoiled from an attempt. Yet, for anyone with a knowledge of physiology and the concept of homeostasis there need be no problem. Whether we are concerned with the maintenance between set limits of blood pressure, of body temperature, or any other of a multitude of physiological measures, the concept necessary to explain the data is that of a *physiological* control system, which is conceived as an organisation situated within the CNS and operating in accordance with the principles outlined earlier in this book.

In proposing the concept of a *behavioural* control system to account for the way a child maintains his relation to his attachment figure between certain limits of distance or accessibility, no more is done than to use these well-understood principles to account for a different form of homeostasis, namely one in which the set-limits concern the organism's relation to features of the environment and in which the limits are maintained by behavioural rather than physiological means. The maintenance of a child within certain set limits in relation to an attachment figure is, of course, one example only of what can be called environmental homeostasis. Other examples, already referred to in Chapter 5, include maintenance of a brooding bird within set distance of nest and eggs, or of any animal within its environment of adaptedness.

Once the concept of a behavioural control system has been grasped, it will be realised that the particular forms of behaviour that are employed to maintain the organism within whatever limits are set are of secondary importance, merely alternative means towards a specified end. Whether a child moves towards a mother by running, walking, crawling, shuffling or, in the case of a thalidomide child, by rolling is thus of very little consequence compared to the set-goal of his locomotion, namely proximity to mother. Since the methods of locomotion are alternatives of one another, there need be no surprise that they are not positively correlated, as those who think in terms of stimulus-response theory have mistakenly assumed attachment theory must predict. The ill-founded criticism of the theory to which this assumption has led has been well answered by Sroufe and Waters (1977).

By proposing that a child's attachment behaviour is controlled by a behavioural system conceived as an organisation existing within the child, attention shifts from the behaviour itself to the organisation that controls it. This organisation, conceived as a permanent, indeed a central, feature of the child's personality, is never idle—a point emphasised by Bretherton (1980) in a most valuable contribution.[1] In order for a control system to perform its function effectively it must be equipped with sensors to keep it informed of relevant events, and these events it must continuously monitor and appraise. In the case of an attachment control system the events being monitored and appraised fall into two classes: those which indicate the presence of potential danger or stress (internal or external), and those concerning the whereabouts and accessibility of the attachment figure. In the light of certain of these appraisals, experienced as feeling uneasy, unwell, insecure, anxious or possibly terrified, action to increase proximity is called for. The particular actions suitable to the circumstances are then decided upon and continue until such time as the system's sensors indicate that the child's situation has changed appropriately, experienced by him as feeling comforted and secure.

In reaching the decision to utilise certain actions rather than others the attachment system is conceived as drawing on the symbolic representations, or working models, of the attachment figure, the general environment and the self, which are already stored and available to the system. It is by postulating the existence of these cognitive components and their utilisation by the attachment system that the theory is enabled to provide explanations of how a child's experiences with attachment figures come to influence in particular ways the pattern of

---

[1] In her article Inge Bretherton elaborates ideas that were only half formulated in the first edition of this work and illustrates them with a block diagram of how a control system of the kind proposed might be organised.

attachment he develops.

In thus postulating the existence of an internal organisation with a number of highly specific features, the theory proposed can be seen as having the same basic properties as those that characterise all the various forms of structural theory, of which psychoanalysis is one and Piagetian theory another, and that differentiate them from behaviourism in its many forms. It is, moreover, these structural properties that enable the theory to be extended, as for example in Chapter 4 of Volume 3, so that it takes into account, and offers explanations of, the various defensive processes, beliefs and activities that, since Freud's earliest papers (1894, 1896), have been at the centre of psycho-analytic interest.

Proximity-keeping behaviour of other kinds

Another matter dealt with insufficiently in the first edition and which has given rise to misunderstanding is the distinction that must be drawn between attachment behaviour and any other form of behaviour that entails an individual attaining or maintaining proximity to a particular other. For example, a child will often seek proximity to a playmate, just as an adult will seek proximity to a companion whose interests he shares. In neither case would such proximity keeping count as attachment behaviour. Nor when an exuberant child approaches his mother asking for a game would that be classifiable as attachment behaviour. Bretherton (1980) is correct when she points out that what I had in mind when defining attachment behaviour was the output of what might be called a safety-regulating system, namely a system the activities of which tend to reduce the risk of the individual coming to harm and are experienced as causing anxiety to be allayed and a sense of security to be increased.

Thus it is inaccurate to describe attachment behaviour solely in terms of attaining and maintaining proximity to a particular individual. This, however, need not give rise to difficulty since there are a number of criteria which serve to distinguish proximity promoting behaviour that is part of the output of the attachment system from similar behaviour which is part of the output of some other system. Almost always it would be elicited in, and terminated by, situations of different kinds, it would be embedded in sequences of behaviour of a different sort, engaged in in a different mood and accompanied by the expression of different affect. Only rarely I believe would the judgment be in doubt.

In defining attachment behaviour as the output of a safety-regulating system emphasis is placed on the important biological function attributed to it, namely that of protecting the mobile infant and growing child from a number of dangers, amongst which in man's environment of evolutionary adaptedness the danger of predation is likely to have been paramount. To an ethologist a proposal of this kind is obvious enough. To clinicians and developmental psychologists, however, unused to distinguishing cause and function and unused also to thinking in evolutionary terms, not only has the proposal come as strange but it has sometimes appeared to be of little practical relevance.

A principal reason why I, by contrast, emphasise this aspect of attachment theory is that on whether we attribute a useful biological function to attachment behaviour or regard it as an irrelevant, infantile characteristic, as has been the tradition of secondary-drive dependency theories, turns our whole approach to our fellow humans.

When the attachment to a preferred person of an infant, a child or an adult is viewed in the way proposed, the ensuing behaviour is likely to be respected as being as intrinsic to human nature as are, say, sexual behaviour or eating behaviour. As a result, when a clinician meets with an individual who is responding to separation or loss with various mixtures of protest, anger, anxiety or despair, he is likely to recognise the behaviour as made up of the natural, even if perhaps inconvenient, responses that any human being would be expected to show in the type of situation that the individual concerned is in. The clinician is likely then to take relevant action of whatever kind lies within his power.

When, however, attachment behaviour and responses to separation and loss are viewed in terms of one or another of the learning theories, the scene looks very different. When a baby has been recently fed, crying is seen as merely demanding attention and picking him up as likely to result in his crying more. When a child is protesting loss of his principal attachment figure and is demanding her return, he is regarded as having been spoilt. An adolescent or adult who is apprehensive lest he be deserted by his attachment figure is regarded as over-dependent, hysterical or phobic. The clinician's actions are likely then to be as disapproving as they are irrelevant. It was in fact considerations of these kinds that led me to question the relevance to clinical problems of any of the traditional forms of learning theory and to adopt an ethological approach as the one best fitted to help understand the clinical phenomena with which every psychiatrist is faced, whether he works with children, with adolescents or with adults.

One objection, raised by Rajecki and others in a review article (1978), to the proposal that attachment behaviour serves a protective function is that the behaviour is sometimes directed towards objects that afford no protection, such as a dummy mother in the case of monkeys or a favourite blanket or toy in the case of humans. This, however, is not an objection of substance. When the conditions in which a young animal is reared deviate from the norm it is not unusual for behaviour to be directed towards inappropriate objects. For example, sexual behaviour may be directed towards a member of the same sex, towards a member of another species, or towards a fetish. Yet no one would dream of suggesting that, because in these cases the behaviour fails to result in reproduction, sexual behaviour itself is without that function.

Attachment-caregiving: one type of social bond

In this volume attention is focussed on one special type of social relationship, that of attachment to a caregiver. Since there is a tendency to extend the use of the word 'attachment' to several other relationships, it is desirable to specify more exactly how it is being used here.

Following Hinde (1979) and Bretherton (1980), a social relationship can be said to exist between two individuals when each partner has constructed programmes of dyadic interaction that are shared with the other. Such relationships take many forms. For example, they differ on the type of principal shared programme and on whether the parts played in it by each partner are similar or complementary, on the number of different shared programmes, on how well meshed each of the programmes is, on how idiosyncratic they are, and on how long they are expected to continue. Thus, there are many relationships, such as buying goods from a shopkeeper, that are likely to be restricted in scope and fleeting in time; others, such as a working relationship, may be more extensive and/or more prolonged; yet others, such as a family relationship, may include not only a broad range of shared programmes but also a commitment by each partner to continue the relationship indefinitely. The term 'social bond', because it implies some sort of binding engagement, is applicable only to those few social relationships to which both parties are committed.

Parent-child relationships, unless aborted by death or adoption, are commonly assumed by society as well as felt by the partners to be committed ones; although, until a child has some concept of the future, commitment on his side is no more than an assumption made by his parents.

Like many other sorts of social relationship, the parent-child relationship is a complementary one. Thus, the behaviour of a mother is usually quite different to that of her child. Nevertheless, in the ordinary course of events the behaviour of the one is the complement of that of the other. This brings us back to attachment.

In this volume we have been examining one half only of what is normally a shared dyadic programme, the other half being maternal caregiving. Since a bond is a property of two parties, the bond with which we are concerned should be designated as one of attachment-caregiving.[1]

There is a strong case, based on the usage of the past twenty years, for restricting the term attachment to the behaviour typical of child to parent and the behavioural system responsible for it, and to avoid using it to describe the complementary behaviour and behavioural system of the parent. Adopting this convention both parties can be said to be bonded. Attachment is then limited to behaviour normally directed towards someone conceived as better able to cope with the current situation; whilst caregiving specifies the complementary behaviour directed towards someone conceived as less able to do so. In most attachment-caregiver relationships, and notably those of child and parent, the roles of the partners do not change. Nevertheless continuity of role is not inevitable. In marriages, for example, changes of role are probably common and healthy; role change can occur also when a grown-up son or daughter cares for a parent in old age. By contrast, the reversal of roles between child, or adolescent, and parent, unless very temporary, is almost always not only a sign of pathology in the parent but a cause of it in the child (see Volume 2, Chapters 16, 18; Volume 3, Chapters 11, 12, 19).

The study of caregiving as a behavioural system, differing somewhat between mothers and fathers (Lamb, 1977), is an

---

[1] Hinde (1979) draws attention to the mistake of applying the term 'attachment' not only to the behavioural system within the child but also to the social bond he makes with his mother.

enterprise calling for attention. Elsewhere (Bowlby, 1982) I suggest it will be fruitful to study its development within a conceptual framework similar to that adopted here for the development of attachment behaviour, namely as the product of interaction between a strong genetic bias to develop certain types of behaviour and the particular sequence of environments, from infancy onwards, within which development takes place.

One further point needs to be emphasised. A mother–child relationship, or a father–child relationship, contains more than one shared dyadic programme. There is, for example, a feeding-fed shared programme in which the behaviour of one partner commonly meshes in a complementary way with that of the other. Another type of shared programme is that of playmates in which the parts played by the partners are often, at least ostensibly, similar. Yet another type, complementary again, is that of learner–teacher. Thus, a parent–child relationship is by no means exclusively that of attachment-caregiving. The only justification, therefore, for referring to the bond between a child and his mother in this way is that the shared dyadic programme given top priority is one of attachment-caregiving.

*   *   *

In conclusion let me outline the picture of personality development proposed. A young child's experience of an encouraging, supportive and co-operative mother, and a little later father, gives him a sense of worth, a belief in the helpfulness of others, and a favourable model on which to build future relationships. Furthermore, by enabling him to explore his environment with confidence and to deal with it effectively, such experience also promotes his sense of competence. Thenceforward, provided family relationships continue favourable, not only do these early patterns of thought, feeling and behaviour persist, but personality becomes increasingly structured to operate in moderately controlled and resilient ways, and increasingly capable of continuing so despite adverse circumstances. Other types of early childhood and later experience have effects of other kinds, leading usually to personality structures of lowered resilience and defective control, vulnerable structures which also are apt to persist. Thereafter on how someone's personality has come to be structured turns his way of responding to subsequent adverse events, among which rejections, separations and losses are some of the most important.

References

Ahrens, R. (1954). 'Beitrag zur Entwicklung des Physiognomie- und Mimikerkennens.' *Z. exp. angew. Psychol.*, **2**, 3, 412–54.

Ainsworth, M. D. (1962). 'The effects of maternal deprivation: a review of findings and controversy in the context of research strategy.' In *Deprivation of Maternal Care: A Reassessment of its Effects*. Public Health Papers No. 14. Geneva: WHO.

Ainsworth, M. D. (1963). 'The development of infant–mother interaction among the Ganda.' In *Determinants of Infant Behaviour*, Vol. 2, ed. B. M. Foss. London: Methuen; New York: Wiley.

Ainsworth, M. D. (1964). 'Patterns of attachment behaviour shown by the infant in interaction with his mother.' *Merrill-Palmer Q.*, **10**, 51–8.

Ainsworth, M. D. S. (1967). *Infancy in Uganda: Infant Care and the Growth of Attachment*. Baltimore, Md: The Johns Hopkins Press.

Ainsworth, M. D. S. (1969). 'Object relations, dependency and attachment: a theoretical review of the infant–mother relationship.' *Child Development*, **40**, 969–1025.

Ainsworth, M. D. S. (1972). 'Attachment and Dependency: A Comparison.' In J. L. Gewirtz (ed.), *Attachment and Dependence*. Washington, D.C.: Winston (distributed by Wiley, New York).

Ainsworth, M. D. S. (1973). 'The development of infant–mother attachment'. In *Child Development and Social Policy (Review of Child Development Research*, Vol. 3), ed. B. M. Caldwell and H. N. Ricciuti. Chicago: University of Chicago Press.

Ainsworth, M. D. S. (1982). 'Attachment: retrospect and prospect.' In *The Place of Attachment in Human Behavior*, ed. C. M. Parkes and J. Stevenson-Hinde. New York: Basic Books, London: Tavistock Pubns.

Ainsworth, M. D. S., and Bell, S. M. (1969). 'Some contemporary patterns of mother–infant interaction in the feeding situation.' In *Stimulation in Early Infancy*, ed. J. A. Ambrose, New York and London: Academic Press.

Ainsworth, M. D., Blehar, M. C., Waters, E., and Wall, S. (1978). *Patterns of Attachment: Assessed in the Strange Situation and at Home*. Hillsdale, N.J.: Lawrence Erlbaum.

Ainsworth, M. D., and Boston, M. (1952). 'Psychodiagnostic assessments of a child after prolonged separation in early childhood.' *Br. J. med. Psychol.*, **25**, 169–201.

Ainsworth, M. D., and Bowlby, J. (1954). 'Research strategy in the study of mother–child separation.' *Courr. Cent. int. Enf.*, **4**, 105.

Ainsworth, M. D. Salter, and Wittig, B. A. (1969). 'Attachment and exploratory behaviour of one-year-olds in a strange situation.' In *Determinants of Infant Behaviour*, Vol. 4, ed. B. M. Foss. London: Methuen; New York: Barnes & Noble.

REFERENCES

Altmann, J. (1980). *Baboon Mothers and Infants*. Cambridge, Mass.: Harvard University Press.

Altmann, J., Altmann, S. A., Hausfater, G., and McCluskey, S. A. (1977). 'Life history of yellow baboons: physical development, reproductive parameters, and infant mortality.' *Primates*, **18**, 315–30.

Ambrose, J. A. (1960). 'The smiling and related responses in early human infancy: an experimental and theoretical study of their course and significance.' Ph.D. Thesis, University of London.

Ambrose, J. A. (1961). 'The development of the smiling response in early infancy.' In *Determinants of Infant Behaviour*, Vol. 1, ed. B. M. Foss. London: Methuen; New York: Wiley.

Ambrose, J. A. (1963). 'The concept of a critical period for the development of social responsiveness.' In *Determinants of Infant Behaviour*, Vol. 2, ed. B. M. Foss. London: Methuen; New York: Wiley.

Ambrose, A. (1969). Contribution to discussion in *Stimulation in early infancy*, pp. 103–4, ed. A. Ambrose. New York and London: Academic Press.

Anderson, J. W. (1972). 'Attachment behaviour out of doors.' In *Ethological Studies of Child Behaviour*, ed. N. Blurton Jones. Cambridge: Cambridge University Press.

Andrew, R. J. (1964). 'The development of adult responses from responses given during imprinting by the domestic chick.' *Anim. Behav.*, **12**, 542–8.

Appell, G., and David, M. (1961). 'Case-notes on Monique.' In *Determinants of Infant Behaviour*, Vol. 1, ed. B. M. Foss. London. Methuen; New York: Wiley.

Appell, G., and David, M. (1965). 'A study of mother–child interaction at thirteen months.' In *Determinants of Infant Behaviour*, Vol. 3, ed. B. M. Foss. London: Methuen; New York: Wiley.

Appell, G., and Roudinesco, J. (1951). Film: *Maternal Deprivation in Young Children* (16mm; 30 mins; sound). London: Tavistock Child Development Research Unit; New York: New York University Film Library.

Arend, R. A., Gove, F. L., and Sroufe, L. A. (1979). 'Continuity of individual adaptation from infancy to kindergarten: a predictive study of ego-resiliency and curiosity in pre-schoolers.' *Child Development*, **50**, 950–59.

Arnold, M. B. (1960). *Emotion and Personality*. Vol. 1, *Psychological Aspects*; Vol. 2, *Neurological and Physiological Aspects*. New York: Columbia University Press; London: Cassell, 1961.

Aubry, J. (1955). *La Carence des soins maternels*. Paris: Presses Universitaires de France.

Balint, A. (1939). *Int. Z. Psychoanal. u. Imago*, **24**, 33–48. Eng. trans. (1949): 'Love for the mother and mother love.' *Int. J. Psycho-Anal.*, **30**, 251–9. Reprinted in *Primary Love and Psycho-analytic Technique*. London: Tavistock Publications, 1964; New York: Liveright, 1965.

Bateson, P. P. G. (1966). 'The characteristics and context of imprinting.' *Biol. Rev.*, **41**, 177–220.

Bayliss, L. E. (1966). *Living Control Systems*. London: English Universities Press; San Francisco: Freeman.

REFERENCES

Beach, F. A. (ed.) (1965). *Sex and Behavior*. New York and London: Wiley.

Benedek, T. (1938). 'Adaptation to reality in early infancy.' *Psychoanal. Q.*, **7**, 200–15.

Benedek, T. (1956). 'Toward the biology of the depressive constellation.' *J. Am. psychoanal. Ass.*, **4**, 389–427.

Benjamin, J. D. (1963). 'Further comments on some developmental aspects of anxiety.' In *Counterpoint*, ed. H. S. Gaskill. New York: International Universities Press.

Berenstein, L., Rodman, P. S., and Smith, D. G. (1982). 'Social relations between fathers and offspring in a captive group of rhesus monkeys (Macaca mulatta). *Animal Behaviour*, **30**.

Berlyne, D. E. (1958). 'The influence of the albedo and complexity of stimuli on visual fixation in the human infant.' *Br. J. Psychol.*, **49**, 315–18.

Berlyne, D. E. (1960). *Conflict, Arousal and Curiosity*. New York and London: McGraw-Hill.

Bernfeld, S. (1944). 'Freud's earliest theories and the school of Helmholtz.' *Psychoanal. Q.*, **13**, 341–62.

Bernfeld, S. (1949). 'Freud's scientific beginnings.' *Am. Imago*, **6**.

Bettelheim, B. (1967). *The Empty Fortress: Infantile Autism and the Birth of the Self*. New York: The Free Press; London: Collier/Macmillan.

Bielicka, I., and Olechnowicz, H. (1963). 'Treating children traumatized by hospitalization.' *Children*, **10** (5), 194–5.

Bischof, N. (1975). 'A systems approach toward the functional connections of fear and attachment.' *Child Development*, **46**, 801–17.

Bishop, B. Merrill (1951). 'Mother–child interaction and the social behavior of children.' *Psychol. Monogr.*, **65**, No. 11.

Bishop, G. H. (1960). 'Feedback through the environment as an analog of brain functioning.' In *Self-organizing Systems*, ed. M. C. Yovits and S. Cameron. Oxford: Pergamon.

Blauvelt, H., and McKenna, J. (1961). 'Mother–neonate interaction: capacity of the human newborn for orientation.' In *Determinants of Infant Behaviour*, Vol. 1, ed. B. M. Foss. London: Methuen; New York: Wiley.

Block, J. H., and Block, J. (1980). 'The role of ego-control and ego-resiliency in the organization of behavior.' In *Minnesota symposium on child psychology*, Vol. 13, pp. 39–101, ed. W. A. Collins. Hillsdale, N.J.: Lawrence Erlbaum.

Bolwig, N. (1963). 'Bringing up a young monkey.' *Behaviour*, **21**, 300–30.

Boniface, D. and Graham, P. (1979). 'The three year old and his attachment to a special soft object.' *J. Child Psychol. Psychiat.*, **20**, 217–24.

Bower, T. G. R. (1966). 'The visual world of infants.' *Scient. Am.*, **215**, December, 80–97.

Bowlby, J. (1951). *Maternal Care and Mental Health*. Geneva: WHO; London: HMSO; New York: Columbia University Press. Abridged version, *Child Care and the Growth of Love*. Harmondsworth: Penguin Books, 2nd edn, 1965.

Bowlby, J. (1953). 'Some pathological processes set in train by early mother–child separation.' *J. ment. Sci.*, **99**, 265–72.

REFERENCES

Bowlby, J. (1958). 'The nature of the child's tie to his mother.' *Int. J. Psycho-Anal.*, **39**, 350–73.

Bowlby, J. (1960a). 'Separation anxiety.' *Int. J. Psycho-Anal.*, **41**, 89–113.

Bowlby, J. (1960b). 'Grief and mourning in infancy and early childhood.' *Psychoanal. Study Child*, **15**, 9–52.

Bowlby, J. (1961a). 'Separation anxiety: a critical review of the literature.' *J. Child Psychol. Psychiat.*, **1**, 251–69.

Bowlby, J. (1961b). 'Processes of mourning.' *Int. J. Psycho-Anal.*, **42**, 317–40.

Bowlby, J. (1963). 'Pathological mourning and childhood mourning.' *J. Am. psychoanal. Ass.*, **11**, 500–41.

Bowlby, J. (1964). 'Note on Dr Lois Murphy's paper, "Some aspects of the first relationship".' *Int. J. Psycho-Anal.*, **45**, 44–6.

Bowlby, J. (1982). 'Caring for children: some influences on its development.' In *Parenthood*, ed. R. S. Cohen, S. H. Weissman, and B. J. Cohler, New York: The Guilford Press.

Bowlby, J., Robertson, J., and Rosenbluth, D. (1952). 'A two-year-old goes to hospital.' *Psychoanal. Study Child*, **7**, 82–94.

Brackbill, Y. (1958). 'Extinction of the smiling response in infants as a function of reinforcement schedule.' *Child Dev.*, **29**, 115–24.

Brazelton, T. B., Koslowski, B. and Main, M. (1974). 'The origins of reciprocity in mother–infant interaction.' In *The Effect of the Infant on its Caregiver*, ed. M. Lewis and L. A. Rosenblum. New York: Wiley-Interscience.

Bretherton, I. (1980). 'Young children in stressful situations: the supporting role of attachment figures and unfamiliar caregivers.' In *Uprooting and Development*, ed. G. V. Coelho and P. J. Ahmen. New York: Plenum Press.

Bretherton, I. and Beeghly-Smith, M. (in press). 'Talking about internal states: the acquisition of an explicit theory of mind.' *Developm. Psychol.*

Brody, S. (1956). *Patterns of Mothering: Maternal Influence during Infancy*. New York: International Universities Press; London: Bailey & Swinfen.

Bronson, G. (1965). 'The hierarchical organization of the central nervous system: implication for learning processes and critical periods in early development.' *Behav. Sci.*, **10**, 7–25.

Burlingham, D., and Freud, A. (1942). *Young Children in War-time*. London: Allen & Unwin.

Burlingham, D., and Freud, A. (1944). *Infants without Families*. London: Allen & Unwin.

Cairns, R. B. (1966a). 'Attachment behavior of mammals.' *Psychol. Rev.*, **73**, 409–26.

Cairns, R. B. (1966b). 'Development, maintenance, and extinction of social attachment behavior in sheep.' *J. comp. physiol. Psychol.*, **62**, 298–306.

Cairns, R. B., and Johnson, D. L. (1965). 'The development of interspecies social preferences.' *Psychonomic Sci.*, **2**, 337–8.

Caldwell, B. M. (1962). 'The usefulness of the critical period hypothesis in the study of filiative behavior.' *Merrill-Palmer Q.*, **8**, 229–42.

Caldwell, B. M. (1964). 'The effects of infant care.' In *Review of Child*

REFERENCES

Development Research, Vol. 1, ed. M. L. Hoffman and L. N. W. Hoffman. New York: Russell Sage Foundation.

Call, J. D. (1964). 'Newborn approach behavior and early ego development.' *Int. J. Psycho-Anal.*, **45**, 286–94.

Casler, L. (1961). 'Maternal deprivation: a critical review of the literature.' *Monogr. Soc. Res. Child Dev.*, **26**, 1–64.

Chance, M. R. A. (1959). 'What makes monkeys sociable?' *New Scient.*, 5 March.

Cohen, L. B., DeLoache, J. S., and Strauss, M. S. (1979). 'Infant visual perception.' In *Handbook of Infant Development*, ed. J. D. Osofsky, pp. 393–438. New York: Wiley.

Connell, D. B. (1976). 'Individual differences in attachment: an investigation into stability implications and relationships to structure of early language development.' Doctoral thesis, Syracuse University.

Darwin, C. (1859). *On the Origin of Species by means of Natural Selection.* London: John Murray.

Darwin, C. (1872). *The Expression of the Emotions in Man and Animals.* London: John Murray.

David, M., Ancellin, J., and Appell, G. (1957). 'Étude d'un groupe d'enfants ayant séjourné pendant un mois en colonie maternelle.' *Infs.-sociales.*, **8**, 825–93.

David, M., and Appell, G. (1966). 'La relation mère-enfant: Étude de cinq "pattern" d'interaction entre mère et enfant à l'âge d'un an.' *Psychiat. Enfant*, **9**, 445–531.

David, M., and Appell, G. (1969). 'Mother–child relation.' In *Modern Perspectives in International Child Psychiatry*, ed. J. G. Howells. Edinburgh: Oliver & Boyd.

David, M., Nicolas, J., and Roudinesco, J. (1952). 'Responses of young children to separation from their mothers: I. Observations of children aged 12–17 months recently separated from their families and living in an institution.' *Courr. Cent. int. Enf.*, **2**, 66–78.

Dawkins, R. (1976). *The Selfish Gene.* Oxford: Oxford University Press.

Décarie, T. Gouin (1965). *Intelligence and Affectivity in Early Childhood.* New York: International Universities Press.

Décarie, T. Gouin (1969). 'A study of the mental and emotional development of the thalidomide child.' In *Determinants of Infant Behaviour*, Vol. 4, ed. B. M. Foss. London: Methuen; New York: Barnes & Noble.

Decasper, A. J., and Fifer, W. P. (1980). 'Of human bonding: newborns prefer their mothers' voices.' *Science*, **208**, 1174–76.

Denny-Brown, D. (1950). 'Disintegration of motor function resulting from cerebral lesions.' *J. nerv. ment. Dis.*, **112**, No. 1.

Denny-Brown, D. (1958). 'The nature of apraxia.' *J. nerv. ment. Dis.*, **126**, No. 1.

Deutsch, H. (1919). Eng. trans.: 'A two-year-old boy's first love comes to grief.' In *Dynamic Psychopathology in Childhood*, ed. L. Jessner and E. Pavenstedt. New York and London: Grune & Stratton, 1959.

DeVore, I. (1963). 'Mother–infant relations in free-ranging baboons.' In

Maternal Behavior in Mammals, ed. H. L. Rheingold. New York and London: Wiley.

DeVore, I. (ed.) (1965). *Primate Behavior: Field Studies of Monkeys and Apes*. New York and London: Holt, Rinehart & Winston.

DeVore, I., and Hall, K. R. L. (1965). 'Baboon ecology.' In *Primate Behavior*, ed. I. DeVore. New York and London: Holt, Rinehart & Winston.

Dollard, J., and Miller, N. E. (1950). *Personality and Psychotherapy*. New York: McGraw-Hill.

Dunn, J. F. (1979). 'The first year of life: continuity in individual differences.' In *The First Year of Life*, ed. D. Shaffer and J. Dunn. London: Wiley.

Egeland, B., and Sroufe, L. A. (1981). 'Attachment and early maltreatment.' *Child Development*, 52, 44–52.

Erikson, E. H. (1950). *Childhood and Society*. New York: Norton; London: Imago, 1951. Revised edn, New York: Norton, 1963; London: Hogarth, 1965; Harmondsworth: Penguin Books, 1965.

Ezriel, H. (1951). 'The scientific testing of psycho-analytic findings and theory: the psycho-analytic session as an experimental situation.' *Br. J. med. Psychol.*, 24, 30–4.

Fabricius, E. (1962). 'Some aspects of imprinting in birds.' *Symp. zool. Soc. Lond.*, No. 8, 139–48.

Fagin, C. M. R. N. (1966). *The Effects of Maternal Attendance during Hospitalization on the Post-hospital Behavior of Young Children: A Comparative Study*. Philadelphia: F. A. Davis.

Fairbairn, W. R. D. (1952). *Psychoanalytic Studies of the Personality*. London: Tavistock/Routledge. Published under the title of *Object-Relations Theory of the Personality*. New York: Basic Books, 1954.

Fantz, R. L. (1965). 'Ontogeny of perception.' In *Behavior of Non-human Primates*, Vol. 2, ed. A. M. Schrier, H. F. Harlow, and F. Stollnitz. New York and London: Academic Press.

Fantz, R. L. (1966). 'Pattern discrimination and selective attention as determinants of perceptual development from birth.' In *Perceptual Development in Children*, ed. A. J. Kidd and J. L. Rivoire. New York: International Universities Press; London: University of London Press.

Flavell, J. H. (1961). 'The ontogenetic development of verbal communication skills.' Final Progress Report (NIMH Grant M2268).

Flavell, J. H. (1963). *The Developmental Psychology of Jean Piaget*. Princeton, N.J., and London: Van Nostrand.

Formby, D. (1967). 'Maternal recognition of infant's cry.' *Dev. Med. Child Neurol.*, 9, 293–8.

Fossey, D. (1979). 'Development of the mountain gorilla (Gorilla gorilla berengei): the first thirty-six months.' In *The Great Apes*, ed. D. A. Hamburg and E. R. McCown. Menlo Park, Calif.: Benjamin/Cummings Pub. Co.

Fox, R. (1967). *Kinship and Marriage*. Harmondsworth: Penguin Books.

REFERENCES

Freedman, D. G. (1961). 'The infant's fear of strangers and the flight response.' *J. Child Psychol. Psychiat.*, **2**, 242–8.

Freedman, D. G. (1964). 'Smiling in blind infants and the issue of innate versus acquired.' *J. Child Psychol. Psychiat.*, **5**, 171–84.

Freedman, D. G. (1965). 'Hereditary control of early social behavior.' In *Determinants of Infant Behaviour*, Vol. 3, ed. B. M. Foss. London: Methuen; New York: Wiley.

Freedman, D. G., and Keller, B. (1963). 'Inheritance of behavior in infants.' *Science*, **140**, 196–8.

Freud, A., and Dann, S. (1951). 'An experiment in group upbringing.' *Psychoanal. Study Child*, **6**, 127–68.

Freud, S. (1894). 'The neuro-psychoses of defence (1).' *S.E.*, **3**.[1]

Freud, S. (1895). *Project for a Scientific Psychology. S.E.*, **1**.

Freud, S. (1896). 'Further remarks on the neuro-psychoses of defence.' *S.E.*, **3**.

Freud, S. (1900). *The Interpretation of Dreams. S.E.*, **4**.

Freud, S. (1905). *Three Essays on the Theory of Sexuality. S.E.*, **7**.

Freud, S. (1910). *Five Lectures on Psycho-analysis. S.E.*, **11**.

Freud, S. (1914). 'On narcissism: an introduction.' *S.E.*, **14**.

Freud, S. (1915a). 'Instincts and their vicissitudes.' *S.E.*, **14**.

Freud, S. (1915b). 'Repression.' *S.E.*, **14**.

Freud, S. (1920a). *Beyond the Pleasure Principle. S.E.*, **18**.

Freud, S. (1920b). 'The psychogenesis of a case of homosexuality in a woman.' *S.E.*, **18**.

Freud, S. (1921). *Group Psychology and the Analysis of the Ego. S.E.*, **18**.

Freud, S. (1922). 'Psycho-analysis.' *S.E.*, **18**.

Freud, S. (1925). *An Autobiographical Study. S.E.*, **20**.

Freud, S. (1926). *Inhibitions, Symptoms and Anxiety. S.E.*, **20**.

Freud, S. (1931). 'Female sexuality.' *S.E.*, **21**.

Freud, S. (1939). *Moses and Monotheism. S.E.*, **23**.

Freud, S. (1940). *An Outline of Psycho-analysis. S.E.*, **23**.

Frommer, E. A., and O'Shea, G. (1973). 'Antenatal identification of women liable to have problems in managing their infants.' *British J. Psychiatry*, **123**, 149–56.

Fuller, J. L., and Clark, L. D. (1966a). 'Genetic and treatment factors modifying the post-isolation syndrome in dogs.' *J. comp. physiol. Psychol.*, **61**, 251–7.

Fuller, J. L., and Clark, L. D. (1966b). 'Effects of rearing with specific stimuli upon post-isolation behavior in dogs.' *J. comp. physiol. Psychol.*, **61**, 258–63.

Géber, M. (1956). 'Développement psycho-moteur de l'enfant Africain.' *Courr Cent. int. Enf.*, **6**, 17–28.

[1] The abbreviation *S.E.* in this list of references and in the text denotes the Standard Edition of *The Complete Psychological Works of Sigmund Freud*, published in 24 volumes by the Hogarth Press Ltd, London. All quotations from Freud in the present work are taken from this edition.

REFERENCES

George, C., and Main, M. (1979). 'Social interactions of young abused children: approach, avoidance and aggression.' *Child Development*, **50**, 306–18.

Gesell, A. (ed.) (1940). *The First Five Years of Life*. New York: Harper; London: Methuen, 1941.

Gewirtz, H. B., and Gewirtz, J. L. (1968). 'Visiting and caretaking patterns for kibbutz infants: age and sex trends.' *Am. J. Ortho-psychiat.*, **38**, 427–43.

Gewirtz, J. L. (1961). 'A learning analysis of the effects of normal stimulation, privation and deprivation on the acquisition of social motivation and attachment.' In *Determinants of Infant Behaviour*, Vol. 1, ed. B. M. Foss. London: Methuen; New York: Wiley.

Goldman, S. (1960). 'Further consideration of cybernetic aspects of homeostasis.' In *Self-organizing Systems*, ed. M. C. Yovits and S. Cameron. Oxford: Pergamon.

Goodall, J. (1965). 'Chimpanzees of the Gombe Stream Reserve.' In *Primate Behavior*, ed. I. DeVore. New York and London: Holt, Rinehart & Winston.

Goodall, J. (van Lawick-) (1975). 'The behaviour of the chimpanzee.' In *Hominisation und Verhalten*, ed. I. Eibl-Eibesfeld, pp. 74–136. Stuttgart: Gustav Fischer Verlag.

Gooddy, W. (1949). 'Sensation and volition.' *Brain*, **72**, 312–39.

Gordon, T., and Foss, B. M. (1966). 'The role of stimulation in the delay of onset of crying in the newborn infant.' *Q. J. expl. Psychol.*, **18**, 79–81.

Gough, D. (1962). 'The visual behaviour of infants during the first few weeks of life.' *Proc. R. Soc. Med.*, **55**, 308–10.

Gray, P. H. (1958). 'Theory and evidence of imprinting in human infants.' *J. Psychol.*, **46**, 155–66.

Griffin, G. A., and Harlow, H. F. (1966). 'Effects of three months of total social deprivation on social adjustment and learning in the rhesus monkey.' *Child Dev.*, **37**, 533–48.

Grodins, F. S. (1963). *Control Theory and Biological Systems*. New York: Columbia University Press.

Gunther, M. (1961). 'Infant behaviour at the breast.' In *Determinants of Infant Behaviour*, Vol. 1, ed. B. M. Foss. London: Methuen, New York: Wiley.

Haddow, A. J. (1952). 'Field and laboratory studies on an African monkey, *Cercopithecus ascanius schmidti* Matschie.' *Proc. zool. Soc. Lond.*, **122**, 297–394.

Haldane, J. S. (1936). *Organism and Environment as Illustrated by the Physiology of Breathing*. New Haven, Conn.: Yale University Press.

Hall, K. R. L., and DeVore, I. (1965). 'Baboon social behavior.' In *Primate Behavior*, ed. I. DeVore. New York and London: Holt, Rinehart & Winston.

Halverson, H. M. (1937). 'Studies of the grasping responses of early infancy.' *J. genet. Psychol.*, **51**, 371–449.

Hamburg, D. A. (1963). 'Emotions in the perspective of human evolution.' In *Expression of the Emotions in Man*, ed. P. Knapp. New York: International Universities Press.

Hamburg, D. A., Sabshin, M. A., Board, F. A., Grinker, R. R., Korchin, S. J., Basowitz, H., Heath, H., and Persky, H. (1958). 'Classification and rating of emotional experiences.' *Archs. Neurol. Psychiat.*, **79**, 415–26.

Hampshire, S. (1962). 'Disposition and memory.' *Int. J. Psycho-Anal.*, **43**, 59–68.

Harcourt, A. (1979). 'The social relations and group structure of wild Mountain gorillas.' In *The Great Apes*, ed. D. A. Hamburg and E. R. McCown. Menlo Park, Calif.: Benjamin/Cummings Publ. Co.

Harlow, H. F. (1958). 'The nature of love.' *Am. Psychol.*, **13**, 673–85.

Harlow, H. F. (1961). 'The development of affectional patterns in infant monkeys.' In *Determinants of Infant Behaviour*, Vol. 1, ed. B. M. Foss. London: Methuen; New York: Wiley.

Harlow, H. F., and Harlow, M. K. (1962). 'Social deprivation in monkeys.' *Scient. Am.*, **207** (5), 136.

Harlow, H. F., and Harlow, M. K. (1965). 'The affectional systems.' In *Behavior of Nonhuman Primates*, Vol. 2, ed. A. M. Schrier, H. F. Harlow, and F. Stollnitz. New York and London: Academic Press.

Harlow, H. F., and Zimmermann, R. R. (1959). 'Affectional responses in the infant monkey.' *Science*, **130**, 421.

Hartmann, H. (1939, Eng. trans. 1958). *Ego Psychology and the Problem of Adaptation*. London: Imago; New York: International Universities Press.

Hayes, C. (1951). *The Ape in Our House*. New York: Harper; London: Gollancz, 1952.

Hebb, D. O. (1946a). 'Emotion in man and animal: an analysis of the intuitive processes of recognition.' *Psychol. Rev.*, **53**, 88–106.

Hebb, D. O. (1946b). 'On the nature of fear.' *Psychol. Rev.*, **53**, 250–75.

Hediger, H. (1955). *Studies of the Psychology and Behaviour of Captive Animals in Zoos and Circuses*. London: Butterworth; New York: Criterion Books, 1956.

Heinicke, C. (1956). 'Some effects of separating two-year-old children from their parents: a comparative study.' *Hum. Relat.*, **9**, 105–76.

Heinicke, C., and Westheimer, I. (1966). *Brief Separations*. New York: International Universities Press; London: Longmans Green.

Held, R. (1965). 'Plasticity in sensori-motor systems.' *Scient. Am.*, **213** (5), 84–94.

Hersher, L., Moore, A. U., and Richmond, J. B. (1958). 'Effect of postpartum separation of mother and kid on maternal care in the domestic goat.' *Science*, **128**, 1342–3.

Hetzer, H., and Ripin, R. (1930). 'Fruehestes Lernen des Saueglings in der Ernaehrungssituation.' *Z. Psychol.*, **118**.

Hetzer, H., and Tudor-Hart, B. H. (1927). 'Die frühesten Reaktionen auf die menschliche Stimme.' *Quell. Stud. Jugenkinde*, **5**.

Hinde, R. A. (1959). 'Behaviour and speciation in birds and lower vertebrates.' *Biol. Rev.*, **34**, 85–128.

Hinde, R. A. (1961). 'The establishment of the parent–offspring relation in birds, with some mammalian analogies.' In *Current Problems in Animal Behaviour*, ed. W. H. Thorpe and O. L. Zangwill. London: Cambridge University Press.

REFERENCES

Hinde, R. A. (1963). 'The nature of imprinting.' In *Determinants of Infant Behaviour*, Vol. 2, ed. B. M. Foss. London: Methuen; New York: Wiley.

Hinde, R. A. (1965a). 'Rhesus monkey aunts.' In *Determinants of Infant Behaviour*, Vol. 3, ed. B. M. Foss. London: Methuen; New York: Wiley.

Hinde, R. A. (1965b). 'The integration of the reproductive behaviour of female canaries.' In *Sex and Behavior*, ed. F. A. Beach. New York and London: Wiley.

Hinde, R. A. (1970). *Animal Behaviour: A Synthesis of Ethology and Comparative Psychology* 2nd edition. New York: McGraw-Hill.

Hinde, R. A. (1979). *Towards Understanding Relationships*. London and New York: Academic Press.

Hinde, R. A., Rowell, T. E., and Spencer-Booth, Y. (1964). 'Behaviour of socially living rhesus monkeys in their first six months.' *Proc. zool. Soc. Lond.*, **143**, 609-49.

Hinde, R. A., and Spencer-Booth, Y. (1967). 'The behaviour of socially living rhesus monkeys in their first two and a half years.' *Anim. Behav.*, **15**, 169-96.

Holst, E. von, and Saint Paul, U. von (1963). 'On the functional organization of drives.' *Anim. Behav.*, **11**, 1-20.

Illingworth, R. S. (1955). 'Crying in infants and children.' *Br. med. J.*, (*i*), 75-8.

Illingworth, R. S., and Holt, K. S. (1955). 'Children in hospital: some observations on their reactions with special reference to daily visiting.' *Lancet*, 17 December, 1257-62.

Itani, J. (1963). 'Paternal care in the wild Japanese monkey, *Macaca fuscata*.' In *Primate Social Behavior*, ed. C. H. Southwick. Princeton, N.J., and London: Van Nostrand.

James, W. (1890). *Principles of Psychology*. New York: Holt.

Jones, E. (1953). *Sigmund Freud: Life and Work*, Vol. 1. London: Hogarth; New York: Basic Books.

Jones, E. (1955). *Sigmund Freud: Life and Work*, Vol. 2. London: Hogarth; New York: Basic Books.

Kaila, E. (1932). 'Die Reaktion des Säugling auf das menschliche Gesicht.' *Annls. Univ. âbo.*, Series B, **17**, 1-114.

Kawamura, S. (1963). 'The process of sub-culture propagation among Japanese macaques.' In *Primate Social Behavior*, ed. C. H. Southwick. Princeton, N.J., and London: Van Nostrand.

Kellogg, W. N., and Kellogg, L. (1933). *The Ape and the Child: A Study of Environmental Influence upon Early Behavior*. New York: McGraw-Hill (Whittlesey House Publications).

Kessen, W., and Leutzendorff, A. M. (1963). 'The effect of non-nutritive sucking on movement in the human newborn.' *J. comp. physiol. Psychol.*, **56**, 69-72.

King, D. L. (1966). 'A review and interpretation of some aspects of the infant-mother relationship in mammals and birds.' *Psychol. Bull.*, **65**, 143-55.

Klaus, M. H., and Kennell, J. H. (1982). *Parent-infant Bonding*. (Second edition). Saint Louis, Missouri: C. V. Mosby Co.

REFERENCES

Klein, M. (1948). *Contributions to Psycho-analysis* 1921–1945. London: Hogarth; New York: Anglobooks, 1952.

Koford, C. B. (1963a). 'Group relations in an island colony of rhesus monkeys.' In *Primate Social Behaviour*, ed. C. H. Southwick. Princeton, N.J., and London: Van Nostrand.

Koford, C. B. (1963b). 'Rank of mothers and sons in bands of rhesus monkeys.' *Science*, **141**, 356–7.

Korner, A. F. (1979). 'Conceptual issues in infancy research.' In *Handbook of Infant Development*, ed. J. D. Osofsky. New York: Wiley.

Kris, E. (1954). Introduction to *The Origins of Psycho-analysis*. Letters to Wilhelm Fliess, drafts and notes: 1887–1902, by Sigmund Freud, ed. by M. Bonaparte, A. Freud, and E. Kris. London: Imago; New York: Basic Books.

Lamb, M. E. (1977). 'The development of mother–infant and father–infant attachments in the second year of life.' *Developmental Psychology*, **13**, 637–48.

Langer, S. (1967). *Mind: An Essay on Human Feeling.* Baltimore, Md: The Johns Hopkins Press.

Langmeier, J., and Matejcek, Z. (1963). *Psychika deprivace v detsvi.* Prague: Statni Zdravotnické Nakladatelstvi.

Levine, R. A., and Levine, B. B. (1963). 'Nyansongo: a Gusii community in Kenya.' In *Six Cultures: Studies of Child Rearing*, ed. B. B. Whiting. New York and London: Wiley.

Levine, S. (1966). 'Sex differences in the brain.' *Scient. Am.*, **214** (4), 84–92.

Levy, D. M. (1937). 'Studies in sibling rivalry.' *Res. Monogr. Am. orthopsychiat. Ass.*, No. 2.

Levy, D. M. (1951). 'Observations of attitudes and behavior in the child health center.' *Am. J. publ. Hlth.*, **41**, 182–90.

Lewis, M., and Kagan, J. (1965). 'Studies in attention.' *Merrill-Palmer Q.*, **11**, 95–127.

Lewis, M., Kagan, J., and Kalafat, J. (1966). 'Patterns of fixation in the young infant.' *Child Dev.*, **37**, 331–41.

Lewis, W. C. (1965). 'Coital movements in the first year of life.' *Int. J. Psycho-Anal.*, **46**, 372–4.

Light, P. (1979). *Development of a Child's Sensitivity to People.* London: Cambridge University Press.

Lipsitt, L. P. (1963). 'Learning in the first year of life.' In *Advances in Child Development and Behavior*, Vol. 1, ed. L. P. Lipsitt and C. C. Spiker. New York and London: Academic Press.

Lipsitt, L. P. (1966). 'Learning processes of human newborns.' *Merill-Palmer Q.*, **12**, 45–71.

Livingston, R. B. (1959). 'Central control of receptors and sensory transmission system.' In *Handbook of Physiology*, Section I. *Neurophysiology*, Vol. 1, ed. J. Field, H. W. Magoun, and V. E. Hall. Prepared by the American Physiological Society, Washington. Baltimore, Md: Williams & Wilkins; London: Baillière, Tindall & Cox.

Londerville, S., and Main, M. (1981). 'Security of attachment, compliance and maternal training methods in the second year of life.' *Developmental Psychology*, **17**, 289–99.

Lorenz, K. Z. (1935). 'Der Kumpan in der Umvelt des Vogels.' *J. Orn. Berl.*, **83**. Eng. trans. in *Instinctive Behavior*, ed. C. H. Schiller. New York: International Universities Press, 1957.

MacCarthy, D., Lindsay, M., and Morris, I. (1962). 'Children in hospital with mothers.' *Lancet*, (*i*), 603–8.

Maccoby, E. E., and Masters, J. C. (1970). 'Attachment and dependency.' In *Manual of Child Psychology* (3rd edn), ed. P. H. Mussen. New York and London: Wiley.

McFarland, D. J. (1971). *Feedback Mechanisms in Animal Behaviour*. London and New York: Academic Press.

McFarlane, J. A. (1975). 'Olfaction in the development of social preferences in the human neonate.' In *Parent–infant Interaction*. Ciba Foundation Symposium 33 (new series), 103–17. Amsterdam: Elsevier.

McGraw, M. B. (1943). *The Neuromuscular Maturation of the Human Infant*. New York: Columbia University Press; London: Oxford University Press.

MacKay, D. M. (1964). 'Communication and meaning: a functional approach. In *Cross-cultural Understanding: Epistemology in Anthropology*, ed. F. S. C. Northrop and H. H. Livingston. New York: Harper.

MacKay, D. M. (1966). 'Conscious control of action.' In *Brain and Conscious Experience*, ed. J. C. Eccles. Berlin: Springer Verlag.

MacLean, P. D. (1960). 'Psychosomatics.' In *Handbook of Physiology*, Section I. *Neurophysiology*, Vol. 3, ed. J. Field, H. W. Magoun, and V. E. Hall. Prepared by the American Physiological Society, Washington. Baltimore, Md: Williams & Wilkins; London: Baillière, Tindall & Cox.

Mahler, M. S. (1965). 'On early infantile psychosis.' *J. Am. Acad. Child Psychiat.*, **4**, 554–68.

Main, M. (1973). 'Exploration, play and level of cognitive functioning as related to child–mother attachment.' Dissertation submitted to John Hopkins University for degree of PhD.

Main, M., and Townsend, L. (1982). 'Exploration, play and cognitive functioning as related to security of infant–mother attachment.' *Infant Behavior and Development*.

Main, M., and Weston, D. (1981). 'The quality of the toddler's relationship to mother and father: related to conflict behavior and the readiness to establish new relationships.' *Child Development*, **52**, 932–40.

Main, M., and Weston, D. (1982). 'Avoidance of the attachment figure in infancy: descriptions and interpretations.' In *The Place of Attachment in Human Behavior*, ed. C. M. Parkes and J. Stevenson-Hinde. New York: Basic Books; London; Tavistock Publications.

Martini, H. (1955). *My Zoo Family*. London: Hamish Hamilton; New York: Harper.

Marvin, R. S. (1977). 'An ethological cognitive model for the attenuation of mother–child attachment behavior.' In *Advances in the Study of Communication and Affect*, Vol. 3, The Development of Social Attachments, ed.

REFERENCES

T. M. Alloway, L. Krames and P. Pliner. New York: Plenum.

Marvin, R. S., Greenberg, M. T., and Mossler, D. G. (1976). 'The early development of conceptual perspective-taking: distinguishing among multiple perspectives.' *Child Development*, **47**, 511–14.

Mason, W. A. (1965a). 'The social development of monkeys and apes.' In *Primate Behavior*, ed. I. DeVore. New York and London: Holt, Rinehart & Winston.

Mason, W. A. (1965b). 'Determinants of social behavior in young chimpanzees.' In *Behavior of Nonhuman Primates*, Vol. 2, ed. A. M. Schrier, H. F. Harlow, and F. Stollnitz. New York and London: Academic Press.

Mason, W. A., and Sponholz, R. R. (1963). 'Behavior of rhesus monkeys raised in isolation.' *J. psychiat. Res.*, **1**, 229–306.

Matas, L., Arend, R. A., and Sroufe, L. A. (1978). 'Continuity of adaptation in the second year: the relationship between quality of attachment and later competence.' *Child Development*, **49**, 547–56.

Mead, M. (1962). 'A cultural anthropologist's approach to maternal deprivation.' In *Deprivation of Maternal Care: A Reassessment of its Effects*. Public Health Papers No. 14. Geneva: WHO.

Medawar, P. B. (1967). *The Art of the Soluble*. London: Methuen; New York: Barnes & Noble.

Meier, G. W. (1965). 'Other data on the effects of social isolation during rearing upon adult reproductive behaviour in the rhesus monkey (*Macaca mulatta*).' *Anim. Behav.*, **13**, 228–31.

Meili, R. (1955). 'Angstentstehung bei Kleinkindern.' *Schweiz. Z. Psychol.*, **14**, 195–212.

Mićić, Z. (1962). 'Psychological stress in children in hospital.' *Int. Nurs. Rev.*, **9** (6), 23–31.

Miller, G. A., Galanter, E., and Pribram, K. H. (1960). *Plans and the Structure of Behavior*. New York: Holt, Rinehart & Winston.

Moltz, H. (1960). 'Imprinting: empirical basis and theoretical significance.' *Psychol. Bull.*, **57**, 291–314.

Morgan, G. A., and Ricciuti, H. N. (1969). 'Infants' responses to strangers during the first year.' In *Determinants of Infant Behaviour* Vol. 4, ed. B. M. Foss. London: Methuen; New York: Barnes & Noble.

Moss, H. A. (1967). 'Sex, age and state as determinants of mother–infant interaction.' *Merrill-Palmer Q.*, **13**, 19–36.

Murphy, L. B. (1962). *The Widening World of Childhood*. New York: Basic Books.

Murphy, L. B. (1964). 'Some aspects of the first relationship.' *Int. J. Psycho-Anal.*, **45**, 31–43.

Murray, H. A. (1938). *Explorations in Personality*. New York: Oxford University Press.

Nagera, H., and Colonna, A. B. (1965). 'Aspects of the contribution of sight to ego and drive development.' *Psychoanal. Study Child*, **20**, 267–87.

Newson, J., and Newson, E. (1963). *Infant Care in an Urban Community*. London: Allen & Unwin.

Newson, J., and Newson, E. (1966). 'Usual and unusual patterns of child-rearing.' Paper read at annual meeting of British Association for the Advancement of Science, September.

Newson, J., and Newson, E. (1968). *Four Years Old in an Urban Community.* London: Allen & Unwin.

Osofsky, J. D., ed. (1979). *Handbook of Infant Development.* New York: John Wiley.

Pantin, C. F. A. (1965). 'Learning, world-models and pre-adaptation.' In *Learning and Associated Phenomena in Invertebrates*, ed. W. H. Thorpe and D. Davenport. Animal Behaviour Supplement, No. 1. London: Baillière, Tindall & Cassell.

Pelled, N. (1964). 'On the formation of object-relations and identifications of the kibbutz child.' *Israel Ann. Psychiat.*, **2**, 144–61.

Piaget, J. (1924, Eng. trans. 1926). *The Language and Thought of the Child.* London: Routledge & Kegan Paul; New York: Harcourt, Brace.

Piaget, J. (1936, Eng. trans. 1953). *The Origins of Intelligence in the Child.* London: Routledge & Kegan Paul; New York: International Universities Press.

Piaget, J. (1937, Eng. trans. 1954). *The Construction of Reality in the Child.* New York: Basic Books. Also published under the title *The Child's Construction of Reality.* London: Routledge & Kegan Paul, 1955.

Piaget, J. (1947, Eng. trans. 1950). *The Psychology of Intelligence.* London: Routledge & Kegan Paul; New York: Harcourt, Brace.

Piaget, J., and Inhelder, B. (1948, Eng. trans. 1956). *The Child's Conception of Space.* London: Routledge & Kegan Paul; New York: Humanities Press.

Pittendrigh, C. S. (1958). 'Adaptation, natural selection and behavior.' In *Behavior and Evolution*, ed. A. Roe and G. C. Simpson. New Haven, Conn.: Yale University Press; London: Oxford University Press.

Polak, P. R., Emde, R., and Spitz, R. A. (1964). 'The smiling response to the human face: I, Methodology, quantification and natural history; II, Visual discrimination and the onset of depth perception.' *J. nerv. ment. Dis.*, **139**, 103–9 and 407–15.

Popper, K. R. (1934, Eng. trans. 1959). *The Logic of Scientific Discovery.* New York: Basic Books; London: Hutchinson.

Prechtl, H. F. R. (1958). 'The directed head turning response and allied movements of the human baby.' *Behaviour*, **13**, 212–42.

Prechtl, H. F. R. (1963). 'The mother–child interaction in babies with minimal brain damage.' In *Determinants of Infant Behaviour*, Vol. 2, ed. B. M. Foss. London: Methuen; New York: Wiley.

Prechtl, H. F. R. (1965). 'Problems of behavioral studies in the newborn infant.' In *Advances in the Study of Behavior*, Vol. 1, ed. D. S. Lehrman, R. A. Hinde, and E. Shaw. New York and London: Academic Press.

Premack, D., and Woodruff, G. (1978). 'Does the chimpanzee have a theory of mind?' *The Behavioral and Brain Sciences*, **1**, 515–26.

Pribram, K. H. (1962). 'The neuropsychology of Sigmund Freud.' In *Experimental Foundations of Clinical Psychology*, ed. A. J. Bachrach. New York: Basic Books.

REFERENCES

Pribram, K. H. (1967). 'The new neurology and the biology of emotion: a structural approach.' *Am. Psychol.*, **22**, 830–8.

Provence, S., and Lipton, R. C. (1962). *Infants in Institutions*. London: Bailey & Swinfen; New York: International Universities Press, 1963.

Prugh, D. G., *et al.* (1953). 'Study of the emotional reactions of children and families to hospitalization and illness.' *Am. J. Orthopsychiat.*, **23**, 70–106.

Pusey, A. (1978). 'Age-changes in the mother–offspring association of wild chimpanzees.' In *Recent Advances in Primatology*, ed. D. J. Chivers and J. Herbert, Vol. 1, pp. 119–23. London: Academic Press.

Rajecki, D. W., Lamb, M. E., and Obmascher, P. (1978). 'Towards a general theory of infantile attachment: a comparative review of aspects of the social bond.' *The Behavioral and Brain Sciences*, **1**, 417–64.

Rapaport, D. (1953). 'On the psycho-analytic theory of affects.' *Int. J. Psycho-Anal.*, **34**, 177–98.

Rapaport, D., and Gill, M. M. (1959). 'The points of view and assumptions of metapsychology.' *Int. J. Psycho-Anal.*, **40**, 153–62.

Reynolds, V., and Reynolds, F. (1965). 'Chimpanzees of the Budongo Forest.' In *Primate Behavior*, ed. I. DeVore. New York and London: Holt, Rinehart & Winston.

Rheingold, H. L. (1961). 'The effect of environmental stimulation upon social and exploratory behaviour in the human infant.' In *Determinants of Infant Behaviour*, Vol. 1, ed. B. M. Foss. London: Methuen; New York: Wiley.

Rheingold, H. L. (1963a). 'Controlling the infant's exploratory behaviour.' In *Determinants of Infant Behaviour*, Vol. 2, ed. B. M. Foss. London: Methuen; New York: Wiley.

Rheingold, H. L. (ed.) (1963b). *Maternal Behavior in Mammals*. New York and London: Wiley.

Rheingold, H. L. (1966). 'The development of social behaviour in the human infant.' *Monogr. Soc. Res. Child Dev.*, **31**, No. 5, 1–17.

Rheingold, H. L. (1968). 'Infancy.' In *International Encyclopedia of the Social Sciences*, ed. David L. Sills. New York and London: Collier/Macmillan.

Rheingold, H. L. (1969). 'The effect of a strange environment on the behaviour of infants.' In *Determinants of Infant Behaviour*, Vol. 4, ed. B. M. Foss. London: Methuen; New York: Barnes & Noble.

Rheingold, H. L., Gewirtz, J. L., and Ross, A. W. (1959). 'Social conditioning of vocalizations in the infant.' *J. comp. physiol. Psychol.*, **52**, 68–73.

Rheingold, H. L., and Keene, G. C. (1965). 'Transport of the human young.' In *Determinants of Infant Behaviour*, Vol. 3, ed. B. M. Foss. London: Methuen; New York: Wiley.

Rickman, J. (1951). 'Methodology and research in psychopathology.' *Br. J. med. Psychol.*, **24**, 1–7.

Robertson, J. (1952). Film: *A Two-year-old Goes to Hospital* (16 mm; 45 mins; sound; guidebook supplied; also abridged version, 30 mins). London: Tavistock Child Development Research Unit; New York: New York University Film Library.

Robertson, J. (1953). 'Some responses of young children to loss of maternal care.' *Nurs. Times*, **49**, 382–6.

REFERENCES

Robertson, J. (1958). Film: *Going to Hospital with Mother* (16 mm; 40 mins; sound; guidebook supplied). London: Tavistock Child Development Research Unit; New York: New York University Film Library.

Robertson, J. (ed.) (1962). *Hospitals and Children: A Parent's-Eye View.* London: Gollancz; New York: International Universities Press, 1963.

Robertson, J., and Bowlby, J. (1952). 'Responses of young children to separation from their mothers.' *Courr. Cent. int. Enf.*, **2**, 131–42.

Robertson, J., and Robertson, J. (1967). Film: *Young Children in Brief Separation*, No. 1: 'Kate, aged 2 years 5 months, in fostercare for 27 days.' (Guide booklet.) London: Tavistock Institute of Human Relations; New York: New York University Film Library.

Robson, K. S. (1967). 'The role of eye-to-eye contact in maternal–infant attachment.' *J. Child Psychol. Psychiat.*, **8**, 13–25.

Romanes, G. J. (1888). *Mental Evolution in Man.* London: Kegan Paul.

Rosenblatt, J. S. (1965). 'The basis of synchrony in the behavioral interaction between the mother and her offspring in the laboratory rat.' In *Determinants of Infant Behaviour*, Vol. 3, ed. B. M. Foss. London: Methuen; New York: Wiley.

Rosenblum, L. A., and Harlow, H. F. (1963). 'Approach-avoidance conflict in the mother surrogate situation.' *Psychol. Rep.*, **12**, 83–5.

Rosenthal, M. K. (1967). 'The generalization of dependency behaviour from mother to stranger.' *J. Child Psychol. Psychiat.*, **8**, 117–33.

Rowell, T. (1965). 'Some observations on a hand-reared baboon.' In *Determinants of Infant Behaviour*, Vol. 3, ed. B. M. Foss. London: Methuen; New York: Wiley.

Rutter, M. (1981). *Maternal Deprivation Reassessed* (second edition). Harmondsworth, Middlesex: Penguin.

Ryle, G. (1949). *The Concept of Mind.* London: Hutchinson; New York: Barnes & Noble, 1950.

Sade, D. S. (1965). 'Some aspects of parent–offspring and sibling relations in a group of rhesus monkeys, with a discussion of grooming.' *Am. J. phys. Anthrop.*, **23**, 1–18.

Sameroff, A. J., and Cavanagh, P. J. (1979). 'Learning in infancy: a developmental perspective.' In *Handbook of Infant Development*, ed. J. D. Osofsky, pp. 344–92. New York: Wiley.

Sameroff, A. J., and Chandler, M. A. (1975). 'Reproductive risk and the continuance of caretaking casualty.' In *Review of Child Development Research*, Vol. 4, ed. F. D. Horowitz and others, pp. 187–244. Chicago: University of Chicago Press.

Sander, L. W. (1962). 'Issues in early mother–child interaction.' *J. Am. Acad. Child Psychiat.*, **1**, 141–66.

Sander, L. W. (1964). 'Adaptive relationships in early mother–child interaction.' *J. Am. Acad. Child Psychiat.*, **3**, 231–64.

Sander, L. W. (1969). 'The longitudinal course of early mother–child interaction: cross-case comparison in a sample of mother–child pairs.' In *Determinants of Infant Behaviour*, Vol. 4, ed. B. M. Foss. London: Methuen; New York: Barnes & Noble.

REFERENCES

Sander, L. W. (1977). 'The regulation of exchange in the infant–caregiver system and some aspects of the context–concept relationship.' In *Interaction, Conversation, and the Development of Language*, ed. M. Lewis and L. A. Rosenblum. New York: Wiley.

Schachter, S. (1959). *The Psychology of Affiliation: Experimental Studies of the Sources of Gregariousness*. Stanford, Calif.: Stanford University Press; London: Tavistock Publications, 1961.

Schaffer, H. R. (1958). 'Objective observations of personality development in early infancy.' *Br. J. med. Psychol.*, **31**, 174–83.

Schaffer, H. R. (1963). 'Some issues for research in the study of attachment behaviour.' In *Determinants of Infant Behaviour*, Vol. 2, ed. B. M. Foss. London: Methuen; New York: Wiley.

Schaffer, H. R. (1966). 'The onset of fear of strangers and the incongruity hypothesis.' *J. Child Psychol. Psychiat.*, **7**, 95–106.

Schaffer, H. R., ed. (1977). *Studies in Mother–infant Interaction*. London: Academic Press.

Schaffer, H. R. (1979). 'Acquiring the concept of the dialogue.' In *Psychological Development from Infancy: Image to Intention*, ed. M. H. Bornstein and W. Kessen, pp. 279–305. Hillsdale, N.J.: Lawrence Erlbaum.

Schaffer, H. R., and Callender, W. M. (1959). 'Psychological effects of hospitalization in infancy.' *Paediatrics*, **24**, 528–39.

Schaffer, H. R., and Emerson, P. E. (1964a). 'The development of social attachments in infancy.' *Monogr. Soc. Res. Child Dev.*, **29**, No. 3, 1–77.

Schaffer, H. R., and Emerson, P. E. (1964b). 'Patterns of response to physical contact in early human development.' *J. Child Psychol. Psychiat.*, **5**, 1–13.

Schaller, G. (1963). *The Mountain Gorilla: Ecology and Behavior*. Chicago: University of Chicago Press.

Schaller, G. (1965). 'The behavior of the mountain gorilla.' In *Primate Behavior*, ed. I. DeVore. New York and London: Holt, Rinehart & Winston.

Schaller, G. B. (1967). *The Deer and the Tiger*. Chicago: University of Chicago Press.

Schmidt-Koenig, K. (1965). 'Current problems in bird orientation.' In *Advances in the Study of Behavior*, Vol. 1, ed. D. S. Lehrman, R. A. Hinde, and E. Shaw. New York and London: Academic Press.

Schneirla, T. C. (1959). 'An evolutionary and developmental theory of biphasic processes underlying approach and withdrawal.' In *Nebraska Symposium on Motivation*, ed. M. R. Jones. Lincoln, Nebr.: University of Nebraska Press.

Schneirla, T. C. (1965). 'Aspects of stimulation and organization in approach/withdrawal processes underlying vertebrate behavioral development.' In *Advances in the Study of Behavior*, Vol. 1, ed. D. S. Lehrman, R. A. Hinde, and E. Shaw. New York and London: Academic Press.

Schur, M. (1960a). 'Discussion of Dr John Bowlby's paper, "Grief and mourning in infancy and early childhood".' *Psychoanal. Study Child*, **15**, 63–84.

REFERENCES

Schur, M. (1960b). 'Phylogenesis and ontogenesis of affect- and structure-formation and the phenomenon of the repetition compulsion.' *Int. J. Psycho-Anal.*, **41**, 275–87.

Schutz, F. (1965a). 'Sexuelle Prägung bei Anatiden.' *Z. Tierpsychol.*, **22**, 50–103.

Schutz, F. (1965b). 'Homosexualität und Prägung.' *Psychol. Forsch.*, **28**, 439–63.

Scott, J. P. (1963). 'The process of primary socialization in canine and human infants.' *Monogr. Soc. Res. Child Dev.*, **28**, 1–47.

Sears, R. R. (1972). 'Attachment, dependency and frustration.' In *Attachment and Dependency*, ed. J. L. Gewirtz. New York and London: Wiley.

Sears, R. R., Rau, L., and Alpert, R. (1965). *Identification and Child Rearing*. Stanford, Calif.: Stanford University Press; London: Tavistock Publications, 1966.

Seay, B., Alexander, B. K., and Harlow, H. F. (1964). 'Maternal behavior of socially deprived rhesus monkeys.' *J. abnorm. soc. Psychol.*, **69**, 345.

Shipley, W. U. (1963). 'The demonstration in the domestic guinea-pig of a process resembling classical imprinting.' *Anim. Behav.*, **11**, 470–4.

Shirley, M. M. (1933). *The First Two Years*. 3 vols. Minneapolis: University of Minnesota Press; London: Oxford University Press.

Sluckin, W. (1965). *Imprinting and Early Learning*. London: Methuen; Chicago: Aldine.

Sommerhoff, G. (1950). *Analytical Biology*. London: Oxford University Press.

Southwick, C. H. (ed.) (1963). *Primate Social Behavior*. Princeton, N. J.,and London: Van Nostrand.

Southwick, C. H., Beg, M. A., and Siddiqi, M. R. (1965). 'Rhesus monkeys in North India.' In *Primate Behavior*, ed. I. DeVore. New York and London: Holt, Rinehart & Winston

Spiro, M. E. (1954). 'Is the family universal?' *Am. Anthrop.*, **56**, 839–46.

Spiro, M. E. (1958). *Children of the Kibbutz*. Cambridge, Mass.: Harvard University Press; London: Oxford University Press.

Spitz, R. A. (1946). 'Anaclitic depression.' *Psychoanal. Study Child*, **2**, 313–42.

Spitz, R. A. (1950). 'Anxiety in infancy: a study of its manifestations in the first year of life.' *Int. J. Psycho-Anal.*, **31**, 138–43.

Spitz, R. A. (1955). 'A note on the extrapolation of ethological findings.' *Int. J. Psycho-Anal.*, **36**, 162–5.

Spitz, R. A. (1965). *The First Year of Life*. New York: International Universities Press.

Spitz, R. A., and Wolf, K. M. (1946). 'The smiling response: a contribution to the ontogenesis of social relations.' *Genet. Psychol. Monogr.*, **34**, 57–125.

Sroufe, L. A. (1979). 'The coherence of individual development.' *American Psychologist*, **34**, 834–41.

Sroufe, L. A. (1982). 'Infant–caregiver attachment and patterns of adaptation in pre-school: the roots of maladaptation and competence.' In *Minnesota Symposium in Child Psychology*, Vol. 16, ed. M. Perlmutter. Minneapolis: University of Minnesota Press.

REFERENCES

Sroufe, L. A., and Waters, E. (1977). 'Attachment as an organizational construct.' *Child Development*, **48**, 1184–99.

Stern, D. N. (1977). *The First Relationship: Infant and Mother.* London: Fontana. Open Books.

Stevenson, H. W. (1965). 'Social reinforcement of children's behavior.' In *Advances in Child Development and Behavior*, Vol. 2, ed. L. P. Lipsitt and C. C. Spiker. New York and London: Academic Press.

Stevenson, O. (1954). 'The first treasured possession.' *Psychoanal. Study Child*, **9**, 199–217.

Strachey, J. (1962). 'The emergence of Freud's fundamental hypotheses.' (An appendix to 'The neuro-psychoses of defence'.) *S.E.*, **3**.

Strachey, J. (1966). 'Introduction to Freud's *Project for a Scientific Psychology.*' *S.E.*, **1**.

Tennes, K. H., and Lampl, E. E. (1964). 'Stranger and separation anxiety in infancy.' *J. nerv. ment. Dis.*, **139**, 247–54.

Thomas, H. (1973). 'Unfolding the baby's mind: the infant's selection of visual stimuli.' *Psychological Review*, **80**, 468–88.

Thomas, H., and Jones-Molfese, V. (1977). 'Infants and I scales: inferring change from the ordinal stimulus selections of infants for configural stimuli.' *J. of Experimental Child Psychology*, **23**, 329–39.

Thorpe, W. H. (1956). *Learning and Instinct in Animals.* 2nd edn, 1963. Cambridge, Mass.: Harvard University Press; London: Methuen.

Tinbergen, N. (1951). *The Study of Instinct.* London: Oxford University Press.

Tinbergen, N. (1963). 'On aims and methods of ethology.' *Z. Tierpsychol.* **20**, 410–33.

Tinbergen, N., and Tinbergen, E. A. (1982). *About 'autistic' children and how they might be cured.* London: Allen & Unwin.

Tizard, B., and Hodges, J. (1978). 'The effect of institutional rearing on the development of eight year old children.' *J. Child Psychol. Psychiat.*, **19**, 99–118.

Tobias, P. V. (1965). 'Early man in East Africa.' *Science*, **149**, No. 3679, 22–33.

Tomilin, M. I., and Yerkes, R. M. (1935). 'Chimpanzee twins: behavioral relations and development.' *J. genet. Psychol.*, **46**, 239–63.

Tomkins, S. S. (1962–63). *Affect, Imagery, Consciousness.* Vol. I, *The Positive Affects*; Vol. II, *The Negative Affects.* New York: Springer; London: Tavistock Publications, 1964.

Trivers, R. L. (1974). 'Parent–offspring conflict.' *American Zoologist*, **14**, 249–64.

Turnbull, C. M. (1965). *Wayward Servants: The Two Worlds of the African Pygmies.* New York: Natural History Press; London: Eyre & Spottiswoode.

Tustin, A. (1953). 'Do modern mechanisms help us to understand the mind?' *Br. J. Psychol.*, **44**, 24–37.

Ucko, L. E. (1965). 'A comparative study of asphyxiated and non-asphyxiated boys from birth to five years.' *Dev. Med. Child Neurol.*, **7**, 643–57.

REFERENCES

Vaughn, B., Egeland, B., Sroufe, L. A., and Waters, E. (1979). 'Individual differences in infant–mother attachment at 12 and 18 months: stability and change in families under stress.' *Child Development*, **50**, 971–5.

Vernon, D. T. A., Foley, J. M., Sipowicz, R. R., and Schulmans, J. L. (1965). *The Psychological Responses of Children to Hospitalization and Illness.* Springfield, Ill.: C. C. Thomas.

Vickers, G. (1965). 'The end of free fall.' *The Listener*, 28 October, p. 647.

Walters, R. H., and Parke, R. D. (1965). 'The role of the distance receptors in the development of social responsiveness.' In *Advances in Child Development and Behavior*, Vol. 2, ed. L. P. Lipsitt and C. C. Spiker. New York and London: Academic Press.

Washburn, S. L. (ed.) (1961). *The Social Life of Early Man.* New York: Wenner-Gren Foundation for Anthropological Research, Inc.; London: Methuen, 1962.

Washburn, S. L. (1968). Letter to the Editor 'On Holloway's "Tools and Teeth".' *Am. Anthrop.*, **70**, 97–100. (Holloway, R. L., 'Tools and teeth: some speculation regarding canine reduction.' *Am. Anthrop.*, **69**, 63–7, 1967.)

Washburn, S. L., Jay, P. C., and Lancaster, J. B. (1965). 'Field studies of Old World monkeys and apes.' *Science*, **150**, 1541–7.

Waters, E. (1978). 'The reliability and stability of individual differences in infant–mother attachment.' *Child Development*, **49**, 483–94.

Waters, E., Wippman, J., and Sroufe, L. A. (1979). 'Attachment, positive affect, and competence in the peer group: two studies in construct validation.' *Child Development*, **50**, 821–9.

Watson, J. S. (1965). 'Orientation-specific age changes in responsiveness to the face stimulus in young infants.' Paper presented at annual meeting of American Psychological Association, Chicago.

Weisberg, P. (1963). 'Social and nonsocial conditioning of infant vocalizations.' *Child Dev.*, **34**, 377–88.

Weiss, P. (1949). 'The biological basis of adaptation.' In *Adaptation*, ed. J. Romano. Ithaca, N.Y.: Cornell University Press; London: Oxford University Press, 1950.

Weiss, R. S. (1982). 'Attachment in adult life.' In *The Place of Attachment in Human Behavior*, ed. C. M. Parkes and J. Stevenson-Hinde. London: Tavistock Publications. New York: Basic Books.

White, B. L., Castle, P., and Held, R. (1964). 'Observations on the development of visually-directed reaching.' *Child Dev.*, **35**, 349–64.

White, B. L., and Held, R. (1966). 'Plasticity of sensorimotor development in the human infant.' In *The Causes of Behavior: Readings in Child Development and Educational Psychology*, 2nd edn, ed. J. F. Rosenblith and W. Allinsmith. Boston, Mass.: Allyn & Bacon.

Whyte, L. L. (1960). *The Unconscious before Freud.* New York: Basic Books; London: Tavistock Publications, 1962.

Williams, G. C. (1966). *Adaptation and Natural Selection.* Princeton, N.J.: Princeton University Press.

Wilson, E. O. (1975). *Sociobiology: the New Synthesis.* Cambridge, Mass.: Harvard University Press.

REFERENCES

Winnicott, D. W. (1953). 'Transitional objects and transitional phenomena.' *Int. J. Psycho-Anal.*, **34**, 1–9. Reprinted in *Collected Papers* by D. W. Winnicott. London: Tavistock Publications, 1958.

Wolff, P. H. (1959). 'Observations on newborn infants.' *Psychosom. Med.*, **21**, 110–18.

Wolff, P. H. (1963). 'Observations on the early development of smiling.' In *Determinants of Infant Behaviour*, Vol. 2, ed. B. M. Foss. London: Methuen; New York: Wiley.

Wolff, P. H. (1969). 'The natural history of crying and other vocalizations in early infancy.' In *Determinants of Infant Behaviour*, Vol. 4, ed. B. M. Foss. London: Methuen; New York: Barnes & Noble.

Wolkind, S., Hall, F., and Pawlby, S. (1977). 'Individual differences in behaviour: a combined epidemiological and observational approach.' In *Epidemiological Approaches in Child Psychiatry*, ed. P. J. Graham, pp. 107–23. New York and London: Academic Press.

Yarrow, L. J. (1963). 'Research in dimensions of early maternal care.' *Merrill-Palmer Q.*, **9**, 101–14.

Yarrow, L. J. (1967). 'The development of focused relationships during infancy.' In *Exceptional Infant*, Vol. 1, ed. J. Hellmuth. Seattle, Wash.: Special Child Publications.

Yerkes, R. M. (1943). *Chimpanzees: A Laboratory Colony*. New Haven, Conn.: Yale University Press; London: Oxford University Press.

Young, J. Z. (1964). *A Model of the Brain*. London: Oxford University Press.

Young, M., and Willmott, P. (1957). *Family and Kinship in East London*. London: Routledge & Kegan Paul; New York: The Free Press.

Yovits, M. C., and Cameron, S. (eds.) (1960). *Self-organizing Systems*. Oxford: Pergamon.

Zahn-Waxler, C., Radke-Yarrow, M., and King, R. A. (1979). 'Child rearing and children's pro-social initiations towards victims of distress.' *Child Development*, **50**, 319–30.

Author Index

Subject Index

activation of behavioural systems,
18–20, 22, 66–7, 72, 74–6, 85–
103, 110, 111, 113–14, 119,
122–3, 125–9, 134–5, 137,
142–3, 145, 148–53, 155, 157–
164, 167–74, 179, 237, 261

adaptation
process of, 14, 37, 41, 46–7, 50–
57, 59, 128, 145, 156, 348
unit of, 38–9, 45, 54–6, 59, 128,
131–3, 141, 145

adaptedness, state of, 14, 47, 50–1,
53–6, 59–60, 64, 66, 145, 173

adolescent, behaviour of, 144, 179,
190, 207

affectional systems (Harlow), 165,
232

affiliation, 229

aim of behaviour, 22, 136, 138–9,
172, 177n
see also object of behaviour; predictable outcome; termination of behavioural systems

alarm behaviour, 48, 69, 72, 95,
101, 151, 159, 171, 184,
187, 189–90, 192–8, 201–3,
206–9, 212–16, 221–3, 226–
227, 239–41, 243, 248–50,
259–61, 267, 279, 281, 287,
296, 302–3, 307, 313, 321,
324–30, 333–8, 348
caused by strangeness, 170, 201,
203, 209, 221, 223, 239, 248–
249, 267, 281, 287, 296, 324–
329, 333–9

alternating behaviour, 98–100

altruism, 131–3

ambivalent behaviour, 6, 7
see also alternating behaviour

anaclitic relationship, 30

animal studies, 7, 39–40, 44–6,
48–50, 55, 60–3, 66–9, 71–6,
79–80, 86–95, 98–101, 121,
122, 124–7, 132, 133, 141–
153, 157–71, 180–99, 211–
216, 219–23, 225–8, 230–3,
235, 238–40, 243, 247–51,
277, 278, 309, 311–13

birds, 7, 19, 39–40, 44–6, 48–50,
55, 60, 66–9, 71–4, 76, 79,
86–91, 94, 95, 98–101, 124–
127, 133, 135, 141–4, 147–50,
152–3, 159, 161–3, 166–71,
181–3, 211, 219–23, 231–3,
238, 251

fish, 66, 87–8, 98

insects, 45, 48n, 55, 57, 60, 74–6,
79–80, 90, 132

mammals
carnivores, 45, 49, 62, 81,
128–9, 147, 150–3, 181,
212–13, 215, 221–2, 227–8
primates, 45, 49, 61–3, 66,
71, 79, 100, 121, 122, 132,
142n, 151, 153, 157–8, 165–
166, 183–99, 203, 212–16,
219, 221–2, 227, 228n, 232–
233, 238–40, 243, 247–50,
277–8, 309, 311–13
rodents, 48–9, 79, 90–4, 142,
151, 152, 157, 181, 212,
233, 238
ungulates, 45, 132, 164, 180–
182, 212–13, 215, 231
relevance of, 6, 7, 12–13, 37–40,
44–57, 168, 171–3, 183–4,
198–9, 211, 216–22
Freud's view, 12–13
reptiles, 168, 183

ant, 45

anthropological studies, 3, 59, 61,
63

anxiety
at eight months (Spitz), 327–9